The
INSTRUMENT
FLIGHT
TRAINING
MANUAL

as developed by
Professional
Instrument
Courses, Inc.

Peter Dogan

This Book is Dedicated
To All Instrument Pilots —
Present and Future.

The
INSTRUMENT
FLIGHT
TRAINING
MANUAL

as developed by
Professional
Instrument
Courses, Inc.

Peter Dogan

July 1994 Revised Printing by P.I.C., Inc.

Second Edition, May, 1991

Peter Dogan, Professional Instrument Courses, Inc.
Aviation Center
30 Plains Rd., Essex, CT 06426
Tel: (203) 767-8263

Library of Congress Cataloging-in-Publication Data

Dogan, Peter, 1947-1991
    The instrument flight training manual as developed by Professional Instrument Courses, Inc. Peter Dogan—2nd Ed.

    p. cm. Includes bibliographical references and index.
    ISBN 0-916413-12-8
    1. Instrument flying.   I. Professional Instrument Courses, Inc.   II. Title.
TL711.B6D64   1991   629.132'5214-dc20   91-13802 CIP

Telecommunications and Typography by Michael R. Burrows, Typographer, Glendale, CA 91204

Printed in the United States of America by Merrill Corporation, Los Angeles, CA 90021

published
by
AVIATION BOOK COMPANY
25133 Anza Drive
Santa Clarita, CA 91355
Tel: (805) 294-0101

Introduction

This book grew out of the Professional Instrument Courses, Inc. (P.I.C.) program for the instrument rating. It embodies the lessons we have learned from years of experience in producing well-qualified, successful instrument pilots. It is meant to provide a solid introduction for the beginner and a valuable overall refresher for the rated pilot, presented in a quickly understood form.

Developed from the P.I.C. instrument flight training *Workbook*, this manual follows a well-organized, step-by-step program that allows the student to systematically build the conceptual skills needed in IFR flying. It is not, however, intended to be used only by the instrument student. Rather, it discusses each topic in sufficient depth to be informative to the active IFR pilot.

It is important to point out that using this book for training is *not* the same as taking the P.I.C. Instrument Flight Training Course. The P.I.C. program provides intensive, individualized training at the student's location. The company has trained thousands of pilots from all of the 50 states and, at the time of writing, is preparing more private pilots for the instrument rating than any other organization in the United States.

P.I.C. uses an unconventional training approach that brings the instructor to the student's home base, wherever it may be. The instructor stays in a local motel and sets up a simulator in the student's home. Half the required training hours are logged on the simulator, the rest in flights from the local airport. Thanks to the carefully organized curriculum and experienced professional *teachers*, most of P.I.C.'s clients receive the rating by the end of the scheduled 10 days.

The P.I.C. program is full-time professional training—not a "cram course." It includes more instruction during the 10-day program than most courses offer, even when spread over many months. On completion, clients are fully qualified *to use the rating in actual weather*—to fly instruments in the system safely, legally and confidently. This manual presents the material covered in the P.I.C. course, as well as additional review and background matter for the rated instrument pilot.

Several chapters begin with anecdotes—"war stories" if you like—to provide the reader with a sense of the real environment of IFR flying. These stories are printed in italics and may be skipped if the reader wishes to move directly to the technical material. Certain more advanced subjects are also printed in italics and may be omitted without sacrificing continuity. They are included for the special interest of some readers.

Most of this manual is written directly to the student, as if it were a self-instruction manual. However, make no mistake, you cannot teach yourself to fly instruments any more than you can be made into a safe IFR pilot by inadequate instructors. Our experience and that of our many students has proven that instrument flying has to be *taught* in a methodical, organized and dedicated program by competent instructors who are truly teachers, not just pilots.

Some sections are addressed directly to the CFII. These portions may also be read profitably by students and rated pilots seeking to deepen their understanding of the IFR system. Sections headed "To The CFII" may also be useful if you are practicing with the help of a safety pilot or are serving as a safety pilot yourself.

It has been said often that the instrument is the most difficult of all the ratings a pilot can seek. Difficult and challenging it is, but it is often made more of a hardship than it need be by unnecessarily complex and disorganized presentations of the material. This manual, as does the P.I.C. program, seeks to ease the burden by applying what we have found to be effective and lasting teaching techniques.

Peter Dogan
Essex, Connecticut

Introduction, 2nd Edition

I began the first edition of the *Instrument Flight Training Manual* shortly after founding P.I.C., over a decade ago. At that time, most general aviation instrument training was informal and took many months. People viewed intensive training with suspicion. Instruction was given mostly in airplanes, and many pilots did not believe in simulator training. This was despite the fact that professional pilots, military and civilian, were trained on a full time basis, with heavy simulator use.

During the 80's, attitudes about instrument training changed and training methods evolved. Today there is hardly a pilot who doesn't know that training on a full time, intensive basis, with the help of a simulator, saves time and money and improves learning efficiency. General aviation is embracing the modern attitudes towards instrument training that the professional pilot has had for many years.

In the 80's, more and more pilots recognized the instrument rating as a practical necessity. Today they use their airplanes more for necessary transportation and have lost their willingness to sit out weather delays in airport motel rooms.

The airspace became more complicated and the ATC system more demanding. Today it requires a higher level of professionalism than in 1980. Even under VFR, the instrument pilot is more comfortable with rapid fire, mandatory communications than his non-rated colleague. More complex airspace (ARSA's, for example) has made many VFR pilots think twice about entering busy areas.

As a tougher liability climate placed more pressure on insurers during the decade, they encouraged their policyholders to upgrade their tickets. The instrument rating became a condition of insurance in some cases.

For all these reasons, the FAA predicts a continuing rise in the proportion of instrument rated pilots. As interest in instrument training has increased, the training "consumer" has become more educated and the demand has grown for high quality, efficient, professional level training. Professional level refresher training is also much more in demand in general aviation than it was a decade ago.

While P.I.C. has grown with these trends and emerged as one of the leaders in its field, I hope that this completely revised version of the *Instrument Flight Training Manual* will be helpful to all general aviation pilots in building their skills and improving their use and enjoyment of the airspace.

This Second Edition, based like the first on the P.I.C. Instrument Rating Course, has been fully edited and updated and contains several completely new sections. The illustrations have been brought up to date, all the quizzes have been revised and expanded, and there is a new chapter on area navigation. While the first edition became the standard guide for new and experienced instrument pilots, this revision is designed to maintain that role in the new general aviation environment.

I am thankful to the hundreds of P.I.C. instructors who have taught in the P.I.C. program over the years and who contributed, directly and indirectly, to this book. Erik Lunde, our excellent operations manager, worked especially hard on double checking the new edition. And I offer a special thanks to Janice Knestout Colvin for her valuable editorial assistance.

Peter Dogan
Essex, Connecticut
January, 1991

CONTENTS

Introduction

Introduction to the Second Edition

Preface   VFR HEADACHES, IFR COMFORTS

Chapter 1   THE RATING—WHY YOU NEED IT, AND HOW TO GET STARTED 1

         Requirements for the Rating 2
         Why There Aren't More Instrument Pilots 3
         How to Choose Your Training Program 4
         What Makes a Good Instructor 6
         The Role of the Simulator..................................7
         Instrument Skills.. 7

Chapter 2   THE FLIGHT INSTRUMENTS—KNOWING AND USING THEM 9

         The Gyro Instruments 10
         The Pressure Instruments 17
         The Magnetic Compass 23
         The Engine Instruments 25
         Instrument Quiz 26

Chapter 3   ATTITUDE INSTRUMENT FLYING 29

         The Instrument Scan 29
         Pitch, Power, and Trim 30
         Instrument Classification...................................32
         The Six Configurations 33
         Turns 42
         Partial Panel 46
         Rate Climbs and Descents 48
         Unusual Attitudes 49
         To The CFII..50
         Attitude Flying Quiz 52

Chapter 4   IFR PLANNING AND PROCEDURES............................53

         Weather or Not to Go 58
         Plane and Pilot Fitness 63
         Legal Requirements 64
         The Airspace Structure 65
         The Flight Plan 67
         The IFR Clearance......................................72
         ATC Communications 76
         Cockpit Organization....................................77
         To The CFII..78
         Flight Planning Quiz 79

Chapter 5   VOR EQUIPMENT, ORIENTATION AND TRACKING 81

       The VOR System 83
       DME and TACAN 85
       VOR Testing 86
       VOR Orientation 87
       VOR Interpretation and the HSI 95
       Tracking 98
       Intercepting a Specified Course 101
       The Five T's 101
       To The CFII 102
       VOR Quiz 103

Chapter 6   ADF EQUIPMENT, ORIENTATION AND TRACKING 107

       The Equipment 108
       The Poor Man's RMI 109
       Intercepting a Specified Bearing 111
       Tracking Inbound 115
       Tracking Outbound 118
       The Procedure Turn 119
       To The CFII 120
       ADF Quiz 121

Chapter 7   HOLDING 123

       Holding Pattern Terminology 125
       Holding at a VOR 125
       Entries 127
       Compensating for the Wind 129
       The Holding Clearance 132
       Holding at Other Types of Fixes 134
       To The CFII 138
       Holding Quiz 140

Chapter 8   NONPRECISION APPROACHES 141

       Neatness Counts 142
       "Cleared for the Approach" 143
       Straight-in and Circle-to-Land 146
       Approach Architecture 149
       The Final Descent on a Nonprecision Approach 149
       Other Nonprecision Approaches 151
       Full Approaches and Straight-in Approaches 154
       An Actual Approach 156
       The DME Arc 158
       To The CFII 162
       Nonprecision Approach Quiz 163

Chapter 9   PRECISION APPROACHES 165

      The Localizer 168
      The Glide Slope 169
      Other Equipment 171
      Technique 174
      The Missed Approach 178
      To The CFII 181
      Precision Approach Quiz 182

Chapter 10   AREA NAVIGATION 187

      The Equipment 188
      Using RNAV 189
      RNAV Clearance 190
      RNAV Approaches 192
      Limitations of VOR/DME RNAV 193
      LORAN-C 193
      Limitations of LORAN-C 194
      The Future of RNAV 194
      RNAV Quiz 195

Chapter 11   EMERGENCIES 197

      Are You Ready? 197
      Engine Failure 199
      Communications Failure 201
      Electrical Failure 205
      Vacuum Failure 207
      Low Fuel 208
      Thunderstorms and Ice 208

Chapter 12   THE FLIGHT TEST AND AFTER 211

      Tips on Flight Test Preparation 213
      Maintaining Instrument Currency 215

Answers to Quizzes 218

Appendices . . . .

A. OBSTACLE CLEARANCE AND THE TERPS MANUAL 230
B. THE BASIC IFR CHECKLIST 233
C. ACRONYM LIST 234
D. SELECTED FEDERAL AVIATION REGULATIONS 236
   Excerpts from Parts 61 and 91
E. GLOSSARY OF TERMS 253
   Excerpts from the Airman's Information Manual

Bibliography 273

Index 274

VFR HEADACHES, IFR COMFORTS

The deepest appeal of flying lies in the freedom it offers. We can "slip the surly bonds of earth" for a few glorious hours, to soar magically in the sky and to enjoy an eagle's view of the world below. Flying has practical advantages too, of course. The salesman can make more calls in a day, and the executive saves precious time traveling to meetings. The vacationer is independent of inconvenient airline schedules. But even the pragmatic pilot who claims to use flying only as a handy business tool secretly revels in the freedom of the sky, of going when and where he likes, answering to no one but himself. A friend of mine says his favorite pastime is flying over traffic jams.

To the non-instrument rated pilot, however, aviation offers only limited freedom. This was illustrated forcefully on a recent trip I made from Long Island, New York, to Palm Beach, Florida. Three of us planned to go in two airplanes, meeting at fuel stops and spending the night together in a hotel near the airport in Savannah, Georgia.

My friends, John and Margery, would take their Piper Dakota, while I flew a Cessna 182. We planned a leisurely two-day trip, VFR, and hoped for good weather. The two airplanes were about equal in airspeed so we saw no problem in staying together.

The chosen day dawned murky and discouraging. A stationary front covered the Northeast, and a typical winter inversion blanketed the region with hazy stagnant air. The visibility was variously reported between two and five miles. The area forecast

had correctly predicted a 2000 foot overcast with tops at 4000.

The weather south of Virginia was predicted to improve. The skies would be clear and the visibilities excellent for the rest of the trip to Florida. There was just a chance of low ceilings and lingering precipitation from a low-pressure region moving off the coast of North Carolina.

John has nearly 1000 hours of pilot time but no instrument rating. A seasoned scud runner, he was disappointed but optimistic as we studied our weather briefing, which I regarded more grimly, hating to fly VFR in such poor conditions.

"It's only the first few hundred miles," John said cheerfully, "and it's all coastline. We'll just stay low over the beach until we get past the messy weather."

"You can," I shrugged, "But I think I'll file and fly on top. Let's just meet at Patrick Henry for an early lunch."

Patrick Henry Field, in Newport News, Virginia, was about 400 miles south, roughly three hours away at 130 knots. I phoned in a flight plan with a route through the New York TCA and down the coast of New Jersey, Delaware, and Maryland. Meanwhile John and Margery took off and began their scud running trip to the same destination.

My clearance was ready when I called ground. My departure was uneventful, and I turned towards the Kennedy VOR at my assigned altitude of 6000 feet about ten minutes after takeoff.

The visibility on top was excellent. The horizon was clear in every direction and sunlight glistened on the shining white tops. I wore sunglasses to cut the glare of the brilliant, reflected light. Below me, a little round rainbow followed along, dancing on the cloud tops.

I descended into the undercast as I passed Chesapeake Bay and spent half an hour in solid IFR. One vector from Norfolk Approach gave me an intercept heading for the ILS, and the glide slope slid me out of the clouds at about 1000 feet. The visibility was poor, perhaps two miles, but the brilliant approach light system stood out boldly, blazing a clear trail to the threshold.

I have been on many IFR flights, but I still feel a thrill of excitement and satisfaction at the magic of breaking out of the clouds with nothing in front but the lights and the big, wide runway, the culmination of planning, organization, and careful execution. The sense of achievement from ending exactly on course is perhaps the greatest pleasure of IFR flight.

Two minutes later, I was on the ground in exactly the flight planned time. I was at the gas pump when John landed and taxied in.

"What a trip!" he exclaimed after shutting down beside me. "We ducked down to 500 feet just off the beach," he said, "to get under the TCA. Kennedy was landing to the north and it was a little creepy sneaking under the heavy jets on approach. Then, when I tried to climb back to a decent altitude, the visibility immediately went to zero.

"I stayed between 500 and 1000 feet and although we could see the water out the side, sometimes we couldn't see anything in front. It got tense at times when we came close to helicopter traffic and some other light plane lunatics like me going the other way. I could really use an hour or two to relax after that flight." Of course, John's flight was not only unsafe, but frankly illegal.

In the Flight Service Station we learned that North Carolina was still covered with a lingering band of rain and heavy cloud about 150 miles wide. I filed my IFR flight plan to Savannah, but John needed more detail. As he looked carefully at the charts and forecasts, the Flight Service specialist eyed him appraisingly.

"Are you VFR?" he asked. At John's nod he erupted gleefully with, "You can't go!" as if his analysis of the weather carried the weight of law.

John, an old hand at dealing with non-pilot Flight Service people, shrugged and finished his examination of the charts. The system was moving from west to east, but no tops reports were available. Outside he said, "I can probably climb over that narrow band, or get around it to the west. It's getting better all the time, and the worst that can happen would be a delay or a detour."

After lunch, John and Margery departed and headed towards the weather as I awaited my clearance. It was the last I was to see of them for almost a week.

I resumed my pleasant IFR trip in marginal VFR conditions. A hundred miles south, I reached the edge of the weather, a solid mass of dark gray cloud reaching nearly from the ground to the high overcast above. Clearly no VFR flight could duck under or climb over it. I plunged into it and soon heard the familiar pounding of rain on the fuselage. For an hour, I flew on the gauges, bouncing around slightly in light turbulence before it dissipated to the south. I emerged into the dregs of the storm — broken clouds and damp, limited visibility. For the rest of the flight to Savannah, the weather improved steadily until, once again, I shot an instrument approach, this time just for practice, in good VFR conditions.

I fueled the aircraft, tied it down and went to the hotel. Later that night, as I waited for John and Margery, my phone rang, and I heard the story of their VFR odyssey.

"I took one look at that weather," John said, "and made a classic 180°. I didn't know who to call for assistance, but Margery finally found the frequency for Washington Center in an old handbook stuck behind the seat. I'm not used to talking to center controllers but did finally manage to explain our predicament.

"Washington Center told me Raleigh-Durham, 80 miles west, was still IFR, and I didn't want to go all the way back to Patrick Henry. We had plenty of fuel, so he gave us a vector northwest to a little field he thought might be VFR, but he had no definite information. That vector put us on a course 90° to our original route, but at least we weren't going backwards, and there was still a chance of an end-run around the weather to the west. A little later, some pilot reported that our new destination was in fact VFR.

"Washington handed us off to Raleigh-Durham Approach, which told me that Raleigh-Durham was now VFR, its weather having just gone to 1200 broken. At 4500 feet, we had broken clouds below us and an overcast above. We decided to try for Raleigh-Durham, which was closer to our route than the little place we were headed.

"The controller gave us a vector and a warning, 'Descend at your discretion. My minimum vectoring altitude is 2500 feet. Below that . . . I don't know.' I couldn't even descend to 2500, because we would have been in the broken clouds. I had to hope to get over the airport and spiral down through a hole."

John was an inveterate scud runner, and I could picture him taking these developments in stride, but I knew Margery was a somewhat anxious flier, and I could imagine the tension building in their cockpit. She would probably alternate between a stony silence and an incessant stream of nervous questions, both of which would ultimately irritate her husband.

John continued, "As we got close to Raleigh, the visibility between layers improved to the south. We were approaching the western edge of the IFR conditions. Fayetteville, 100 miles south, was reporting VFR with a scattered layer at 1000 feet. I caught a glimpse of the Raleigh-Durham airport through the clouds below us but decided to try for Fayetteville.

"The new hourly weather showed Fayetteville unchanged, and Florence, our next possible airport, had improved to marginal VFR. I thought of continuing, but the negative factors began to outweigh the positive. It would soon be dark. Daytime marginal VFR is one thing, but scud running at night in unfamiliar country is quite another. We would have reached Florence with only two hours of fuel, and if the weather hadn't improved, I could have been stuck. On top of everything, Margery was pretty tired and started complaining and talking too much. With all these discouraging factors, I decided to stop for the night. We landed through the scattered layer just as it was getting dark. So here we are in Fayetteville, 300 miles from Savannah."

I would have been uncomfortable taking such chances as he had, and was relieved that he had stopped when he did. We arranged to meet in West Palm Beach the next afternoon, and I advised him to get an early start, as bad weather was due to move over northern Florida around noon the next day.

I left Savannah early without bothering to file IFR and reached my destination by midday. John got to Jacksonville by late morning but not in time to beat the low pressure system that moved over northern Florida from the Gulf. The weather stalled and became a stationary front that hung on for several days, covering the region with low ceilings, insurmountable tops, and impenetrable cloud masses. When we spoke by phone on the last day before they finally reached West Palm Beach, he was quite discouraged.

"Maybe I need an instrument rating," he admitted. "The gas I wasted and the hotel bills I paid on this trip alone would pay a good part of the training. It's a strain constantly punching at soft spots in the weather, planning and replanning, and thinking in terms of 'outs.' And Margery hates the guesswork of wondering where she's going to sleep each night."

I commiserated with him and agreed that the rating would be a good addition to his pilot ticket. I used gentlemanly restraint in not pointing out that my trip had gone exactly as planned. And even though I needed the rating for its successful completion, I had spent only a small part of the 10 hour trip in the clouds and had not had to shoot a single low instrument approach. The trip was a routine bit of travel, not an uncertain adventure.

CHAPTER ONE

THE RATING — WHY YOU NEED IT, AND HOW TO GET STARTED

Without an instrument rating, a pilot is at the mercy of the weather. If flying's prime value is its freedom, then an instrument rating should be on every license.

A significant number of general aviation accidents involve non-instrument rated pilots continuing VFR flight into worsening weather. Flying closer and closer to the terrain to avoid a lowering overcast and continuing flight into deteriorating visibility are two dangerous traps. The pilot who relies on his ability to make the proverbial one-eighty gets a nasty surprise when the visibility has gone down behind him as well as in front.

The pressure to continue a flight can be strong. The cost and inconvenience of an unscheduled hotel stay, the need to get to a pressing meeting or long awaited vacation, and the negative reflection on one's skill implied by "turning back" are factors which may be difficult to eliminate from one's thinking.

The instrument rating helps you keep to your schedules. If you fly on business, you can't afford to tell associates, clients or customers that "I'll be there if the weather is good." And you can't afford delays in getting back to home base. Non-instrument rated business pilots often must drive or fly commercially, when flying their own plane would be far more efficient.

Spending a few vacation nights in Jacksonville when you want to be in Palm Beach can destroy the pleasure of a long anticipated trip. By contrast, the satisfaction of planning and completing the trip in weather is a pleasure and an ego booster for every pilot.

A pilot's passengers are more enthusiastic about flying if they regularly reach their planned destinations. With reduced uncertainty, they enjoy their flying more, as does the weather-liberated pilot.

Over the years, the instrument rating is a significant money saver. Since it allows more use of the airplane, a smaller percentage of the fixed cost can be allocated to each flight hour, reducing the overall price of flying — and instrument rated pilots enjoy lower insurance premiums than their non-rated counterparts.

The rating cuts down on the time and money wasted by weather delays. Bills for unscheduled restaurant meals and nights in motels have a way of mounting up. And, if you have ever left your airplane at a socked-in airport, flown home commercially, and then returned for the airplane when the weather improved, you know how expensive and inconvenient that can be. If you rent airplanes, the FBO's feelings also become a consideration — as do his charges. For a frequent flyer, the cost of instrument training is quickly offset by the savings in reliability it offers.

The greatest advantage of the instrument rating is that it enhances your confidence and safety. You feel more comfortable in the increasingly complex ATC system. Calling center is no longer a major project but a routine task. The language of radio communications becomes second nature to you, and your understanding of ATC and the airspace system improves your confidence as it expands the usefulness of your airplane.

Perhaps most important, the instrument rating removes the temptation to scud-run. The instrument pilot prefers to file and fly in the system, rather than spend a chancey trip dodging clouds and poking around in poor visibility, for VFR flight in marginal conditions is dangerous for any pilot, no matter how skilled.

Instrument training does improve a pilot's skills, whether or not he flies hard IFR. He knows and understands his airplane intimately and learns to control it with greater precision. Holding altitude and heading precisely become second nature to him and staying aware of his position becomes a natural part of his flying. He flies his airplane more like a skilled professional and less like a "weekend flyer."

However, make no mistake: The instrument rating is *not* a magic carpet that allows pilots to complete 100% of their trips on schedule. Sometimes the weather is bad enough to stop everyone, even the airlines. One of the important skills you will learn during instrument training is a more sophisticated approach to "go/no go" decisions, both before the flight and en route.

Requirements for the Rating

The instrument rating can be added to either a private or commercial pilot certificate. When an instrument rated private pilot upgrades to a commercial certificate, the commercial ticket automatically bears the instrument rating.

The instrument rating applies to specific *categories* of aircraft, as indicated on the certificate by the words "instrument airplane." If your license says "Private Pilot, Airplane Single Engine Land, Instrument Airplane" and you then become licensed in helicopters, you are not automatically instrument qualified in a helicopter.

If you add a multi-engine rating to your certificate, you will be required to demonstrate the ability to control the twin engine airplane by reference to instruments. This will include shooting a single engine approach. You have the right to decline this part of the multi-engine flight test, but if you do, your multi-engine privileges will be limited to VFR flight.

Legal requirements for the instrument rating are divided into three areas: ground instruction, flight instruction and skill, and flight experience. Requirements for these are spelled out in FAR 61.65 (see Appendix).

To receive the instrument rating, a pilot must pass written and flight tests. The applicant for the written test must have received certain ground instruction specified by FAR 61.65 or have completed a home study course acceptable to the FAA. It is technically *not* necessary to have an instructor's sign-off to be allowed to take the written exam. However, if you don't, the FAA must approve your home study course before you are allowed to take the test. It is usually easier to get an instructor's sign-off.

The applicant must take the written test and receive satisfactory results from the FAA exam grading facility, in Oklahoma City, before taking the flight test. Since grading the test and mailing time takes one to three weeks, the written should be taken before beginning a ten-day flight training course. However, some computerized testing companies are now approved by the FAA to administer the written test and grade it immediately, allowing a person to start flight training sooner, and to better retain the material.

There is a significant shift in emphasis from the material learned for the written test to that needed to actually use the instrument rating. Most examiners recognize this and give a thorough oral exam with the flight test. Consequently, a well-planned instrument course includes nearly as much ground school material as flight and simulator work, even though the student has already passed the written.

There is some controversy within the industry about preparing for the written exam through a weekend "cram course" (please, never refer to any aviation course as a "crash course"). The argument against such courses is that they "only prepare you for the test" and that material rapidly assimilated is just as rapidly forgotten.

The opposing opinion is that an intensive course is more effective because the forgetting process begins *during* a longer, more drawn out program. This view holds that the written test is merely an obstacle for the aspiring instrument pilot and should be passed by the most expeditious means.

If the practical course is thorough and is aimed at instrument proficiency rather than merely "getting the rating," it should fill any gaps and correct any misconceptions created by the written test preparation. The practical course, not the written test preparation, should prepare the pilot to fly instruments safely and effectively, regardless of how he prepared for the written. If it is conducted well, the applicant can pass the oral and flight tests without undue pressure and may even find them to be anticlimactic.

An applicant for the rating must have logged at least 125 hours of total pilot time, including all the dual and solo hours flown as a student pilot. The 125 hour total must include at least 50 hours cross-country flight as pilot in command, beyond the student pilot level. For this purpose, a flight qualifies as "cross-country" if a landing is made at an airport at least 50 nautical miles from the departure point.

Because of the total hour requirement, a pilot beginning a full time instrument rating course should have already logged at least 85 hours, including 45 hours of pilot-in-command cross-country time after receiving the private certificate. Then the time logged during the course can complete the requirements.

The rules require 40 hours of instrument experience, of which 15 must be instruction from a CFII. Technically, this means that a pilot may present himself for the flight test with 25 hours of hood time flown with a safety pilot and only 15 hours of instruction. However, in practice, *at least* 40 hours with a current, competent instrument *instructor* are needed to achieve the necessary proficiency.

Of the 40 hours of logged instrument experience, 20 may be instruction from a CFII in an authorized ground trainer. This sensible provision permits the economies of time and money afforded by modern simulator technology. It saves fuel and operating cost, and, as will be discussed later, allows learning to progress faster because the simulator is a far better teaching tool than the airplane. (We use the word "simulator" to mean "ground trainer," although the FAA defines the two slightly differently.)

The final requirement is that the applicant must pass oral and flight tests given by an FAA inspector or an FAA-designated examiner.

Why There Aren't More Instrument Pilots

At the end of a recent year, the FAA listed 292,184 private and 145,842 commercial pilots in the United States. Of these, 39,962 private (14%) and 125,145 commercial (86%) pilots were instrument rated.

It is not surprising that most commercial pilots are instrument rated. The commercial certificate allows the holder to fly for hire, but without the instrument rating, he may exercise the privilege only in the daytime and on trips of 50 nautical miles or less — a serious limitation.

It is surprising that more private pilots do not hold the instrument rating, given the many advantages it offers. In a recent 12-month period, the FAA issued 13,512 new instrument ratings, 5,409 to private pilots and 8,103 to commercial pilots. So the percentage of instrument rated pilots is not increasing rapidly. When you, as a private pilot, receive your rating, you will join an elite fraternity consisting of less than 15% of all private pilots.

Perhaps one reason why so few new instrument ratings are issued is the difficulty encountered by most pilots seeking it. Many parts of the country do not have organized, well established training programs for the rating. Local flight schools are often part of fixed base operations which are also engaged in several other businesses. The manager is concerned with selling airplanes, fuel, maintenance services and charter flights. Often the flight instructor doubles as a charter pilot; many a flight lesson has been canceled because the instructor is away on an air taxi mission. The instructor may prefer to cancel the lesson and take the charter flight because it is an easier way to build time for the airline job he one day hopes to have.

Most instruction at local flight schools is primary flight training, giving the instructors little chance to learn how to teach instruments. Merely holding the rating does not qualify an inexperienced instructor to conduct an effective training course, even if he is sincerely dedicated to the task.

Unfortunately, many schools and individual instructors attempt instrument training without benefit of a curriculum. Effective training is therefore impossible, because in such a situation there is no way to ensure that everything will be covered and the rating will be finished on schedule. Training tends to drift with no clear end in sight. Thus it happens that for many students the main difficulty in getting an instrument rating is not in mastering the skills but in tolerating the frustration of coping with broken schedules, inexperienced, uncommitted instructors, and nonexistent course organization. Many students simply give up. Others get the rating after many months of unnecessarily arduous and expensive training.

The average number of hours required to obtain the instrument rating nationwide is 65, more than 60% above the requirement. This may even be an optimistic figure, since it does not include the many students who log far more time and never receive the rating. All in all, the statistics speak poorly for the overall quality of instrument training in the United States.

How To Choose Your Training Program

Instrument training is not usually marketed to "educated consumers," and yet choosing wisely is the pilot's responsibility. Unfortunately, when he shops for an instrument course, the pilot often doesn't know what questions to ask. He may choose on the basis of price alone or he may assume that all courses are created equal and hire the nearest CFII. If he has a disappointing experience, with a small prospect for improvement, he will struggle through anyway or quit in frustration only when he has learned too late to evaluate competitive programs.

In choosing an instrument training program, there are some guidelines that will help the prospective student who considers the "Brand-X School of Aviation." Choosing an instrument course is like choosing any educational program. The main considerations are the quality and thoroughness of the instruction. Convenience and cost are two other features to examine.

In evaluating an instrument training program, here is a suggested checklist to help make the correct "go/no go" decision.

—*Note the word program*. Instrument training is like instrument flight: to be successful, it must be fully and carefully planned. A course with no curriculum is like an aircraft in the soup without navigation gear. If you want to get the rating on schedule, enroll in a course which follows a course plan. Ask to see *in writing* your exact training sequence and the approximate time devoted to each phase of the curriculum. Once started, you should be able to plan the date you will receive the rating. During training, insist that the schedule and curriculum be adhered to, and records kept of your progress through it.

If the school has no written curriculum, go elsewhere. Don't be like so many people who periodically "get some dual" and log 40, 60, or 80 hours of hood time without significant progress towards the rating. The lack of a syllabus causes gaps, delays and confusion. Unplanned courses may go 200% or 300% beyond the time scheduled, with corresponding effects on the budget.

—*Is instrument instruction an important part of the school's business?* Will they agree not to cancel your lessons in favor of charter flights or rental pilots? If the FBO also fixes aircraft, sells gas, rents airplanes and flies charter, you are less likely to get first class treatment, unless the "school" has also specifically provided for a professionally conducted instrument program. How many instrument students finished the course last year at this operation and what was the average time required? Request the names of one or two graduates, and speak to them before committing yourself.

—*Does the program include ground instruction?* Even though you passed the written exam (remember the written?), ground school is an esssential part of an instrument rating course. A 30-minute ground briefing can save hours of frustrating hood time. Half an hour or more of ground school for each flight hour is reasonable for thoroughly covering all the material.

Expect to pay for ground instruction. If you don't pay for it, you probably won't get it, and your course will consequently be longer, more expensive and more frustrating than necessary.

—*Check the instructor's background.* Just being a Certificated Flight Instructor, Instrument (CFII) is no guarantee that he is well qualified. The CFII is an easy credential to obtain, easier than the CFIA (certificated flight instructor, airplane) and easier than the instrument rating itself. The "double-eye" can be earned in a week or less, with 250 hours total time, no actual weather time, and no teaching experience. Compare this with the much more stringent requirements for charter pilots under Part 135 of the FAR's: 500 flight hours for VFR operations, 1200 for IFR work, and an instrument proficiency check every six months.

Ideally, your instructor should be committed to teaching, not just to building time for the airlines or making extra money. High pilot time is not necessarily a sign of a good teacher either, but instructing experience is. You are hiring a teacher, not a pilot, and you should look for the qualifications you would expect in a high school or college teacher. Has he signed off ten or twelve instrument pilots in the last year, or will he be learning his job at your expense? Most instructors are somewhere in between, and the more recent experience with the curriculum you will be using, the better.

—*Will you fly in actual instrument conditions?* Training in IFR weather is valuable experience, and you should be sure that if nature provides the opportunity, your school will take full advantage of it. Believe it or not, there are flight schools that forbid IFR flight during IFR training, and there are CFII's who have never been in weather and are unwilling to try it.

—*Does the program use a simulator?* If so, you will save gas, money, and a significant amount of time, because a simulator is a far better teaching device than an airplane. It allows normal conversation; it can be stopped "in mid-air" to discuss or clarify a point; and it can be instantaneously moved to any spot on the chart to repeat an exercise or begin a new one. IFR procedures are learned many times faster in a simulator than is possible in the airplane. FAR Part 61 allows up to half the 40 hours required for the rating to be instruction in a simulator, and a well-conceived program will take advantage of this.

Like an airplane, the simulator must be regularly maintained and properly operated if it is to serve you well. A dusty Link C-3 dating from the 1930's with most of the instruments broken, or an instructor who isn't familiar with simulator instruction, can cancel the benefits available from this type of training.

—*Convenience.* Once you are satisfied that you are considering a good training program, you still must think about convenience. How far and how often will you have to drive for instruction? How much time will you be committing? Will it be ten consecutive days, full time, or every Saturday morning for a year? Will there be delays, cancellations or waiting time? Will part of every session be spent in regaining proficiency lost owing to inactivity?

We often hear arguments about the value of concentrated training. Anything you learn quickly, detractors claim, you will forget just as quickly, once the course is over.

It is true that flying instruments is not like riding a bicycle. You must practice it to stay proficient; in fact, it is strictly a case of "use it or lose it." The level of skill a pilot keeps after finishing instrument training depends on how much and how carefully he practices his new skills.

Consider two pilots who begin instrument training at the same time. One enrolls in a concentrated course (perhaps a full time program) and receives his rating between ten and sixty days later. The other trains once or twice a week for nine months. After nine months, the first pilot has actively flown instruments for more than half a year and has accumulated substantial experience. The second is just taking his check ride, receiving his new instrument ticket and getting ready to begin enjoying the benefits of the rating. Obviously, the one who took the concentrated course is, at that moment, a better qualified instrument pilot.

When substantial time passes between lessons, proficiency is lost *during* the training period. This leads to repetition, frustration and the previously mentioned national average of 65 flight hours for the rating. The repetition also results in unnecessary expense.

All professional training programs provide more intensive training than do most FBO flight schools. Full time training is accepted as the norm in most fields. Management and technical seminars in industry and the professions are usually presented as continuous full time programs. Can you imagine the Navy or Air Force training their aviation cadets in two hour sessions once or twice a week?

Not everyone can take advantage of full time instrument training. But with planning, you may be able to arrange a fairly concentrated training program. For effectiveness, try to make your training experience as concentrated as possible, with three sessions per week as a minimum.

—*Cost.* Cost is often the most difficult factor to evaluate. The advantage of a lower hourly price quickly evaporates if the "cheaper" course is even a few hours longer than a concentrated one. Furthermore, it is difficult to balance cost against quality when you are acquiring knowledge that will affect your safety for years to come. "You get what you pay for."

If one program offers better quality training than another, it will not be significantly more expensive in the long run. You will get good value for your money, and since better training takes less time, you may pay less overall. Taking the trouble to insist on first class flight training will make you more proficient, enhance your safety, and give you greater satisfaction from flying. In the long run, it may also force an improvement in the overall quality of aviation training.

What Makes A Good Instructor

The CFII's goal is to help his student develop new habit patterns, some of which are physical but most of which are mental. To do this, he must understand exactly what these patterns consist of, be able to break them down into the smallest possible units, and communicate them to the student. A good instructor is specific in his explanations and corrections. The more precise they are, the more effective they will be. For example, it is better to correct a heading problem by identifying the scanning error which causes it than merely by offering a vague "watch your heading." In fact, the latter comment can aggravate the problem if it results in the student's fixating on the directional gyro when his fault is omitting the attitude indicator when leveling the wings.

A good instructor understands the learning process and empathizes with the student. From previous experience, he understands the student's problems and overcomes them with a broad repertoire of teaching techniques. He is never judgmental. He rewards good performance with positive feedback, and he takes responsibility for the success of the teaching process.

The good instructor works to maximize progress towards the goal of training: to transmit skills and information. Like many professionals, he learns that the more he knows and the more skilled he becomes, the less he actually has to do. His comments and corrections go right to the heart of matters. Words and motion are not wasted on superfluous topics. His experience and expertise become a lever, allowing large changes with small efforts.

No learning environment, including the cockpit, is a place for abuse, ridicule or angry scolding. There may be a student somewhere who learns better when he is abused, treated with contempt, and constantly faced with impossible challenges. If he does exist, he is rare. Most people learn better when they are treated respectfully, when the instructor explains new material carefully and in detail, and when he corrects faults or misconceptions with patience and precision. An effective instructor understands this.

The Role of the Simulator

The relationship between the simulator and the aircraft in IFR training causes confusion for some instructors and pilots without simulator experience. I often hear the criticism that the simulator does not "fly" like an airplane. In fact, it has an important role in instrument training which does not depend on its handling exactly like a particular aircraft.

The simulator is used to teach scan and visualization of position. For this, it is a far better *teaching tool* than the airplane. It is easier to learn in a comfortable chair, with no distracting noises louder than the air conditioner, than in a noisy, vibrating cockpit, where the instructor must shout to be heard and the student must yell to ask questions. Furthermore, none of the instructor's attention is lost in scanning for traffic.

The simulator allows you to concentrate on one thing at a time. Good teaching technique requires that errors be clearly identified by the instructor, understood by the student, and corrected. If the student falls behind the airplane, his confusion, frustration and fatigue may increase to the point where learning is impossible. In a moving airplane there is no time for the quiet, detailed conversation that best gets such points across. The simulator, on the other hand, can be put on hold, and the exercise can be repeated as many times as necessary. Most simulators can be "frozen," or stopped in mid "flight" with instrument indications intact, while problems or misunderstandings are discussed. You can't do that in an airplane!

A common teaching fault lies in asking a student to fly a procedure that he doesn't fully understand and attempting to explain things in the airplane. Hold entries are particularly difficult to teach in a loud and bucking airplane. Typically, in the air, the instructor assigns a hold on the way to the holding fix. If the student has had trouble visualizing the entry, he is confused at the fix and the instructor must either abandon the exercise or give such instructions as "Turn to a heading of 030°; start the clock; change the OBS to 210°." Either way, the student learns nothing about figuring hold

entries. To try the entry again, he must waste many minutes flying several miles away from the fix, turning and flying back to it, hoping he understands what to do.

The simulator also excels for teaching approach techniques. Consider a challenging VOR approach, one with the final approach fix (FAF) at the VOR and calling for a turn at the FAF. Crossing the fix, you must turn to a new heading, start the watch, change the OBS setting, reduce the power to descend, and report to the tower. Many students have trouble at this point and usually forget one or more of the tasks required. When they are practicing in the airplane, they must continue the prescribed approach, fly the missed approach, and begin the entire procedure again. Three tries in an hour is about average in normal airplane practice. And there is always the possibility that ATC will limit the number of approaches because of traffic. In the simulator, by moving back to the FAF instantaneously, the difficult part of the procedure can be practiced repeatedly and rapidly. Making ten repetitions in 20 minutes is not unreasonable.

Ideally, procedures are taught so thoroughly in the simulator that the student is never confused or disoriented when he goes to the airplane. In the airplane, he concentrates on integrating new procedures with his previous skills, and on improving precision. He doesn't waste time getting lost or trying to understand something he should have learned on the ground.

The simulator also makes you independent of the weather. Although training in actual weather is good experience, serious ice or thunderstorms occasionally prevent it. A flexible curriculum allows continuing on the simulator while waiting for conditions to improve. Thanks to this flexibility, a well-organized instrument program might lose a day to weather less than once in 50 ratings. The typical student finishes on schedule with no weather delays.

Instrument Skills

Instrument instruction depends on careful organization. The key to effective teaching in this field is to break down component skills into the smallest possible units and to present them in logical sequence, in the simplest possible way. Taking the mystery out of IFR facilitates learning.

No single skill or facet of instrument flying is complicated or difficult in itself. It is the complex combination of movements, decisions, and reactions that makes it challenging. The role of the curriculum is to organize the many parts of the subject into digestible chunks, and to present it in a simple, coherent, easily understood order. It can be broken into three major areas: **scan**, **visualization**, and "**the system**." In practice these areas overlap, but for learning purposes, they make convenient divisions.

Scan starts with the techniques of flying the airplane on the gauges — holding heading and altitude, climbing and descending to specific altitudes and turning to particular headings at predetermined airspeeds. It is the fundamental skill to be mastered before progressing to more advanced work.

Visualization refers to instrument navigation. It involves forming a mental picture of your position in relation to fixes and courses, usually with reference to a chart. Visualization is essential for cross country travel, holding, and

approach work. The student should be given specific techniques for mentally picturing his position. Navigating also increases the instrument scan. In the learning process, you must first have the ability to control the airplane on instruments with little or no conscious effort and then enlarge the scan to include the navigation instruments.

The system means air navigation methods and includes a knowledge of the FAR's, IFR procedures, the ATC system, and proper interpretation of charts and approach plates. The instrument pilot needs a thorough knowledge of the system to use the rating effectively.

There is a substantial overlap of visualization skills onto this part of the IFR curriculum, and they are a prerequisite for it. Especially in approach work, position visualization and an understanding of the system go hand in hand.

I hope you are excited about instrument flying and are looking forward to proceeding with your training. It is a satisfying and mind-expanding activity — immersion in a discipline that will greatly enhance your personal confidence and freedom.

CHAPTER TWO

THE FLIGHT INSTRUMENTS— KNOWING AND USING THEM

This chapter and the next are the most important in the book. If what they teach is learned thoroughly, the subsequent material will come easier as you learn navigation and the system. How well you master attitude flying by reference to instruments will determine, more than any other factor, how successful you will be as an instrument pilot. Attitude flying is the foundation of all IFR skills and must be done well for the later work to go well. You can't stay ahead of the IFR situation if you are behind the airplane. How true this is was borne out by the experience of one of my students.

Lyndon Thomas was upset the first time he called. He had been pursuing the instrument rating for a year, and his training was not going well. "I've got 65 hours of instrument time," he said, "and my instructor signed me off for the flight test. He says I'm completely ready, but I failed the test in the first ten minutes. The examiner said I need a lot more training. He said I fly like a harelipped cow. Now I don't know what to believe or who to trust."

Lyndon lived in San Antonio, and I was scheduled to teach an instrument rating there the following week. I arranged an evaluation with him the day after it ended.

We met at my motel, which was close to the airport where Lyndon kept his airplane. At first I was baffled. I showed him our syllabus and there was nothing he hadn't covered. I had him get a weather briefing for a

hypothetical flight, and he knew exactly what to ask for. He had an excellent shorthand and kept right up with the briefer. He knew all the symbols on the chart and the approach plates even down to such items as TCH and SSALSR. I quizzed him on approaches and hold entries, and he seemed knowledgeable. I wondered how he could have failed the flight test.

The first clue came from his logbook, but I missed it at the time. He had five or six hundred hours in various types, with about 100 in his new airplane, a Pressurized Centurion. His instrument time was all in the P-210 with the same instructor, and, sure enough, they had done everything specified in the flight test guide. The odd thing was the sequence; advanced maneuvers were thrown in with basic airwork practically from day one, and consecutive flights were often devoted to quite different subjects.

At the airport, Lyndon continued to make a good impression. He was a careful pilot with plenty of respect for the complexity of his airplane. He preflighted meticulously and went through his checklists methodically and thoroughly. I relaxed and found myself enjoying the modern, well equipped airplane.

It was nearly noon as we began the takeoff roll. San Antonio's early morning stratus layer had burned off and some scattered cumulus were forming. Tops were about 6000 feet, and clear blue sky sparkled around the isolated puffs. From my ten days in the area, I knew it would probably become broken with tops as high as 13,000 feet by late afternoon. Turbulence below the clouds could be quite noticeable.

"Let's climb above this stuff," I suggested.

Immediately after takeoff Lyndon became very busy. He raised the gear over the runway end and chose a climb setting of 31 inches for the turbocharged engine. He gave the red mixture control knob a couple of twists before noticing that, owing to a lag in the gauge, the manifold pressure had dropped to 29 inches. His hand darted back to the throttle and returned the power to 31 inches. Next, he backed the prop off to 2500 RPM, only to see the manifold pressure increase to 32 inches, necessitating another throttle adjustment. He adjusted the elevator trim and gave the rudder trim a couple of turns to the right. Finally, his hand went back to the mixture.

He looked like a whirling dervish in the cockpit, and I began to see the problem. With no set techniques for flying the airplane, he fiddled with the controls almost at random, sometimes starting one task before finishing the last. He flew inefficiently and put far too much effort into aircraft control. His attitude control was wild, and the heading and altitude had to take care of themselves. He had no time to scan for traffic. While Lyndon understood IFR procedures, he had never been taught to fly the airplane properly.

Below the clouds the air was bumpy, but it smoothed out at 6000 feet. "Level off at 6500," I said.

It boggled my mind to watch him try to level off. He fooled with the power, the prop, the mixture, the elevator and rudder trim for close to five minutes while we porpoised between 6000 and 7000. I hadn't assigned a heading, but it was still disconcerting to see the nose swinging 60° around the horizon.

We tried some airwork exercises. At 140 knots, I said, "Hold your present heading and slow to 100." Lyndon took four minutes to stabilize the airplane at the slower speed, and I watched almost in disbelief as the altitude fluctuated 400 feet and the heading varied by 30°.

Lyndon's training had skipped the basics and made his whole repertoire weak. Although his problems were magnified by the complexity of his airplane, his lack of concentration on the fundamentals would have been equally important in a 172.

It is worth spending time to master basic aircraft control.

Lyndon's story had a happy ending. I only spent three more days in San Antonio, working with him on basic aircraft control. We determined "the numbers"

for his 210 and developed techniques for transitions from one configuration to another. Lyndon discovered that good techniques simplified his work and gave him more time to navigate, plan and, yes, scan for traffic.

After basic airwork, we went rapidly through advanced procedures. Lyndon was already well acquainted with IFR charts, weather, and other parts of the instrument pilot's arsenal. With the basic skills mastered, we quickly completed a thorough review. He passed his flight test just before I left for home; a week and a half after his original failure. His examiner, a suntanned old cowboy, was the same one he had had previously. When the test was over, he said, "I congratulate you on such progress in so short a time. I wouldn't have believed you could do it, after flying so poorly on your first check ride."

Most modern airplanes have a standard basic instrument panel, the six basic flight instruments, arranged in two rows of three each, which the instrument pilot needs to understand thoroughly (figure 2-1).

The Gyro Instruments

The gyro instruments are the attitude indicator, also called the artificial horizon; the heading indicator, also known as the directional gyro or DG; and the turn and bank or turn coordinator instrument.

The attitude indicator and directional gyro use the principle of gyroscopic rigidity in space; that is, a rapidly spinning object tends to resist being forced off its axis, regardless of twisting forces applied to it. The airplane, in effect, pitches, rolls, and turns around the instrument, while the gyro's axis remains undisturbed, resulting in the proper instrument indications.

This principle can be seen in a child's toy gyroscope. When the string is pulled and the rotor is set spinning, the top will balance on a pencil point. If you tip the pencil from side to side, the gyro will not tip with it but will stay upright as long as it is spinning rapidly. It will begin to waver and eventually fall as its speed bleeds off.

A gyroscope will tend to turn at right angles to a force applied to twist it off its axis. This can be felt by turning your wrist with the toy gyroscope in your hand. It resists movement in the direction of turn and wants to go at right angles to the way it is twisted. The same principle is seen in any rapidly rotating object, such as an

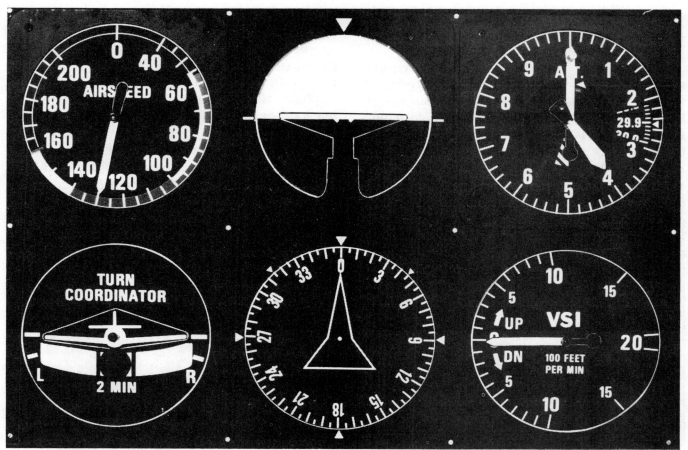

Figure 2-1

engine. Hold a chain saw or other small motor in one hand and try turning it. It shows a definite tendency to turn perpendicular to the direction you expect. These examples illustrate gyroscopic **precession**, an unavoidable phenomenon which causes errors to develop in the attitude and directional gyro indicators because of friction in the "gimbals" (suspension bearings that allow the gyros's axes to remain undisturbed while the airplane yaws, pitches and rolls around them).

In most light aircraft, the attitude and directional gyros are spun at high speed by an engine driven air pump. The pump creates a negative pressure (vacuum) or a positive pressure, depending on the preference of the airframe manufacturer, but the system is commonly called a vacuum pump in either case. Air is directed against paddle wheel-like cutouts on the outer rim of the gyro rotors, causing them to spin at high speed.

The suction gauge on the instrument panel measures the generated pressure and gives an indication of the health of the vacuum system. Its reading is the difference between atmospheric pressure and the pressure in the vacuum system. It should be checked prior to IFR flight according to manufacturer's recommendations. The usual specification is 4.5 to 5.5 inches of mercury (in. Hg; Hg is the chemical symbol for mercury) at runup RPM. If it reads too low, the instruments will be insufficiently stable and their indications sloppy and unreliable. An out of limits vacuum indication, whether too high or too low, is a sign of trouble which could lead to damage to the system and be a precursor to vacuum failure.

Air from the engine driven vacuum pump to the gyro instruments is kept clean by filters in the vacuum lines. The filters eventually become clogged, spoiling the performance of the two instruments and requiring disassembly and cleaning. If there is a lot of smoking in the cockpit, the instruments will need overhaul sooner.

The Attitude Indicator

In the middle of the top row of the panel is the artificial horizon, or attitude indicator, the central element of an instrument pilot's scan. In IFR flight, the AI replaces the natural horizon, showing the relationship of the nose and wings to the horizontal plane.

After startup, the attitude indicator should erect and become stable within two minutes (the FAA recommends a maximum of five minutes). At this point you can adjust it to show level flight. Use the knob at the lower portion of the instrument to align the wings of the symbolic airplane with the 90° bank indices (corresponding to 0° of pitch). This preliminary adjustment should be refined in flight when you determine your level-flight pitch attitude at cruise power.

During taxi, after the gyros have reached full

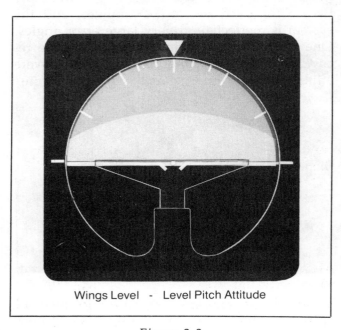

Wings Level - Level Pitch Attitude

Figure 2-2

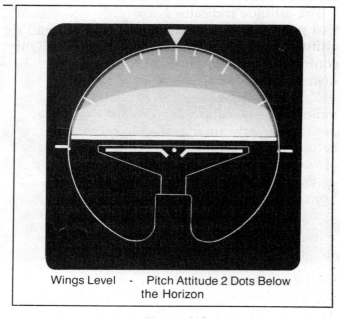

Wings Level - Pitch Attitude 2 Dots Below
the Horizon

Figure 2-3

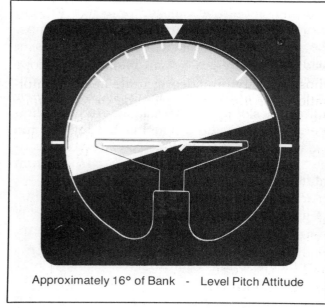

Approximately 16° of Bank - Level Pitch Attitude

Figure 2-4

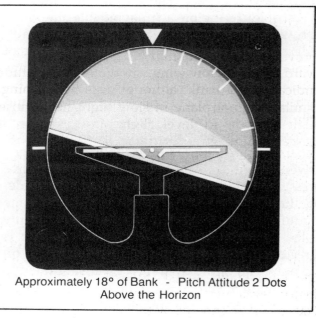

Approximately 18° of Bank - Pitch Attitude 2 Dots
Above the Horizon

Figure 2-5

speed with normal suction/air pressure, applying the brakes should cause a noticeable pitch down movement in the attitude indicator. Turning should not reveal any indication of bank if the wings are level. If the AI does show bank in a taxi turn, excessive friction in the gimbal bearings is indicated, calling for the instrument to be cleaned or overhauled. Five degrees of such "slop" is the maximum permissible amount; even a smaller amount makes attitude control difficult.

The attitude indicator is the only instrument that gives *direct* information about the aircraft's attitude. Each conscious movement of the flight controls, changing pitch or bank, is therefore made with reference to this instrument.

The bank index on the face of the attitude indicator marks off the first 30° in 10° increments and shows one mark each for 60° and 90° of bank. Pitch attitude may be judged as a number of "dots" (using the dot that represents the nose of the symbolic airplane) above or below the horizon (figures 2-2 through 2-5). On some instruments, short lines above and below the horizon indicate degrees of pitch attitude.

In a bank, the horizon bar remains parallel to the horizon; the symbolic airplane, rigidly attached to the instrument case, rolls with the real airplane showing the bank against the horizon bar in the background. If you pitch up, the horizon bar drops, causing the symbolic airplane to appear "above the horizon."

Notice that a bank does not necessarily indicate a turn, and a nose high attitude does not prove you are climbing. An airplane in a forward slip has a low wing, shown on the attitude indicator as a bank, although it is not turning. Similarly, an airplane in slow flight has a nose high attitude in level flight and even in a descent. The attitude indicator merely shows the airplane's *attitude* in relation to the horizon.

Older attitude indicators are accurate within limits, and if these limits are exceeded, may tumble and become useless for controlling the airplane. The limits, however, are far greater than would ever be encountered in normal flight. The pitch limit is usually 60° to 70°, and the bank limit is 100° to 110°. Many newer instruments are "non-tumbling"; they can take 360° of pitch and roll with relatively little error because there are no internal stops to limit travel.

If you have ever spun an airplane with an uncaged attitude indicator, you may have seen it spinning uselessly like a pinwheel, coming to rest on its side or upside down. With the conventional pendulous vane erecting system, the gyro may take an hour or more to re-erect after becoming fully tumbled. The correction rate with the rotor at operating RPM is not more than 3° of pitch or roll per minute, and the system is ineffective at very large error angles. One reason for practicing unusual attitude recovery on partial panel is that in a severe attitude, the attitude indicator could become useless.

Small precession errors do occur in the attitude indicator, but if the instrument is in good condition, you have to look closely to detect them so they pose no danger. At the end of a 180° turn the attitude indicator may show up to 5° of bank. This error will be removed at 2° or 3° per minute by the gyro's self-erecting system after you return to level flight.

An old or worn attitude indicator may suffer some precession error after even a small turn, showing wings level when, in fact, the airplane is still slightly banked. This may result in a slight, undesired additional turn.

The Directional Gyro

Below the attitude indicator is the heading indicator, also called the directional gyro or DG (figure 2-6). It does not sense the airplane's heading directly, but has an internal gyroscope whose stability provides accurate heading information *once it is initially set to the correct heading*. The airplane's heading is shown at the top of the instrument. We need the DG for heading control because of the errors that occur in the magnetic compass during turns, speed changes, and even in rough air.

The face of the DG is a compass rose divided into 5°, 10° and 30° segments. Often, 45° divisions are marked on the circumference of the instrument to further simplify visualizing the compass rose. To turn right 45°, for example, just notice the course under the reference mark 45° to the right and turn to that heading.

Figure 2-6

Calculate compass reciprocals by glancing diametrically across the instrument from the heading whose reciprocal you need. Using the DG in this way cuts down on cockpit arithmetic, always a worthwhile goal. Consulting the DG also makes clear which runway goes where as you approach an airport, which can be especially valuable on a circling approach.

Check the DG before takeoff. When it has spun up, set it to the magnetic compass prior to taxi and check it against runway heading just before takeoff. This checks the DG for excessive precession and also protects you against the danger and embarrassment of departing from the wrong runway at an unfamiliar field.

Gyroscopic precession is a problem in using the directional gyro. A normal DG will precess, or drift off its heading, and should regularly be checked against the magnetic compass in straight, level, unaccelerated flight. Three degrees of precession in 15 minutes is the maximum permissible error for normal operations.

The DG will tend to precess more when several turns are made, as in a holding pattern or during an approach. *The DG should always be checked before and during an instrument approach.*

Like the attitude indicator, the directional gyro has limits and will become unreliable if the airplane is banked too steeply. Beyond fifty-five degrees of bank, the DG will lose accuracy and may spin wildly.

If the aircraft has a heading control autopilot, the DG includes a pointer, or heading bug, which is moved to the desired heading by a knob at the lower edge of the instrument. When turned on, the autopilot holds the heading to which the bug is set. While hand flying the airplane, some pilots set the bug as a reminder of the desired heading before beginning a turn. It reminds them to stop turning as it reaches the top of the instrument. When tracking a VOR or localizer course, the course is set in the OBS; the heading bug can be adjusted to reflect the wind correction required to remain on course.

The horizontal situation indicator (HSI) is a combined DG and VOR display. It has several extra indicators in addition to the heading bug, including the course selector, TO-FROM indicator and CDI. However, the heading indicator function of the HSI works just like that of an ordinary DG. (The navigation uses of the HSI are covered in Chapter Five.)

The VOR display portion of the HSI is electric. The heading indicator part may be vacuum driven or electric. The pilot should know which type he has, to better understand and deal with system failures. To determine which you have, turn on the master switch momentarily, prior to engine start. If the warning flag, usually marked ''HDG,'' disappears, the DG is electric.

If the HSI is all electric, a vacuum failure will not affect it, while an electrical failure will put it completely out of service. If it is combined vacuum/electric, an electrical failure will disable the navigation portion but not the heading function.

The Turn Instrument

The third and final gyro instrument is found at the lower left corner of a standard panel and is often called the turn and bank indicator.

In modern light airplanes, the gyro in the turn instrument is driven, not by vacuum, but by electricity, so that if the vacuum system fails, the pilot still has a means of knowing and controlling his bank attitude. Conversely, if he loses his turn instrument in an electrical failure, the vacuum instruments continue to work.

Figure 2-7

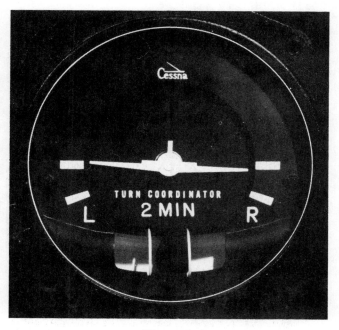

Figure 2-8

Two distinct types of turn instrument are installed in today's general aviation fleet, the older **turn indicator**, also known as the turn and bank indicator (figure 2-7), and the more modern turn coordinator (figure 2-8).

The turn indicator is the familiar "needle and ball" instrument, with a pointer that shows direction and rate of turn. Rate of turn is expressed as the number of *degrees of heading change per second*; it indicates the time required to turn from one heading to another.

In instrument flight all turns are made at 3° per second (standard rate) or less; steeper turns are considered dangerous. For very small turns — 5° or 10° of heading change — a less than standard rate is used. Turn indicators usually have little squares with peaked caps, referred to as "doghouses," to indicate standard rate turns to left and right.

Newer aircraft have a **turn coordinator** which replaces the older instrument's needle with a miniature airplane that dips a wing to indicate the direction and rate of turn. Two hash marks show standard rate to left and right.

In both instruments, a gyro wheel is suspended with its axis parallel to the airplane's lateral axis, positioned by a spring of calibrated strength, in gimbals so the whole assembly can pivot around the airplane's longitudinal axis.

As the wheel spins, any yawing by the airplane causes the wheel to react (precess) by tipping left or right in the gimbals. The more rapid the yaw, the bigger the precessional force, the further the tipping gyro stretches the spring, and the bigger the displacement of the turn needle or airplane symbol.

On turn coordinators, the gimbal axis is canted about 30° above horizontal, which causes an exaggerated reaction when the airplane changes bank angle. This was originally intended to provide data for a wing-leveling autopilot, but it was found that the active display during roll caught pilots' eyes. Many people now think the turn coordinator is easier to use than the older turn indicator. The damping of stray oscillations in rough air is better in turn coordinators than in turn indicators.

Two important points about turn coordinators: (1) The exaggerated reaction caused by the canted gimbal axis only occurs when the airplane is *changing* bank angle, not in a constant angle of bank; and (2) although the miniature airplane turn symbol suggests a banking airplane, it does *not* necessarily mean the airplane is in a bank (any more than the turn needle in a turn and bank indicator does); what the symbol really displays over the long term is *rate of yaw*.

The ball part of the turn instrument, some-

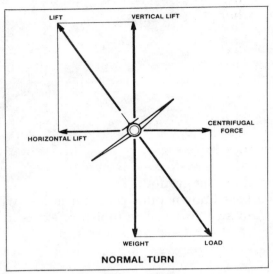

Figure 2-9

times called the slip-skid indicator, is the same in the two types of instrument. It is simply a heavy ball in a curved glass tube filled with kerosene to dampen its movements. In a turn, the ball's position in the tube is controlled by the balance between gravity (acting downward toward the center of the earth) and centrifugal force (acting toward the outside of the turn). Its purpose is to show whether or not the airplane is in coordinated flight.

In any turn, the airplane is affected by its weight and by centrifugal force. The weight pulls the airplane towards the earth, and centrifugal force pulls it towards the outside of the turn. The resultant is a net force pointing downward at an angle to the vertical, referred to as the total *load* (figure 2-9).

A turn is said to be coordinated if the airplane is banked just enough so that the resultant force is directed straight toward the floor of the cockpit. In a coordinated turn the ball will rest in the center of its tube.

If the ball moves towards the inside of a turn, the airplane is not turning fast enough for its degree of bank and is said to be slipping. This is corrected by applying rudder to increase the rate of turn. If the ball moves towards the outside of the turn, the airplane is turning too fast for the degree of bank and is said to be skidding. The usual cause is too much rudder pressure.

In slipping and skidding turns, the turn instrument will show the actual rate of turn. Its accuracy is not disturbed by uncoordinated flight.

To help visualize slipping and skidding errors, picture a race car on a steeply banked track. If it travels too fast, turning too rapidly for the degree of bank, it will *skid* towards the outside of the track. If it is driven too slowly, not turning fast enough, it will *slip* towards the inside of the track.

Coordinated flight has several advantages. Most stall-spin accidents result from uncoordinated maneuvers at low airspeed in the turn from base to final. Similar dangers exist in departure turns, if the airspeed is allowed to diminish too much, and in strong turbulence. Coordinated flight is also far more comfortable than flight in which the airplane's occupants are subjected to a lot of unnecessary lateral forces. It will therefore greatly reduce the incidence of airsickness among your passengers.

In coordinated flight at a given airspeed, the turn rate is directly proportional to the bank angle. The steeper the bank, the faster the airplane will turn. At a given airspeed, a standard rate turn will always be achieved with a particular angle of bank.

The bank angle required for a given turn rate depends on the airspeed. The higher the airspeed, the more bank is necessary for a standard rate turn. To visualize this, picture a Piper J-3 Cub and an F-15 fighter, both banked 30°. The Cub will complete a circle in far less time than the faster aircraft.

The bank angle required for a coordinated standard rate turn is about 15% of the airspeed. A Mooney or Bonanza flying an approach at 100 knots would bank 15° for a standard rate turn, while the same airplane would bank 22° to turn at the same rate when cruising at 150 knots. In very fast airplanes, it may be necessary to bank more than 30° to achieve a 3° per second turn, and this is considered unsafe. In such situations the bank is limited to 30° and turns are made at less than standard rate.

It is important to recognize the differences between the turn instrument and the attitude indicator. The attitude indicator gives direct information about *angle of bank*, which is not necessarily the same as turn information. The turn instrument gives *rate-of-turn* information but says nothing about the angle of bank, except in coordinated flight, where the bank angle associated with a given rate of turn depends upon speed.

What about the old story of the pilot who lost all his gyros and was inspired to quickly hang his tie from the ceiling of the cockpit? Supposedly, he maneuvered the machine so that the tie hung towards the floor and brought himself to safety. Sorry. The tie would behave just like the ball. In any coordinated flight attitude, it would hang towards the floor of the aircraft, even in a steep bank.

To check the turn instrument prior to IFR takeoff, observe its indications during taxi turns. As you turn a few degrees left or right, you should see corresponding turn indications on the turn instrument, and the ball should roll toward the outside of the turn. If you turn 90° onto a perpendicular taxiway at a normal taxi speed, you will be turning at considerably more than standard rate; the instrument should show this.

The Pressure Instruments
The Pitot-Static System

An airplane's pressure instruments — the airspeed indicator, altimeter and vertical speed indicator — are driven by the pitot-static system, which includes the pitot tube, the static port or ports, plumbing to transmit pressure to the pressure instruments and, often, an alternate static source.

The pitot tube receives ram pressure from outside the airplane for use by the airspeed indicator. It is prone to various problems, starting with the pilot's forgetting to remove its protective cover before flight. (Incidentally, if you don't have a fancy red cover, a perfectly serviceable substitute can be made from the finger of an old glove). The pitot tube seems to be an especially attractive hiding hole for beetles and other crawling insects; one insect can effectively disable an airspeed indicator. Care should be taken when taxiing in the snow, especially in a low wing airplane, because pitot heads have

been known to intercept a snow bank and clog, even when there was no bump felt in the cockpit.

A blocked pitot tube cannot always be detected during the preflight, but a quick glance at the airspeed during the takeoff roll can flag it in time to discontinue the takeoff.

The pitot system can be completely or partially blocked by water in heavy rain. This will result in a jumpy airspeed needle or one that does not return to zero when the airplane is stopped on the ground.

The best known pitot problem is ice, which can form any time visible moisture exists in the presence of sub-freezing temperatures. The preflight should therefore always include a check of the pitot heat. Just click on the master switch and pitot heat; the ammeter should immediately show a significant jump. (With a left needle type ammeter, this check can only be done after start-up.) A more positive check is to feel the pitot tube with your hand; it should be warm to the touch in less than a minute, but don't wait too long to touch it for you would unnecessarily drain the battery and risk a burn.

Pitot heat should be used as a preventative measure, not a cure. Switch it on any time you expect to enter visible moisture when the outside air temperature may reach 0°C or colder.

Static ports are usually located in the pitot head or on the fuselage. Airplanes with static ports on both sides of the fuselage reduce the risk of a blocked system by half.

The static system also includes tubes to transmit ambient pressure from the ports to the instruments and, usually, an alternate static source for use in the unlikely but dangerous event that the static ports become blocked. The alternate source can be opened to allow cabin pressure into the static system. As part of an IFR preflight, open the valve and observe a slight jump in the three pressure instruments. (Not all aircraft exhibit this jump, but if yours does, check for it before each flight.)

The alternate static source is inside the cockpit, where the pressure is usually lower than outside the airplane, owing to the Bernoulli effect of air rushing over tiny openings in the cabin. *Altimeter and airspeed indications are therefore somewhat high on most aircraft when using the alternate static source*, typically 10 to 50 feet of altitude and 5 to 10 knots of airspeed. Airspeed and altitude correction charts provided in the pilot's handbook show adjustments necessary with the alternate source open.

When using the alternate static source, shade your altitudes on the side of safety and use higher than normal approach speeds, especially if your static system has been disabled by ice. If you are carrying structural ice, your stall speed will be higher than usual. Some owner's manuals and pilot's operating handbooks list additional instructions for use of the alternate static source, such as closing vents and windows, to minimize the pressure difference between inside and outside the cockpit.

The most definite indication of a blocked static system would be an altimeter showing a constant reading regardless of pitch inputs. If the airplane has no alternate static source and the static ports do ice over, you may be able to let cabin pressure into the system by reaching under the panel and slipping the hose off the VSI. If this fails, break the glass on the VSI. This may be possible with a heavy ring, but these instruments are sturdily constructed and might require an implement, such as a metal tool or the fire extinguisher, to crack the glass. As a last resort, try ramming it with the screwdriver end of a fuel tester or the corner of your clipboard. You could break the airspeed indicator or the altimeter, but the VSI is the most expendable pressure instrument, the only one not required by regulations, and, incidentally, the cheapest to replace. If you are ever actually in this situation, reduce unnecessary anxiety among your passengers by explaining why you are "attacking" the instrument panel — before you go at it.

The Altimeter

The altimeter (figure 2-10) is a simple mechanism, and yet, some aspects of its operation can be confusing.

An altimeter is basically a barometer calibrated in feet instead of inches of mercury. The static system transmits atmospheric pressure from outside the airplane to the altimeter. Sealed chambers called "aneroid cells" inside the instrument expand and contract with pres-

sure changes, and a mechanical linkage moves the hands in response.

What is meant by *inches of mercury*? A barometer measures atmospheric pressure by determining the height of a column of mercury required to produce the same pressure. Mercury was chosen for this role because it is the heaviest liquid known. A lighter liquid, such as water, would be too awkward to use.

The fifty miles of air above us exerts about the same pressure at the surface of the earth as would a thirty inch column of mercury. The exact value varies with changes in the weather. At sea level, the average, or standard, barometric pressure is 29.92 in. Hg (Hg is the chemical symbol for mercury).

With an increase in altitude, since there is less air above you, the pressure is less and is therefore equivalent to fewer inches of mercury. Atmospheric pressure decreases approximately one inch of mercury for each 1000 foot increase in altitude. We define a *pressure plane* as a level of the atmosphere where the pressure has a certain specified value. Above a particular plane, the pressure is lower; below it, the pressure is higher.

The altimeter gives your height above the pressure plane that is specified in the Kollsman window, which you set with the knob at the

Figure 2-10

lower left of the instrument. If the Kollsman setting is the current sea level pressure, i.e., the current altimeter setting, the altimeter reads your altitude above sea level.

Notice that the altimeter setting at an airport is the local barometric pressure, *adjusted to sea level*, not the actual atmospheric pressure at the observation point. On a standard day in Denver, where they are five thousand feet above sea level, the actual atmospheric pressure would be approximately 24.92 inches of mercury. However, the correct altimeter setting is 29.92, just as it is anywhere else.

An important check, prior to IFR flight, is to put the correct altimeter setting in the Kollsman window and compare the altimeter reading with field elevation. The difference should be small, certainly less than seventy-five feet, which is the FAA's suggestion for the maximum allowable error.

When performing this check, bear in mind, of course, that "field elevation" is defined as the highest point on any usable runway, and the elevations at other places may vary considerably. The field elevation at Burbank, California, for example, is 775 feet, but the touchdown zone elevation at the approach end of runway 33 is about 80 feet less. Consider this factor before condemning the altimeter for excessive error.

Assuming you are going to conduct an IFR flight with a 50 foot altimeter error, would you prefer the altimeter to read 50 feet too high, or 50 feet too low? A reading that is too *low* would be preferable. If you shoot an approach to minimums and level off when the altimeter shows your minimum descent altitude, you will actually be on the high side of the safe altitude. If the altimeter reads too high, you should *add the amount of the error to the minimum altitude on approach*.

Have you ever come out to the airplane and found the altimeter reading higher than you left it? Perhaps it read field elevation when you taxied in and now reads several hundred feet above the ground. Assuming nobody tampered with your aircraft, what caused the altimeter reading to change? Apparently the barometric pressure has fallen. Sensing lower pressure, the altimeter "thinks" it has climbed to a higher altitude. If you put in the current altimeter setting you should read the field elevation again.

The same reasoning applies if you find your altimeter reading to be a few hundred feet below ground height — higher pressure has moved into the area.

Pressure changes can cause problems in flight. If the pressure drops, your altimeter will read higher, and you would descend to maintain the indicated altitude. Remember the old rule, "From high to low, look out below." If the pressure were to change several tenths of an inch, which is not unusual on a long flight, and the altimeter setting were not updated, you could find yourself seriously below a minimum altitude, either en route, or worse, in the approach environment.

Each controller is required to give you the local altimeter setting at least once while you are in his sector. *Enter the setting each time you receive it* and you will avoid "look out below" worries.

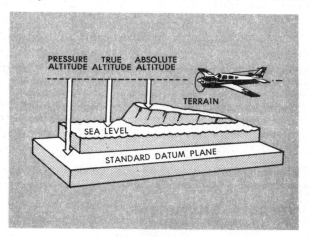

Figure 2-11

Pilots are concerned with several types of altitude (figure 2-11). The number read off the altimeter is called **indicated** altitude and agrees with true altitude when you have entered the local altimeter setting and there is no instrument error or nonstandard pressure lapse with altitude. Actual height above mean sea level (MSL) is called **true** altitude. *True altitude should be used by all aircraft below 18,000 feet and is the basis for IFR separation.*

Height above the terrain is called **absolute** altitude, and the conventional aneroid altimeter knows nothing about this. The only instruments for determining absolute altitude are the radar altimeter and the good old human eyeball. An aid to remembering the meanings of true and absolute altitude is that the "a" in absolute stands for "AGL", above ground level.

Pressure altitude is the height above the pressure plane where the pressure is 29.92 inches of mercury, known as the standard datum plane. It is equal to true altitude on a standard day. To determine the pressure altitude, simply enter 29.92 in your Kollsman window and read the indicated altitude.

Because encoding altimeters report pressure altitude, you don't have to worry about the altimeter setting on your mode "C" equipment. The ATC computer converts the reported pressure altitude to the true altitude seen by the controller on the radar screen, by applying the local altimeter setting.

At 18,000 feet and above, altitudes are called Flight Levels in the United States and are based on pressure altitudes in hundreds of feet. For example, Flight Level two-niner zero means a pressure altitude of 29,000 feet. As an aircraft climbs through 18,000 feet, the altimeter is changed from the local setting to 29.92. The altitude where the reference change is made to pressure altitudes is determined by the national aviation authority, the FAA in the U.S., and in some countries is as low as 4,000 feet.

When atmospheric pressure varies greatly from standard, there is a considerable difference between true and pressure altitudes. On a low pressure day, there could be a conflict between aircraft at the top of the low altitude airspace structure using true altitudes and those near the bottom of the high altitude structure, using flight levels. For example, if the pressure were to drop to one inch below standard, an aircraft at Flight Level 180, at a pressure altitude of 18,000 feet, would actually have a true altitude of only 17,000.

To avoid this problem, FAR 91.121 and the *Airman's Information Manual* give a table of "lowest usable flight levels," listed according to the current altimeter setting. If the pressure actually were a full inch below standard, all aircraft in the high altitude structure would be

prohibited from using Flight Levels lower than 190 (figure 2-12.)

At or above 18,000 feet MSL — to 29.92 inches of mercury (standard setting). The lowest usable flight level is determined by the atmospheric pressure in the area of operation as shown in the following table:

Altimeter Setting (Current Reported)	Lowest usable flight level
29.92 or higher	180
29.91 to 29.42	185
29.41 to 28.92	190
28.91 to 28.42	195
28.41 to 27.92	200

Figure 2-12

Density altitude is pressure altitude corrected for non-standard temperature. At the 29.92 in. Hg. pressure plane, 15°C. (59°F.) is the "standard" temperature, and, on a standard day, the temperature decreases predictably with altitude. For any given pressure altitude, there is a corresponding standard temperature. When the temperature varies from standard, aircraft performance is affected. Density altitude is a computed value which accounts for temperature and pressure variations and is used in calculating expected performance.

High temperature and high altitude both reduce air density and airplane performance. Engine output suffers in thinner or warmer air, and lift, which also depends on air density, decreases. On a hot day, an airplane will need a longer takeoff roll, climb slower and have a lower indicated airspeed than in cooler temperatures.

Density altitude provides a practical method of evaluating these factors and is found by using a computer or a density altitude table published in your operating handbook (figure 2-13). Density altitude is considered in making performance calculations and is especially important to pilots at high-elevation airports and in hot climates, or where the airplane's weight and the runway length are critical. Density altitude is also the basis for calculating *true airspeed*, which you show on IFR flight plans.

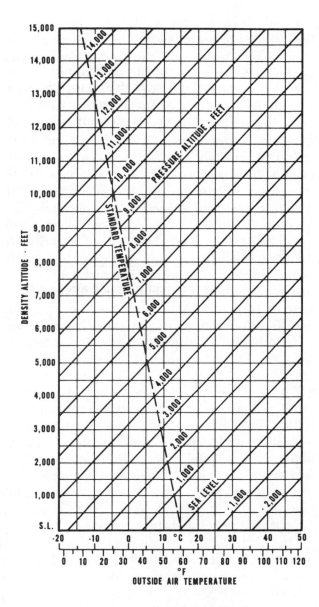

Figure 2-13. Density altitude chart

The Vertical Speed Indicator

Like the altimeter, the VSI (figure 2-14) is built around a chamber or aneroid cell which expands and contracts in response to pressure changes. A system of gears and levers moves the needle on the face of the instrument. The chamber receives ambient pressure from the static system. Unlike the altimeter, the VSI case also receives static pressure from the static system through a tiny opening often called a "calibrated leak."

In level flight, the pressures outside and within the VSI chamber are equal and a properly working instrument will read zero.

At the start of a climb, the pressure in the VSI diaphragm begins to drop. However, the pressure outside the chamber and inside the case does not drop as rapidly, because of the small size of the calibrated leak. A pressure differential is created, and the chamber contracts, moving the hand on the face of the VSI to indicate a climb. The pressure differential exists as long as the climb continues, because air can never escape through the calibrated leak as fast as through the larger opening to the chamber. At the completion of the climb, the pressure within the chamber stops changing immediately, but it takes several seconds to equalize the pressure in the casing through the calibrated leak, which accounts for the lag in *rate* information given by the VSI.

Trend information is available immediately at the start of a climb or descent because a pressure differential occurs as soon as the airplane begins an altitude change. However, do not develop the bad habit of relying on the VSI for pitch information. It provides accurate rate (and therefore pitch) information only in smooth air during level flight or in a sustained constant-rate climb or descent. For this reason, the VSI is

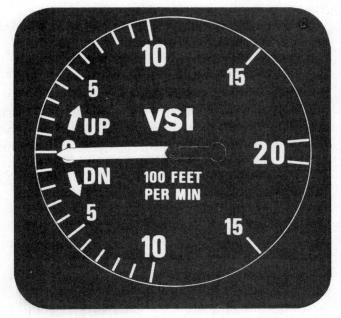

Figure 2-14

useful only as a backup instrument in most regimes of flight.

During the preflight check, observe the VSI reading on the ramp. After tapping it gently, use whatever it shows as the zero rate indication throughout the flight. If necessary, the small adjusting screw on the lower left side of most VSI's can be used to move the needle to zero on the ground.

Figure 2-15

The Airspeed Indicator

The airspeed indicator (figure 2-15) is one of the oldest and most important of the flight instruments. For the instrument pilot on an approach it is critical for calculating the time to the missed approach point and for ensuring that the airspeed stays comfortably above the stall.

Older instruments show airspeed in statute miles per hour, with knots given on a smaller inner scale. Since 1976, knots have been shown on the outer scale, with miles per hour relegated to the smaller ring on most airplanes. This is primarily because nautical miles and knots are used in planning and conducting IFR flights. Low altitude charts show distances in nautical miles, and ATC specifies speeds in knots. If you have been using statute miles in your flight planning, get in the habit of thinking in nautical miles and knots.

Like the altimeter and VSI, the airspeed indicator is a pressure gauge. It measures the *dynamic* pressure of the airstream rushing against the moving airplane. The pitot tube receives dynamic pressure *and* static pressure, so pressure in the pitot system is the sum of the two. The airspeed indicator can be thought of as a device that mechanically *subtracts* static system pressure from pitot pressure, leaving a measure of dynamic pressure only. A mechanical linkage moves the needle on the dial and displays the dynamic pressure sensed as the **indicated airspeed**.

Indicated airspeed may involve an error owing to the position of the pitot tube. This error is slight at the angles of attack used during instrument flight. The actual error at various airspeeds is given by a table in the operating manual, and the corrected value is **calibrated** airspeed. For instrument flight, indicated and calibrated airspeed may be used interchangeably.

Flight plans call for **true** airspeed, which is calibrated airspeed corrected for density altitude. The airspeed indicator is calibrated to indicate true airspeed under standard conditions at sea level. At higher altitudes and temperatures, the air pressure is reduced. Since the indicated airspeed reflects dynamic pressure, it drops in relation to the true airspeed as the altitude or temperature increases.

True airspeed may be determined with a flight computer or the rotatable true airspeed ring on some airspeed indicators. A good rule of thumb is that true airspeed is 2% higher than indicated for each 1000 feet of altitude. For example, let's calculate your true airspeed if you are indicating 150 knots at 5000 feet. Two per cent of 150 is three knots, so add three knots to your indicated airspeed for each 1000 feet of altitude. At 5000 feet this comes to fifteen knots, so an estimate of true airspeed is 165 knots.

True airspeed should be entered on the flight plan, and you should report to ATC if it varies from the flight plan value by 5% or ten knots, whichever is greater.

The difference between indicated and true airspeed is important on a timed approach to a high altitude airport. Suppose the approach has a ten mile final approach course at an altitude of 8000 feet. If your indicated airspeed is 100 knots, your *true* airspeed will be about 116, shortening the time to the missed approach point by almost a minute. If you based your groundspeed calculation on the indicated airspeed rather than true, you would be a mile and a half past the airport when the time expired, well beyond the protected obstacle clearance area.

Here is a tricky question from the instrument rating written test: "You are climbing to altitude maintaining cruise, climb, pitch, attitude, and power setting. At 8000 feet, you notice that your airspeed has increased 7 knots and you increase the pitch attitude (i.e., raise the nose). At 9000 feet, the airspeed shows another 5 knot increase. What does this condition indicate?"

The answer to this gem is that the pitot tube is probably blocked. The opening iced over suddenly, or it was blocked by a floating particle, trapping the pressure in the pitot system. As the aircraft climbed, the pressure in the static system declined, while pitot pressure, which normally decreases with increasing altitude for a given speed, stayed the same because of the blockage. Therefore, the difference sensed by the airspeed indicator increased. If the pilot kept raising his nose in an attempt to lower the airspeed, he would eventually stall the airplane. The tipoff would be that the airspeed would not respond to pitch changes.

This situation has caused several recorded accidents and provides an interesting insight into the workings of the pitot-static system. However, a blocked pitot tube does not always produce this indication. If the ram air opening is blocked but the water drain hole remains open, the pressure within may escape, resulting in a "zero" airspeed reading.

As preflight checks, the airspeed indicator should be checked for a zero reading on the ramp and a positive reading during the takeoff roll.

The Magnetic Compass

The DG is needed because the magnetic compass bounces around in turbulence and during pitch changes, and also because it exhibits **dip errors** during speed changes and turns.

Dip errors occur because the compass tries to align itself vertically as well as horizontally with the earth's magnetic lines of force, which slant downward towards the poles. The compass *lags* about 30° on a north heading in a standard rate turn at mid-latitudes; it *leads* by about the same amount when heading south during a turn. When a right turn is begun from a heading of 360°, the compass will initially swing 30° in the opposite direction, then begin following the turn, and will finally catch up as the heading reaches 090°. When a turn to the right from a heading of 180° is begun, the compass will swing 30° almost immediately, showing a heading of 210° when the nose of the airplane has barely started to move. The compass will turn more slowly than the airplane, so that it reads approximately correctly as the heading passes through west.

To remember that the compass lags on northerly headings and leads on southerly headings, draw a circle representing all the directions, with north on top. Write the word "lag" at the top and "lead" at the bottom. The memory aid is that "lead" also spells the name of a very heavy metal — which sinks to the bottom (figure 2-16).

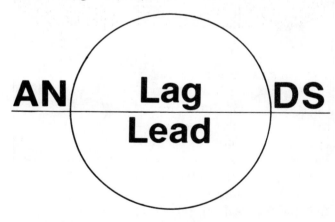

Figure 2-16

Another memory aid for this is popular in Louisiana: the South Leads, the North Lags. Provincial, perhaps, but effective. Yankees will have to find something else.

Magnetic dip also causes errors during speed changes. These acceleration and deceleration errors are greatest on east and west headings and are zero on north and south headings.

When, on an east or west heading, the airplane accelerates, the compass swings slightly to the north. When it decelerates, the compass swings slightly to the south.

The memory jogger for acceleration error is ANDS (accelerate north, decelerate south) (figure 2-16).

An Intuitive Explanation of Those Annoying Compass Errors

You can make a model compass to help understand dip errors. Push a pencil through a styrofoam cup to represent the magnetized iron bars, as illustrated in figure 2-17. Mark "N" on the side of the cup with the "eraser" end of the pencil; mark "S" on the side with the pencil point. Facing the "N" side of the cup, mark "E" 90° away on the left, and "W" 90° away on the right.

Figure 2-17

Remember that in the airplane, the compass is ahead of you and you see the back side of the compass card; this means that the "N" is actually on the south side of the card, the "W" is on the east side, and so on. Also bear in mind that in the northern hemisphere, the north ends of the magnetized bars in the compass are always trying to "dip", or tilt down and align themselves with the vertical component of the earth's magnetic field.

In your model, the pointed end of the pencil points toward magnetic north.

*First, we'll discuss northerly turning error: Hold the cup so you're facing the "N" and imagine that the airplane is flying north. If you roll into a turn to the right ("bank" the cup to the right), you can see that the north (pencil point) end of the bar could "dip" downward by simply rotating around the now-inclined pivot. This clockwise rotation of the card produces an initial indication of a turn from north toward **west** . . . but in turning right from north, you're actually turning toward **east**! As the turn continues, the "dip" influence makes the compass indication lag behind the airplane's progress in the turn.*

*Now hold the cup so you're facing the "S", and imagine that the airplane is flying south. If you roll into a turn to the right (bank the cup to the right again), the north (pointed pencil) end of the bar can again "dip" downward by rotating around the inclined pivot . . . and as the pointed end rotates to the low side of the turn, you see a turn toward west indicated again. You're actually turning toward west this time, but the combination of the turn and dip makes the compass **race ahead** of the airplane's real progress in the turn.*

The error is about equal in degrees to your latitude as you pass through north or south in a standard rate turn. Thus, at 35° North Latitude, the compass would be about 35° behind the airplane as you passed through north (or ahead of the airplane as you passed through south). The error diminishes as you turn further away from north or south, and is completely gone as you pass through east or west headings.

Difficulty in interpolating the amount of error at intermediate headings makes it extemely difficult to make accurate turns using the compass. You're better off to use timed standard rate turns if you're operating with a failed DG.

Now we'll examine acceleration error. Hold the cup so you're facing the "W" and imagine you're flying west. Remember that the compass is pivoted at the top. If the airplane's speed were to increase, the bottom of the compass card (the open end of the cup) would swing back toward you during the acceleration. Once again, the compass can rotate around the pivot to "dip." As you rotate the cup counterclockwise on its now-tilted axis to lower the north (pencil point) end, you'll see an indication of a turn toward north. If you slow down, the card will swing forward (open bottom of the cup moves away from you) during deceleration, the card will rotate clockwise to dip the north (pencil point) end down, and you'll see a turn toward **south** indicated.

This acceleration error is greatest when you're headed exactly east or west during rapid speed changes. The further you are from east or west, or the more gradually you change speed, the smaller the error. It is gone entirely on headings of north and south.

Moral of the story: Don't expect an accurate reading from the compass if you're changing speed, changing heading, or are in rough air. Pick a time when none of these factors perturb the compass, read it, and set the DG.

The Engine Instruments

Like the flight gauges, the engine instruments are part of the instrument pilot's scan. The instruments that indicate power output are used in controlling the airplane, and the others are important monitors of the equipment's health. It is easy to forget the ammeter or the temperature and pressure gauges, especially at busy times in the IFR cockpit, but you do so at your peril. They can give valuable warnings of potential engine or instrument failures.

The Power Instrument(s)

The power instrument is the tachometer in a fixed pitch propeller airplane and the manifold pressure-tachometer combination in a controllable prop machine. In either case, the power instrument is consulted at each power adjustment.

The tachometer measures the speed of engine rotation. As engine RPM increases, the needle moves clockwise on the face of the tachometer. The reading can be interpreted as a percentage of sea level brake horsepower by referring to the manufacturer's power setting chart.

The small numbers in the center of the tachometer, where the "miles traveled" indicator would be on a car's speedometer, give the accumulated hours of engine operation. You may have noticed that they consistently run slower than the airplane's "Hobbs" type hour meter. This is because the tachometer gauge counts engine revolutions, registering an "hour" after a certain number of revolutions, regardless of elapsed time. "Tach time" corresponds to clock time at a certain speed, usually near cruise setting. At slower speeds, "tach time" moves more slowly. During instrument approach practice or touch and goes, the tach may show only .6 or .7 after an hour of flying.

The manifold pressure gauge is a barometer that records the pressure inside the engine intake manifold. With the engine off, the gauge shows atmospheric pressure, about 30" Hg. at sea level. When the engine is running, the fuel-air mixture is sucked from the intake manifold into the cylinders. Since the flow of air into the manifold is restricted by the throttle valve in the carburetor, the pressure is lower inside the manifold than outside. The more the throttle is opened, the less restriction exists at the carburetor and the more nearly the manifold pressure approaches the outside pressure.

In a normally aspirated (non-turbocharged) engine, the manifold pressure will be slightly lower than ambient pressure at full throttle. At a constant throttle setting, the manifold pressure decreases with altitude about one inch for each thousand feet, just like atmospheric pressure. Therefore, at higher altitudes, it is impossible to maintain the power settings that are possible near sea level.

Turbochargers compress the intake air so that the manifold pressure may exceed atmospheric pressure. In some cases, safety precautions must be observed to avoid engine damage from "overboosting" (using too much manifold pressure). As the altitude increases, the maximum possible manifold pressure decreases. Above the *critical altitude*, full throttle, even with the supercharger, will not provide enough manifold pressure to produce the rated horsepower.

Where a manifold pressure gauge is used to set engine power, the tachometer registers propeller RPM as set by the prop control. The prop control sets a governor which controls the propeller pitch, or angle of attack into the airstream. This determines the work each revolution must do and hence the speed at which the engine turns. The ideal propeller setting in a climb is different from that in level flight and we usually follow the manufacturer's recommendations in adjusting the propeller setting.

Engine Temperature and Pressure Gauges

Engine power loss or failure is even more

serious to the instrument pilot in the clouds than to the VFR flyer on a sunny day. Since some warning of engine problems is often given by the temperature and pressure gauges, they should be included in the instrument scan. Unusual readings, especially when they reflect sudden changes, are cause for concern and may be sufficient reason to terminate a flight.

Low oil pressure may indicate an engine leak or other lubrication problem, which would shortly result in engine failure. Low oil pressure combined with high oil temperature is an almost certain sign of leakage. The temperature increases when there is less oil circulating in the engine to absorb the available heat or when bearing failures or similar troubles increase frictional heat.

The cylinder head temperature gauge is likely to warn of engine damage due to overheating in a climb before the oil temperature gauge does. A high cylinder head temperature in a climb indicates too much load on the engine or insufficient cooling airflow and can be remedied by opening cowl flaps, increasing speed, using a reduced power setting, or a richer mixture, all of which improve engine cooling.

Although cylinder head temperature does react to mixture setting, monitoring it is not the best way of leaning the mixture. An exhaust gas temperature gauge provides better information for mixture control.

The Ammeter

There are two types of ammeter in use today — center zero and left zero. The center zero type shows whether electricity is flowing into or out of the battery. A positive reading indicates that the battery is being charged by the alternator. A zero reading indicates that the battery is fully charged and that the alternator is running all the electrical equipment currently in use.

A negative reading means that the load on the electric system is causing a net drain on the battery, which could indicate a complete or partial alternator failure. The electrical load should be reduced until the ammeter shows a positive reading. If this can't be done, reduce the electrical load to an absolute minimum and terminate the flight as soon as possible.

The left zero type of ammeter shows the amount of electricity being delivered to the system by the alternator or generator and is often called a load meter. This kind is easier to read, because a healthy reading with a positive load is quite easy to see on the dial. In the event of an alternator failure, the ammeter reading drops for no apparent reason. Be aware of the normal load for various operating regimes and alert to such unexpected reductions in current draw.

Since electrical failure is almost always heralded by the ammeter, it is vital to keep this gauge in your scan. If the alternator does fail, seeing the indication immediately can mean the difference between losing all electrical power suddenly and being able to conserve enough for a safe approach at your destination. (See Chapter Eleven for a discussion of electrical failure.)

Flight Instruments Quiz

The following questions refer to most light airplanes:

1. What system drives the AI?
2. How is the AI checked for proper operation prior to flight?
3. Does the AI tell the pilot when a turn is coordinated?
4. What system(s) drive(s) the DG?
5. Which type of turn instrument do you have, and what system drives it?
6. What are the two important points to remember about turn coordinators?
7. What happens to the ball in the turn coordinator during a slip? During a skid?
8. How many static ports do you have and where are they located?
9. What instrument(s) become(s) inoperative when the pitot tube is blocked?
10. What instrument(s) become(s) inoperative when the vacuum pump fails?
11. How often should the DG be checked during an IFR flight?
12. How do you activate the alternate static source?

13. What would cause the altimeter reading to change on its own while in a parked airplane or during flight?
14. Define indicated altitude, true altitude, absolute altitude, pressure altitude, and density altitude.
15. What information does the VSI provide?
16. Define indicated airspeed, calibrated airspeed, and true airspeed.

17. Why do dip errors occur on the magnetic compass?
18. What is the key power instrument in a fixed pitch propeller airplane? In a controllable pitch propeller airplane?
19. Which type ammeter do you have, and what is its normal reading?
20. It is 0° C. at 6000 feet pressure altitude; your calibrated airspeed is 120 knots. What is your true airspeed?

CHAPTER THREE

ATTITUDE INSTRUMENT FLYING

The Instrument Scan

Our sense of balance and spatial orientation is a combination of visual perception and of "kinesthetic sense," which is rooted in the semi-circular canals of the middle ear. However, under certain circumstances, such as flight in cloud or total darkness, the kinesthetic sense can be completely unreliable. Without an outside reference such as the horizon as a backup, it is common to have *feelings* that you are in a flight attitude quite different from your aircraft's real situation. Such confusion is called *vertigo* and it can be deadly. You must learn to disregard these feelings and doggedly believe the indications on the instrument panel.

In instrument flight, your most important tools are your *eyes*, which must move continuously as they read, compare and absorb the information from all the gauges on the panel. Only as you comprehend and analyze what you see, do you decide what control pressures to apply and where to look next. Hearing the engine and a change in the rush of passing air may alert you to an unintentional dive or imminent stall, and your sense of smell may give the first warning of a fire, but these senses are relatively unimportant. For the instrument pilot, the sense of sight is primary.

To demonstrate the importance of visual information and the unreliability of your kinesthetic sense, cover all three gyro instruments the next time you are under the hood and try some shallow turns. You may be surprised at how quickly you induce a severe unusual attitude.

A simpler demonstration of the importance of vision in maintaining balance is to stand on one foot and shake your head vigorously. Most people have no trouble balancing this way *with their eyes open*. Now try it with your eyes closed. The average person remains steadily upright less than two seconds.

If an airplane could be flown by concentrating on only one instrument, flight on the gauges would be easy. However, there are six basic flight instruments, plus navigation and engine gauges to monitor, and many other duties that claim the pilot's attention. Each task is simple by itself, but to consistently perform them all correctly, at the proper time and in the proper sequence, takes disciplined training and regular practice. The key element of the game is the constant eye movement that makes up the **scan**.

Scanning is therefore your basic and most important skill. Nothing else approaches it in importance. Smoothness in controlling the airplane, efficient communication, and good cockpit organization are necessary, but they are all quite useless without a good scan, which is the first skill to learn and the one you must constantly work at hardest to maintain, for it deteriorates quickly with disuse during any break from IFR flying.

There is no ideal scan pattern for all pilots or all situations. There are recommended patterns, but most pilots develop individual habits to maximize their efficiency. In developing a scan pattern, however, you should remember that if your eyes are not moving, even for a short period, you are making a common mistake called *fixating*. Another common error is *omitting* one or more instruments from the scan. Both of these errors will be mentioned frequently in our later discussions of manuevers.

Pitch, Power and Trim

Good management of pitch and power is basic to safe instrument flying and should be understood and exhaustively practiced in your training. Let's begin with a disagreement.

One of aviation's oldest and most emotionally charged arguments involves whether "pitch controls airspeed and power controls altitude," or the reverse. Most pilots realize that the practical tasks of flying an airplane involve combinations of the two, yet the old argument persists. Even mature pilots whose sanity is not otherwise in question may bring outlandish amounts of energy to this debate on rainy Saturdays. Why such concern? Because pilots want to be sure of what makes the airplane fly most effectively, especially in situations when they must make quick decisions to obtain best performance.

The basic relationships among power, altitude, angle of attack and airspeed can be proved mathematically and demonstrated in flight. Airspeed depends on the angle of attack, which is related to pitch attitude under constant power. (Pitch is the airplane's attitude in relation to the ground plane; angle of attack is the angle at which it meets the relative wind.) Therefore, pitch can be said to control airspeed.

A power change will not affect the airspeed if the angle of attack is held constant. At any airspeed, a certain amount of power is required to maintain level flight. This relationship is expressed graphically in the familiar "power curve." An excess of power over that needed for level flight at a particular airspeed will result in a climb, while a deficit of power will cause a

descent. Clearly then, power controls altitude, or rate of climb or descent. Increase the power at a constant angle of attack, and the ship climbs or reduces its sink rate; throttle back, and it goes down or slows its climb (figure 3-1).

While these basic facts can be mathematically verified and demonstrated under controlled conditions, they are not the whole story. Other factors also govern an aircraft in flight and their relationships are complex enough to make actual flying technique vary from the theoretical ideal. In practice an interplay between pitch and power controls airspeed and altitude.*

Sometimes, you consciously control altitude with power and airspeed with pitch, in accordance with theory. In slow flight, for example, you cannot control altitude with pitch. If you raise the nose, the airspeed drops off and the airplane may stall. If it doesn't, the increase in drag associated with an increased angle of attack causes a deficit of power and a descent. If you lower the nose, the airspeed increases, but drag decreases, an excess of power develops, and when a steady state is reached the airplane climbs. This is why slow flight, the "back side of the power curve," is also known as the "region of reverse command." We cushion a soft field landing, not by raising the nose, but by applying a slight burst of power just at touchdown.

During a visual landing approach, you judge your position relative to the runway by the apparent location of the threshold in the windshield. Pitch changes would alter this location and make it difficult to judge your altitude and rate of closure with the runway. Therefore, you establish airspeed with a constant pitch attitude and make any necessary sink rate adjustments with power changes. If you realize that you are too low, you *must* add power. Raising the nose would produce only the illusion of a higher altitude and the reality of decaying airspeed towards a potential "low and slow" accident

---

*For an excellent discussion of power, altitude, angle of attack and airspeed, see Wolfgang Langewische's, *Stick and Rudder*. For the mathematical relationships, see William Kershner's, *The Advanced Pilot's Flight Manual*, or H.H. Hurt Jr.'s, *Aerodynamics For Naval Aviators*.

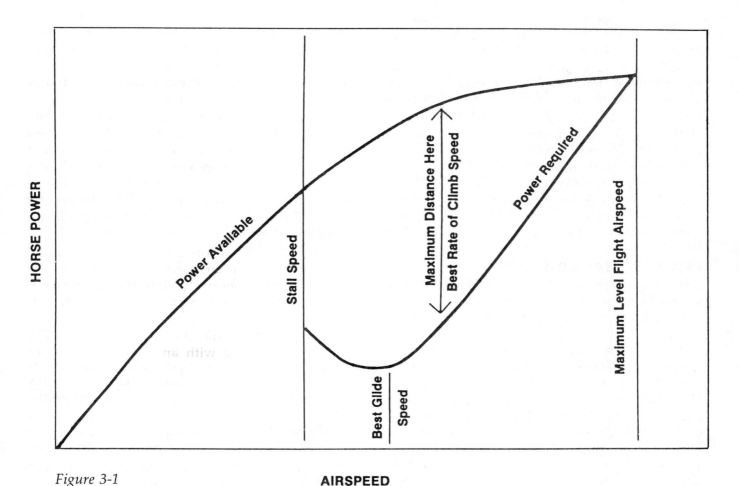

HORSE POWER

Power Available

Stall Speed

Maximum Distance Here

Best Rate of Climb Speed

Power Required

Maximum Level Flight Airspeed

Best Glide Speed

Figure 3-1

AIRSPEED

situation. In the extreme case you might exceed the critical angle of attack and stall the airplane.

In some regimes of flight it is more efficient to control altitude with pitch and make power adjustments only if the airspeed gets out of hand as a result. "Level cruise flight," for example, is actually a series of tiny climbs and descents, in which the pilot constantly corrects minor altitude excursions. Slight descents are usually accompanied by airspeed buildups and climbs by airspeed decay. Therefore, pitch corrections for altitude control tend to bring both the airspeed and altitude back to the desired values. In cases where altitude excursions are caused by masses of rising or descending air, the airspeed may not change, and power adjustments are required to return to the desired altitude. A good rule of thumb is to *use pitch to correct altitude excursions of less than 100 feet. Above that, also make a power change.*

As we shall see later, a similar technique is used on the ILS. Airspeed is *set* with pitch, and rate of descent is *set* with power, but minor glide slope adjustments are made with slight elevator movements. So your use of the throttle and elevator will depend not only on physics but on the maneuver you are conducting.

Good technique requires theoretical knowledge and practical experience. Pitch and power experiments, such as deriving a power curve for your airplane, practicing slow flight, and perfecting short field techniques, will repay the time invested with improved confidence and proficiency.

Another important aspect of airplane control is trim management.

Trim adjusts tail-down force, which in turn controls the angle of attack. Within the speed range used in instrument flight, trim sets *airspeed*.

You can prove this to yourself by a simple experiment. Trim a conventional airplane for hands-off level flight. When the airspeed and altitude are stable, increase power one inch of manifold pressure (or 100 RPM) and watch the results. The nose rises slightly, and the airplane climbs *at the same airspeed*. Now reduce the power below the original level-flight setting. The airplane drops its nose and descends, again at the original speed. If you make additional small power reductions, the sink rate increases while the airspeed stays approximately constant. Eventually the power will be so low that the tail will rise, the nose will drop and the airspeed will increase, but not until you are well outside the performance envelope that normally governs IFR flying.

This demonstration shows that for instrument flight, *it is necessary to touch the trim only when making an airspeed change.* Do not develop the bad habit of fiddling with the trim when not changing the airspeed. You can save yourself a lot of extra and often useless work.

Instrument Classification

In developing your scan pattern, you can simplify things by classifying the basic instruments in a logical way. A convenient system divides them into *control* and *performance* groups.

(*The control and performance system is not the only one in use today. The FAA favors dividing the instruments into pitch, bank and power groups and further classifies them into primary and supporting functions. A weakness of this system is that it is complicated: an instrument's classification varies according to the maneuver being conducted. For example, the attitude indicator is considered "primary" for pitch or bank during* changes *in pitch or bank, but becomes a "supporting" instrument when a constant condition of flight (such as a climb, descent, or turn) is established. The pitch, bank and power grouping can be confusing, as some instruments fall into more than one category. While interesting and internally consistent, this classification system is confusing and cumbersome in training.*)

The control instruments show the attitude and power settings directly and are used in making control inputs. Since it is the only instrument that gives direct information on the airplane's attitude, the attitude indicator is the one control instrument among the basic six. Consult it every time you make a change in pitch or bank. The power indicator (the tachometer or manifold pressure gauge) is the control instrument for power setting.

Precise aircraft control requires that attitude changes be made to specific values. For example, the attitude for a climbing turn might be one dot (or 5° if the instrument is marked to show degrees of pitch) above the horizon, and 15° of bank. To set the attitude exactly, use the instrument that shows pitch and bank attitude directly — the attitude indicator. Similarly, to make power changes precisely to predetermined values, consult the power indicator each time you move the throttle.

Note that it is better to use "dots" than "bar-widths" for setting pitch attitude on the attitude indicator. This is because the "dot" of the symbolic aircraft's fuselage is always in the proper position for this use — the "bar" of the wings cannot be used for setting pitch when the airplane is banked.

The results of attitude and power changes are evaluated on the performance instruments, which give indirect indications of the aircraft's attitude. The performance instruments are the airspeed indicator, altimeter, turn coordinator (or turn indicator), directional gyro, and vertical speed indicator.

Let's consider the start of a climb to see how one uses the control and performance instruments. Initiate the climb by increasing pitch on the attitude indicator and applying power with reference to the power instrument. Then use the performance instruments to check for decreasing airspeed, increasing altitude, the proper climb rate, constant heading and coordinated flight. The airspeed indicator, altimeter, VSI, DG and turn instrument show that the climb is progressing properly on a constant heading. You would make any necessary adjustments on the attitude indicator.

The attitude indicator is the keypoint of the scan. Its central position on the panel thus points up its importance. A typical scan pattern includes the attitude indicator as every second or third instrument looked at. Because it is so critical, the attitude indicator is also the place where many errors are made.

As previously mentioned, the two most common scanning errors are *fixating* and *omitting*. Fixating on the attitude indicator can cause a variety of problems. Holding the required bank angle by staring at the attitude indicator will keep a turn going at a constant rate, but it may result in your turning past the desired heading. It can be humbling to hear the controller ask you, "Seven two one five foxtrot, *where* are you going?"

Omitting the attitude indicator, even in straight and level flight, makes it hard to hold heading and altitude. Heading and altitude are not held by use of the DG and altimeter, which, as performance instruments, only show the results of control inputs, but by keeping the wings level and the pitch attitude steady on the attitude indicator. If you omit this central instrument, your heading is likely to wander. If you omit it when making a control input, you almost certainly will not get the desired performance.

Omitting the attitude indicator is a common fault, especially for new instrument pilots. I suspect one reason is the difficulty in learning to *trust* the tiny mechanical dial in place of the familiar natural horizon of VFR flying. If this is so, it can be overcome with practice and persistence. Another reason may be impatience to see the results of the changes one has initiated. It can be very tempting to *begin* a turn or descent and to stare at the DG or altimeter so as to nail the desired number. Doing so will only put you "behind the airplane" and leave you "chasing the needles."

The Six Configurations

Attitude flying, the basic collection of instrument skills, requires flying accurate courses at specified altitudes, making turns at a specified rate, and climbing and descending, on course, at particular rates and airspeeds. The instrument pilot must develop the precise habits of flying "by the numbers."

In normal circumstances, a particular pitch and power setting will produce the same performance each time it is used. This is summarized in the expression,

"**attitude + power = performance**."

With a given power setting and pitch attitude, you can always expect a certain airspeed and rate of climb or descent. If you know the performance you want and the attitude and power setting to achieve it, you can control the aircraft with great precision.

Flying by the numbers makes your job easier. Since particular pitch and power settings will consistently produce predictable performance, your ability to go quickly to memorized settings will reduce your workload and free your attention for other tasks. Determine "the numbers" for your airplane carefully, enter them on your power sheet (figure 3-2), and memorize them. It is an important part of knowing the airplane.

In setting up the power sheet there are choices to make, and they should be decided in favor of simplicity. The fewer numbers to memorize the better. Cruise descent and approach level should use the same power setting, if possible, and approach and climb should be at the same airspeed. In a complex airplane, you can usually limit the prop settings to two, one for climb and the other for the other configurations.

Once you have determined the settings, you may want to use a grease pencil or bits of tape to mark approach level and approach descent on the power indicator as a memory aid. These two configurations seem to be the most easily forgotten for most pilots.

In this portion of the instrument course, you should learn to hold heading and altitude accurately, turn to headings, climb and descend to altitudes and make climbing and descending turns to specified headings and altitudes. The key sign of proficiency is that you make corrections promptly, not that your heading and altitude are always exactly on the mark.

However, do strive for *perfection*. If the heading or altitude is off by the smallest amount, make a correction. If you only require altitude accuracy within 100 feet and heading precision within 10° (*Practical Test Standards*) that is what you will get. By striving for perfection you will develop a more rapid scan pattern and quickly learn to control the airplane to much closer tolerances.

AIRCRAFT _____

	MANIFOLD PRESSURE	RPM	PITCH SETTING	AIRSPEED	VSI
CLIMB					
CRUISE					
CRUISE DESCENT					
APPROACH					
APPROACH DESCENT					
NON-PRECISION DESC.					

Figure 3-2

Climbs

In general aviation aircraft, we usually make *airspeed* climbs, not rate climbs. It is nice to know how to climb at exactly 100 knots *and* 400 feet per minute, but it is not very useful for everyday flying. Instead we pick a power setting and airspeed and accept the rate of climb we get. Rate of climb will vary with aircraft loading, temperature and altitude, and there isn't much we could do about it anyway.

The climb power setting in non-complex airplanes is usually full throttle. In complex airplanes the climb power setting should be determined according to the manufacturer's recommendations.

There are several considerations in choosing a climb airspeed. Most airplanes have three climb speeds for use in various situations.

The best-angle-of-climb airspeed is used for clearing obstacles immediately after takeoff but not for other purposes. Best *rate* of climb is obtained at a higher airspeed and is useful for expediting a climb to altitude.

The climb airspeeds given in pilot's operating handbooks are sea level values, but best-angle and best-rate airspeeds change with altitude.

Best angle of climb increases and best rate of climb decreases with altitude until they are equal at the aircraft's absolute ceiling. When departing a high-elevation airport, check the handbook for the applicable airspeeds.

The best-angle and best-rate-of-climb speeds have several disadvantages. Both require high pitch attitudes, which put a strain on the engine and allow less air into the cowling for cooling. Forward visibility is reduced, making traffic avoidance more chancy and "S" turns advisable on climbout. For en route climbs, best angle and best rate do not afford efficient forward speed.

Cruise climb airspeed is a compromise which permits good engine cooling and visibility, an acceptable rate of climb, and reasonable forward speed. It is specified in many aircraft operating manuals and is usually 15% or 20% above best-rate.

Manage the airspeed after takeoff by accelerating to best rate-of-climb speed. Maintain this airspeed to 1000 feet AGL, and then accelerate to cruise climb. At a short, obstructed airport, use best-angle-of-climb speed to clear the obstacles and then accelerate to best rate of climb speed. The rationale is to clear obstacles as quickly as possible and then to climb expeditiously past the first 1000 feet, where engine failure would be most critical. Since engine failures are most likely to occur during power changes and, statistically, the most likely time for an engine failure is upon the *first* power reduction, it should wait until the nose is lowered at 1000 feet. Although some pilots believe that an earlier reduction lengthens engine life, I personally feel I am doing more for the engine's and my own longevity by climbing to 1000 feet at takeoff power.

Cruise climb airspeed is ideally the same airspeed used for approach, so that no airspeed change — and no trim adjustment — is necessary when starting a missed approach procedure.

To initiate a climb from level flight, apply climb power and raise the nose to the climb pitch attitude on the attitude indicator. As the airspeed bleeds off, trim to eliminate the control pressure and apply right rudder to maintain coordinated flight. Make a final trim adjustment when you reach climb airspeed and confirm that you have the proper power setting.

The power instruments — both tachometers and manifold pressure gauges — have inherent lags. The load on a fixed pitch propeller changes with airspeed so the RPM reading continues to move slightly after a power adjustment. The manifold pressure gauge reading will also move slightly as RPM is changed. Because of this, each power adjustment requires looking at the power gauge twice: Once for an initial setting and again for a final adjustment. Do not fixate on the power gauge while waiting for it to settle down, but continue your scan.

The suggested procedure and scan for starting a climb is: set the power on the power instrument; raise the nose on the attitude indicator; check for decreasing airspeed on the airspeed indicator; check for straight, coordinated flight on the turn coordinator; confirm a constant heading on the DG (the heading may swing to the left if you don't apply rudder smoothly when raising the nose). Finally, with a manifold pressure/tachometer combination, return to the power instrument to confirm the proper setting. With a fixed pitch propeller, simply confirm full throttle. Beyond this, the scan depends on instrument readings and one's individual preference (figure 3-3).

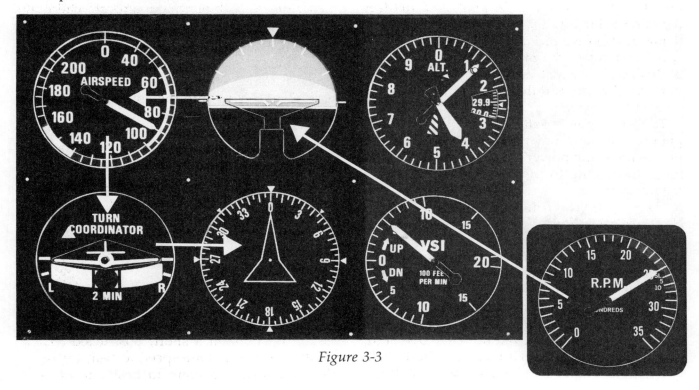

Figure 3-3

To level off from a climb at cruise airspeed, lower the nose to a level flight attitude. Lead the level-off by *10% of the climb rate* so as to stop precisely on the desired altitude. As the airspeed increases, trim off the control pressure and ease up on the right rudder. Reduce power and make a final trim adjustment when you reach cruise airspeed. Be sure to let the airplane accelerate all the way up to anticipated cruise airspeed before reducing power, or you'll make a lot of work for yourself as the airplane slowly accelerates, starts to climb, you retrim, it accelerates some more and climbs again, you retrim, etc. By setting cruise power only when you reach cruise airspeed, you can stabilize the airplane in minimum time. Remember, in instrument flying, patience pays.

Practice climbs and level-offs initially without reference to a specific altitude. As your proficiency develops start leveling off at specified altitudes and make the climbs successively shorter. This will build your ability to react quickly and precisely to the needs of the moment.

The suggested scan and procedure for leveling off from a climb is: note the altimeter (assuming you are leveling off at a specified altitude); lower the nose on the attitude indicator; check for increasing airspeed on the airspeed indicator; check for constant heading on the DG (the heading often swings to the right on level-off). Continue to monitor altitude, airspeed and heading until the desired airspeed is reached, then reduce power on the power instrument (figure 3-4).

To level off at the approach airspeed, as if you had executed a missed approach and were proceeding at a leisurely pace to the holding fix, lower the nose and reduce the power immediately (assuming the climb and approach airspeeds are identical). The scan is then: altimeter, attitude indicator, power instrument.

Commonly made errors to avoid are:

— In leveling off from a climb, students often lower the nose and then reduce power prematurely. In a fast airplane, this will substantially increase the time required to get back to cruise airspeed, and may cause an altitude loss.

— Since it takes a while to make smooth, slow power changes, you may tend to fixate on the power gauge when a power change is made. Learn to set the power, continue the scan, and return to the power instrument for a final adjustment several moments later.

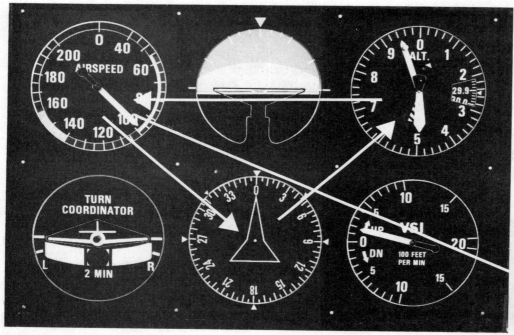

Figure 3-4

— Since an airspeed change is made in starting or ending an en route climb, the trim must be readjusted. However, do not try to make pitch changes directly with the trim. Make them with the yoke, by referring to the attitude indicator, and use the trim to relieve control pressure as the airspeed changes.

— Insufficient right rudder in a climb is a common error. Hold heading by keeping the wings level on the attitude indicator and the ball centered on the turn instrument. *Do not bank right to stay on your heading.*

Level Cruise

Cruise airspeed is the speed the pilot chooses for en route travel, considering his knowledge of the airplane, the manufacturer's recommendations, the acceptable noise level and the amount of fuel consumption. Once chosen, it should be used throughout the en route portions of training.

As described earlier, level cruise flight is actually a series of tiny climbs and descents; the pilot constantly corrects minor altitude excursions. Slight descents are usually accompanied by airspeed buildups and climbs by airspeed decay, so that small pitch corrections tend to bring both the airspeed and altitude back to desired values. In turbulence, the airspeed may not change much as the altimeter bounces around, and power adjustments are needed to correct the altitude. A useful rule of thumb is to *correct altitude excursions of less than 100 feet with pitch alone — for larger corrections, make a power change as well.*

In cruise, an abnormally low airspeed suggests a nose-high attitude; an increasing altimeter and positive reading on the VSI will corroborate this. Use the attitude indicator, the control instrument for pitch, to lower the nose. Trying to correct the pitch attitude by reference to the airspeed indicator is less effective because the airspeed does not respond immediately to pitch changes. When you lower the nose, the airspeed increases only gradually. If you press the yoke until the airspeed goes back to normal, the nose will be well below the cruise attitude and the airplane will be diving. Only the attitude indicator gives a direct indication of the aircraft's attitude. If you're still in doubt, in partial panel work you will come to appreciate the difficulty of controlling pitch with only the performance instruments.

The recommended scan for straight-and-level flight is: attitude indicator, DG, attitude indicator, VSI, altimeter. The airspeed indicator and turn instrument are added every few cycles for backup information. As in most maneuvers, the attitude indicator is the hub of the scan pattern. The VSI and altimeter are checked together, almost as one instrument. The VSI will give the earliest sign of a change in altitude, even before it is evident on the altimeter, since the VSI provides an instantaneous indication of a *trend* in altitude. Any adjustments in pitch or bank are made with reference to the attitude indicator (figure 3-5).

Practice holding altitude and heading exactly for ten minutes. It is useful to use odd altitudes and headings, such as 4320 feet and 127°. In this exercise, try for perfection, not 100 feet and 10° off. Make small corrections at the first sign of heading or altitude variation.

Common errors to avoid:

— Difficulty in heading control is often due to omitting not the DG but the *attitude indicator*. With the wings level and the ball centered, the heading won't change.

On some attitude indicators it is advisable to refine the 0° bank angle on the top index after setting it by leveling the "wings" in relation to the horizon bar. The wings and horizon bar may be too thick for a precise setting. Heading difficulty sometimes comes with trying to use the horizon bar for sensitive bank information.

— In turbulence, you may have a tendency to fiddle with the trim as the airplane is buffeted. This is self-defeating. Even in rough air the airplane's stability will allow it to hold altitude quite well. The ups and downs due to short-term turbulence tend to cancel out. Make necessary pitch adjustments with the yoke, referring, as you do, to the attitude indicator. Trim is needed only when you make an airspeed change.

To improve your flight technique, develop a light touch on the yoke. Practice flying with your thumb and one finger. If you have difficulty, interlace a pencil with the four fingers of your left hand. In training, this "crutch" will

Figure 3-5

make it impossible to take a white-knuckled death grip on the control.

— Flying unwanted vertical S's through the assigned altitude comes from trying to adjust pitch by referring to the altimeter or VSI. These are *performance* instruments and "chasing" either needle will only result in continuous — and infuriating — vertical S's through the desired altitude. Make all pitch corrections with reference to the attitude indicator.

Cruise Descent

According to the *Airman's Information Manual*, descents should be made at the "optimum" rate down to the last 1000 feet and completed at 500 feet per minute. In most situations single-engine aircraft may find 500 feet per minute to be the optimum rate, as it gives the pilot time to plan and provides good passenger comfort. For our purposes, cruise descent is conducted at 500 feet per minute and at the same airspeed as the cruise configuration.

A descent is started by reducing the power and lowering the nose to the cruise descent attitude. Since the trim is already set for the desired airspeed, most airplanes will automatically nose over to the proper attitude.

A typical procedure and scan for the descent entry is: reduce power on the power instrument; lower the nose on the attitude indicator; check for constant airspeed; check the attitude indicator; check the DG for constant heading (with the power reduction, some left rudder may be needed; the heading may have a tendency to swing to the right); check the attitude indicator; check for decreasing altitude on the altimeter and for the proper rate on the VSI; check the attitude indicator. Finally, re-check the power instrument and return to the attitude indicator. Once again, the attitude indicator is the hub of the scan (figure 3-6).

During the descent, the airspeed and power

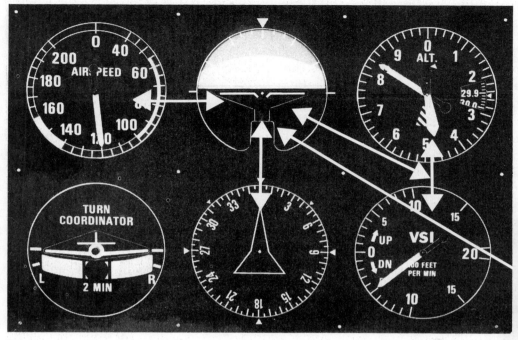

Figure 3-6

should be at the prescribed values. A typical scan pattern is: attitude indicator, airspeed, attitude indicator, altimeter and VSI, attitude indicator, DG. The most common discrepancies are a high descent rate combined with a high airspeed, which is corrected by raising the nose, and a low airspeed combined with an insufficient descent rate, corrected by lowering the nose. If only the airspeed or only the sink rate is wrong, owing to unusual atmospheric conditions, pitch and power adjustments are needed.

To level off from a descent, raise the nose and add power 50 feet or 10% of the descent rate above the target altitude. Set the symbolic airplane on the horizon line and hold it there, while increasing power to the cruise level setting.

Common errors to avoid:

— Since there is no airspeed change in beginning or recovering from a cruise descent, no trimming is necessary. Trimming only increases pilot workload, creates unwanted control pressures and spoils airplane performance.

— Fixating on the power instrument can be a problem in starting and ending descents. Set the power, continue the scan, and return to the power instrument for a final adjustment a few moments later.

— In recovering from a descent, failure to lead the level-off properly will cause the airplane to descend through the altitude. This fault may be due to omitting the altimeter as the altitude approaches.

Approach Level

This configuration is used on approach. Even though you may slow to this speed some distance from the approach fix, you should be completely prepared to land the airplane in this configuration. Being too far ahead of the airplane may waste a little time, but it is insurance against falling behind the flight and risking more serious consequences.

In a complex airplane, lower the gear when you slow to approach speed. While it is arguably more efficient to keep the wheels up to the final approach fix, lowering them further out cuts down your workload at later, more critical, phases of the appproach. Completing your landing checklist when you first slow down in the approach environment provides more insurance that it will be done than leaving it, say, until you reach the final approach fix. Thus, it reduces the chance of a gear up landing.

Another advantage to lowering the gear when you first slow down is that it means you need to remember only three approach power settings: approach level, approach descent, and non-precision descent (described later), all with the gear down. If you keep the wheels up until the final approach fix, you will additionally need approach level and approach descent settings for the clean configuration — more work and more to remember. Finally, in some very clean airplanes, gear up descent or even level flight at approach airspeed would necessitate such a low power setting that you would risk overcooling the engine.*

If possible, use no flaps. Lowering the flaps is just another task (and raising them again is one more chore during the missed approach phase, should it be necessary). Use an approach flap setting if descending without it requires reducing the power so much that you risk harmful cooling of the engine. Another reason for flaps on approach would be if the no-flap pitch attitude is high enough to impair forward visibility. In most cases, no more than one notch (about 10°) of flaps need be used.

The approach airspeed should be chosen carefully. It should be slow enough to allow a comfortable deceleration for landing once visual contact is established. It should also be in the flap operating range so that if a short field landing is planned, the flaps can be lowered as soon as you are on visual final for the runway. The airspeed should be fast enough so that the control response is good, and not mushy, as it would be at very low speeds. Course tracking is easier at higher speeds, and the airplane is less susceptible to the effects of turbulence and

*The procedure discussed here works best for new instrument pilots flying typical light high performance airplanes. We recognize that the majority of airlines, many corporate operators, and others require that the gear be extended at glide slope intercept or the final approach fix. As your experience increases, you may wish to change techniques.

crosswinds. Ideally, the approach speed is the same as the climb speed, so that little or no trimming is required in the event of a missed approach.

The approach speed should not be near the bottom of the power curve. If it is, raising the nose to recover a small amount of altitude can cost so much airspeed that the airplane slips into the region of reverse command. Then it will not climb even a few feet without an application of power. This forces the pilot to play with the throttle on approach, a burdensome extra task.

In most single-engine airplanes, the ideal approach speed is 90 or 100 knots. In light twins it is usually about 120 knots.

The procedure and scan for slowing from cruise to approach speed begins with the power instrument to reduce the power to the approach setting. In fast airplanes, use a lower setting initially to facilitate deceleration. Once the approach airspeed is reached, increase the power again.

Use the attitude indicator to set the approach pitch attitude and to ensure that the wings are level. You may not be able to see the difference between the cruise and approach pitch attitudes, but the nose will tend to *drop* when power is reduced, and the attitude indicator should be used to keep it up. Trim to reduce the control pressure as the speed bleeds off.

Continue the scan with the turn instrument to ensure that the ball is centered, then go to the attitude indicator, the VSI and the altimeter for any inadvertent change in altitude, recheck the attitude indicator and then the airspeed indicator for declining airspeed. At the gear-operating speed, extend the gear to assist in further deceleration. If you choose to use approach flaps, lower them as soon as permitted by the aircraft manual. Each time a drag-producing item is lowered, check the VSI and altimeter for variations in altitude and make pitch adjustments on the attitude indicator.

When the transition to the approach configuration is complete, the scan becomes the same as for cruise level. Complete the landing checklist. "GUMPS" is a good reminder for gas (fuel on proper tank, fuel pump and carburetor heat on, if required), undercarriage (gear down), mixture (rich for landing and a possible go-around), propeller forward, and seat belts fastened. At the approach level power setting, some propellers will surge above redline if they are roughly "firewalled" — advance the control slowly and it won't be a problem.

Practice slowing from cruise to approach speed and accelerating from approach to cruise repeatedly until it can be done quickly and smoothly with no variation in altitude or heading.

Common errors to avoid:

— Heading problems can be due to several factors. Omission of the attitude indicator is one. Another is the "heavy left hand syndrome," which causes a turn when you shift your attention away from the central panel to the power instrument. This can be avoided by maintaining a light touch and checking the attitude indicator each time the power gauge is used. With a large power reduction, left rudder may be needed to keep the ball centered. Without it, the heading may drift even with the wings level. Do not omit the turn instrument after reducing the power.

— Altitude problems are also common in speed changes. Keep the VSI and altimeter in the scan and make necessary corrections on the attitude indicator.

— Excessive use of trim is an occasional error. Since the airspeed is changing, the trim must be adjusted, *but not prematurely*. Use it to relieve the control pressure, not to set pitch attitude.

— Do not omit going through the landing checklist when slowing from cruise to approach speed. Make the checklist a habit in all your practice. Conscientious practice and the development of an iron-clad habit will ensure that you remember it, even when a critical situation draws your attention away from basic flying chores.

Approach Descent

The approach descent uses the same airspeed as approach level and a descent rate which is approximately that required for an ILS glide slope. At 90 or 100 knots, this is about 500 feet per minute in a "no-wind condition." At 120 knots, it is about 650 feet per minute.

The transition to approach descent is similar to the change from cruise level to cruise descent:

reduce the power with reference to the power indicator and check the attitude indicator for the proper pitch attitude. Check the airspeed indicator for unwanted speed changes. Check the attitude indicator, and check the heading on the DG. Then go back to the attitude indicator. By this time, the VSI should be showing the desired rate of descent so check the VSI and altimeter. Check the attitude indicator and make a final power adjustment, if necessary, on the power instrument. Review your "GUMPS" check.

To level off from approach descent to approach level, raise the nose on the attitude indicator and simultaneously apply power with reference to the power indicator. Begin the level-off some 50 feet above the desired altitude. Remember that on approach, you would rather be 50 feet high than one foot low, so shade the altitudes on the high side, especially in turbulent conditions. Leveling here demands that you plant the nose on the attitude indicator horizon, lest you drift below an MDA or DH or — almost as bad — balloon significantly above one. Make the horizon line your target and use whatever pressure will do the job.

In addition to the transitions between approach level and approach descent, practice the transition from approach descent to climb, simulating a missed approach. The procedure is: apply takeoff power (no need to check the power gauge unless your manual forbids full throttle at low altitudes); raise the nose on the attitude indicator; check the VSI for an upward trend; check the airspeed indicator for a safe climb speed. If the airspeed is too low, the nose is too high: lower it on the attitude indicator. When you have confirmed a positive rate of climb and are not dangerously slow, raise the flaps and gear. If climb power is less than the takeoff setting, make the power reduction and adjust the propeller as you leave 1000' AGL.

Common errors to avoid:

— In changing between approach level and approach descent most errors are similar to those between cruise level and cruise descent and that section can be consulted here.

— The transition from approach descent to climb often causes difficulty, and should be practiced carefully until it is consistently smooth. Your top priority is *to get away from the terrain*. The sequence of steps is specific: power, pitch, VSI, airspeed indicator. Initiate the climb promptly when you reach the simulated decision height or missed approach point, without variation in airspeed or heading. If the approach and climb speeds are the same, no trimming is required.

Nonprecision Descent

This is not an *im*precise descent (everything in instrument flying is done with precision), but the descent configuration used on nonprecision approaches. On such approaches you want to reach the minimum descent altitude well before the missed approach point, so you will be out of the clouds and in a good position for the final descent to landing. If the missed approach point is on the airport, a mile out is a minimum distance from which to see the runway and make a normal landing. At 90 or 100 knots, this means 40 seconds before the time is up, and on many approaches this would be impossible if the descent rate were only 500 feet per minute.

A nonprecision descent calls for your normal approach airspeed and a higher descent rate; 1000 feet per minute is normal. It also requires a lower power setting than an approach descent. Airspeed control is the key to success. If the nose is too low or the power is too high, your forward speed will build and shorten the time, defeating the purpose of descending faster.

In some airplanes, the engine would be overcooled if the power were merely reduced enough to achieve the desired descent rate. In these cases, partial flap extension should be used to slow the airplane down and protect the engine.

The most frequent error in performing this maneuver is allowing a buildup of airspeed. Learn to hold the nose at the desired pitch attitude with reference to the attitude indicator and to monitor the airspeed indicator. Since a large power reduction may be involved, a trim adjustment may be necessary.

Turns
Normal Turns

Accurately turning and recovering from turns, as well as holding a heading, are impor-

tant skills. Practice them until they are as much a part of your instrument repertoire as the six configurations.

IFR turns are made at standard rate, which means 3° per second, so that a complete 360° turn takes two minutes. The only exceptions to the standard rate rule are for very small turns, which are performed at a slower rate, high speed turns that would require more than 30° of bank for standard rate, and steep turns which are practiced as a highly beneficial training exercise, but never used in normal operations. *Never vary the rate of turn in order to hasten or delay completion of a turn.*

Standard rate turns require a bank equal to approximately 15% of the airplane's airspeed in knots. Use coordinated aileron and rudder to produce this bank indication on the attitude indicator. In very fast aircraft (over 200 knots) do not exceed 30° of bank, even though the turn is less than standard rate. Steeper banks in instrument flight are considered dangerous because of the large amount of back pressure needed to hold altitude and because the airplane may have a tendency to roll even steeper.

With the bank established, cross check the turn instrument for coordination and rate of turn. If the rate of turn is not correct, adjust the bank on the attitude indicator. If the ball is out of center, center it with rudder pressure.

With the proper coordinated turn established, check the VSI for steady altitude, keeping in mind that although the VSI lags in reporting *rate* information, it does instantaneously show the *trend* of any altitude change. A recommended scan for initiating a turn is shown in figure 3-7.

In a bank, a component of lift is diverted horizontally and some back pressure is needed to maintain altitude. In standard rate turns, which use only shallow banks, this factor is negligible, yet many pilots unconsciously apply *excessive* back pressure. This is a habit we develop in primary training. The most common turning error in IFR training is an inadvertent *climb*.

If you maintain altitude in the turn, there will be a slight drop in airspeed, owing to the slightly increased pitch attitude required to hold altitude, but the airspeed loss is negligible and does not need correction with a power adjust-

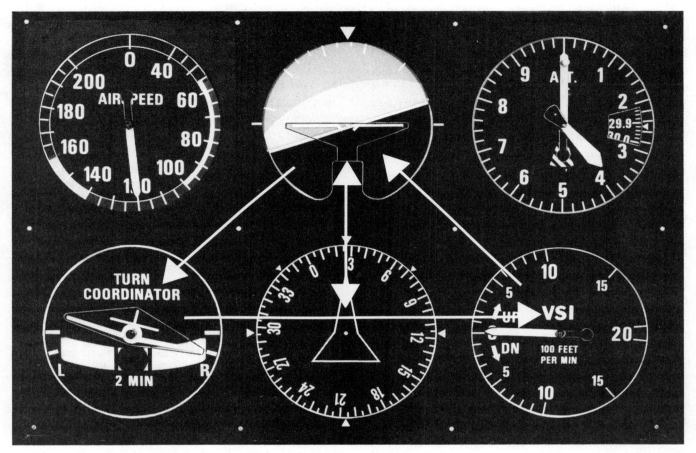

Figure 3-7

ment.

As the aircraft approaches the desired heading, use the DG to lead the rollout by approximately *one half the angle of bank*. For example: in a 20° bank, start rolling out 10° prior to the desired heading. During the rollout use the attitude indicator to accurately determine the wings level position.

For small heading changes, the angle of bank should not exceed the number of degrees of turn. To turn 10°, bank no more than 10°. A greater bank would result in overshooting the heading.

Before practicing turns, it is advisable to calibrate the turn instrument. It is surprising how many of them are slightly out of calibration. Make a level 360° turn with the instrument showing exactly standard rate. Time the turn carefully. If full circle comes out in exactly two minutes, the turn instrument is accurate. If it is

more than five seconds off, try again with the instrument showing slightly more or less than standard rate. Repeat the exercise until you know exactly how the instrument reads in a true two minute turn. Calibrate the turn instrument in both directions. Often it will be accurate one way and slightly off the other. If it is more than 10 seconds off in either direction, the turn instrument should be repaired.

Practice turns at first without reference to the heading. Establish the turn, continue it a few seconds, and then recover, using the attitude indicator to return to wings level. The objective is to get used to leveling the wings on the attitude indicator, rather than the DG.

When you are adept at starting and stopping turns with the correct scan, add heading control to your repertoire. Learn to lead the rollout by one half the angle of bank on the DG and watch the attitude indicator as you level the wings.

Again, you will find it helpful to zero out out the bank angle by referring to the bank index at the top. With a little practice you will recover with a consistent roll rate and invariably end on the desired heading.

In response to simulated radar vectors, practice smaller and smaller turns to headings, watching for accurate rollout, turning in the proper direction, and altitude control.

Common errors to avoid:

— When turning to a heading, the most common error is to watch the DG as the desired heading approaches, and then apply pressure to level the wings. When the heading is reached and the pressure is released, the airplane may remain banked if you have not used the attitude indicator. It may, as a result, continue to turn after you stop paying attention to the DG, or it may have rolled two or three degrees through level and may turn slowly back the other way.

Learn to lead the rollout by half the angle of bank and then give your full attention to the attitude indicator. Once you develop this habit, you will rollout on headings consistently and, with level wings, will have no trouble holding heading.

— The most common altitude problem in turns is an inadvertent climb. Most private pilots are taught that in a bank some lift is diverted horizontally so that back pressure is needed to hold altitude, which is true. Consequently, many pilots unconsciously haul back on the yoke *excessively* each time a turn is started. Since *very little* back pressure is needed in a shallow or medium bank turn, the result is often a climb.

— Turning the wrong way is a surprisingly common problem. If you have this tendency, develop a procedure for verifying which way you are going to turn. Tapping the appropriate foot works for some pilots; for others, putting little ''left'' and ''right'' tags on the instrument panel is effective. When turning to vector headings, make a habit of looking at the DG and making sure the intended turn is less than 180°. If it is more than 180°, the controller may be giving you a long turn for traffic separation, but he should be queried to make sure you didn't misunderstand him.

— Overbanking during turns at approach speed is a common error. If the airplane cruises at 150 knots and makes approaches at 100, the bank angle for a standard rate turn at cruise will be approximately 22° and at approach only 15°. If you roll to the steeper bank angle at the slower speed and do not correct, you are probably omitting the turn coordinator, which should be the second element in the scan.

— Overbanking during small turns can cause an erratic flight path. For accurate course control, learn to make shallow banks for small turns. All turns should be coordinated. A turn of 1° or 2° requires a 1° or 2° bank and a bit of rudder pressure. If you roll to 15° of bank for a 5° turn, the result will likely be ''S'' turns through the course and an uncomfortable fishtailing of the airplane.

— Stopping the rollout prematurely can cause heading control problems. There is a difference in behavior between the turn indicator and the turn coordinator. The needle of the *indicator* shows only rate of turn while the symbolic airplane of the *coordinator* indicates rate of turn *and* direction and rate of *roll*. Watch the turn coordinator as you recover from a normal turn. During the rollout, the turn coordinator shows a turn in the opposite direction and returns to level when the roll is stopped. This causes trouble if you incorrectly watch the turn coordinator during turn recovery, for it gives the impression that you have over-controlled and have started a turn in the opposite direction. To avoid this, use the attitude indicator as your control instrument during the rollout.

Climbing and Descending Turns

When assigned a climbing or descending turn, you are expected to accomplish the altitude and heading changes simultaneously. However, you are not required to *initiate* them together. To simplify the maneuver you can initiate the climb or descent and then begin the turn. Practice is required to be able to end the climb without stopping the turn, and vice versa.

In practicing climbing and descending turns, begin by starting the climb or descent and *then* the turn. Gradually smooth out your technique to the point where you can use the attitude indicator to initiate the pitch and bank changes simultaneously. Practice climbing and descending turns in which you do not reach the altitude and heading simultaneously but must level either the pitch or bank without changing the other.

Keep in mind that if you reach the altitude before the heading, you may lower the nose to level off, and inadvertently level the wings, stopping the turn before reaching the heading. Conversely, if you reach the heading first, you may level the wings and inadvertently lower the nose. This is really like patting your head and rubbing your belly. Pay attention to the specific elements of the scan where the problems are occurring.

Steep Turns

Steep turns are those that require more than 30° of bank. They are considered unsafe for instrument flight but are valuable as training maneuvers. The 45° bank turn sharpens the scan and increases awareness of the function of the attitude indicator in controlling pitch and bank.

In a *steep* turn, considerable lift is diverted horizontally and significant back pressure is required to maintain altitude. The need for back pressure does not increase uniformly during the turn entry but rises sharply between 30° and 45° of bank. To maintain altitude during the turn, make small pitch adjustments on the attitude indicator until the VSI reads zero and the altimeter is steady. Note the pitch attitude and hold it for the remainder of the turn. Trim should not be used during steep turns, because it would have to be readjusted at the end of the turn and would increase the tendency to "balloon" (climb) at the completion of the turn.

The recovery from a steep turn must be initiated well before the desired heading is reached. The rule of leading the rollout by one half the

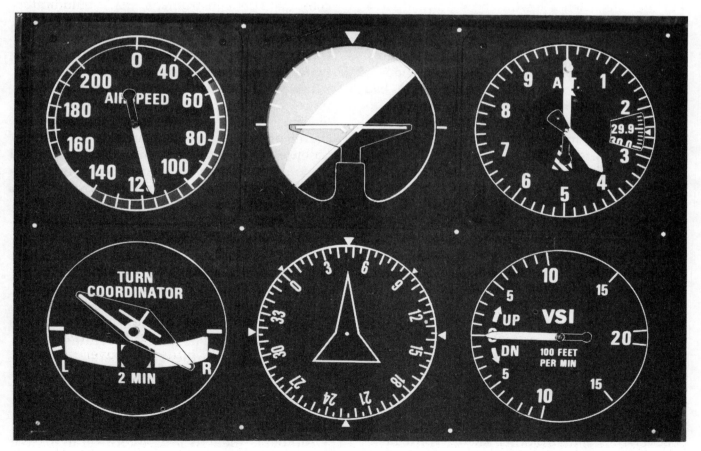

Figure 3-8

angle of bank still applies. The recovery from a 45° bank turn should thus start 20° to 25° before the heading is reached. Back pressure must be smoothly released during the recovery to avoid "ballooning."

In practicing 360° steep turns, start by turning at a smaller bank angle. You might even begin with 360° standard rate turns and use the exercise to calibrate the turn coordinator. Then go to 30° of bank and notice the slight increase in back pressure necessary to hold altitude. Determine the required pitch attitude and hold it on the attitude indicator (figure 3-8). Be prepared to hold much more back pressure when you go to 45° of bank. In some aircraft you will have to continue increasing back pressure for a few seconds after the 45° bank is established, as the airspeed bleeds off and stabilizes.

Common errors to avoid:

— Steep turns are merely a training exercise, but they do teach a lesson about scan. If bank control is a problem, direct your attention to the bank index on the attitude indicator.

— Holding "top rudder" is a common fault. It slows the rate of turn and makes the maneuver seem easier, but it is an uncomfortable, bad habit. Use the turn instrument and resume coordinated flight.

— At the start of the turn, excessive back pressure is often applied, resulting in a climb during the first 30° of roll. The need for back pressure develops slowly during the first 30° of roll and sharply between 30° and 45°.

— Holding altitude during the turn depends on discovering the proper pitch attitude for turns in each direction and holding it on the attitude indicator. Chasing the altimeter or VSI has even more disastrous results in a steep turn than in a normal turn.

— During the rollout there is a tendency to climb. Back pressure should be released as the wings are leveled. Then, as the airspeed increases (you lost airspeed because of the high angle of attack in the turn) the nose will tend to rise and attention will have to be paid to the altimeter and attitude indicator to avoid an inadvertent climb. Another factor worth mentioning here is that we have trouble remembering where "neutral" is. Although you *think* you relaxed all of the back pressure, you may un-

consciously hold a little. You may have to "push nose down against your own muscles" to obtain the right attitude on the attitude indicator.

— Do not trim during the steep turn. A 360° steep turn is so short that it is more efficient to hold the back pressure manually than to trim for the turn and retrim at its completion.

— Precessional error in some attitude indicators causes problems during steep turns. These errors will cause the indicated "target" pitch attitude to change as heading changes. The error is usually largest 180° from the entry heading. A fast scan and continuous refinement of the indicated pitch attitude that results in zero vertical speed will keep ahead of this problem.

Partial Panel

The so-called partial panel consists of the three pressure instruments and the electric turn coordinator, the instruments that would remain in use after a vacuum system failure (figure 3-9). This section discusses partial panel work as a training exercise and describes techniques for flying the airplane in a partial panel situation. Additional procedures for dealing with a partial panel emergency are discussed in Chapter Eleven.

The disadvantage of partial panel is the absence of a control instrument for pitch and bank attitude. You must make control inputs with reference to the performance instruments, which are not ideal for the purpose. The pitot-static instruments report data which lags somewhat behind attitude variations, and the angle of bank associated with a standard rate turn on the remaining gyro instrument varies with speed.

Your control movements, therefore, must be smooth and gradual. Begin each maneuver with a slight change and observe the instrument reactions, then make further adjustments accordingly. Maneuvering in this condition requires a more rapid scan pattern and more trial and error, because there is no direct indication of attitude.

Although there is less information for the pilot, flight techniques on partial panel are the same as with a full panel. To reduce the airspeed, for example, reduce the power and raise

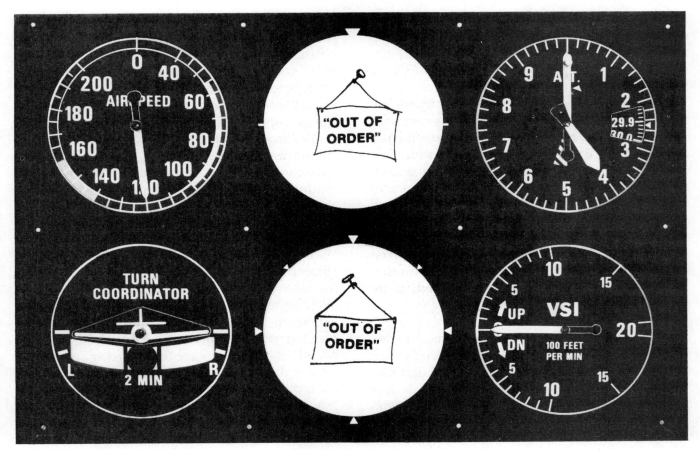

Figure 3-9

the nose. The airspeed indicator will react almost immediately, and the VSI will indicate any tendency to descend. Apply back pressure to stabilize the airspeed and altitude and *retrim* for the new airspeed. To increase the airspeed, increase the power. The airspeed indicator will show an almost immediate reaction, and the VSI will indicate any tendency to climb. Apply forward pressure to stabilize airspeed and altitude, and retrim for the new airspeed.

As on full panel, a descent requires simultaneous reduction of pitch and power. Make the adjustment to the correct power setting (knowing "the numbers" for the six configurations is invaluable here) and allow the nose to settle. If the airplane was trimmed properly for level flight at the original airspeed, it will now descend at the same airspeed and at the desired rate.

A climb involves pitch and power changes. Move the throttle to the climb-power setting

and raise the nose smoothly until the airspeed drops to the desired value. As in a full panel climb, adjust the pitch to maintain the proper airspeed.

Partial Panel Turns

Timed Turns. Partial panel turns are made with reference to the turn needle or turn coordinator. Since there is no direct information about angle of bank, it is important that the turn be coordinated. As on full panel, the altimeter and VSI must be cross checked to verify that altitude is constant in the turn.

When making timed turns with a turn coordinator, remember that during the rollout the instrument will show an apparent turn in the opposite direction, because it reacts to *roll* as well as to heading changes. To overcome this problem, use a light touch on the controls and familiarize yourself with the behavior of your particular instrument. A rule of thumb is to neutralize the ailerons when the turn coordinator shows a nearly standard rate turn in the direction of roll. This will usually result in a level flight attitude.

Turning to a heading is accomplished with the magnetic compass and clock. Since, owing to dip errors, the compass is unreliable in a turn, a standard rate turn is made for a certain number of seconds. To make a timed turn to a heading, ask yourself a series of questions:

Which way? The numbers on the magnetic compass card are backwards compared to their arrangement on the compass rose or map. To decide which way, visualize the compass rose or look at the ADF indicator to orient your turn.

How many degrees? Use mental arithmetic or count them on the ADF.

How many seconds? Since you are planning a standard rate turn, divide the number of degrees by 3. An alternate method is to count ten seconds for each 30° of turn on the ADF dial. Do *not* start the turn immediately and try to do the arithmetic while turning. Very few people can. You can afford to be patient, if it leads to your being right.

Turn. If you are using a clock with a sweep second hand, start the turn entry when it reaches a quarter-minute position. When the time is up, begin the recovery.

For small turns, 15° or less, turn at *half* standard rate and count seconds aloud. To turn 10°, for example, establish a half standard rate turn on the turn instrument and count off six seconds.

Compass Turns. If you understand compass errors, and are willing to work at it, you can learn to make fairly accurate turns with the magnetic compass alone, especially if you are turning to one of the four cardinal points.

During standard rate turns on north or south headings, the lag/lead error is approximately equal to the latitude, so lead the rollout by your latitude, plus the normal number of degrees allowed for rollout. For example, in St. Louis (approximately lat. 38° N.), if you are turning with 15° of bank, lead the rollout by approximately 45° (38° + 15°/2 = 45.5°). On east or west headings, the lag/lead error is zero, so lead the rollout by your normal one half the angle of

bank. For headings other than the cardinal points, lag/lead error must be figured by interpolation.

In making compass turns, it is also necessary to be familiar with the individual instrument you are using, as compasses vary widely in the amount of error. I have even seen some that, in a turn from north to east, not only show an initial turn in the wrong direction but swing all the way around through west and south before coming to rest on the proper heading.

Rate Climbs and Descents

We normally make airspeed climbs by using climb power and a desired airspeed and accepting whatever rate we get. However, it is a useful exercise to practice climbing at a specified rate, as shown by the VSI, and timing the climbs to reach desired altitudes. Five hundred feet per minute is a good rate for this exercise and can be achieved by most general aviation aircraft.

To practice this, you first need to know what power setting will give you 500 feet per minute at your normal climb airspeed. Set up a normal climb and allow the VSI to settle. If the rate of climb is higher than desired, reduce the power slightly. If the airplane is trimmed for the desired airspeed, a slight oscillation will occur and a stable climb at the same airspeed and a lower rate will eventually result. Experiment until the correct power setting for 500 feet per minute is determined. With the power setting known, establish the aircraft at an altitude and cover the altimeter. Use the new power setting to climb at normal climb airspeed for, say, four minutes. An altitude gain of 2000 feet should result. The value of this exercise is in learning to carefully control pitch attitude so that the airspeed is constant and the rate of climb averages 500 feet per minute. Chasing the VSI will cause disastrous oscillations in airspeed because of the long lag in the instrument's reaching an accurate rate indication.

Timed descents are easier, since the power settings for 500 foot per minute descents are already known. They also may have more practical value as, in the event of an altimeter failure, you are more likely to want to descend out of the clouds than to climb.

Practice timed descents as timed climbs, with the altimeter covered. Again, the most common error is to chase the VSI.

Unusual Attitudes

An unusual attitude may be caused by turbulence, improper control pressures and inattention, or a failure of the trim mechanism. Severe unusual attitudes may exceed the limits of the attitude indicator and DG and recoveries should therefore be practiced on partial panel.

There are two types of unusual attitudes: nose high and nose low. If the trim control is intact and the airplane is not banked, the aircraft will tend to recover automatically from extreme pitch attitudes. Owing to its inherent longitudinal stability, it will enter a decreasing oscillation, the nose dropping as airspeed bleeds off and rising as airspeed builds, and eventually return to its original airspeed and attitude. This type of movement is called a **phugoid oscillation**.

The most dangerous unusual atitude is the descending turn. Because of the bank, a steep dive will tend to develop and the airspeed can rapidly build to dangerous levels. If the turn exceeds medium bank the airplane will tend to continue rolling more steeply, accelerating the spiral dive and increasing the chances of exceeding the design load factor.

The danger for the unwary pilot who finds himself unexpectedly on partial panel and who hears the buildup of wind over the cockpit and sees his airspeed high in the yellow as the altitude plummets is that he will reflexively pull back on the yoke, tightening the spiral, increasing the descent rate and airspeed even more, and possibly applying destructive structural loads.

Practicing unusual attitude recoveries is an important part of instrument training. In setting up practice spirals for a student or another pilot, the instructor or safety pilot can have him look into his lap so the hood blocks his view of the panel. A couple of clearing turns (especially including a good look below) will assure that there is no traffic nearby and will also serve to disorient the student.

Before entering the spiral, the instructor can fly "over the top," allowing airspeed to decay almost to the stall and entering the maneuver like a "lazy eight." If the aircraft is turned over to the student at the top of the "eight," he will see a very low but increasing airspeed and may misinterpret his attitude to be a sharp climb, possibly approaching the stall. If he makes this mistake, emphasize that he must look for the *trend* of the airspeed, not just its value.

Another, more realistic, way to practice unusual attitude recoveries is to have the student induce the unusual attitudes himself. Have him attempt to make turns to left and right while looking into his lap. In a very short time a true unusual attitude will be established and the student can then return his attention to the panel to make the recovery.

In a spiral dive, the airspeed will eventually be high and increasing, and the turn coordinator will be pegged in the direction of the turn. The steps for recovery are:

1. Reduce power to eliminate the accelerating thrust of the engine. Also, the propeller will produce some drag.

2. Level the wings. Do not attempt to raise the nose while the airplane is banked. This would tighten the spiral and increase the stress on the airframe.

3. Raise the nose. At high airspeeds, strong control pressure is unnecessary. The nose will tend to rise and without a direct indication of pitch attitude it is easy to over-control, which could cause a high pitch attitude and a near-stall condition. Level flight is reached when the altitude stops decreasing. If it starts to increase, the airplane is climbing and you should dampen this tendency with light forward pressure.

Steep climbs are not usually a problem in light general aviation aircraft. If the airplane is banked, the nose will generally drop by itself and you will soon be in a steep spiral. If the airplane is not banked, the nose may rise until the airspeed decays, at which time the nose will drop and a phugoid oscillation will occur until the airplane settles at the airspeed for which it is trimmed.

In the case of "runaway" electric trim, the nose-high attitude may persist and become dangerous. The instructor can try to simulate this for a student, but he should keep talking in a loud voice as he twists the trim wheel, or the student will hear it and spoil the surprise.

The steps for recovery from a nose-high unusual attitude are:

1. Apply power to increase airspeed and avoid the stall.

2. Lower the nose to increase airspeed and avoid the stall. Level flight is reached when the altitude stops increasing.

3. Level the wings. With low airspeed there is no danger of overstressing the airframe if the nose is lowered with the airplane banked. *But be alert to the danger of entering a spiral dive.*

These exercises should help you to do something that is vital to safe, smooth instrument flying — visualizing the airplane's actual attitude as revealed by the instruments. *Unusual* attitudes are fortunately just that. But when your gauges tell you that you have entered that realm, you should be able to "see" the airplane's position as readily as if you could see the real horizon and the ground. It takes thought and practice. It may also save your life.

Stalls

To practice stalls under the hood, start with stalls by visual reference. Make two 90° clearing turns, with the instructor looking for traffic, and slow the airplane to just above the stall speed. With practice, the airspeed will be just above the stall as the second turn is completed. Progress to stalls by instrument reference, performing exactly the same maneuver, and finally advance to stalls on partial panel. Practice stalls in the approach configuration, and climb power stalls as they might occur following power application during a missed approach.

To The CFII

In teaching basic instruments, learn to focus on the student's scan. Teach by directing his eyes to the proper instrument at the proper time. Break the scan into its component parts, and give clear, specific explanations, especially when offering a correction. For example, if a student has trouble leveling the wings and still insists that he *is* using the attitude indicator as you taught him, he may actually be using the instrument *incorrectly*. After rolling the miniature airplane symbol parallel with the horizon line, he should confirm the zero degree bank

angle by checking the bank index at the top of the instrument. If he doesn't, the airplane might stay in a slight bank because the thickness of the airplane wings and horizon line make it difficult to exactly determine the wings level position. This is the kind of subtle problem that you should learn to identify and correct.

As a skilled instrument instructor, you will recognize scan problems from flaws in your students' performance and improve their performance by correcting the scan. An instructor who can analyze why the airplane is behaving as it is and can link the problem to what the student is watching and/or neglecting, actually seems to be "inside" the student's head. "You were watching such and such, weren't you?" "How did you know *that?*"

The answer usually is that responding to particular instruments yields particular results. The right instruments thus produce the right results, and the instructor should acknowledge good performance as well as errors. *Positive feedback* reinforces correct technique and is an excellent teaching tool.

Instrument practice takes concentration and precision. Tension often develops during training and causes fatigue and lapses in attention. A tight grip on the yoke causes unnecessary errors, such as the "heavy left hand syndrome," in which the airplane turns left every time the pilot's attention is diverted from the center of the panel. Returning immediately to the attitude indicator each time the scan leaves the basic panel for the radios or power instrument is an antidote for this error, but a relaxed grip prevents it.

During practice sessions, take breaks to focus on relaxing. Encourage the student to fly with a light touch, keeping just a thumb and finger on the yoke, if possible. Practice turns and configuration changes without the hood, and try to develop a relaxed posture.

Comfort in the cockpit is all-important. Be sure the student can reach the controls easily and can see all the gauges without straining. Move the seat as far forward as necessary. Many pilots are more comfortable with a cushion on the seat or supporting their lower back. Take the time to make him comfortable. It will reduce fatigue and improve his performance and safety.

If you are using a simulator, estimate the power settings that will produce desired speeds and rates in the airplane, rather than having the student memorize two sets of numbers. Adjust the simulator to correspond to the airplane's performance. Have the student go through the power sheet, and carefully record the power settings, pitch attitudes, airspeeds and climb/descent rates for each configuration. Thoroughly familiarize him with each configuration, and practice transitions until they are smooth and automatic.

In the airplane, determine the actual settings for the six configurations without using the hood. Then, with the student under the hood — and you watching for traffic — begin practicing airspeed, altitude and heading changes, using the verified numbers. At first, do pitch and power exercises without regard to heading. As his proficiency grows, do the exercises on a constant heading. Finally, combine them with turns.

With proper ground and simulator preparation, basic attitude flying can usually be mastered in two three- or four-hour flights. However, practicing turns and configuration changes for this long can be tedious and tiring. You can use several exercises in your practice sessions to break the monotony, provide a rest, and give useful insight into aircraft and instrument performance. Conduct them visually to give your student a welcome respite from the "dreaded hood."

The *phugoid oscillation demonstration* illustrates the airplane's longitudinal stability. After a couple of clearing turns, drastically raise the nose until airspeed drops nearly to the stall. In the process, you will gain several hundred feet. Release the yoke and allow the nose to drop. As the pitch attitude drops, the altitude will decrease, and the airplane will enter a dive; do not let the airspeed get higher than the middle of the yellow arc. (Do not get too close to the red line — airplanes have broken up in flight owing to flutter from unbalanced control surfaces, at speeds *below* V_{ne}.) Use rudder pressure to counteract the tendency to turn owing to "P-factor;" for this demonstration, resist touching the yoke.

Just when you think you will have to intervene to prevent overspeeding, the nose will rise and the airspeed will decrease. Lost altitude will be recovered. As the airplane climbs, the airspeed will bleed off, but not as much as the first time. Before it becomes dangerously low, the nose will drop again and the airspeed will rise.

The oscillations in airspeed and altitude will continue, getting smaller with each cycle. Eventually, you will return to level cruise flight at the original airspeed. The altitude typically will end up within two or three hundred feet of the start of the exercise.

The turn instrument vs. the attitude indicator. To illustrate the differences between these instruments, here are two simple exercises. From straight and level flight, initiate a 5° to 10° bank to the left. By applying right rudder, force the turn instrument back to level. You are now banked left, as shown on the attitude indicator, while flying straight ahead, according to the turn instrument. The *attitude indicator shows the aircraft's attitude, while the turn instrument shows the rate of turn.* Add more right rudder, and you can actually turn right while banking left.

Next, from straight-and-level flight, apply rudder to skid the aircraft to the left, while holding the wings level with the ailerons. The attitude indicator now reads wings level, while the needle shows a left turn.

None of these situations, of course, is an example of coordinated flight; they are just used to illustrate the differences between control and performance instruments.

Pitch attitude vs. climb performance. This is basically a slow flight demonstration of the differences between control and performance instruments. After appropriate clearing turns, slow the airplane to a speed near the stall. To maintain level flight, increase the power to a near-cruise setting and hold a very high angle of attack. You may feel that you are lying on your seat back. Observe the attitude indicator. It should show a nose high attitude, even though the VSI indicates level flight. Reduce the power slightly and you can descend with the same high pitch setting.

Unusual Attitudes. In unusual attitude recoveries, as in all partial panel work, emphasize light control pressures and a rapid instrument scan.

The greatest danger is in overcontrolling and creating another unusual attitude during the recovery.

The best method of setting up unusual attitudes is to allow the student to induce them himself, as described in the main text. If you prefer to set them up yourself, use discretion with the airplane, entering the maneuvers smoothly and, staying within the airspeed and g-force limits. Check with the student periodically to be sure he is not getting sick — and don't spend longer than necessary setting up the unusual attitudes. Always do unusual attitude recovery practice *last* on any training flight. Then if there must be a quick return to the airport, you will not lose valuable training time.

Instrument Scan. During IFR practice, remind the student to include the engine gauges and ammeter in the scan. This is the best time to develop this potentially lifesaving habit.

Attitude Flying Quiz

1. Trim sets a desired (attitude, altitude, or airspeed).
2. List the control instruments.
3. List the performance instruments.
4. What are the two most common scanning errors?
5. What are the six configurations?
6. In a climb, airspeed is controlled by … (pitch or power?)
7. What are the steps to level off from a climb?
8. During level cruise, what is the rule of thumb used to correct altitude excursions?
9. What is the recommended scan for straight-and-level flight?
10. You are in level flight, at cruise airspeed. What are the steps to initiate a climb?
11. You are in level flight, at cruise airspeed. What are the steps to initiate a descent?
12. What are the steps to level off from a descent?
13. What is the most frequent error when performing a nonprecision descent?
14. Turns on instruments are made at a standard rate. What is that rate? How long does it take to complete a turn at this rate?
15. How do you check the accuracy of the turn instrument?
16. Partial panel turns are made with reference to what instrument?
17. What instruments remain in use after a vacuum system failure?
18. Define phugoid oscillation.
19. What are the steps to recover from a nose-high unusual attitude?
20. What are the steps to recover from a nose-low unusual attitude?

CHAPTER FOUR

IFR PLANNING AND PROCEDURES

This chapter begins with the story of a flight. Give it a different pilot, plane, and location, and this trip could be like one you will make when the IFR rating is yours to use. This isn't a "war story," unless you want to consider a routine, successful trip a victory over the possibilities of a white-knuckler. In IFR flying, hazards are most frequently dealt with before they occur— through planning.

In this case, once I knew where and when I wanted to fly, I surveyed the most likely routes to take, checked out the general weather picture by means of the local newspaper and TV weather reports, and, with an idea of conditions in mind, got down to business.

When I had dialed the local Flight Service number, I was relieved to find that this time I was not greeted by the recorded announcement, "Please stand by, all briefers are busy." A human briefer came on the line, and I heard the click as he keyed his mike. The local phone number connects to the Flight Service Station (FSS) at Bradley Field, in Hartford, Connecticut, through a nearby VOR, and communications are relayed by radio. While I was speaking into my home phone, the briefer was sitting at a console, talking into a radio microphone.

"Windsor Locks Flight Service. O'Brien."

"Skylane seven eight nine papa fox," I said, "planning an IFR trip from Bradley to Syracuse, New York, in about two hours, on Victor 203 and Victor 2. I'd like a briefing, please."

"Stand by."

I could picture the briefer turning to his computer terminal and typing a code to call up a standard set of sequence reports and terminal forecasts for perhaps two dozen airports in the region.

"Bradley," he said after a pause, "is estimated five hundred, sky obscured two miles in light rain and fog. Temperature three eight, dew point three six. Wind one five zero at five. The forecast is five hundred overcast, two miles in light rain and fog, chance of two hundred overcast one half mile in rain and fog. That's good until zero four hundred Zulu.

"Syracuse is one thousand overcast and eight miles. Wind two three zero at one five. Forecast until one seven zero zero Zulu is one thousand two hundred overcast, ten miles, with southwest wind at ten knots. Occasionally three miles visibility in snow showers. Until one nine zero zero Zulu, forecast is five hundred overcast, two miles in snow. Wind two seven zero at fifteen gusting two five. Until zero zero Zulu expect two thousand broken, ten miles. Wind three three zero at fifteen. After that, VFR."

Since the standard FAA weather briefing format has the briefer begin with flight precautions from the area forecast, my man was departing from the rules. I suspected that he was nearing the end of his shift and would not offer a complete briefing.

I copied his words on my weather briefing sheet as he spoke, using my private shorthand to keep up with his rapid delivery. When he paused, I realized he wasn't offering any more information and that I would have to ask for whatever else I wanted.

"Read me the synopsis, please," I said.

His second "stand by" was not surly but studiedly neutral. A moment later, I heard, "A large low pressure area south of Nantucket will be moving out to sea early tomorrow. A cold front over western New York and Pennsylvania is moving eastward. High pressure over Ohio will move into upper New York State by late this afternoon. There is a chance of icing in clouds and precipitation."

Even as I hastily copied, I realized that our bad local weather was due to the onshore wind from the low to the southeast. The rapid deterioration and then improvement predicted for Syracuse indicated the expected time of the cold front passage. It would behoove me to reach Syracuse before the cold front—I'd have to get going pretty soon to do so.

Provided I reached Syracuse before the front, it looked like a routine trip. "Chance of icing in clouds and precipitation" is a standard prediction included in most winter area forecasts by defensive forecasters. It is never correct to cancel a flight solely on the basis of such flight precautions, even if they are listed as meteorological advisories for light aircraft (AIRMETs) or significant meteorological information (SIGMETs). Before canceling, I would want to see a truly terrible synopsis and terminal forecasts, or bad sequences or pilot reports (PIREPs). PIREPs, of course, are the best source of en route information, as they report observed conditions from the vantage point of the airplane, something no forecast or sequence report can do.

"Any pilot reports for my route?"

This time, I didn't even hear a "stand by," just a click. In a moment, O'Brien returned. "Over Albany, a Piper Saratoga reported on top at six thousand, clear above. That's all I've got."

The tops report was very good news. I didn't relish a 2-hour trip in the clouds with temperatures near freezing, but with the tops below 6000, I would feel comfortable going up and down through the layer. Another good sign was that there were no reports of icing.

So the flight was a go. Time now to pick an alternate destination, just in case—and because the law says so.

I would need an alternate because my destination didn't meet the FAR requirement of a forecast of at least 2000 feet and 3 miles visibility from 1 hour before to 1 hour after my estimated time of arrival—not the Syracuse forecast as it was between 1700 and 1900 Zulu. The regs also stipulate requirements that prospective alternates must meet—conditions we will go into later

in this chapter—regarding weather conditions, the types of approach available there and other factors. To make the selection easier, I called upon my taxes-paid resource person on the other end of the line.

"I need an airport forecasting better than 600 and two between 1700 and 1900," I said.

"Cleveland looks good," he said, obviously scanning his readily available data. "They're forecasting two thousand broken and ten for that period."

"I don't think I want an alternate on the other side of the front. Does anything look good east of Syracuse?" If I wound up going to my alternate, the last thing I wanted was to tackle a cold front.

O'Brien seemed to be warming up and genuinely trying to be helpful. "The front shouldn't reach Albany until 2000 Greenwich," he said. "They're forecasting twelve hundred and six until then."

"Thanks," I said, turning to my flight plan form, "I'll give you an IFR flight plan now."

"Go ahead."

I could see the two of us, each poised over his own copy of the same form with its boxes arranged to profile the who, where, when, how and with-what of every flight. No questions were called for—only the answers.

"Seven eight nine papa foxtrot, C-182 slash Tango, one three zero knots, Bradley, 1530 Zulu, six thousand feet, direct Chester, Victor-203 Albany, Victor-2 Syracuse, direct. Destination Syracuse, one plus 30, five hours fuel, alternate Albany, name Dogan, on file at Air Kaman, two on board, aircraft is blue on white."

"Okay, have a good day," and the Flight Service man clicked off.

At the airport, I performed my preflight, started the engine and tuned the number one comm to 118.15, the Bradley automatic terminal information service (ATIS) frequency.

"Bradley International Airport information Delta. One five zero zero Zulu weather. Indefinite ceiling five hundred, sky obscured, visibility two, light rain and fog, temperature three four, dew point three two, wind one five zero at ten, altimeter two niner seven eight. ILS Runway Two Four in use, landing Runway Two Four, departing Runway One Five. Advise controller on initial contact you have information Delta." There had been no significant changes since the last hour.

I next called clearance delivery, using my number two radio. "Bradley Clearance, Skylane seven eight nine papa fox, IFR to Syracuse."

Evidently, they were waiting for me; the clearance

came back as I unkeyed the mike. I have learned that it pays to have pencil in hand when calling clearance delivery.

As always, the clearance came in a particular order, setting out everything I would need to know to get from the Bradley runway to the runway at Syracuse, even if I lost communications at liftoff. In such a case, this clearance plus my filed flight plan—with its stipulation of my alternate—plus the rules ATC and I would both follow would provide information on my whereabouts at all times. The man at clearance delivery quickly went through the seven-part clearance, and I followed my customary method of copying, or not copying, as the case required. Why and/or why not to copy will be detailed later in the chapter.

"November seven eight nine papa fox (part one, which I didn't copy) is cleared to the Syracuse Hancock International Airport (part two, which, again, I didn't copy) as filed (part three, which I copied). After departure Runway One Five, turn left heading three six zero, radar vectors to Chester (part four, which I copied, keeping in mind that I would make sure not to start the turn, at least until I was at the circling minimum for the airport to ensure terrain and obstacle clearance. I also recognized that I'd probably receive no vectors at all to the Chester VOR, but would be expected to navigate direct, on my own. (Why, then, "radar vectors"? More later.)

"Climb and maintain two thousand, expect six thousand one zero minutes after departure (part five, which I copied, knowing full well that my clearance to 6000 would probably come sooner than departure plus ten). Contact departure control on one two five point three five (part six, which demanded only the copying of the numbers—what else could they stand for?). Squawk five two four seven (part seven, again copying only the numbers, for the same reason)."

Using my memory (not a great challenge in this case) and my shorthand, I repeated the clearance and was rewarded with "readback is correct, have a good flight."

So far, so simple. Since this was a controlled airport, I wouldn't have to deal with what would have been part eight—my release and void times and the possible Drawbridge Factor. Again, more about that later.

Having thanked clearance delivery, I turned to ground control, 121.9, on my number one radio. Ground's response would verify that I had transmission and reception on both radios.

"Bradley Ground, Skylane seven eight nine papa fox at Air Kaman with Delta and clearance. Ready to taxi."

"Nine papa fox, taxi to Runway One Five, intersec-tion Charlie. Wind is one five zero at eight, altimeter two niner seven niner."

"Nine papa fox requests full length." Nothing is more useless on takeoff than runway behind you, especially into IFR.

"Nine papa fox, taxi to Runway One Five via Sierra. Hold short of Runway Two Four."

I advanced the throttle and rolled onto the taxiway. As I reached the hold line at Runway Two Four, I heard, "cessna nine papa fox, cross Runway Two Four."

At the runup pad, I carefully set up the radios. I like to do as much as possible of the necessary twisting and fiddling while on the ground, not right after takeoff, when I am entering the soup and transitioning to flight on instruments. I put the tower frequency in one comm radio and the departure frequency in the other.

I set the frequency for the Chester VOR on the number one nav and was able to identify it on the ground. I set the OBS for the approximate course to Chester, the authoritative "radar vectors to Chester" given in my clearance notwithstanding.

My second nav radio was now set to identify the first intersection, with its OBS twisted to the appropriate radial. As usual, I did not plan to alternate my tracking between the first and second navs, even though setting those frequencies in advance might put me a little ahead of things. I knew that if I did, somewhere, some day, when I would least expect it, I'd find myself—quite candidly—tracking on the wrong instrument, no doubt distracted by other things becoming pressing or going wrong, causing ATC to wonder just where I thought I was going.

To this rule of mine, there is an exception. More later.

Finally, I set the squawk code in the transponder, which I was leaving on standby until being cleared onto the runway—no sense further cluttering the already loaded radar screen—and set the frequency for the compass locator at the destination into the ADF. Talk about getting ahead of the situation! Thus did my radios serve as a sort of checklist for the clearance—all I needed to do was to be sure that each one was properly tuned.

So now, my radios were set and the clearance made sense as being a good way to get to where I wanted to go. Had it not been, had I been left without a clearance to my destination, or had there been a fix or an element more confusing than comforting, I would have inquired for verification or clarification and even, perhaps, have embarked upon negotiations to straighten things out, as is one's right as pilot in command. A correct readback is not an acceptance, neither is taxiing to the runway. Now I was ready to signal acceptance, although good sense would have called for raising questions as early as possible.

"Bradley Tower, Cessna seven eight nine papa fox is ready on One Five."

"Nine papa fox, position and hold, traffic landing Runway Two Four."

I switched on the transponder, and, as I turned onto the centerline of Runway One Five, I checked the DG against the runway heading. Perfect. Through the mist, I watched a small Learjet gracefully touch down from left to right across my windshield. The sound of its engines seemed to trail several hundred feet behind the airplane. A moment later, the tower called, "Cessna seven eight nine papa fox, cleared for takeoff."

"Nine papa fox cleared for takeoff," I acknowledged, jotting down the time—1529 Zulu—on my clipboard. I advanced the throttle and began rolling.

As I entered the clouds at 600 feet, the tower directed, "Seven eight nine papa fox, proceed on course, contact departure, one two five point three five. Have a good flight."

"Nine papa fox." I resisted calling departure before making my turn to 360. I follow the rule—aviate, navigate, and then communicate. With the aviating and navigating done for the moment, I switched radios and reported:

"Bradley Departure, Cessna seven eight nine papa fox is with you out of one thousand two hundred for two thousand."

"Nine papa fox, Bradley Departure, radar contact. Join Victor-203 on course, climb and maintain six thousand."

"Out of one thousand five hundred for six, nine papa fox," I said as I centered the needle for Chester, which I soon passed, established on Victor-203. Halfway to Albany, Bradley Departure advised, "Cessna seven eight nine papa fox, contact Albany Approach now, one two five point zero."

"One two five point zero, nine papa fox."

Switching channels, I reported, "Albany Approach, Cessna seven eight nine papa fox is with you at six thousand."

"Nine papa fox, Albany Approach, ident. Albany altimeter is two niner eight five."

I hit the ident button and immediately heard, "Nine papa fox, radar contact. Maintain six thousand."

At this point, I was enjoying a benefit that had been a great help a few years back during the time of the General Aviation Reservation System—TEC, or "tower en route control." TEC was allowing me to pass between Bradley and Albany without being under center jurisdiction; only approach control facilities were necessary. More about that later, too.

As I crossed the Albany VOR, I received another hand-off, "Cessna nine papa fox, contact Albany Approach now on one one eight point zero five." Albany Approach's jurisdiction is divided into sectors, each handled by a different controller. Although I dialed a new frequency and spoke to a new voice, I knew that he sat in the same room as the first controller, perhaps at his elbow.

"One one eight point zero five, nine papa fox." Switching radios again, I reported, "Albany Approach, Cessna seven eight nine papa fox is with you at six thousand."

"Nine papa fox, Albany Approach, radar contact. Albany altimeter two niner eight five."

"Nine papa fox."

The next communication came as I approached Utica. "Cessna nine papa fox, contact Griffiss Approach now, one one eight point five, so long."

"One one eight point five, nine papa fox." Switching again, I reported, "Griffiss Approach, Cessna seven eight nine papa fox is with you at six thousand."

"Nine papa fox, Griffiss, radar contact. Griffiss altimeter is two niner niner zero."

I was flying in brilliant sunshine, above an undercast that I estimated to be 2000 feet below me. My distance measuring equipment (DME) showed a groundspeed of 125 knots, 10 knots slower than my true airspeed. Since the only PIREP I had received during my briefing had been from the early morning, I decided to perform a service for my fellow pilots and make one of my own. "Griffiss Approach," I transmitted, "Seven eight nine papa fox requests permission to leave the frequency for two minutes." I knew from experience that pilot reports made to ATC facilities are not always relayed to the FSS, where they are the most help to pilots on the ground.

"Roger, nine papa fox," came the reply, "report back on the frequency."

I was tracking Victor-2 to the Utica VOR. My chart showed I could contact Utica Flight Service either on frequency 122.65, or by calling on 122.1 and listening on the VOR frequency. I opted for 122.65, judging that it would be less congested. "Utica Radio," I called, "Cessna seven eight nine papa fox, on 122.65."

I had to repeat the transmission twice before hearing

the response, "Seven eight nine papa fox, Utica Flight Service."

"Cessna Skylane seven eight nine papa fox is twenty-five miles east of Utica on Victor-2," I reported, "I have a PIREP for you."

"Go ahead," the FSS specialist replied immediately, and I imagined his pencil poised over the red PIREP form.

"We're on top at six thousand, tops of the undercast at four thousand, clear above," I reported, "air is smooth."

"Roger, nine papa fox," the FSS acknowledged, "Thank you for your pilot report."

A moment later I reported back with Griffiss Approach Control.

Passing Utica, I listened to the Syracuse ATIS on the second radio, keeping one ear cocked for a transmission from Griffiss on number one.

"Hancock International Airport information Uniform. One six zero zero Zulu weather, measured ceiling eight hundred overcast, visibility six in fog. Wind two six zero at one four. Temperature two six, altimeter two niner niner two. ILS Runway Two Eight in use, landing and departing Runway Two Eight. Advise you have Uniform." I was pleased to hear that the destination weather was not significantly different from what had been forecast.

The hand-off to Syracuse Approach came a few minutes later, "Nine papa fox, contact Syracuse Approach now, one two four point two."

"One two four point two, nine papa fox." Switching frequencies, I reported, "Syracuse Approach, Cessna seven eight nine papa fox is with you at six thousand with Uniform."

"Nine papa fox, Syracuse, radar contact. Descend and maintain three thousand, expect vectors for ILS Runway Two Eight. Wind is two three zero at one three, altimeter two niner niner four." As usual with radar working, I would be routed directly to the approach and saved the time-consuming flight to the VOR and the published transition to the outer compass locator.

"Out of six thousand for three thousand, nine papa fox," I replied, after reducing power to begin the descent. I set my number one radio for the localizer and continued tracking Victor-2 on the number two.

A little later the controller came back, "Nine papa fox, descend and maintain two thousand, intercept the localizer and track it inbound." The localizer intercepts Victor-2 a few miles outside the marker, so no radar vectors were necessary.

"Out of three for two, nine papa fox."

As the CDI swung and I turned to track the localizer I heard, "Nine papa fox, your position is six miles from the outer marker, cleared for the ILS Runway Two Eight approach, maintain one thousand eight hundred until established on the localizer, contact tower now, one two zero point three."

"One two zero point three, cleared for the approach, one thousand eight hundred until established, nine papa fox."

As I worked to center the CDI, I flicked the transmit switch to tower, "Syracuse Tower, Cessna seven eight nine papa fox is with you at one thousand eight hundred."

"Nine papa fox, Syracuse Tower, report the Kirki outer marker."

"Nine papa fox."

I intercepted the glide slope at the charted altitude of 1800 feet and a moment later saw the blue light of the outer marker. As the audio portion became audible I keyed the mike and reported, "Nine papa fox, Kirki inbound."

"Nine papa fox, cleared to land Runway Two Eight. Wind two four zero at one five."

I acknowledged the clearance and concentrated on keeping my needles square. Breaking out 800 feet above the airport, I saw the runway ahead in the windshield and was on the ground a minute later.

With the throttle closed and the airplane slowing on the runway, I listened to the tower's last instruction, "Cessna nine papa fox, turn left or right next intersection, Ground point seven when clear." Ground control frequencies are usually 121.6, 121.7, 121.8 or 121.9; controllers routinely omit the "121."

I took the left turn, crossed the hold lines and switched to 121.7, "Syracuse ground, Cessna seven eight nine papa fox clear of the active, taxi to Sair Aviation."

"Nine papa fox, ground, taxi to Sair."

It was cold in Syracuse, and the wind was blowing. As I entered the ramp, no lineman was in sight. Switching from ground, I tuned the unicom frequency, 122.95, and called the operations office, "Sair Unicom, Cessna seven eight nine papa fox." A lady's voice acknowledged and awaited my request. "I'd like fuel and directions to parking," I said.

"Yes sir," she said, "Somebody will be right out." A moment later I saw a fuel truck lurch into motion, the driver pointing me towards the tiedown area. Another routine but satisfying IFR flight was completed.

There is more to flying IFR in today's increasingly complex ATC system than merely controlling the airplane on instruments. The goal of instrument training is to make you a complete instrument pilot, able to competently plan and conduct IFR flights and to answer affirmatively each of the following questions:

Am I confident?

Am I safe?

Am I legal?

Confidence depends on knowledge and experience. A familiarity with charts and publications, an understanding of Flight Service procedures, and an ability to communicate clearly and easily with ATC build the pilot's sense of comfort under IFR.

Safety depends on your skill at controlling the airplane and at navigating accurately with the help of radio aids. It also involves weather analysis and evaluating your equipment's capabilities. Furthermore, knowing which situations to venture into and which to avoid is a primary skill of the instrument pilot.

Legal requirements are important. Not only does compliance protect you from running afoul of the FAA, but the regs, in many cases, reflect good, common-sense safety procedures. Knowing and complying with them increases the likelihood of a long and satisfying IFR career.

A lot of the factors that go into a successful IFR flight occur before the airplane ever leaves the ground.

Weather Or Not To Go?

It has been said that each IFR flight is one continuous go/no-go decision. This does not mean that you should, at any moment, be prepared to turn tail and run, but rather that you must never stop evaluating your situation and considering your options. Every flight will begin with your decision to go or to cancel, before you ever leave your living room.

Most weather is flyable, if you have enough information, knowledge, and skill. With reliable equipment, this is a realistic view in today's modern system. In most areas, there are very few days when the well-equipped instrument pilot cannot make a planned trip. There are times, of course, when massive gatherings of thunderstorms or widespread icing conditions preclude a particular

trip, but such conditions are the exception. If the trip is planned far in advance, you will monitor overall weather conditions and will know of any major storms that are likely to invade the area. Assuming that the TV or newspaper weatherman says nothing to rule out the flight, the next step is to get a thorough weather briefing. For most pilots, this means a phone call to Flight Service.

To obtain and evaluate the necessary information, you must understand the current FAA weather briefing system. Weather information is collected, analyzed, and reported by the National Weather Service (NWS), which is part of the United States Department of Commerce. Flight Service is part of the FAA within the U.S. Department of Transportation and is one of the many clients of the NWS.

The best way to build a mental picture of the weather affecting your flight is to examine the charts, reports, and forecasts at a FSS or NWS office. Unfortunately, most briefings must be obtained by telephone, as relatively few airports have FSSs, and their number is being reduced. NWS offices are even sparser. If you do go to an FSS, be sure to examine as much of the raw data as possible, including the charts posted in the back, where pilots are not usually invited.

The burden of obtaining adequate weather information lies with you, the pilot. Flight Service briefers are not weather forecasters and are supposed to provide the weather information they have without analysis or opinion. Most Flight Service personnel, furthermore, are not pilots and may not understand the amount and types of information you need to fully evaluate the weather. Therefore, it is imperative that you know what information you want.

Some pilots, especially those with relatively little experience, are intimidated by Flight Service personnel. This is unfortunate and, to a pilot planning an IFR flight, could be dangerous if it prevented him from getting complete information. Remember that Flight Service briefers exist solely for the convenience of pilots like yourself. It is perfectly acceptable to ask them to read slower so you can copy better, or to have them repeat an item you missed. It is also okay to ask for as much information as you think you need. If, as sometimes may happen, a briefer offers a grudging or incomplete briefing, it is not because you are keeping him from more important work. It is more likely that he rose on the wrong side of the bed. Giving you weather information is his primary duty, and you have the right to be insistent and assertive in getting the information you want.

According to the FAA briefing format, to get all the facts, it should be sufficient to tell the telephone briefer your aircraft type and number, departure point, route and destination, estimated time of departure, and whether you plan to go IFR. However, the thoroughness of the briefing will depend on local custom, how busy the facility is, and even the mood of the individual briefer. After the initial briefing is provided, you should be prepared to request whatever additional information you want. The better you understand the reports and forecasts that are available, the more specific you can be in your questions and the better will be the briefing you receive.

From the pilot's point of view, weather information is not ideally organized. You need certain information, such as the expected ceiling and visibility at the destination, the location of acceptable alternates, and the possibility of adverse weather such as icing, storms, high winds, or turbulence. This information must be pieced together from a multitude of available reports and forecasts, such as area forecasts, route forecasts, terminal forecasts, sequence reports, pilot reports, radar reports, radar summary charts, winds aloft forecasts, and prognostic charts. To get a good briefing you need to understand what information you want and also how it is organized in the current weather reporting system.

A checklist is helpful to ensure a complete briefing and to systematically record the information. As you fill in the blanks, the list automatically alerts you to any missing items. The P.I.C. weather briefing sheet (figure 4-1) offers a good format and is convenient to use.

It is usually inadvisable to call for a weather briefing between 10 minutes before and 5 minutes past the hour. During this 15-minute interval, the computer contains either sequence reports 1 hour old or none at all while the data is being changed.

The first item a briefer gives you should be "flight precautions," an advisory of adverse conditions. These are usually in the form of **AIRMETs** or **SIGMETs**, and, if they are discouraging enough for you to cancel your flight, that information will mark the end of the briefing. However, it is rarely appropriate to cancel a trip solely on the basis of an advisory.

SIGMETs and AIRMETs (SIGMETs are significant, generally more serious than AIRMETs) are amendments to the **area forecast** and are issued when adverse conditions are known or predicted to exist. Like other forecasts, they are subject to error and you must request additional information to determine the importance you will assign to the advisory.

SIGMETs for turbulence, icing, and thunderstorms are routinely issued for large areas and long time periods, but these phenomena are frequently local and transitory. The dangers implied by the existence of a SIGMET must be evaluated in the light of additional information.

Assuming the briefing continues, the next item of importance is the **synopsis**, the big picture. The P.I.C. weather sheet has an outline map on which to draw the highs, lows, and fronts that the briefer will describe. This provides an overview of the weather and a framework within which to consider more detailed information. You should ask the briefer for the valid time of the weather depiction chart he is using. If the chart is several hours old, try to determine how much the indicated weather has moved.

Current weather in the form of **sequence reports** should be obtained for the departure airport and destination, the alternate airport, if one has been selected, and one or more en route airports. If possible, sequence reports for 2 or 3 hours previous to the current issue, as well as any special reports in that period, should be obtained, to compare the actual trend of the weather with that forecast. To do so means calling flight service each hour for several hours before your flight, since old sequence reports are discarded as they are replaced. In changing conditions, forecasts are often correct about the severity of the weather but wrong about the rate and time of change. A series of sequence reports gives a clue as to how the weather is changing, as well as evidence of the forecast's accuracy.

All control zones, and some airports without control zones, have official weather observers who report the weather at least during part of the day. Observations are made just before each hour

PIC Professional Instrument Courses INC.

SYNOPSIS

CURRENT WEATHER					FORECAST WEATHER			
LOCATION	CEILING	VISIBILITY	WIND	ALTIMETER	TIME	CEILING	VISIBILITY	WIND

WINDS ALOFT		
LEVEL	LOCATION	LOCATION
3		
6		
9		
12		

FREEZING LEVEL _____

_____

_____

RADAR SUMMARY _____

_____

_____

_____

NEAREST VFR _____

SIGMETS - AIRMETS _____

_____

_____

PIREPS _____

_____

CLOUD TOPS _____

_____

_____

NOTAMS _____

_____

© PIC 1984

Figure 4-1. Weather Briefing Form

so briefings given just after the hour contain the most recent information. Be sure to copy the entire sequence for each location, as it may be the last information you will have in the event of communication failure. Sequence reports for several en route locations will give you an idea of what to expect if you should have to land short of your destination. If your trip is westward and bad conditions are moving in from the west, reports for stations west of your destination will give you an idea of how bad and how far away the approaching problems are.

Terminal forecasts are issued for the area immediately surrounding an airport and cover a 24-hour period broken into segments. They are not available for all hourly reporting airports, but you should obtain them for as many locations as possible. Copy the entire forecast, as the trend it describes is more likely to be accurate than the predictions for particular time periods. If reported conditions are radically different from the forecast, the value of the forecast is downgraded, and you must use more of your own knowledge and experience to evaluate the trend of the weather.

Terminal forecasts are issued three times daily at the following times—in the Eastern and Central time zones, at 0940Z, 1440Z, and 2140Z; in the Mountain and Pacific time zones, at 0940Z, 1540Z, and 2240Z. (All times are "Zulu,"— Coordinated Universal Time (UTC), formerly known as Greenwich Mean Time (GMT).)

Next, following the briefing sheet, obtain the **winds aloft forecast**. (For those with a Jeppesen subscription, the United States Flight Planning Chart shows a map of locations for which winds and temperatures aloft are forecast.) For a flight of some length, you may want the information for more than one location and for various altitudes.

Winds aloft forecasts will be an element in your choice of altitude. The temperature forecasts are an indication of the predicted freezing level and a means of estimating your true airspeed. Remember that true airspeed depends on altitude and temperature.

Cloud top information is valuable but often hard to get. To avoid ice or turbulence, or just to enjoy the sunshine when the world below is clouded over, you may want to choose an altitude on top. Or, for practice, you may want to fly within a cloud layer. The only sources of actual

tops information are **PIREPs**. Prediction of tops is sometimes included in the area forecast, and PIREPS are often not available from Flight Service. A telephone call to the local approach control facility may yield the information. You can get the phone number from the FSS.

During the winter months, check the forecast freezing level, which is contained in the area forecast and can also be inferred from the temperatures in the winds aloft forecast. Direct reports of the freezing level are provided by upper air observation stations (balloons). The reports are identified by the word **RADAT** and are included in the remarks section of the 0000Z and 1200Z sequence reports from selected stations.

A typical RADAT report is—RADAT 75090, meaning 75% relative humidity at the freezing level of 9000 feet MSL. When temperature inversions exist, the rising balloon may cross a 0 C. isotherm, enter warmer temperatures, and reach another freezing level higher up. In such cases, the report might read: RADAT 75L045090, meaning there were two crossings of the 0 isotherm, at 4500 and 9000 feet, and the relative humidity was 75% at the lower of the two. Observed freezing level data is plotted on **freezing level charts**, and lines are drawn showing where the freezing level can be expected in various geographic locations. You can also get an idea of where icing has actually been encountered through PIREPs.

Airframe icing can occur in clouds or precipitation whenever the temperature is at or below freezing. The likelihood of icing decreases below 20 Fahrenheit. The severity depends on water droplet size, so the worst icing is likely in precipitation within cumulus clouds.

Entering "known icing conditions" is illegal and hazardous without proper certificated equipment. If your plans include the possibility of an icing encounter, be sure you have an out. You should be sure of your ability to descend below the freezing level if precipitation is likely, or at least to get out of the clouds if ice should begin to form. High ceilings, a high enough freezing level or low tops are possible outs. It is not wise to rely on climbing very far to get out of icing conditions in a light airplane, because ice on the airframe can rapidly destroy your ability to climb.

Weather radar displays precipitation and is useful in determining the location, intensity, and movement of showers and storms. Since there is a correlation between heavy rain and turbulence, radar reports give indications of areas to be avoided.

Radar provides no information about cloud cover or turbulence per se. Even though heavy rain usually means turbulence or thunderstorms, pilots using **3M Stormscopes*** have learned that there are exceptions. Stormscope-equipped Skyhawks have reported flying safely through areas that were avoided by radar-equipped heavy jets. But if you are not so equipped, it is better to avoid such areas.

In clear weather, airmass thunderstorms, which develop and dissipate rapidly with no particular organization, can be seen and avoided. However, you cannot see embedded thunderstorms. Since you cannot rely on ATC to help you avoid them, give a wide berth to areas of reported embedded storms. Frontal thunderstorms are longer lasting and often form impenetrable lines. Such conditions often require postponing a trip until the storms have passed.

Some FSSs can produce a printed facsimile of a ground-based weather radar scope simply by dialing a telephone access number. Others have color TV monitors showing actual radar returns. This instantaneous information is extremely valuable in pinpointing the location of storms in an area. Just remember that they may have moved by the time you get there.

The **radar summary chart** is a collection of weather radar reports graphically displayed on a map of the United States. These charts are prepared once an hour, but the fast-changing nature of thunderstorm activity requires that you pay particular attention to the direction and speed of area and cell movement in areas where significant weather is depicted. This will give you an idea of where the rough weather might be when you get there.

Continuing with the briefing, you should inquire where the "nearest VFR" will be, to give yourself a direction to fly in the event of total electrical failure (see Chapter Eleven).

---

*The Stormscope detects and displays areas of atmospheric electrical discharge, which correlates closely with turbulence.

As we have seen, PIREPs are the most reliable source of information about cloud tops, icing, and turbulence. They are valuable in evaluating forecasts because they reflect actual conditions. Be sure to record the position and altitude of the reporting aircraft. If icing or turbulence is involved, the reporting criteria (light, moderate, severe, etc.) are based on the effect on the airplane, so the aircraft type is also important. Light chop to a Boeing 737 can be severe turbulence to a Cessna 172.

While PIREPs are valuable, the PIREP system is imperfect, because it depends on pilots volunteering information to Flight Service, something they should do more often. Also note that the absence of PIREPs early in the morning is not necessarily revealing, because most pilots are then still in bed.

Do not rely solely on the Notice to Airmen (**NOTAM**) information offered by the Flight Service briefer. Additional NOTAMs may be listed in the FAA's be-weekly NOTAM publication. Flight Data Center (FDC) NOTAMs cover changes in instrument approaches and are listed in the same publication. If you don't have a copy, ask the briefer to check his for you. If you use Jeppesen charts, the Chart NOTAM section of the manual gives, according to the publisher, "an abbreviated NOTAM service, which highlights significant changes affecting Jeppesen charts." These include FDC NOTAMs, covering changes in IFR minimums and equipment. However, a notice significantly warns the pilot to "ask for other pertinent NOTAMs prior to flight."

Another way to obtain a briefing, and for many pilots, the most convenient and effective one, is by means of their personal computer. The FAA offers a computer weather service called Direct User Access Terminal (**DUAT**). The basic service, which includes complete weather briefing information and flight plan filing, is free. There are no subscriber or service charges, and the government even makes the service available over toll free lines.

The FAA provides DUAT through private contractors who compete for your business through advertising, quality of service, and price. Any FSS office can give you the toll free or local access numbers of the current contractors.

DUAT offers advantages both for the FAA and

for the pilot. For the government, letting you "talk" to a computer briefing system, even on their nickel, is a lot cheaper than providing a live telephone briefer. And for you, you can forget forever that annoying recorded message, "....all briefers are busy...."

To access DUAT, you need a personal computer, telecommunications software, and a 300-, 1200-, or 2400-baud modem. If you have a printer, you can also forget about those hurriedly scribbled weather notes. Just capture your DUAT briefing in a file, print it after you hang up, and study it at your leisure.

The system is so user-friendly that even an inexperienced computer user should have very little trouble becoming comfortable with it. If you do have difficulty, DUAT has an extensive online help feature. The FAA says that the average pilot can get a briefing and file a flight plan in 15 minutes when he first uses the system, and that the time required drops to seven minutes as he becomes more familiar with it. DUAT is so easy to use that the FAA expects it to account for nearly half of all pilot briefings within a few years.

DUAT provides all the standard weather reports and forecasts in coded form, so it's an opportunity to bone up on the NWS weather codes that you learned for the instrument rating written exam. An alternative is to use DUAT's plain English option, which the contractors provide for a price.

Other "value-added" services, those for which the contractor charges, include weather and radar charts, automatic station identifier decoding, special use airspace alerts, route optimization computations, airport information, and a variety of others. The system is new at the time of writing, and is expected to develop in part according to user demand.

Since DUAT allows you to get a complete weather briefing and file your flight plan directly through your computer, you may never have to call Flight Service again.

Plane and Pilot Fitness

With the weather briefing completed, consider it in the light of all other factors affecting the flight. Even on a beautiful blue sky day you might cancel a flight if the engine runs rough on one magneto or if you have a terrible hangover. Equipment condition and your frame of mind are important considerations in planning any flight.

A pilot I know once planned to rent a Turbo Arrow, an airplane in which he was checked out, but in which he was not really comfortable. The weather was "soft" IFR, with a 2000-foot overcast at the departure point and destination, but with high terrain in between that precluded a VFR trip. He would have to file and fly in the clouds for the enroute part of the trip.

"I was a little uneasy about the flight," he told me, "because of the relatively unfamiliar airplane and the fact that I would have to be on the gauges. But there would be no instrument approach, since the destination was VFR, so I decided to go ahead.

"At the airport, the FBO acted surprised that I still planned to go and told me I couldn't rent the airplane to fly IFR. Well, the trip was important to me and I got mad. We had words, and finally he gave me the keys. During the preflight, I found myself thinking harsh thoughts about what a crummy businessman that operator was.

"I made a couple of mistakes copying the clearance but finally got it straight and taxied out. Takeoff went normally, but as I climbed out, I realized that half my attention was still on my anger at the FBO. All of a sudden, I asked myself if I should continue the trip with my attention divided. Just before entering the clouds, I called departure and made a return to the airport."

This pilot canceled a trip he would have been comfortable making if he hadn't been in a bad mood. A wise decision, I think.

Fatigue is another factor that should be considered before flight. A tired pilot does not have his normal judgment and should resist the temptation to fly when not fully rested. Fatigue has been a cause of many accidents.

Equipment condition should also be reviewed. If the glide slope has been acting up, you might make a trip if the forecast is 800 and three, relying on a nonprecision approach as your "out." But if there is a chance of 300 and a half, the ILS capability would be essential, and the trip should be canceled.

An IFR trip might be reasonable in marginal VFR conditions with only one working nav-comm. But if the weather were forecast hard IFR, losing the one radio would jeopardize the flight and would be cause to cancel before takeoff.

An IFR night flight would show dubious judgment if the cockpit lighting were poor or suspect.

The philosophy used in the go/no-go decision is partially one of evaluating your outs. Ask yourself, "What would I do if....?"

When you fly VFR in ceiling and visibility unlimited (CAVU) conditions, you probably plan what your actions will be if the engine quits. Frequent practice at power-off landings and your knowledge of the airplane's glide characteristics will give you a fair chance at a safe landing. On IFR flights, the possible problems are more numerous and the decisions more subtle. The following are some examples:

You might fly in the clouds above the freezing level—if you know you can descend below it or if the cloud bases are high enough to allow you to get out of the moisture.

You might go to an airport forecasting below minimums—if you know there are others nearby that have better forecasts or lower minimums.

You might fly in an area of scattered thunderstorms—if the visibility is good or if you are equipped with radar or a Stormscope.

The go/no-go decision is complex and finally comes down to your judgment, when you've taken into account all the factors affecting the flight.

Legal Requirements

One important factor to consider in the go/no-go decision is whether the flight will be legal. If it is not legal, there is a good chance it won't be safe either.

On an IFR flight, both the pilot and the airplane must meet certain legal requirements. In addition to the equipment required for day or night VFR as listed in FAR 91.205, your airplane must have five working flight instruments (of the basic six, only the VSI is not mandatory) as well as a clock and magnetic compass, and communication and navigation equipment "appropriate to the ground facilities to be used." There is no specific requirement for radio equipment, but as a practical matter in the low altitude structure, you will need at least a two-way radio and one VOR receiver. Dual nav-comms are virtual necessities for hard IFR flying, and an ADF, a glide slope receiver, and DME enhance your capability even further. FAR 91.215 requires a Mode C (altitude reporting) transponder if you plan to fly above 10,000 feet, within 30 miles of a primary airport in Class B airspace, or in or above Class C airspace.

Naturally, the airplane must have a current annual inspection. The transponder and encoding altimeter must have been checked within the previous 24 calendar months (FARs 91.411 and 91.413).

FAR 91.411 also requires that, for IFR flight in controlled airspace, the altimeter and static system must have been checked by qualified personnel within the preceding 24 calendar months. While these are actually two separate checks, they are normally done together. It is a simple procedure and can usually be done by an instrument shop in about an hour. Remember that the altimeter will be pressure tested only up to a certain altitude and may not be used above that altitude.

You should check your aircraft maintenance log to see that both checks are current on your airplane before any IFR flight. As the owner or operator of the airplane, it is your responsibility to see that these inspections are carried out on time. Do not rely on your mechanic or the FBO to complete them automatically. Note that static system and altimeter checks are not normal parts of an annual inspection.

On a new aircraft or one with a rebuilt altimeter, the dates of the static and altimeter checks may differ. In some cases, the altimeter is stored for several months after manufacture and testing, and only the static system is checked when the instrument is installed in the airplane. In this case, the altimeter check would expire a few months before the static check came due.

Each VOR receiver to be used must have been tested within the previous 30 days (FAR 91.171). This test is normally conducted by the pilot and must be logged in some "permanent record," which needn't be in the airframe log but has to be somewhere. See Chapter Five for details of VOR checks.

Finally, the airplane must be carrying the required paperwork—airworthiness certificate, registration, radio station license, operating limitations, and weight and balance data, including an installed equipment list. To remember these items, use the acronym "ARROW." ("A" stands for airworthiness certificate, etc.)

If the airplane is ready to fly IFR, what about the pilot? You must have a current FAA medical certificate and a current biennial flight review (BFR). Passing a flight check for a new rating takes the place of a BFR, so if you received your instrument rating within the past 2 years (24 calendar months), that counts as your BFR. Finally, to fly under IFR you must have a current instrument rating.

Your instrument rating is legally current if you have logged 6 hours of instrument time and flown 6 instrument approaches within the previous 6 calendar months. Three of the hours must have been in category (that is, in an airplane) either in actual weather or under the hood. The other 3 hours and all of the approaches may have been in an aircraft of another category, such as a helicopter, or an approved ground trainer.

If your currency has expired, you may not act as pilot in command of an airplane under IFR. However, for 6 calendar months from the date your currency expired you may become current by meeting the requirements mentioned above. Hood work requires a safety pilot who is rated in the aircraft but who need not be instrument rated, as long as you don't accept an IFR clearance. In a single-engine airplane, he must be licensed as a private pilot, single engine, land. If it is a high performance airplane, his logbook must contain a high performance sign-off. When you practice with a safety pilot, you must record his name in your logbook.

Once currency has lapsed for 6 months, an instrument competency check is required. This is most commonly done with a CFII, but can also be given by an FAA inspector or a designated examiner.

To check your understanding of the currency rule, try this FAA test question, which undoubtedly reaches the corners of the "regulatory envelope": Suppose you are a private pilot, instrument rated in airplanes and helicopters. Within the last 6 calendar months, you have flown 3 hours under the hood in an airplane and another 3 hood hours in a helicopter, but shot no approaches in either. You did, however, shoot six approaches on a ground trainer. Are you current in the airplane, the helicopter, or both?

According to the regulation, you are legally current in both.

It is essential to realize that legal currency does not guarantee that the pilot is proficient enough to handle all IFR situations. Instrument skills deteriorate rapidly with disuse, and each pilot must determine if he is "current" enough to be not only legal but safe. True proficiency means not only being competent to handle routine matters, but being far enough ahead of the airplane to deal satisfactorily with unexpected ones.

The final requirement for IFR flight in controlled airspace is an ATC clearance. You must file a flight plan and receive a clearance.

In uncontrolled airspace, the legal requirements for IFR flight are less restrictive. A current instrument rating is necessary, and the airplane must have the basic IFR instrumentation. No clearance is required, and no reporting; therefore, there is no need for a communication radio. Since there is no constraint to follow a flight plan, no navigation equipment is legally necessary.

An interesting privilege of the instrument-rated pilot is the right to depart a fogged-in uncontrolled airport in zero-zero conditions without phone calls, radio work, or the need for an IFR clearance. He must, however, enter VFR conditions before reaching controlled airspace.

The Airspace Structure

The purpose and extent of controlled and uncontrolled airspace are confusing to many pilots. The Airman's Information Manual describes controlled airspace as "a generic term that covers the different classification of airspace (Class A, Class B, Class C, Class D, and Class E airspace) and defined dimensions within which air traffic control service is provided to IFR flights and to VFR flights in accordance with the airspace classification. Consequently, Class G airspace can be defined as uncontrolled airspace which has not been so designated. This explanation, couched as it is in governmentese, is not very illuminating. A good way to explain the airspace structure is to begin at the beginning and proceed down from the top.

In the beginning, all airspace was uncontrolled. Airplanes flew when and where they chose and took responsibility for collision avoidance. The two principles used were "see and avoid" and, especially in IFR conditions, "big sky small airplane." As the airspace became more crowded and near misses and midair collisions occurred, increasingly broad and complex systems, equipment, and rules were developed to help airplanes avoid each other in flight.

The primary mission of air traffic control is to help separate airplanes in flight. Its mandate to help expedite traffic by providing navigation assistance, weather information, and other services, is secondary. To accomplish this, ATC was given authority over particular areas designated as controlled airspace.

To best understand the arrangement of controlled airspace, consider its function of separating traffic. Faster traffic flying at and above 18,000 feet is considered most in need of ATC assistance to avoid other airplanes. At these altitudes, called **class A airspace**, not only is all airspace controlled, but all flights must be under instrument flight rules.

Between 18,000 and 14,500 feet, all airspace over the continental United States is controlled. This airspace is known as **class E airspace**. ATC services are available at these altitudes but are not mandatory except in IFR weather.

In some remote parts of the west, there is no controlled airspace from the surface to the base of **class E airspace**. Lower flying airplanes are on their own and rely to some extent on chance to avoid other traffic. The hemispheric rule, eastbound aircraft use odd altitudes and westbound aircraft use even, helps somewhat.

In most parts of the country, **transition en route domestic areas** bring controlled airspace down from 14,500 feet. Around airports with instrument approaches, transition areas extend downward to 1200 feet AGL and are shown in magenta on sectionals.

The problem with this arrangement is the difference between VFR visibility minimums in controlled and uncontrolled airspace. In uncontrolled airspace, only 1 mile is required, while in controlled airspace, the requirement is 3 miles (above 10,000 feet, MSL, the requirement is 5 miles in both types of airspace). A pilot who shoots an instrument approach to an uncontrolled airport in poor visibility enters **class G** airspace at 700 feet AGL and can actually be in danger of running into a scud runner in the same area, or into a hungry flight instructor doing "touch and goes" with a student below 700 feet. As long as there is 1 mile visibility, the IFR and VFR pilots are both legal, though the situation may be dangerous.

To eliminate this danger at busier fields, class E airspace was developed. These areas bring controlled airspace down to the surface so that all VFR flights must have 3 miles visibility. Controlled airspace to the surface is created at fields with instrument approaches, and the only requirement for their existence is the presence, on duty, of a certificated weather observer to determine when it is IFR (below 1000/3) in that airspace. The weather observer may be a controller, a Flight Service specialist, or an employee of an operator on the field. The area therefore doesn't need a control tower.

The lateral limits of the surface area (class D and E) are usually a 4 or 5 mile radius, with rectangular protuberances to extend their protection to airplanes on the approach paths. They extend up to 18,000 feet MSL and are outlined on sectional and low altitude enroute charts with dashed lines. In VFR conditions, no clearance is needed to enter class E airspace. It is VFR in class E airspace when the ceiling is at least 1000 feet and there is 3 miles visibility.

The airspace structure is complex, and most of your flying will probably be in controlled airspace. Whether you are in controlled or uncontrolled airspace, you do have to comply with minimum IFR altitudes.

In class G airspace, or when you are flying an off airway route in controlled airspace, it is your responsibility to maintain safe and legal obstacle clearance. This means that you must look at a sectional to determine the highest obstacles along your route of flight, and plan your trip to be at least 1000 feet above the highest obstruction within 4 nautical miles of your flight path. In designated mountainous areas, the requirement increases to 2000 feet. (For Jeppesen subscribers, a map of designated mountainous areas appears in the subscription.)

On an airway flight, there are several minimum altitudes that concern the IFR pilot.

The **Minimum Enroute Altitude (MEA)** guarantees a usable navigation signal from at least one of the VORs defining the airway to which it applies over the entire length of the route. If there is a stretch of airway where the signal may be lost, it will be labeled "MEA gap." In that case, you must dead reckon until you are able to pick up the signal from the next station.

The MEA also provides 1000 feet of obstacle clearance for the entire width of the airway, and 2000 feet in designated mountainous areas.

If you are at the MEA and it increases, you should begin your climb to the new MEA at the point where the change occurs. An exception to this rule is when a **Minimum Crossing Altitude (MCA)** is specified, in which case you should begin climbing early enough to cross the fix at the MCA.

The **Minimum Obstruction Clearance Altitude (MOCA)** offers the same obstruction clearance as the MEA, but guarantees a usable navigation signal only within 22 nautical miles of the VOR. It is intended for use primarily in emergencies, but you *may* descend to this altitude if you are cleared for an approach and you are within 22 nautical miles of the VOR.

The **Minimum Reception Altitude (MRA)** applies to an intersection and is the lowest altitude at which a usable signal is guaranteed from the off airway fix defining that intersection. Do not confuse it with the MEA. Being below the MRA does not imply that you will lose the signal defining the airway.

In some cases a **Maximum Authorized Altitude (MAA)** is specified, and you may not expect clearance for a higher altitude. Some MAA's exist because at a higher altitude you might receive simultaneous signals from two distant stations on the same frequency. This would cause erratic and useless instrument indications. In other cases, the airway may underlie heavy use airspace, such as arrival and departure routes to class B or class C airspace.

The Flight Plan

Once you have assimilated the weather briefing and decided to make the flight, you can complete the flight plan and route log. The back of the P.I.C. weather sheet provides a convenient flight planning form (figure 4-2). Referring to the flight plan:

Box 1: Type. Check IFR. For a flight into improving or deteriorating weather, you may choose to file a composite flight plan. Check VFR and IFR and indicate in box 11 where the change is to occur. If the first part of the flight is VFR, cancel VFR at the changeover point, and request IFR clearance from the nearest FSS. If "VFR on top" is your altitude (see box 7), you still check IFR in box 1.

Box 2: Aircraft identification. Give the full 'N' number.

Box 3: Aircraft type and special equipment. ATC gives each make and model a special four-character identifier. Flight Service can tell you yours. Special equipment suffixes refer to the type of navigation equipment on board and are as follows:

/X - no transponder
/T - transponder with no altitude encoding capability
/U - transponder with altitude encoding capability
/D - DME, but no transponder
/B - DME and transponder, but no alti-

PIC

Professional Instrument Courses, Inc.

Speed	Speed Factor
60	1.0
90	.7
100	.6
120	.5
150	.4
200	.3

FUEL REQUIRED	
ENROUTE	
APPROACH	
ALTERNATE	
RESERVE	
TOTAL	

ATIS		
CODE		
WEATHER		
WIND		
ALTIMETER		
APPROACH		
RUNWAY		

FLIGHT PLAN

1. TYPE (VFR / IFR / DVFR)	2. AIRCRAFT IDENTIFICATION	3. AIRCRAFT TYPE/ SPECIAL EQUIPMENT	4. TRUE AIRSPEED KTS	5. DEPARTURE POINT	6. DEPARTURE TIME PROPOSED (Z) / ACTUAL (Z)	7. CRUISING ALTITUDE
8. ROUTE OF FLIGHT						
9. DESTINATION (Name of airport & city)	10. EST. TIME ENROUTE HOURS / MINUTES	11. REMARKS				
12. FUEL ON BOARD HOURS / MINUTES	13. ALTERNATE AIRPORT (S)	14. PILOT'S NAME, ADDRESS & TELEPHONE NUMBER & AIRCRAFT HOME BASE	15. NUMBER ABOARD			
16. COLOR OF AIRCRAFT	17. DESTINATION CONTACT/TELEPHONE (OPTIONAL)					

Ground Speed: Speed Factor:

Time Off:

FIX	COURSE	DIST.	ETE	ETA	ATA

Further Clearance:

ATC Clears N To: Via:

Altitude: TXP Code:

Departure:

Figure 4-2. Flight Planning Form

tude encoding capability
/A - DME and transponder with altitude encoding capability
/M - TACAN only, but no transponder
/N - TACAN only and transponder, but with no altitude encoding capability
/P - TACAN only and transponder with altitude encoding capability
/C - RNAV and transponder, but with no altitude encoding capability
/R - RNAV and transponder with altitude encoding capability
/W - RNAV but no transponder

Box 4: *True airspeed.* Once you have chosen an altitude (Box 7), the true airspeed can be calculated from your planned indicated airspeed, forecast temperature aloft, and pressure altitude, or obtained from aircraft performance data for the power setting you plan to use. A rule of thumb is that true airspeed exceeds indicated airspeed by 2% for each 1000 feet of altitude. (For a complete description, refer to Chapter Two.)

Box 5: *Departure point.* Each airport's three-character identifier is listed in the *Airport Facility Directory* and at the top of the Jeppesen airport diagram. A "K" preceding the three-character identifier indicates that it is a U.S. airport of entry. The "K" needn't be included on the flight plan.

Box 6: *Departure time.* This should be at least 30 minutes after you file the flight plan. If your departure is delayed, ATC will keep your flight plan on file for 1 hour beyond your proposed departure time. For a multiple leg trip you may file more than one flight plan, each with an estimated departure time. If you realize you are behind schedule and will miss the 1-hour limit at your next departure point, arrange to have the time extended by requesting this from ATC by radio. If ATC is unable to handle your request, obtain permission to leave the frequency and state your desire to the nearest FSS. Times should be in UTC or Zulu time (Z).

To obtain UTC from:

	EST	EDT	CST	CDT	MST	MDT	PST	PDT
add	5	4	6	5	7	6	8	7

Box 7: *Cruising altitude.* Choose your altitude after the route (Box 8) so you can consider the MEAs in your planning. If the trip involves one section with a high MEA and you prefer to stay lower on other sections, you may file a lower altitude initially. ATC will assign a climb before you reach the higher MEA, but if they should forget, it is your responsibility to request the higher altitude.

Weather is an important factor in choosing altitudes. You may wish to stay below the freezing level or above the clouds and turbulence. There is frequently a trade-off between ground-speed and comfort—a higher altitude may offer less turbulence, but a stronger head wind.

Aircraft characteristics and equipment must be considered. How high will your airplane climb efficiently? What altitude offers the best speed and economy? Above 10,000 feet MSL, FAR 91.215 requires a transponder and encoding altimeter. FAR 91.211 requires the crew to use oxygen for any portion of the flight of more than 30 minutes duration at cabin altitudes above 12,500 feet. The crew must always use oxygen above 14,000 feet MSL. Above 15,000 feet MSL, all occupants of the airplane must be provided with oxygen.

IFR altitudes—odd thousands eastbound, even thousands westbound—are mandatory only in uncontrolled airspace. In controlled airspace, in most areas of the country, ATC does not care whether you abide by this rule or not. However, in some areas, they will assign odd altitudes eastbound and even ones westbound, regardless of what you file.

You may file "VFR conditions on top," instead of a specific altitude. If you receive this clearance, you are expected to follow all VFR and IFR regulations. VFR altitudes must be complied with (west-bound traffic even thousands plus 500 feet, eastbound odd thousands plus 500 feet), VFR cloud clearance maintained, and visual traffic avoidance must be exercised. You must also fly your assigned route, report changing altitude, make position reports as required, and observe minimum IFR altitudes as on any other IFR clearance.

"VFR-on-top" can be used instead of a specified altitude. It cannot be assigned unless requested by the pilot and is most commonly used to avoid delays when the volume of traffic puts a strain on available airspace.

Box 8: Route of Flight. Every flight has a departure, an en route, and an approach portion. It is convenient to begin planning your route in reverse, starting with the approach plates and Standard Terminal Arrival Routes (STARs) for your destination. The flight plan should show your route to an initial approach fix (IAF), which is also an airway fix, or to an airway fix from which there is a published transition. From that fix, the word "direct" indicates that you plan to follow a published approach procedure.

Familiarize yourself with the approach plates for your destination, noticing the types of approaches available, the names of fixes, and any unusual features. When the approach controller says, "Report Zigmy," it is comforting to have seen the word before.

If there is a STAR leading to the airport from the direction in which you are flying, look it over. Even if you do not file the STAR, it is likely to be the route you will get.

After studying your destination, check for Standard Instrument Departures (SIDs) from your departure point in the direction you are going. The purpose of SIDs is to establish you in the en route structure and to save writing and talking. If you don't have a particular SID, it may still appear in your clearance, and you will have to copy it, read it back,

and follow it without benefit of the graphic depiction. If there is no SID applicable to your direction of flight, you will normally file direct to a nearby airway fix.

For the en route portion of your flight, check for preferred routes in the Airport/Facility Directory or the Jeppesen Airway Manual. Some preferred routes are not listed, but with a little experience of your area, you will learn them. Flight Service can be helpful in telling you of unpublished preferred routes. Often, if you don't file a preferred route, your flight plan will be changed by ATC.

If there is no preferred route for your flight, simply list the airways and fixes you intend to use from the point you enter the en route phase to the IAF or transition fix at your destination. You may file direct from one VOR to another when no airway is shown between them as long as the distance from fix to fix is less than 80 nautical miles. In doing this, you must consult a sectional chart and provide yourself the required IFR terrain clearance: 1000 feet above the highest obstacle within 4 nautical miles of your route; 2000 feet in designated mountainous areas.

Box 9: Destination. Enter the three-character identifier. You may file an IFR flight plan to a field with no instrument approach, but then an alternate with such an approach is always required (see box 13) regardless of the weather forecasts. To accomplish an IFR arrival at a field with no instrument approach, you must be able to descend from the minimum IFR altitude, make a visual approach, and land in VFR conditions.

Box 10: Estimated time en route. To calculate your estimated time en route (ETE), determine the total mileage from the low altitude chart and estimate your groundspeed from the true airspeed and the winds aloft forecast. You can make a precise estimate using a calculator, wind triangles, and fractional mileages, but the sum of errors due to bad wind forecasts, time to climb, and time spent being vectored, makes a rule of thumb estimate equally useful.

To estimate your groundspeed quickly, determine the net effect of the wind. Will it be a headwind or tailwind, direct or quartering? If it is a direct headwind or tailwind, subtract or add the forecast wind speed at your altitude from or to your true airspeed. If the wind is quartering, use half the forecast value. For a direct crosswind, subtract a quarter of its value from your true airspeed, as you will sacrifice some forward speed by crabbing to stay on course. When these calculations are finished, divide the distance by the groundspeed for a good estimate of your ETE. Once airborne, you can update it with ATC on the basis of your actual experience of the wind.

Prior to an IFR departure, request a time check from ground control. Write down your takeoff time because in the event of a communications failure, ATC will expect you to begin an approach at your destination at your takeoff time plus your ETE.

Box 11: *Remarks*. Indicate any limitations or requests. Examples of remarks are—request customs, no over water, medical evacuation flight, no oxygen.

Box 12: *Fuel on board*. When completing this section, determine if the amount you are carrying meets the requirement of FAR 91.167. You must carry enough fuel to fly first to the destination, then to the alternate, and then to fly an additional 45 minutes at normal cruise power. The "fuel required" box on the P.I.C. flight planning sheet can be used to calculate your fuel requirements. Indicate the fuel on board in hours and minutes.

Box 13: *Alternate airport*. File an alternate to let ATC know what you will do if your radios fail and you are unable to land at your destination.

An alternate is required *unless* your destination has an instrument approach and the weather forecast indicates at least a 2000-foot ceiling and 3 miles visi-

bility from 1 hour before until 1 hour after your estimated time of arrival. If the forecast contains expressions such as "occasionally," "variable to," or "chance of," the worst possibility mentioned must be considered.

A memory aid for the above is "1, 2, 3:" plus or minus 1 hour, 2000 feet, 3 miles.

For an airport to be used as an alternate, the forecast must indicate that its weather will be above **alternate minimums** at your ETA there. (Alternate minimums are shown on Jeppesen airport diagrams for each airport, but *standard alternate minimums* usually apply: 600-2 if you plan to use a precision approach, and 800-2 for nonprecision.) To locate a suitable alternate, ask the Flight Service briefer to check his forecasts for one with the necessary conditions. In many areas, the only airports authorized for use as an alternate are those with an ILS and a control zone.

In bad weather, the location of the closest legal alternate may be the limiting factor on the length of a flight. The fuel needed to get to the alternate reduces the distance you can fly to any proposed destination. On a *really* bad day, there may be no legal alternate within the range of the aircraft; therefore, no legal flight is possible.

After a missed approach, assuming no communications failure occurs, you have several options. You may choose to try the approach again if the ceiling is ragged or if patchy fog is causing frequent changes in visibility. You may elect to hold, in the hope that conditions will soon improve. You can also request clearance to a nearby field where the weather is above minimums. In a really bad weather situation, however, don't try these options so long that you are left without fuel to get where you *know* the weather is good.

On a day bad enough to cause a missed approach, it is quite likely that the alternate will be far away, and not your first choice of backup destination.

However, you *will* have to go there if your radios fail, so you should take the time to use good judgment in choosing it. The alternate should have an ILS, if possible, and be in an area likely to have weather better than the destination. It should *not* be on the other side of a cold front you would then have to penetrate. Considering these factors, your departure airport may turn out to be your best alternate. After all, that is where you left your car. Therefore, make sure of the weather forecast for home base and the fuel required for the round trip—just in case.

Box 15: Number aboard. This includes all passengers and crew.

File the flight plan with Flight Service in person, by telephone, or by radio. In some areas, the "Fastfile" system allows you to file by reading your flight plan to a recording machine on the telephone. In any case, allow at least 30 minutes for the flight plan to be processed and your clearance to become available.

In some cases, it is possible to "pick up" an IFR clearance directly from center or approach control, without the formality of filing a flight plan with Flight Service. This service is provided by controllers on a "workload permitting basis" and its availability may depend on the time of day and local procedures. When airborne and VFR, you can usually get a clearance for an IFR descent directly from ATC. On the ground, you can request a clearance to VFR conditions on top from ground control.

For an IFR flight within approach control airspace, you can obtain a "tower to tower" or "low level direct" IFR clearance directly from ATC. This type of clearance is officially known as "TEC"; TEC routes were greatly expanded following the 1981 controller strike. These routes are shown in the *Airport Facility Directory* and in the *Jeppesen Airway Manual*. The FAA recommends using TEC routes only for flights of less than two hours.

The IFR Clearance

Your filed IFR flight plan is transmitted by Flight Service to a computer at the controlling Air Route Traffic Control Center (ARTCC). Shortly before your proposed departure time, a **flight strip** is produced at the center and held for you. If your departure field is controlled by an approach control facility, the strip is transmitted to them by teletype. The expression "clearance on request" means that the controller has requested your flight strip from the center or approach control. During this process, ATC may alter your proposed flight plan to conform with local traffic flow patterns and eliminate conflicts.

One of the last things you do before blasting off into the murk on an IFR flight is to copy your ATC clearance. It is an important step in your preflight activity and deserves special attention. Understanding clearances, and even practicing reading and copying them with friends or an instructor, can greatly improve your comfort and efficiency at the beginning of a flight.

When at a typical controlled airport, request your clearance from ground control at the same time you call for taxi to the active. Your communications will be something like this:

"Newport Ground, Cessna seven eight nine papa foxtrot is at the terminal, taxi, IFR to Boston."

In reply, you will receive taxi instructions, the weather or designator of the current ATIS, and the words "clearance on request." This means that the controller has requested your clearance from the ARTCC computer and will give it to you as soon as he receives it. Often, it will arrive while you are on your way to the runway. Don't try to copy it while taxiing unless you have a co-pilot, and it is usually not a good idea to stop in the middle of the taxiway. Say the magic words, "Stand by," and copy the clearance when you are safely on the runup pad.

At larger fields, there is a separate "clearance delivery" frequency which is marked "Cpt" on the Jeppesen airport diagram and means "clearance pre-taxi." Copy the ATIS (an airport with clearance delivery will invariably have an ATIS), then call clearance delivery. He will frequently have your clearance ready, so have pencil in hand when you call. After copying the clearance, you can call ground for taxi.

At uncontrolled fields, clearance procedures are more complicated and vary from place to place according to local custom.

One way to get the clearance is to take off VFR and climb to an altitude from which you can reach center or departure control by radio. Just be sure you can safely stay VFR for as long as it takes to get your clearance. Sometimes there can be considerable delay.

At some fields, an ATC frequency is usable on the ground. It may or may not be on the approach plate, but it is usually known to local pilots and the FSS. If there is a bigger field nearby, you may call their tower or ground control, or there may be an approach control frequency that works. At Manassas, Virginia, you call Dulles Clearance Delivery and at Manahawkin, New Jersey, there is an unpublished departure control frequency usable from one corner of the airport only. So, if you're not sure how to pick up your clearance, check around with the local pilots.

If the weather is such that you cannot take off and maintain VFR while picking up your clearance and there is no frequency that is usable on the ground, Flight Service can give it to you by telephone. They will call ATC on another line and relay your clearance to you. It will be a "void time" clearance; that is, it will contain the words "clearance is void if not off by (...time...)." ATC reserves airspace for you only for so long. In uncrowded areas of the Midwest, void times as long as 45 minutes are used. In busier parts of the country, they are more likely to be 5 or 10 minutes. If a void time is too short for you, it is negotiable. You can often get instructions to take off within a 10-minute window, starting 10 minutes into the future. When you first ask for your clearance the FSS may ask, "How soon can you go?" Your release and void times may then be based on your answer, so be realistic, taking into account such things as runup, taxi to the runway, and waiting for the runway to become yours.

When you intend to call for a void time clearance, first finish your preflight, load the airplane, and board your passengers before making the call. In the cold winter months, you may also want to start your bird and warm the engine a few minutes before calling.

When departing an uncontrolled field, jot down your time off, just as at a controlled field. You will need it in case of a communications failure, and ATC may ask for it on your first contact. (Knowing that time can also be a critical help should you find yourself running tight on fuel. Remember that fuel gauges are notoriously unre-

liable, especially when fuel is running short. You should maintain a running calculation of the fuel consumption.)

My worst experience with a void time clearance occurred early one foggy morning at an isolated strip in New England. The nearest telephone was across a drawbridge from the airport. I was given a 10-minute void time and—thank you, Murphy —the bridge was up, so I missed the time. I felt pretty sheepish calling back for a new clearance. When you are given a close void time take the Drawbridge Factor into consideration before accepting it.

There are five steps to receiving an IFR clearance. The first is simply to *copy* it. Set up your pad and use shorthand to simplify what you must write. As you copy, concentrate on the controller's words. *Do not try to understand the clearance as it is read to you.* That would only increase the chances of your falling behind or making a mistake. If something sounds wrong or you do fall behind, don't worry about it. Just write down what you hear. Don't try to interrupt the controller for clarification before he finishes. You can ask him to read slowly, and he will usually comply.

After copying the clearance, *read it back.* Again, don't try to understand it. And don't repeat what you think you heard, only what you have written on your clip-board. Reading back a clearance does not mean you accept it—it is just a check that you have recorded it correctly. It is only on takeoff that you commit yourself to following the clearance you have received.

The third step is to *study* the clearance, especially if it is different from what you filed. Pull out the charts and trace the route from start to finish. Be sure that it makes sense, that the airways actually go to the fixes specified and that the entire route does lead to your destination. For a long trip, this checking may take several minutes, but it is well worth it—yours would not be the first clearance that left a pilot hanging at a point in space, or took him to the wrong destination.

Check the MEAs along the route. Can your aircraft climb that high? Do you want to fly that high in light of the forecast winds aloft?

The fourth step in receiving your IFR clearance is to *request any changes or clarification* you want. For example, if the route is too circuitous, you may request one more direct. If the altitude is too high, you may ask for one that is not up in the strong winds. If the departure frequency is 122.7 or the transponder code has an eight in it*, you can request verification. Don't be shy about asking for clarification; if you made a mistake, you would like to know it *before* takeoff. Controllers make mistakes too. Even if you heard the words "Readback is correct," there is no guarantee that he heard exactly what you read.

When you are sure the clearance is acceptable, the last step is to *set up your radios*. Do as much as possible of your twisting and fiddling on the ground, not right after takeoff when you are entering the soup and transitioning to flight on instruments.

Put the tower frequency in one comm radio and your first departure control or center frequency in the other. Double check—if you are familiar with the area, is it the frequency you expected?

Set one nav radio for the first en route fix, and identify it on the ground if possible. Set the OBS for the approximate course to this fix. Even if your clearance specifies "vectors to Chester VOR," dial in the Chester VOR and enter the course in the OBS. You will be vectored only long enough to clear the traffic or obstructions around the airport and then you will be told to intercept an airway or fly direct. Set the second nav radio to identify the first intersection, and twist the OBS to the appropriate radial.

It is *not* a good idea to set the number two nav to the second en route fix. Always navigate on the number one nav radio, changing frequencies to the fix ahead at each VOR changeover point. If you alternate radios, which *does* allow you to enter your frequencies further in advance, inevitably, some day when other things have already gone wrong, you will start tracking on the wrong instrument. The only exception to the "track only on number one" rule is when you are flying a radial to intercept a final approach course. In that case, track on number two, because you want the approach navaid set into number one, and you don't want to be switching frequencies and resetting

---

*Of course, 122.7 doesn't make sense for departure control because it is designated as a UNICOM frequency. Transponders with 4096 codes have only the digits zero through seven.

OBSs when you should be concentrating on intercepting the approach course.

Don't forget to set the squawk code in the transponder. Turning the transponder from STANDBY to ON or ALT should wait until you are cleared onto the runway.

Since you are trying to do as much as possible of your radio setup before takeoff, you can even finish up by setting the frequency for the NDB at your destination. Notice that the radios themselves serve as a sort of checklist for your clearance: All you have to do is be sure each one is properly tuned. Be coolly meticulous in setting the radios. Frequencies can be confusingly similar, and numbers are all too easily transposed and jumbled, as are OBS settings. Some setting can be done before calling for the clearance; just be sure to recheck.

Make your clearance shorthand as simple as possible. Nobody has to read it except you, so there is no need for complete sentences or for your symbols to be clear to another reader. An informal system of abbreviations—the bare minimum for you to understand what you wrote—is all you should put on paper.

Every IFR clearance contains the same items in the same order, so knowing the format simplifies the job of copying. A typical IFR clearance has seven parts, given in the following form.

1) *Your full identification.* "November seven eight nine papa fox..." You don't have to write down your number, so there are five characters-worth of writing saved. However, be sure the number you hear is correct.

2) *Clearance limit.* "...is cleared to the Syracuse Hancock International Airport..." Since the clearance limit is your destination, you don't have to write that down either, surely you can remember where you are going. If owing to congestion, you are cleared to a point short of your destination, write that down as a reminder. If you haven't received further clearance by that point, you may not proceed beyond it. Sometimes, ATC needs reminding.

3) *Route.* "...as filed." The "as filed" refers only to the route; you still must listen for departure instructions and altitude.

Let's suppose that instead of "as filed" the entire route is read to you: "...Direct Chester, Victor-203 Albany, Victor-2 Syracuse, direct..." The word "direct" is used in this route, as it was on your flight plan, with two different meanings. "Direct Chester" means literally to fly to the Chester VOR by the shortest possible route. Dial in the course to the station and track it inbound. The second usage is a bit more obscure. The syracuse mentioned in the route is the Syracuse VOR, not the Syracuse airport, which is your destination. The word direct means that you are expected to proceed from the VOR to the airport via the published route (i.e., the approach procedure). Checking your approach plates for Syracuse, you will find that the VOR is either an initial approach fix for one or more approaches or that there is a terminal route from it to an IAF.

There are plenty of good abbreviations for copying a route. Many pilots use a capital "D" with an arrow through it for "direct," a "V" for "victor", and anything they can think of for the names of the fixes. In an unfamiliar area, ask the controller to spell the VOR names. He will usually respond by spelling the identifiers only and in the phonetic alphabet. To guard against confusion, study the area a bit when you plan the flight to get an idea of where nearby VORs, airways and intersections are located.

4) *Departure instructions*: "After departure Runway One Five, turn left heading three six zero, radar vectors to Chester..." Just jot down an "l" or a left curving arrow for the direction of turn, the heading, "RV" for radar vectors, and the name of the fix to which you'll be vectored. If you must write the runway number, go ahead, but it seems unnecessary if you are going to taxi to it. If there are parallel runways—right and left —with the same number, be sure you have that safely in mind or on paper.

Departure instructions are one of the most misunderstood parts of the clearance. The expression "radar vectors to Chester" suggests that you will be vectored to your first en route VOR but you will probably be given one or two headings to get you clear of the traffic pattern and then be told to fly direct to the VOR. Recall that any clearance supersedes those previously issued. You are told to expect "radar vectors to Chester" simply as a precaution in case of communications failure. If you should lose your radio right after takeoff, you are expected to fly direct to the fix specified in the vector clearance.

Departure instructions expedite your flight and begin ATC's job of separating you from other IFR traffic at the earliest possible moment. The controller is not responsible for terrain and obstacle clearance right after liftoff. You must know when it is safe to begin your first turn. Maintain the runway heading at least to circling minimums and preferably to the traffic pattern altitude to stay in the clear.

At some airports with high terrain nearby, there are special IFR departure procedures. These appear at the bottom of the airport diagram on Jeppesen charts and in a special listing at the front of government approach plates. The listing is with the non-standard takeoff minimums on the government plates, and an entry is indicated by the "T" within a triangle in the footnote section of the approach plate. Always consult them before an IFR takeoff.

As an example, the Shenandoah Valley airport lies in a beautiful Virginia valley surrounded by high ridges. As protection from these ridges, the departure instructions read, "Climb to the locator outer marker and continue climb in a southwest holding pattern to 4500' before proceeding on course." Ignoring this procedure could place a slow-climbing aircraft dangerously close to the terrain. These departure instructions are not usually included in your clearance; ATC does not have responsibility for terrain clearance in this situation.

Departure instructions are not always issued at the same point in the clearance. Usually, they come just before the route, as in our example, but it is a matter of local custom. At some airports, they will be the last item in the clearance, after the transponder code, and at some, they will not be issued with the clearance at all but by the tower controller just before takeoff.

Another type of departure instruction is the SID. These published procedures are designed to simplify the clearance delivery process by reducing the reading and copying that pilots and controllers have to do. Jeppesen provides SIDs with the approach plates for each airport, while the government issues them in separate flip books. If you use the government approach plate system and don't have the SIDs with you, you can specify "No SIDs" in the remarks section of your flight plan. This, however, does not mean that you won't be given a SID, merely that it will be read to you and you will have to copy and read back the whole thing. Since SIDs can be long and complex, it is advisable to carry them with you.

5) *Altitude*: "...climb and maintain two thousand, expect six thousand one-zero minutes after departure..." A handy notation is "2, 6 - 10." If the expected altitude is specified at a fix (say Chester), the notation would be "2, 6 - CTR." There is no need to copy the zeros in "two thousand"— you know it doesn't mean 200 or 20,000 feet. Since you must climb after takeoff, no special symbol for "climb and maintain" is necessary.

You filed for six, so why the 10 minutes at 2000? ATC does it for their own purposes, and you are usually cleared to your final altitude in a lot less than 10 minutes. They issue the 10 minutes in their perpetual concern with communications failure. If you do lose your comm radios shortly after takeoff, climb to the expected altitude 10 minutes after takeoff.

In areas with little traffic, the altitude may be stated as "...cruise six thousand..." A cruise clearance authorizes you to use the stated altitude, descend at your discretion to the applicable minimum altitude, and fly an approach at your destination. You must report leaving the assigned altitude and cannot return to it without additional clearance.

6) *Frequency*: "...contact departure control on one two five point three five..." Just jot down the number; you know it is not an altitude or a transponder code. Put it in one radio right away, for you will be switching to departure a few hundred feet off the ground,—perhaps just as you enter the clouds.

7) *Transponder code*: "...squawk five two four seven." Again, just write down the number. There is no danger of mistaking it for anything but a squawk code. Enter the code and make sure the transponder is on standby. Turn it on as you are cleared onto the runway.

If you miss part of the clearance, resume copying at the next part. For example, if you fall behind on the route, stop, and then start copying when the altitude is given. Read back what you copied correctly, so that only the section you missed will have to be repeated.

Clearance shorthand is a personal matter, and since no one has to interpret it but you, there are no right or wrong methods, unless your system confuses you.

To copy a clearance efficiently, make six headings down the side of your pad or use the space provided on the P.I.C. route log. Leave one line for each item, except the route, which could take up two or three. With this format set up, only the departure instructions and the route will require more than a single word of writing.

At an airport with no control zone, the departure instructions will begin with "upon entering controlled airspace...." ATC is thus reminding you that they have no authority over your flight in uncontrolled airspace and no responsibility there for your safety.

Clearance copying is one of the most anxiety producing tasks for the low-time instrument pilot. Something about copying what the man says and reading it back correctly makes many otherwise confident and literate people cringe and even freeze with fear, perhaps because of an unconscious feeling that as less-than- experts, they are wasting the controller's valuable time. If you suffer from this, be reassured that you are in good company; many pilots feel as you do. Also, realize that you are not wasting anybody's time. The controller's mission is to facilitate your flight, and that includes reading your clearance as slowly as necessary for you to copy.

ATC Communications

As we have seen, on an IFR flight between two major terminals, the sequence of routine radio contacts will typically be, as follows:

1. ATIS: Copy departure airport information.
2. Clearance delivery: Copy IFR clearance.
3. Ground control: Permission to taxi to the active runway.
4. Tower: Permission to take off.
5. Departure control: Your contact with ATC in the terminal area.
6. Center: You will probably talk to several sectors and possibly more than one center during the flight. For TEC routes you will talk to several approach control sectors and no center.
7. Arrival ATIS: Copy arrival airport information. Try to listen on your second radio, or request permission to leave the center frequency for a minute.

8. Approach control: Approach clearance.

9. Tower: "Cleared to land."

10. Ground: Taxi to the ramp.

11. Unicom: Parking instructions and request fuel.

Each time you are handed off to a new facility, contact the new controller with your full identification and altitude: "Cessna seven eight nine papa fox, with you at six thousand." The response will usually be an acknowledgment and the nearby altimeter setting.

In addition to routine communications, pilots under IFR must make certain reports to ATC. Reports that are required at all times are:

1. Leaving an assigned altitude.

2. When unable to climb or descend at least 500 feet per minute.

3. Missed approach.

4. Change in true airspeed of 5% or 10 knots, whichever is greater.

5. Time and altitude reaching a holding fix.

6. Leaving a holding fix.

7. Loss or impairment of navigation or communications capability.

8. Any information relating to the safety of flight, including hazardous or unforecast weather. Additionally, when not in radar contact, report the following:

9. Final approach fix inbound.

10. Position reports at compulsory reporting points (indicated by solid triangles on en route charts). Position reports include the aircraft identification, position, time over the fix, altitude, estimated time of arrival (ETA) to the next reporting point, and the name of the next succeeding reporting point. A corrected ETA should be reported if it is seen to be in error by 3 minutes. This type of position reporting is rarely necessary, as so much of the United States is covered by radar.

Cockpit Organization

The mysterious and awe inspiring job of flying instruments is nothing more than a collection of simple and mundane habits. In the cockpit, the tasks of flying, navigating, and planning must be coordinated smoothly. Some of the instrument pilot's most important skills resemble those of a good office manager. Finding—and unfolding and setting up—the right chart at the right moment is no less important than being able to fly a

good ILS—and in rough conditions, no less tricky.

A single pilot under IFR can become extremely busy and must budget his time and attention carefully. In planning for good cockpit organization, simplify whenever possible. Unusual and exotic tools and aids are to be avoided rather than sought. The following items will simplify your job:

Lap board - A standard office clipboard will suffice. Avoid knee boards. They are too small, and if they come with built-in lights, velcro fasteners, pencil sharpeners and secret compartments, they are too expensive. A patch of corduroy or thin foam rubber glued to the back of your clipboard will keep it from sliding off your lap.

Approach plate clip - Mounted on your control wheel, this is convenient but not essential. It does eliminate the need to look down to your lap at crucial moments. If you use the bound government approach plates, the large patented clip that holds the whole book open to your page is a marginal solution to a difficult problem.

Timer - Attach the timer to the center of your yoke with a strip of velcro. A stop watch or digital timer is better than a clock with a sweep second hand for timing approaches and holds. With a sweep second hand, it is too easy to remember the second hand position but forget how many minutes have elapsed. When choosing a timer, look for the largest numbers and fewest buttons. Avoid complicated calculators with built-in timing functions. As you cross the FAF with a 20-knot crosswind, you are bound to press the wrong key. Local electronic stores often have good timers at better prices than aviation supply houses.

Pen/pencil - There you are, ready to copy the clearance, your only pen won't work, and your pencil is rolling around on the floor under your seat. Carry several. Mechanical pencils work well and can be clipped to your pocket or lap board.

Approach plates and charts - Carry them with you even when the weather is forecast to be VFR, and keep them within reach. They are no use in the baggage compartment.

Route logs - These are good for planning, figuring, and copying clearances. You can do these things on a napkin from the coffee shop, of course, but a pad of route logs is better.

Headset - A boom mike with a push-to-talk switch on the yoke saves motion and time. Headphones also cut down on cockpit noise and reduce fatigue. For training, a voice-activated intercom eliminates the need to shout in the cockpit, saving energy for instructor and student.

Keep in mind that, difficult as it may now seem to master, the system and the procedures described in this chapter are essentially logical—they work, and they become increasingly easy with familiarity. We began this chapter with a simple IFR flight that was enjoyable in itself to do right. That you will be making such trips is one of the good things you can look forward to as an instrument pilot.

To The CFII

This chapter can be covered early in an instrument course. After mastering basic airwork, plan a hypothetical IFR trip from your home airport and cover this material as it comes up. The sequence of subjects will then be completely natural.

Begin with a weather briefing. Go over each item on the weather briefing sheet in detail, studying its significance. Review the customary format of a weather briefing and the occasional need to question the briefer for additional information.

If you are lucky enough to have an IFR day, call for a weather briefing, with your student listening. Then, using the route for which he will actually plan a trip, let him call Flight Service himself for a briefing.

Weather is one area that no course can cover completely. A thorough knowledge of weather flying only comes with much experience. You can analyze forecasts, refer to low ceilings, ice and thunderstorms, but until your student has seen them for himself, there will be a gap in his knowledge.

However, he can benefit from your experiences and "weather wisdom." Hangar flying can be educational and helpful here. Describe some actual weather encounters, including the forecast, how you made your go/no go decision, what "outs" you planned for yourself, what weather you encountered and what you did as a result.

In planning a cross country flight from the home airport, go over all the en route chart symbols thoroughly. Your student should become proficient at chart reading at this point. Have him prepare a detailed route log and calculate the times and distances to each intersection. Be sure he understands the relationships between indicated airspeed, true airspeed, and groundspeed.

Cover the regulations governing cross country flight. If your student is weak on them or has trouble remembering, schedule extra ground school time. If you drive back and forth to the airport with him, the car is a good place for this type of ground school.

One of the most confusing subjects for all instrument pilots is the concept of controlled and uncontrolled airspace, so study airspace classification and transition areas in terms of of the safety they afford the IFR flight.

Give your student plenty of practice copying clearances. At a busy field, he can listen to ground control or clearance delivery and practice copying other people's clearances. You should also be proficient at imitating ATC, including making up and issuing realistic IFR clearances. Have him practice copying clearances until it comes easily. Many people suffer from undue anxiety over clearance copying, and you can relieve him of this by thoroughly covering the format of a clearance and giving him plenty of experience. When he is capable of copying a clearance easily, slip in some mistakes, such as an altitude above the service ceiling of his airplane. Errors in clearances are not uncommon, and most instrument pilots can cite several examples from their experience.

After completion of this chapter, have your student prepare and file an IFR flight plan each time you fly. For the rest of the course, every flight can begin on a clearance, even if, for simplicity, you cancel shortly after takeoff. The student should do the radio work. If he has trouble staying ahead of the airplane while handling communications, give him plenty of practice during simulator sessions and while driving back and forth to the airport. Every flight after the airwork section can be done on a real or simulated clearance, even if you are merely holding.

Flight Planning Quiz

1. Does weather radar provide information on cloud cover or turbulence?
2. If the aircraft's turn coordinator is inoperative, can you legally fly IFR?
3. How recently must the transponder, altimeter, and static system have been checked?
4. How often must the VOR be checked? How must it be logged?
5. What is class A airspace?
6. What is class D airspace?
7. What paperwork must be carried in the aircraft at all times?
8. To be legally current for IFR flight you must have logged…
9. A transponder and encoding altimeter is required for flight above what altitude?
10. What does a MEA guarantee?
11. What is a MRA?
12. When is oxygen required?
13. Where are preferred routes found?
14. What is the minimum fuel required for an IFR flight?
15. When is an alternate not required?
16. If an alternate is required, what minimum weather must be forecast at the alternate?
17. What is the purpose of designating an alternate on a flight plan?
18. What does a cruise clearance authorize?
19. In box 3 on the IFR Flight Plan, what is the code used for transponder with altitude encoding capability?
20. What is a SID?

CHAPTER FIVE

VOR EQUIPMENT, ORIENTATION AND TRACKING

"I won't soon forget the lessons I learned about VOR orientation on day eight of the ten-day P.I.C. course," relates a recent instrument student. "We had covered VOR navigation with the simulator and in the airplane. I had flown procedure turns, hold entries, and a variety of VOR approaches, and I felt confident in my orientation skills. Little did I realize how easily I could make a potentially serious mistake and how tricky was the little VOR needle.

"I wanted to combine the required 250 nautical mile IFR cross country with a trip to Las Vegas. The total distance was over four hundred miles, but I preferred to fly the extra distance for the pleasure of a stop in the 'glitter city.' My P.I.C. instructor, Tom Seymour, was from the East and not at all averse to the idea.

"Our clearance was as I had filed, and the only unusual circumstance was that Burbank radar was out of service. After carefully noting the clearance, I repeated it to Van Nuys ground control: "Four five six alpha romeo cleared to Las Vegas. After departure Runway One-Six Right, fly runway heading to four thousand, turn left heading zero five zero to intercept Victor two-oh-one to Palmdale, Victor twelve Hector, Victor twenty-one Creso, direct. Maintain nine thousand. Contact Burbank departure on one two zero point four, squawk zero five five three (figure 5-1).

"The MEA on Victor 201 is 8,500 feet; I realized that the straight out climb before turning was

intended to give us needed altitude before intercepting. It was a beautiful, sunny day, and I regretted having to spend much of it under the hood. I was feeling a bit cocky, and, in my haste, I made a couple of mistakes on the pre-takeoff checklist. Tom gave me a gentle admonition about paying attention to detail. He knew, as I have learned, that little mistakes have a way of compounding.

"The tower cleared us for takeoff, and we climbed into the choppy air below the typical winter temperature inversion. Tom handed me the hood, simulating entering the clouds at 200 feet above the runway. My difficulties started almost immediately. The DG read 270°, 110° from the assigned heading. I began a climbing turn to the left before realizing I had forgotten to set the DG against the runway heading while still on the ground. Stopping the turn, I concentrated on setting the DG to the magnetic compass but had difficulty as the compass danced wildly in the rough air. A moment later, rising engine sounds and the wind rushing more loudly over the cockpit alerted me that I had not only stopped climbing, but was in a steep descent.

"I recovered from my first real life unusual attitude, re-established the climb and finished setting the DG. I was 60° east of my heading and probably a lot closer to Victor 201 than I should have been at that point. With alarm I realized we were reaching 4000 feet.

"As I was about to turn left heading 050°, my

concentration was broken by the insistent call of Van Nuys Tower, 'Four five six alpha romeo, Van Nuys Tower, how do you read?' I had evidently missed several calls during the excitement.

" 'Six alpha romeo, loud and clear,' I sputtered into the mike.

" 'Six alpha romeo, I've been calling you for five minutes,' the tower said angrily, 'do you need assistance?'

" 'No,' I said sheepishly, 'everything is okay now.'

" 'Four five six alpha romeo, contact Burbank departure now, one-two-zero-point-four.'

" 'One-two-zero-point-four, six alpha romeo,' I replied, trying to regain my composure. We were almost at 5000 feet, and I decided to make my turn before calling departure control. I remembered Tom's frequent admonitions to 'fly the airplane first, then navigate, then communicate.' Aviate, navigate, communicate, in that order. It made sense to me and I made the 45-second turn to heading 050°.

" 'On the proper heading and, I thought, finally in control of the flight, I flicked the transmitter switch to the number two comm. The speaker immediately erupted with the raucous chatter of a unicom frequency. Disgustedly I checked the frequency on my lap board and set the radio correctly. Another job I should have done on the ground.

" 'Burbank Departure,' I reported, 'Four five six alpha romeo is with you.'

" 'Six alpha romeo, Burbank Departure, Roger. Be advised that Burbank radar is out of service. Report reaching four thousand.' My failure to report altitude on the initial contact left the controller unaware of where I actually was.

" 'Six alpha romeo is leaving seven thousand,' I reported, 'heading 050°.'

" 'Roger, six alpha romeo,' the unruffled controller replied. 'Climb and maintain niner thousand, Palmdale altimeter is 29.95.'

" 'Six alpha romeo,' I breathed, glad to be done, temporarily, with reporting.

" 'After a moment of perfecting the heading and airspeed, I turned my attention to the VOR. I was nonplussed to see yet another neglected checklist item: enter the frequency of the first enroute fix in the number one nav and set the OBS for the course to that fix. With my hood on, I couldn't see Tom's expression, but in my discomfort I imagined him grimacing disgustedly at my disorganization.

" 'I carefully set and identified the Palmdale fre-

quency, 114.5. As I started to set the OBS, I noticed we were reaching 9000 and paused in my navigation work to level the airplane, accelerate and trim for cruise.

" 'With the flight under control I reported once again to Departure Control, 'Six alpha romeo, level at nine thousand.'

" 'Roger, six alpha romeo,' the controller said, 'report intercepting Victor two-oh-one.'

" 'Six alpha romeo.'

" 'In retrospect, it seems that a collection of relatively minor errors had caused chaos in the cockpit. Instrument flying requires careful attention to detail, and chaos tends to grow like a monster and to lead to more errors. And I was yet to make my biggest mistake of the day.

" 'The en route chart showed that Victor 201 is

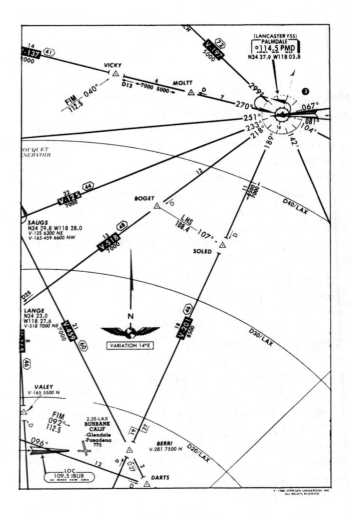

Figure 5-1

*defined by the Palmdale 189° radial, and **I set the OBS to 189°. Heading northeast to intercept the inbound course, I had selected the outbound course** (figure 5-1). The needle was full right, and, concentrating on heading and altitude, I settled back to wait for it to swing off the peg.*

"I knew that we should be near Victor 201 and as the minutes ticked by I became concerned. But I did not realize I had selected the reciprocal of the course and we had already crossed the airway. I worried instead that there was a strong east wind, our intercept angle was too small, and we would pass north of Palmdale before intercepting. Incredibly, I turned farther east.

"In retrospect, these errors are unfathomable, but at the time they seemed like sensible decisions. Almost ten minutes passed before I realized what was wrong. Just as I was about to correct the OBS and make the proverbial 180°, Tom reached over and slipped the hood from my head. Tom had a very dry sense of humor. 'All right,' he said, 'what's wrong with this picture?'

"There were the beautiful Southern California mountains, lush green to the treeline and rocky brown above, a sight I love to see and terrain I love to fly over. The awful part was the mountain, with its peak just above eye level, rising at twelve o'clock and less than three miles.

"The sectional shows that mountain towering to 9,399 feet, 400 feet above our altitude that day. Had I been alone in actual conditions, I surely would have been planted there.

"A miserable story, but with valuable lessons. I learned forever the importance of the checklist and methodical attention to detail. And I learned that the simple VOR display can hide pitfalls for a distracted pilot."

The VOR System

In the 48 contiguous United States, most instrument navigating is done with the aid of a VOR receiver and the very high frequency (VHF) radio signals emitted by ground based VOR's. Virtually all en route navigation and many instrument approaches use these signals, which are broadcast in the frequency range of 108.0 to 118.0 megahertz (MHz), just above the FM radio band.

When using VOR navigation either en route or on approach, develop the habit of identifying

each new station. Turn up the volume when you change the frequency, interpret the Morse code and then turn down the sound at your leisure, with a minimum of movement. If the station has a voice identifier, there is no need to listen to the Morse. However, it is *not* safe to assume you are on the right frequency because you hear someone calling the Flight Service Station that monitors the VOR you want. A FSS may monitor several VOR's.

Do not identify the station just to ensure that you are receiving *something*. If you were receiving nothing, you would probably notice an OFF flag and a dead needle. Identify primarily to ascertain that you have dialed in the *right* frequency. Even if you are *sure* that *you* will never make a mistake, the numbers on digital frequency selectors are known to slip. I know a pilot who once flew to the Pawling VOR instead of the Deer Park VOR. The frequencies differ by only one digit but the VOR's are 60 miles apart.

During VOR maintenance, the identifier is taken off the air as a warning that the station may broadcast unreliable signals.

A VOR signal has two parts, known as the reference phase signal and the variable phase signal. It is transmitted in such a way that the electrical phase angle between the two components differs by the exact number of degrees that the receiving aircraft is away from the station's 360° radial. Thus if you are east of the station, the variable phase signal will be received 90° out of phase with the reference phase signal; south of the station it will be 180° out of phase, etc. Your VOR equipment recognizes the phase difference and uses it to determine its magnetic direction, or course, from the VOR (figure 5-2).

Owing to the nature of VHF radio waves, VOR navigation is only possible along a "line of sight." Obstructions such as mountains will block VOR signals, and at low altitudes, the curvature of the earth may interfere with reception from a distant station. Because of this, instrument charts specify minimum altitudes for proper navigation signal reception.

The IFR en route airspace structure consists of airways, or specified courses, defined by VOR's. Stations usable in the low altitude structure (below 18,000 feet MSL) are classified as **(H)**

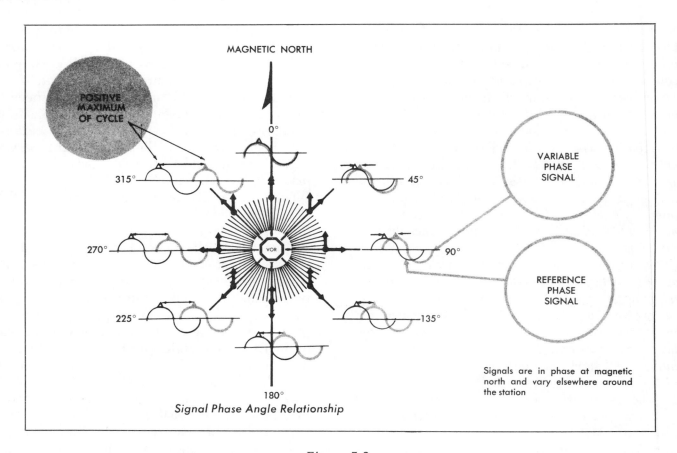

Figure 5-2

and **(L)** class VOR's and are usable for at least 40 miles. Additionally, (H) class stations are usable to a distance of l00 miles above l4,500 feet and to l30 miles above l8,000 feet. The frequencies of most (L) and (H) class VOR's are in the 112.0-118.0 range.

Terminal class (T) VOR's are not usually part of the IFR en route navigation system. Usually located on airports, (T) VOR's are used primarily for instrument approaches. They are nominally usable only within 25 miles, up to 12,000 feet. Most (T) class VOR's have frequencies in the range 108.0-112.0, as do other approach navaids such as localizers, localizer type directional aids (LDA), and simplified directional facilities (SDF).

In some cases the usable range of a VOR may be different from "normal." A restriction over all or part of the station's broadcast area will be noted in the *Airport/Facility Directory*.

Most VOR's have voice communications capability, and Flight Service uses them to talk with aircraft. If a VOR has no voice communications capability, its class designator will end in a "W", e.g. VORW. If a VOR is equipped with a continuous transcribed weather broadcast (TWEB), it is designated with "AB" preceding the class designation, e.g., ABVOR. (Formerly, Flight Service Stations would broadcast an hourly weather report on the VOR frequencies in their jurisdiction at a quarter past each hour. Stations which carried these transmissions were indicated with a "B", e.g., BVOR. However, these hourly broadcasts have been discontinued and the "B" is now an obsolete designation.)

The VOR may be associated with a Limited Remote Communications Outlet (LRCO) which receives pilot transmissions, usually on frequency l22.l, and relays them to the FSS. The FSS transmits on the VOR frequency. Using this method of communication, you transmit on your communication radio, and listen on the VOR for the response. The proper callup is "(Name of FSS), Cessna seven eight nine papa alpha, receiving (. . .) VOR." When the Flight Service man returns your call, he will interrupt the VOR identifier. (If it is a voice identifier, you can tell your passengers that the poor announcer finally got a coffee break.)

You can use this system for all communications with Flight Service, including filing and closing flight plans, requesting weather information, and making pilot reports. However, if a simplex communications frequency is shown above the VOR frequency box on the chart, it is usually easier to call the FSS this way, transmitting and receiving on your communications radio. Most FSS's use 122.2, so if there is more than one frequency shown, choose one of the others — it will be less congested.

On an IFR flight, make pilot reports directly to Flight Service or to Flight Watch, the Enroute Flight Advisory Service (EFAS), on 122.0. Those you give to ATC may not be relayed to the FSS, where pilots on the ground are seeking their weather information. Remember that cloud top information is especially useful and that pilot reports are its best source. On an IFR flight plan, request permission to leave the ATC frequency, make your PIREP, and report back to ATC.

DME and TACAN

For reducing pilot work load, DME is one of the best devices on the market. Like many electronic products, it has steadily improved in quality in the last few years, while its price and weight have declined. When working properly, modern DME continuously pinpoints the airplane's position and even gives a readout of ground speed and/or "time to station." It eliminates the need to keep a careful route log, with ground speed calculations and position estimates. At or above 24,000 feet MSL, FAR 91.205(e) requires DME if VOR navigation is used.

DME also simplifies the identification of en route intersections. On Jeppesen charts, an intersection marked with an arrow and a "D" may be identified by its DME distance from the VOR as well as by the intersecting radial (figure 5-3). Use DME for intersection identification only when flying towards or away from the DME fix. Do not use off-airway stations as DME fixes.

DME accuracy is excellent, usually within three per cent or half a mile. If a fix may be defined by a DME distance or an intersecting radial, the distance is usually more accurate.

Distance measuring equipment operates in conjunction with a ground based transmitter/receiver unit (known as a transponder), part of a Tactical Air Navigation (TACAN) station, and usually collocated with a VOR.

The military services use the TACAN system instead of the civil VOR system. To a properly equipped aircraft, TACAN provides both azimuth and distance information. The VOR receiver cannot use azimuth information from a TACAN station, but the DME does interact with the TACAN to display distance, speed, and time to station.

Many TACAN stations share VOR sites; the combined navaid is called a VORTAC. If the TACAN station has only the distance feature (and not the azimuth feature) then the station is known as a VOR-DME. TACAN and VOR frequencies are paired so that when the VOR frequency is set on the DME, the appropriate TACAN channel is automatically selected. In some aircraft installations, DME tuning is slaved to one or the other NAV receiver, selected by a switch. To the pilot in the cockpit, there is no operational difference between VORTAC and VOR-DME stations. Although NOS charts display a different symbol for VORTAC and VOR-DME stations, Jeppesen charts do not.

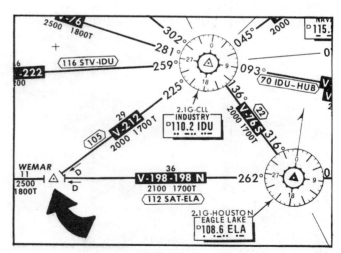

Figure 5-3

DME operates in the UHF range. The airborne equipment sends an electronic interrogation to the ground station, which gives an electronic response. By timing the interval between interrogation and response, the airborne DME calculates how far the signals are traveling. DME equipment can also be paired with a localizer or ILS, so that DME distances may be used as fixes during the approach.

The ground based DME transponder can respond to only a finite number of DME interrogations. If the number of airplanes using a facility exceeds its capacity, the facility will automatically ignore the weaker signals. Airplanes further from the station, and those with weaker airborne equipment, will get periodic dropouts on their distance (and associated) data. If the DME cannot update at least every 20 seconds or so, it reverts to "search," with no data displayed, until it successfully "hits" the ground station again. This can be a problem in busy high density areas.

DME measures the distance between the aircraft and the ground station, *in a straight line*. This is known as **slant range** and is slightly more than the actual horizontal distance. In the extreme case, directly over the station, the DME simply reads the altitude of the airplane in nautical miles. As you pass over the station at 6000 feet, the DME reads one NM. At 18,000 feet, directly over the VOR, the DME reads three NM. Slant range error decreases at greater distances from the station and is considered negligible when the airplane's altitude in thousands of feet is less than the distance in nautical miles (figure 5-4).

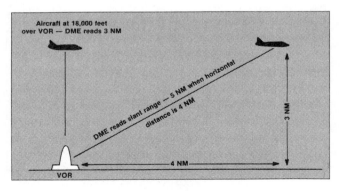

Figure 5-4

DME calculates ground speed and time to station by measuring the rate of change of distance to the station. Therefore, this information is valid only when the aircraft is flying directly towards or away from the station selected.

The DME station has its own identifier. The Morse code is the same as that for the associated VOR, but the pitch is higher, and it is broadcast only approximately twice a minute. You hear three or four repetitions of the VOR ident, and then one from the DME. Be suspicious of DME readings if the identifier is off the air.

In rare cases, there is a risk of receiving azimuth and distance information from different sources. At a few locations the TACAN channel paired with a (T) VOR is used by a nearby military TACAN beacon, allowing you to read azimuth from the VOR and distance from the *non*-collocated TACAN without knowing it, unless you simultaneously identify the VOR and DME. The idents should be the same, and the TACAN ident should fall in a pause between VOR idents. If they overlap, or if the idents are different, they are not collocated and you should ignore the DME. This is usually a problem only outside the official service volume of the (T) VOR (i.e., beyond 25 miles), but it still can be confusing and dangerous.

VOR Testing

To be legal for your IFR flight, each VOR receiver to be used must have been tested within the preceding 30 days (FAR 91.171) and the test logged in some "permanent record." It need not be in the aircraft maintenance logs, but it must be somewhere. If you rent IFR airplanes, you may log the checks in your pilot logbook. Flying clubs and partnerships often log the checks with the Hobbs meter record in the glove compartment. The entry should contain the date, the bearing errors for each instrument, the location where the check was conducted and your signature. A memory aid for this is "DEPS": date, error, place, signature.

There are six ways to test the VOR:

1. *The VOR test facility (VOT) check.* Located at certain major airports, VOT's transmit a 360° radial in all directions. To use the VOT from anywhere on the airport (some VOT's are also usable from the air), select the VOT frequency,

center the CDI with a FROM, and read the error on the OBS. The same check can be conducted centering the needle with a TO. In this case, the needle should center on 180°. To remember which is which, think of "one eighty TO." It sounds like "182," a popular airplane from a well known manufacturer.

On a VOT check the needle should center within 4° of the proper OBS setting.

VOT frequencies are given in the frequency box on the Jeppesen airport diagram and are listed in the *Airport/Facility Directory*.

2. *Designated ground checkpoint*. At certain airports, a circle is painted on the pavement, usually on the ramp or at the runup area. The course TO and FROM a nearby (sometimes on the field) VOR is indicated.

To use a designated ground checkpoint, park on the painted circle (your heading is immaterial) and center the needle. The OBS should read within 4° of the specified course. You can also check your DME indication against the published distance to the station from the checkpoint.

Designated ground checkpoints are listed in the FAA *Airport/Facility Directory*.

3. *Designated airborne checkpoints* are also listed in the FAA *Airport/Facility Directory*. Fly over the checkpoint (it may be a runway intersection, a spot on the ramp, or a building) and center the CDI. The OBS should read within 6° of the specified course.

4. *"Homemade" airborne checkpoint*. If no designated ground or airborne checkpoints are available, use a sectional to find a prominent landmark *on a Victor airway*, preferably more than 20 miles from the VOR. Fly over this landmark and center the CDI. The OBS should read within 6° of the airway course.

5. *Dual VOR check*. You may test the VOR instruments against each other. Tune them both to the same station, and center both needles. They should read within 4° of each other.

The least desirable check, this one will pass two wildly inaccurate instruments, provided they are close to each other; for example, if one is off by 7° and the other is off by 10°, they pass. It will also fail two instruments which would individually pass another type of check. If the

VOT check shows one instrument +3° and the other -3°, they are both legal, but on a dual check, they would be 6° apart and both fail.

6. *Radio shop check*. This is the only type of check not conducted by the pilot. The radio shop broadcasts a test signal, usually on frequency 108.0, and checks the VOR's behavior. The record of the check must be endorsed and signed by the radio shop representative.

VOR Orientation

The central skill in IFR navigation is the ability to form a mental picture of your position in relation to a station or course. Your main objective in this chapter and the next is to learn to *visualize* your position. Additionally, you will learn to accurately track specified courses and perform procedure turns. It is important to *master* this material. If you don't, nothing will go right later on. Don't leave this phase prematurely, or your impatience will come back to haunt you.

The process of *visualization* is most easily accomplished by use of the eight points of the compass (figure 5-5). The eight points are used to specify the aircraft's **position** with respect to a course or station and also its **heading**. Heading is the compass point towards which the airplane is *pointing*, and should not be confused with position. *The VOR display shows aircraft position only*; its indications are not affected by heading.

To visualize your position, imagine the com-

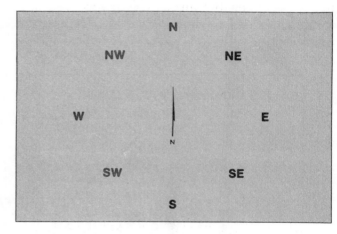

The Eight Points of the Compass

Figure 5-5

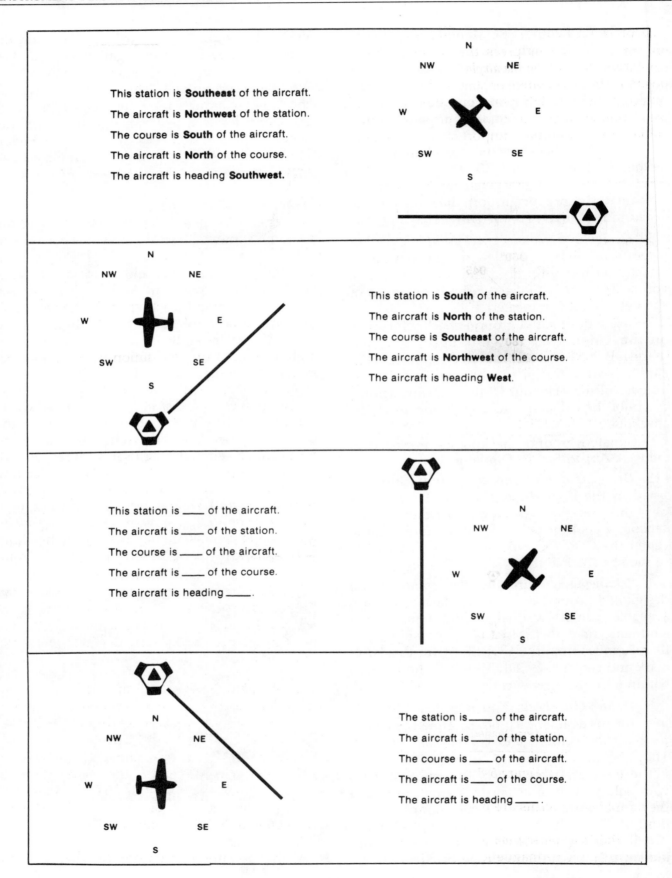

This station is **Southeast** of the aircraft.

The aircraft is **Northwest** of the station.

The course is **South** of the aircraft.

The aircraft is **North** of the course.

The aircraft is heading **Southwest.**

This station is **South** of the aircraft.

The aircraft is **North** of the station.

The course is **Southeast** of the aircraft.

The aircraft is **Northwest** of the course.

The aircraft is heading **West**.

This station is ____ of the aircraft.

The aircraft is ____ of the station.

The course is ____ of the aircraft.

The aircraft is ____ of the course.

The aircraft is heading ____.

The station is ____ of the aircraft.

The aircraft is ____ of the station.

The course is ____ of the aircraft.

The aircraft is ____ of the course.

The aircraft is heading ____.

Figure 5-6

pass points in figure 5-5 as being superimposed on the aircraft. This gives the position of the course or station *from the airplane*. The airplane's position from the course or station is the reciprocal point. In visualizing position, the eight compass points are sufficient; exact numerical values are of secondary importance (figure 5-6).

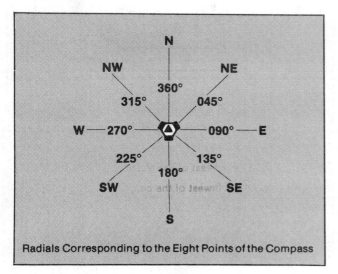

Figure 5-7

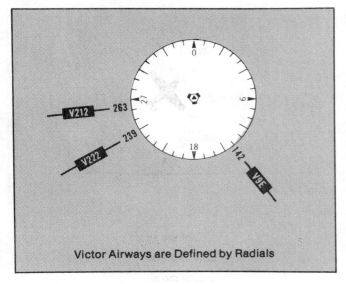

Figure 5-8

The following terms are used in VOR navigation:

A **radial** is a *course from* a VOR station specified in relation to magnetic north (figures 5-7,

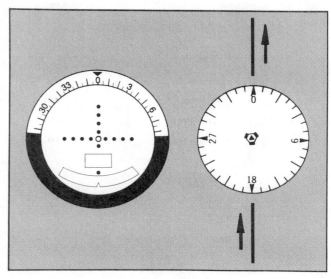

Figure 5-9

5-8). Courses TO the station should not be referred to as radials.

The **omni-bearing selector** (OBS) is used to select a particular VOR course, either FROM or TO the station (figure 5-9).

The **course deviation indicator** (CDI, needle) indicates which side of the selected course the airplane is on. It divides the area around the VOR into two parts (figure 5-10).

The CDI shows angular displacement from the selected course, not actual distance. A half scale deflection indicates 5° off course, a full-scale deflection means at least 10° off course, and usually each dot represents two degrees off course. At 60 miles from the station, each degree off course represents one mile, while at 6 miles from the station each degree represents only one tenth of a mile.

The **TO-FROM flag** indicates the airplane's position in relation to a line perpendicular to the selected course, and passing through the station. Together, the flag and CDI divide the area around the VOR into quadrants (figure 5-11).

The **zone of ambiguity** is the region close to the line which separates the TO and FROM areas. Within this region the TO-FROM flag reads OFF, or NAV on some instruments (figure 5-12).

As the airplane moves from the TO region to

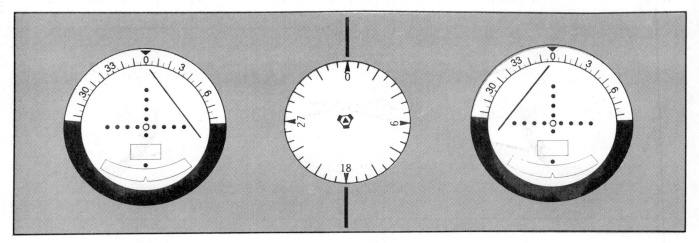

Figure 5-10

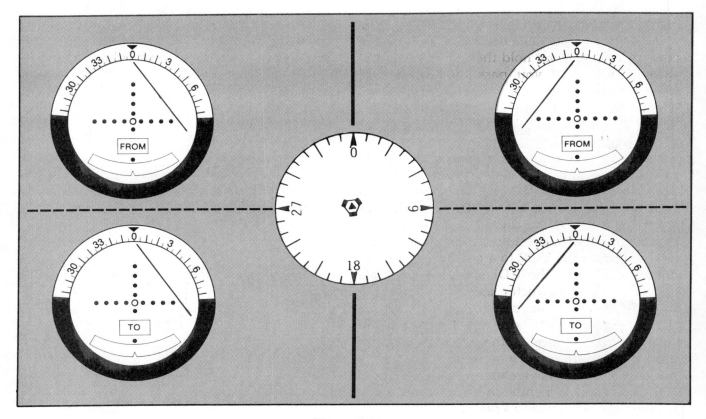

Figure 5-11

the FROM region, the flag changes from TO to OFF (or NAV) to FROM. The speed at which the change occurs depends on the aircraft's distance from the station, because the width of the zone of ambiguity increases with distance from the station. The exact width of the zone varies and is characteristic of the particular instrument. A typical value is 24°.

Although similarly named, the **cone of confusion** is different from the zone of ambiguity. It is the region *directly above* the station, where the radials are so close together that regardless of how well you have been tracking, it is virtually impossible to avoid crossing numerous radials.

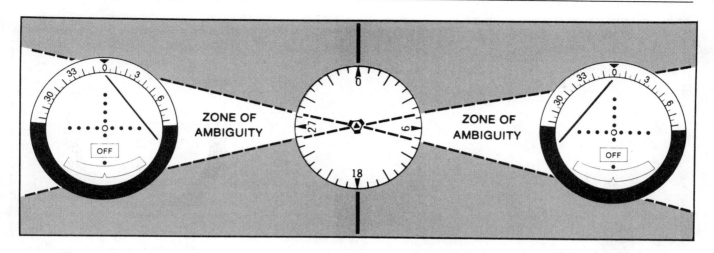

Figure 5-12

The CDI moves randomly as you enter the cone and usually a full scale deflection occurs. Do not chase the needle, but hold the last heading that worked well until you pass the station and emerge from the cone on the other side.

The cone of confusion widens with altitude, so the area of unreliable readings is bigger at higher altitudes. Hence its name.

Notice that no heading information was given in figures 5-9 through 5-12. Again, the CDI and TO-FROM flag give the airplane's position in relation to the course dialed into the OBS and are not affected by the aircraft's heading.

A good diagnostic test for new student evaluations is to set the VOR to a nearby station and twist the OBS so the CDI shows a full scale deflection. The instructor asks which way to turn to intercept the selected course. If the answer given is "left" or "right" and is made solely with reference to the VOR display, he knows he is up against a serious misunderstanding of VOR navigation. The direction of CDI deflection depends only on the course selected and the airplane's position relative to it. The VOR display can tell us only a *compass direction* to the selected course. Whether to turn left or right depends on the airplane's heading.

During training, avoid the words "left" and "right" when referring to *courses*. (These words are unavoidable when talking about turning to a *heading*, as in "turn right heading 360°.") Thinking in terms of compass directions eases orientation problems. Here is one example: you are procedure turn outbound on a course of 170°, following the published procedure on an approach plate clipped to your yoke (figure 5-13).

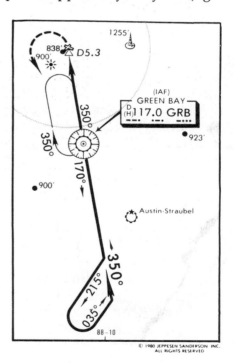

Figure 5-13

The pattern shows a turn to heading 215°, shown on the reader's *left*. Actually, however, a *right* turn is needed. If you think in terms of left and right, you may turn the wrong way, but if you just note that you must turn *west*, there is no chance of confusion.

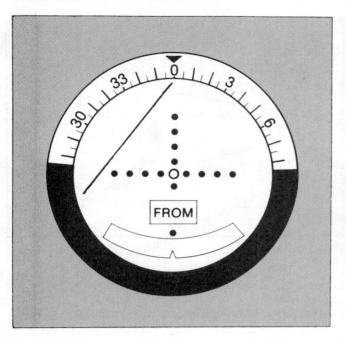

Figure 5-14

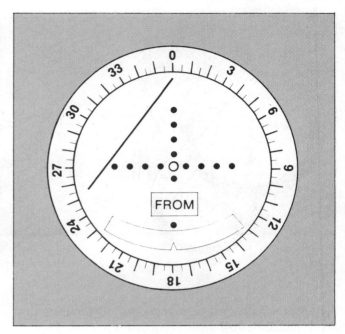

Figure 5-15

Let's take a look at what the VOR display actually shows.

Figure 5-14 shows a standard VOR display. The 360° course is set in the OBS, the TO-FROM flag reads FROM, and the CDI is deflected full scale to the left. The question that most frequently causes confusion is "Which way do I turn to intercept the selected course?" Take a moment to answer this yourself.

As we have noted, "left" and "right" can be misleading answers. The left needle tells us we are *east* of the 360° course. In order to intercept this course we must therefore fly *west*. We can't know whether this requires a left or right turn without knowing the heading of the airplane. From an approximate north heading, a left turn would be correct; from a southerly heading a right turn would be easier.

Herein lies the confusion. Many pilots are taught that the CDI points to the course if the heading approximates the OBS setting, and away from the course if it is approximately opposite. A notion called "reverse sensing" is used to explain this.

In fact, the CDI knows nothing of the location of the selected course. It "senses" and reacts the same way regardless of heading. So to what is it actually pointing? Let's imagine that the OBS,

instead of being exposed only at the top of the instrument, is a continuous ring around its perimeter (figure 5-15). Newer King and Narco instruments are designed this way.

Think of the numbers around the edge of the instrument as courses. The selected course is at the top, its reciprocal is at the bottom, and all those around the sides lead towards or away from it. The CDI points to the courses that lead towards the one selected. In figure 5-15, all the courses between 181° and 359° point the airplane towards the 360° course. The 270° course, at the 9 o'clock position, provides a 90° intercept. Other courses on the left side give smaller intercepts. Both the 330° and 210° courses, for example, give a 30° intercept. You might use 330° if you wanted to track north after interception, 210° if you wanted to track south once the 360° course is intercepted.

The flag tells you which side of the zone of ambiguity you are on. A FROM indicates the side of the zone where the selected *radial* lies; a TO indicates the opposite side. Thus, in figure 5-14 the airplane is on the same side of the course as the 360° *radial*; it is north of the station.

Combining these two pieces of information, we see that the airplane whose instrument is shown in figure 5-14 is in the northeast quad-

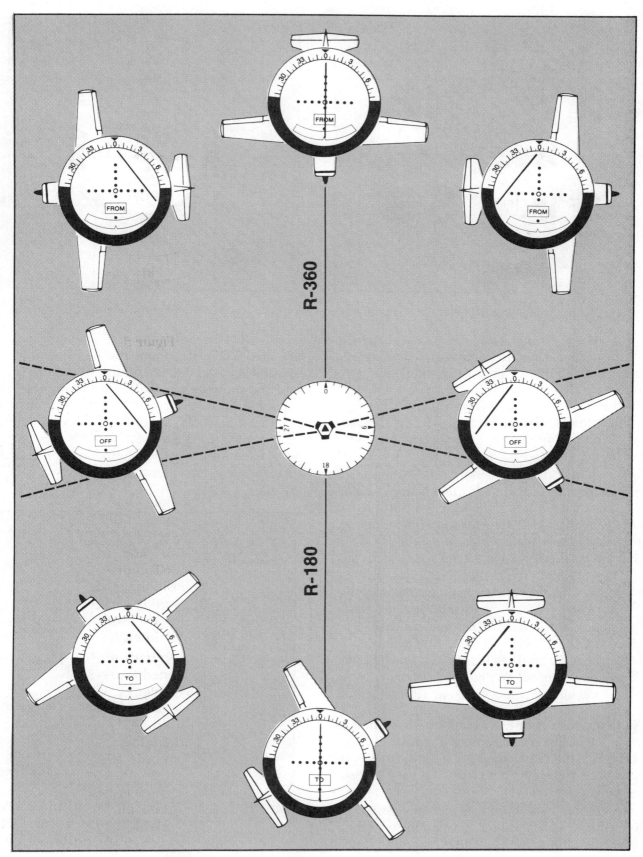

Figure 5-16

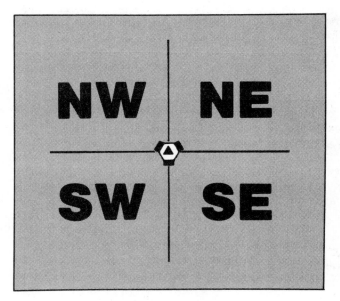

Figure 5-17

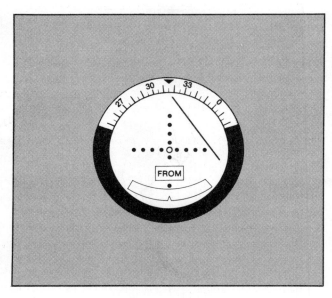

Figure 5-18

rant (figure 5-17). Figure 5-16 shows the flag and needle indications for aircraft in eight positions around a VOR.

If the OBS setting is not one of the four cardinal points, the quadrants will be skewed. The airplane in figure 5-18 is in the west quadrant (figure 5-19).

If the width of the zone of ambiguity is known, the airplane's position can be told within a much smaller range, even with a full scale deflection, although it should be realized that this is an academic exercise, not a practical technique.

Suppose the needle is deflected full scale and the flag says TO or FROM. We already know how to determine our position within 90°. Additionally, since the flag is deflected full scale we know we are not within 10° of the selected radial. Therefore we know our position within 80°. Suppose the zone of ambiguity is known to be 24° wide. Then the fact that the flag is not OFF tells us we are not within 12° of the center of the zone of ambiguity. We now know our position within 68°.

To determine your *exact* position in relation to a VOR station, center the needle with a FROM. This reveals the radial you are on, and, from your knowledge of the compass rose, it is easy to visualize your position.

Intersection orientation is accomplished by determining your position in relation to each of two VOR stations (figure 5-20). Generally, if you

are dual VOR equipped, the number one VOR should be used for en route airway navigation and the number two VOR for identifying intersections. During an instrument approach, the number one VOR should be tuned to the approach navaid (ILS, VOR) and the number two VOR used for navigation to the approach course or for intersection identification.

Figure 5-19

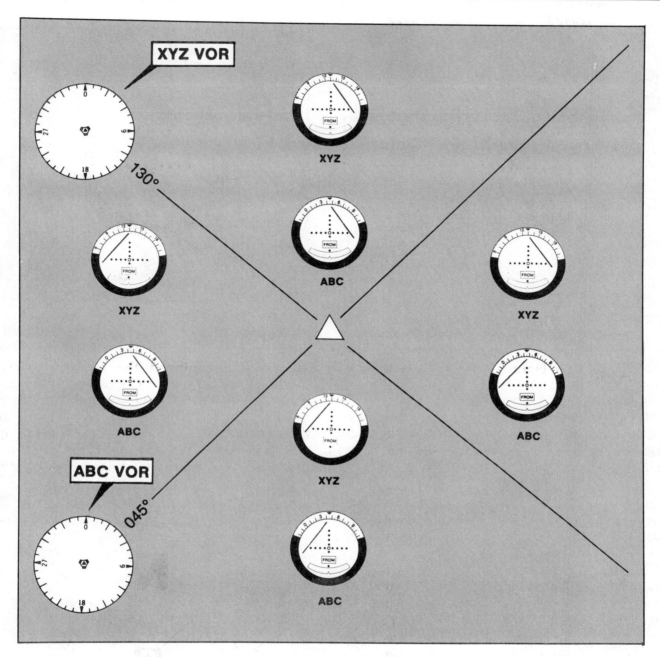

Figure 5-20

VOR Interpretation and the HSI

Exposing the entire OBS ring worked so well, let's experiment some more with redesigning the VOR display. In the example above, the pendulum type needle does not emphasize the fact that the 270° course gives a 90° intercept, and it does not bring out the fact that 210° and 330° are symmetrical, in the sense that they offer the same intercept angle with the selected course. Suppose the needle were to remain vertical as it moved left and right across the face of the instrument (figure 5-21, left). This would give a clearer picture of which courses do what for the airplane's position.

A problem remains, however. In figure 5-21, the needle shows that any westerly course will intercept the 360°. However, the DG shows that

95

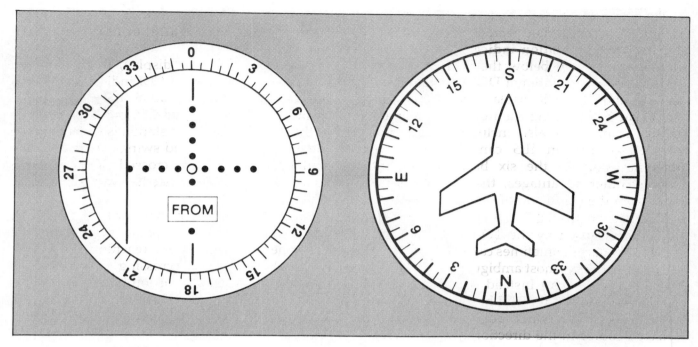

Figure 5-21

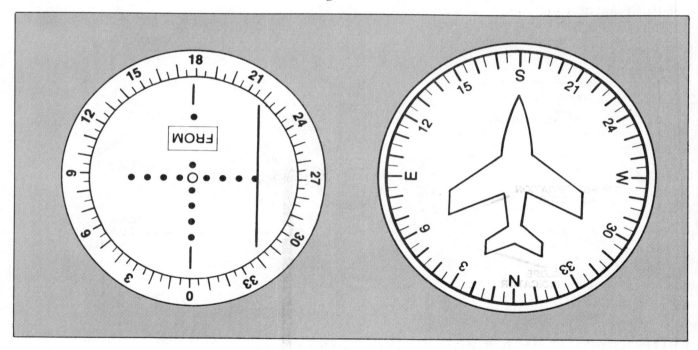

Figure 5-22

the airplane is heading south and a westerly turn is a *right* turn, away from the needle. It would be simpler if we could always intercept the course by turning towards the needle.

This would be so if the VOR unit could be swiveled so that instead of the selected course,

the airplane's heading were at the top. Better yet, suppose the VOR display automatically rotated so that the top reading was always the aircraft's heading. With this arrangement, we could always fly towards the selected course by turning towards the needle (figure 5-22).

The instrument described in principle does exist and, as up-to-date readers know, is called the **horizontal situation indicator**, or **HSI**. It is normally mounted below the artificial horizon in place of a conventional DG. It replaces both the DG and the VOR display and reduces pilot workload by lessening the number of elements in his scan. HSI's also include a glide slope needle so that an ILS can be flown with reference only to the six basic instruments. Among other advantages, the HSI offers freedom from the confusion of "reverse sensing."

The flag on the HSI also cuts the confusion sometimes caused by the TO-FROM flag. (The TO-FROM flag is sometimes called the "ambiguity meter" and like most ambiguity, it occasionally causes problems.) Instead of a conventional TO-FROM display, the HSI has a pointer in line with the CDI bar which points parallel to the selected course in the direction of the station. It can be thought of as a "to" pointer. One design of "to" pointer is shown in figure 5-23.

The HSI simplifies many navigation problems by eliminating the need for the pilot to be concerned with whether he is intercepting a radial (an outbound course) or its reciprocal (an inbound course).

With a conventional display, this distinction reverses the meaning of CDI indications. When intercepting a selected radial, the conventional "windshield wiper" type CDI points to the side of the display where the station is located before the radial is reached and swings away from the station as the radial is crossed. If an inbound course is selected, the needle swings the other way.

On an HSI, the movable portion of the CDI bar is ahead of the airplane symbol on the instrument's glass before reaching the course and behind it after crossing, regardless of whether an inbound or outbound course is selected (figure 5-24). This simplifies interception problems and is especially helpful on a DME arc.

A DME arc is flown as a sequence of tangents to a circle, a sequence of headings at approximately right angles to the radial being crossed. Radials are selected at ten degree intervals. As

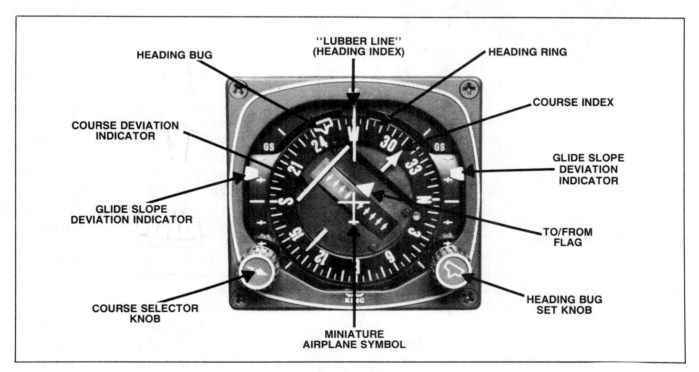

Figure 5-23

Figure 5-24

each radial is intercepted the OBS is advanced ten degrees and the heading changed ten degrees. (See Chapter Eight for a full description of DME arc orientation.) The HSI gives a convenient pictorial display of the angle between the selected radial and the heading, making it easy to hold any wind correction angle. If the arc being flown leads to an inbound course to the VOR, it is more convenient to use a sequence of inbound courses while flying the arc. With an HSI, this requires no mental adjustment on the part of the pilot.

HSI's are expensive and are currently found only in a relatively small number of general aviation aircraft. However, understanding their workings aids in understanding the operation of a standard VOR display.

Tracking

Tracking a specified course and compensating for wind, whether on instruments or visually, is basic to all flying skills. Even before venturing into the traffic pattern, the student pilot practices various ground reference maneuvers. Just tracking a straight road with a strong crosswind teaches a lot about the vicissitudes of the wind.

Route 3 runs due north from our airport. To follow Route 3, we fly over it and point the nose along it. If the wind is out of the west, we are soon east of the road. We turn 30° or 40° towards it, fly back over it and this time crab to the west to counteract the wind. Soon we are west of course. Evidently, our wind correction was too great, so we turn back to a north heading. The wind carries us back over the highway, and we try a smaller crab angle to stay above it. The new heading is successful, and we remain directly over the road, our nose pointed 10° left, into the wind. The heading that compensates for the wind and keeps us on course is known as the *reference heading* (figure 5-25).

Actually, the pilot is unconsciously processing much more information than just the heading. The exercise seems simple because, flying visually, he gets all his information at once and need not distinguish among the various elements of his "scan." The road is his course, and he easily tells if he is on course or east or west of it. Heading information comes from the angle between the road and the long axis of the airplane. To turn, he banks in the proper direction by observing his wings in relation to the horizon or ground plane. He stops the turn by leveling the wings in the same way.

Tracking an instrument course is similar to paralleling a road, but it requires more visualization and training in extracting information from the instruments. On instruments, specific types of information come from the various gauges, and each must be correctly interpreted.

There is a VOR on our local field, and the 360° radial exactly overlies Route 3. The procedure we use to track the highway also puts us on the radial. If we were on top or in the clouds, we

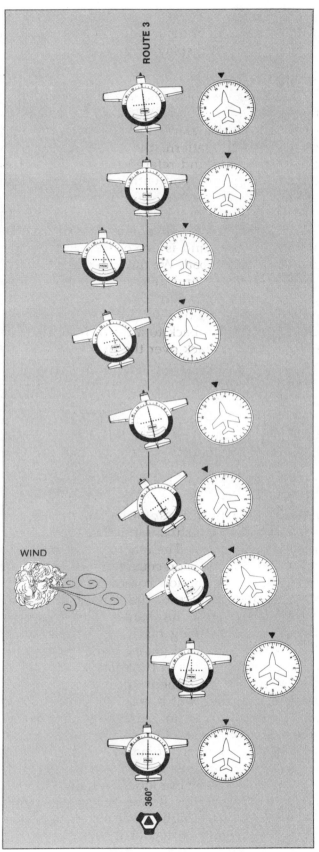

Figure 5-25

could still follow the road by tracking the radial. We would do the same things in response to the same information; only the scan would be different.

Instead of the road, the course is now the radial shown by the CDI. The heading is read on the DG, and any crab is seen as the angle between the actual heading and 360°. To make turns, we use the attitude indicator instead of the natural horizon or ground plane. Here is how the same exercise goes without visual reference (figure 5-25).

We start, as before, by intercepting the course, in this case the radial, and flying the heading that agrees with it (360° is selected in the OBS and the needle is centered). Instead of pointing the nose along the road visually, we turn to 360° on the DG. The west wind carries us east of course, and, instead of seeing the road move to the left side of the airplane, we see the CDI swing left.

We react by turning 30° west to intercept. We set up a 15° bank on the attitude indicator; we check the turn coordinator for standard rate, the VSI for steady altitude, and the DG to see how the heading is progressing. As the heading passes 337° (half the bank angle before the desired heading), we level the wings, again with reference to the attitude indicator. When the attitude indicator shows wings level, we check the DG for the desired 330°.

Now we wait to intercept the course, as shown by the CDI. As the needle swings towards center, we turn back to 345°. Since the needle moves fast this close to the station, we "lead" the turn enough so that we reach 345° just as the needle centers. This is our first approximation to the reference heading.

The correction is too great and we wind up west of course, as shown by the right-deflected needle, so we turn back to 360° and the wind carries us back to course.

Our next try at the reference heading is 350°, and to turn only 10°, we bank 10°, even though the turn is less than standard rate. When the CDI remains steady, we have found the reference heading.

So there are more similarities than differences between tracking a road and a radial. The response to the information is the same, and we maneuver in the same way. Only the source of information, the scan, differentiates one procedure from the other.

To track a course on instruments, whether it be a VOR radial, an NDB bearing, an ILS or even a DME arc, follow the same basic pattern. While each kind of tracking presents its own peculiarities, the differences are primarily in the source of course information. Tracking a road, we look outside; for a radial or localizer, we use the CDI; for an NDB course, we use the ADF; and for an arc, we use the DME.

Once the course information is interpreted, the tracking procedure is basically the same: get on course, fly the heading that agrees with the course, and observe the effect of the wind. Make small changes left and right to bracket the reference heading. Once it is known, heading control has special importance. Always, *if you hold the reference heading, you will stay on course.* The exception, of course, is when the wind changes, as it might as you descend on an approach.

To summarize the VOR course tracking process: In "no-wind" conditions, tracking a specified radial would consist of pointing the airplane towards (or away from) the station on the radial and holding your heading. However, since "no-wind" days are rare, the procedure for tracking becomes more complicated.

There is a particular heading that will exactly compensate for any wind and allow the aircraft to fly the specified course. This is called the *reference heading*. Tracking is the process of determining the reference heading by bracketing or making successive approximations.

Two fine points regarding tracking:

"**Proceed Direct**" is an ATC clearance meaning "go immediately from where you are, straight to the fix specified in the clearance." However, it is not necessary to track the exact radial you are on when you receive the clearance. You may turn towards the fix and track the course you are on after completing the turn. (Figure 5-26). When cleared "direct" to a VOR station the procedure is:

1. Center the needle with a TO.
2. Turn to the heading selected by the OBS. As you make this turn, your position will change, and the needle may move from

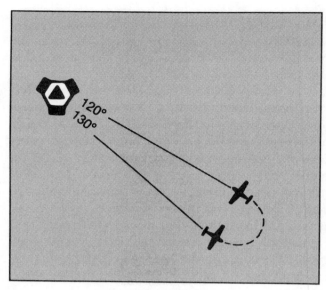

Figure 5-26

center.

3. Re-center the needle.
4. Track the indicated course to the station.

When you make a sharp turn at a VOR from an inbound course to an outbound one, the motion of the airplane will carry it beyond the intended radial. To compensate for this, turn 20° beyond the outbound course, change the OBS setting, and wait for the needle to re-center before turning back to the course (figure 5-27).

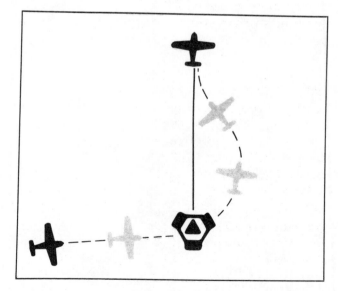

Figure 5-27

Intercepting a Specified Course

What follows is an orientation and tracking exercise which combines the skills discussed in the previous three sections.

To intercept a specified course, first determine your position with regard to the VOR. *Visualize* your position in relation to the specified radial and imagine which way you would turn to intercept it. Pick the compass direction (one of the eight points) that most nearly gives you a 90° intercept and turn to that heading. Do not bother figuring out the exact numerical heading. If you are to track outbound on the intercepted radial, select it on the OBS. If you are to track inbound on the intercepted radial, select the reciprocal course on the OBS. You can do this easily by placing the radial at the reciprocal index (bottom) of the VOR display.

To summarize: "From your present position, intercept the 090° radial, and track it outbound."

1. Determine your position (center the needle with a FROM).

2. Visualize your position in relation to the specified radial. (Assume you are south of the 090° radial.)

3. Turn to the one of the eight points that most nearly provides a 90° intercept to the desired course. (In this case, north.)

4. Twist the OBS to select the desired course.

5. Fly your heading until the needle starts to move, then gauge your turn to the outbound heading so that you reach the heading as the needle centers.

6. Track.

"From your present position, intercept the 090° radial and track it to the station."

The procedure for this assignment is the same as the last *except* that in Step 4:

4. Twist the OBS to select the *reciprocal* of the desired radial (put 090° at the reciprocal index). To fly *inbound* on the course, you need a TO indication. (Intercepting a Victor Airway to a VOR also requires selecting the reciprocal of the published course.)

"From your present position, intercept the 090° radial and track it to the JKLMN intersection."

The first three steps are the same. However, you do not know which direction to turn on the specified radial, until you determine which side of the intersection you are on.

4. Using number two VOR, determine which side of the intersection you are on. Then twist number one OBS to reflect the course you intend to fly after intercepting the specified radial.

5. Twist the number two OBS to select the *radial* of the second VOR station that defines the JKLMN intersection.

6. Intercept the radial and track to the intersection.

The Five T's

When flying an instrument procedure, such as an approach or hold entry, you are extremely busy and need a technique to accomplish all the tasks required by the procedure. A useful technique is called the "Five T's" — a little checklist for the crucial tasks at each turn and each fix (figure 5-28).

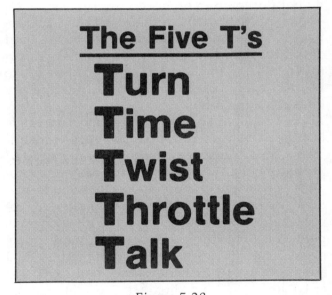

Figure 5-28

Turn. Each time you cross a fix or make a turn, get in the habit of saying "turn". Do nothing else during the turn. When it is completed:

Time. Note the time, or start the stop watch;

Twist. Change the OBS setting and/or change frequencies;

Throttle. Slow down, go down, or both;

Talk. Make any required report.

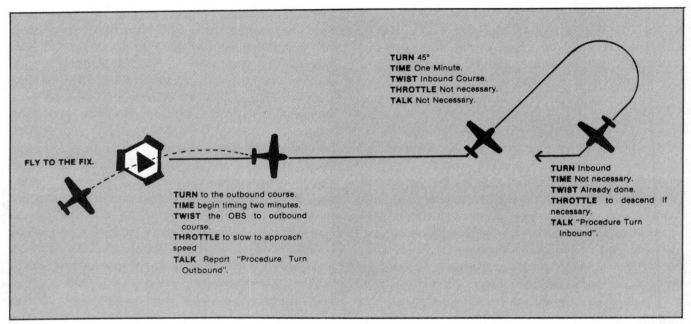

TURN 45°
TIME One Minute.
TWIST Inbound Course.
THROTTLE Not necessary.
TALK Not Necessary.

FLY TO THE FIX.

TURN to the outbound course.
TIME begin timing two minutes.
TWIST the OBS to outbound course.
THROTTLE to slow to approach speed
TALK Report "Procedure Turn Outbound".

TURN Inbound
TIME Not necessary.
TWIST Already done.
THROTTLE to descend if necessary.
TALK "Procedure Turn Inbound".

Figure 5-29

The Five T's not only list the jobs you have to do but put them in order of priority. Notice, for example, that when you are starting an approach, it is more important to begin your descent promptly than to make a timely report to ATC. Get in the habit of saying the Five T's to yourself every time you make a turn and every time you cross a fix.

The Five T's may be the most important single item in an instrument course. So much of instrument flying involves following complicated procedures that procedural errors account for a great percentage of the mistakes made by instrument pilots. In the heat of a complicated approach it is easy to forget even the most obvious part of a procedure. I have seen many pilots neglect the Five T's while crossing the final approach fix, so that they *forget to descend* and arrive over the threshold at 3000' above the airport. The Five T's are a simple and convenient checklist for remembering each step of a complex procedure.

Some pilots have objected to the Five T's as being childish and unnecessary for "grownup" pilots — a silly viewpoint; the Five T's are no more childish than the GUMPS prelanding checklist that most pilots use.

The **procedure turn** is introduced here to provide practice in using the Five T's, and

because it will be needed later, in approach work. It is a technique used when you are tracking a specific course if you want to reverse direction on the same course.

Figure 5-29 illustrates the use of the Five T's in the procedure turn. Notice that each time you go through the Five T's there may not be an action for every one. However, to avoid skipping any important step, it is good practice to say each "T" to yourself every time you make a turn and every time you cross a fix.

To The CFII

This part of the course is primarily concerned with developing mental habits, not flying the airplane. Use such devices as having the student point to the station or the course with his hand, referring to compass directions, not left or right. Continue the exercises until he knows where it is at all times. Minimize periods of straight and level flight, even on the simulator. Instead, pack as many exercises as possible into the time available. Each exercise should be terminated as soon as your student understands it and knows where he is, that is, as soon as the learning goal is achieved.

Tracking errors. The most common cause of inaccurate tracking is looking at the DG instead of the attitude indicator during the roll-out from a heading correction. Since the DG gives no bank information, it is easy to stop rolling while still slightly banked, or to bank slightly the opposite way. In either case, the heading drifts after the pilot thinks the turn is completed. To roll out accurately on a heading, he must lead the roll-out by one-half the angle of bank, and level the wings on the attitude indicator.

Another common error results from impatience. It is the tendency to make large corrections when small ones are not immediately effective. When the student turns towards the course enough, he thinks, to intercept, he should *wait* for the CDI to move. It may take a few moments. Explain that if he were half a mile east of the road he wouldn't expect to be over it immediately just because he turned 30° towards it.

The appropriate intercept angle depends on the distance from the station and the speed of CDI movement. Farther from the station, each needle position represents a larger off-course distance. The CDI moves slower than when you are closer in, and larger intercept angles are called for.

Excessively large course corrections may result in "S" turns through the course. If the student's corrections are too small, he will have trouble intercepting. If he is making excessively large or small course corrections, there are several possible explanations.

He may be watching the CDI as he turns, rather than the DG. In this case, he will continue turning until the CDI moves towards center and may wind up with a 60° or 90° intercept angle, or even turn a full circle. Explain that he should make course corrections to specific headings and that he should turn with reference to the DG and attitude indicator, not the CDI.

He shouldn't always "cut" the same number of degrees, regardless of the distance from the station. Smaller course corrections are required close to the station because the radials are closer together. The needle will move faster as the airplane crosses more radials in a shorter time. A rapidly swinging CDI is not a signal to make larger corrections, but smaller ones.

Course interception exercises. Course interception is primarily a visualization exercise, and

more can be accomplished by concentrating on the mental processes than by flying many miles. Here is an example of where the simulator outshines the airplane as a teaching tool and where a skilled instructor can maximize the use of the simulator.

A good exercise is to have the student fly a "spider web," flying outbound on the 090° radial (for example), intercepting and flying inbound on the 060° radial, intercepting and flying outbound on the 030° radial, etc.

If, in selecting a course which is not a multiple of ten, the student tends to transpose the last two digits, have him twist to the nearest multiple of 10°, then make the remaining small correction. For example, if he habitually dials 331° instead of 313°, have him select 310° first, then twist the last three degrees to 313°.

Procedure turn exercise. The main purpose of this exercise is to start developing the habit of using the Five T's.

For each procedure turn, have the student fly to the fix, turn outbound, slow to approach speed and report. Have him speed up again on procedure turn inbound, to gain more practice in the Five T's and to set himself up to start another exercise when he returns to the VOR. Alternatively, he can descend 500 feet on procedure turn inbound, leveling off before reaching the fix again.

When he is using the five T's reliably on the procedure turns, introduce a wind factor. Teach him to deduce the direction of the wind from the behavior of the CDI and to anticipate corrections during the maneuver. In planning for the wind, it is helpful to have the student indicate the wind direction on the DG with the heading bug.

VOR Quiz
1. What are the classes of VOR and what is the nominal range of each?
2. Is equipment installed at all VOR station sites to permit airborne DME to read distance from the station?
3. When identifying a VORTAC, how do you tell whether the DME portion is usable?
4. Why is it unsafe to use a VOR without properly identifying it?

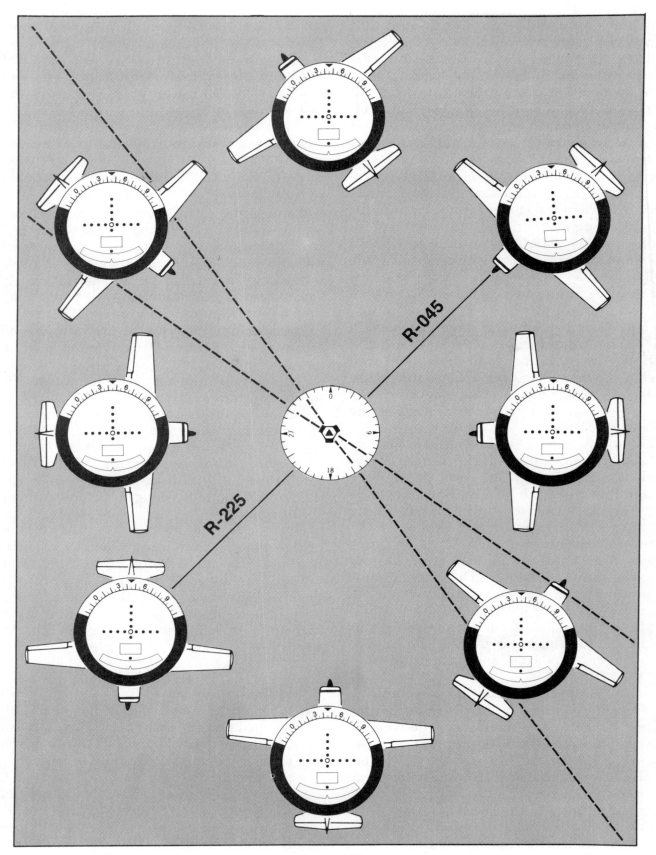

Figure 5-30

5. Is the voice identifier sufficient, or should you also listen to the Morse code?
6. How often must your VOR equipment be checked to be legal for IFR flight?
7. What are the six ways of checking your VOR equipment, and what is the proper method of performing each test?
8. What record must be kept of VOR checks, and where must it be kept?

9. What is a radial?
10. Explain the OBS and the CDI.
11. How does the cone of confusion differ from the zone of ambiguity?
12. What is the HSI?
13. How do you positively locate your position relative to a VOR?
14. What are the steps to fly "direct" to a VOR from an unknown position?

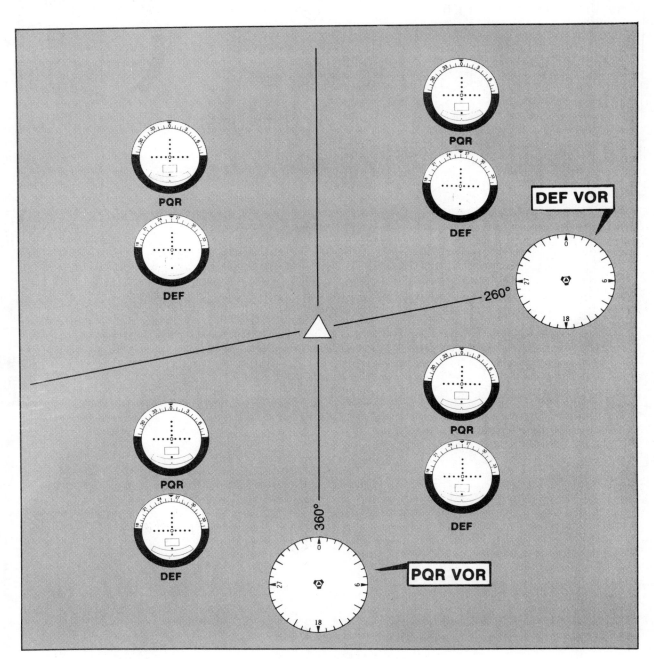

Figure 5-31

15. What are the steps to intercept a specified radial and track it inbound, starting from an unknown position?

16. If your OBS is set to 060° and your aircraft is on the 330° radial, what would the flag indicate? Explain.

17. The TO/FROM indication is "TO", you are 40 miles from the station, and the needle is full right. How would the indications change when the aircraft makes a 180 turn?

18. In figure 5-30 eight airplanes are shown geographically in relation to a VORTAC. The VOR receivers are all tuned to this station and the OBS's are all set to 045°. Draw in the correct CDI positions and the correct TO-FROM flag readings.

19. In figure 5-31, VOR displays are shown for four aircraft positions around an intersection. Fill in the correct flag and needle indications.

20. What are the Five T's?

CHAPTER SIX

ADF EQUIPMENT, ORIENTATION AND TRACKING

In many wide open areas in the center of America, the non-directional radio beacon (NDB) is an important navigation aid. A glance at a midwest low altitude chart shows airport after airport with an NDB on the field and no VOR within miles. Of 76 instrument approach equipped airports in Iowa, 66 have NDB approaches, and 34 have no other type of approach procedure.

Many NDB's are weak, with only limited range, and many NDB approaches don't allow you much below VFR minimums, but they do offer a safe means of descent and a way to locate the airport in marginal VFR or soft IFR conditions.

In the United States there are hundreds of uncontrolled airports served by NDB approaches which would otherwise be inaccessible on IFR days. For such fields, the NDB offers relatively inexpensive installation and low maintenance where more sophisticated facilities would be prohibitively costly. Sometimes an owner or major user of an airport will establish an NDB at his own expense. For cost reasons, the beacon is often on the field rather than on leased property beneath the final approach course. At more affluent fields, the Outer Compass Locator (LOM) is a small NDB that gives valuable information during an ILS approach.

Although NDB approaches offer less course accuracy than other instrument approaches, many have minimums of 500 foot ceiling and one mile visibility, allowing arrivals in fairly bad weather. Terrain clearance, however, on straight-in NDB approaches is greater than on VOR approaches with the same structure (see the Appendix for details of obstacle clearance).

With the widespread establishment of VOR's, the old low/medium frequency "colored" (Green and Red ran east and west, Amber and Blue ran north and south) airway system has long been replaced in the 48 states by the present Victor Airway system. However, in parts of Alaska, Canada, and some foreign countries, low frequency beacons still form the en route airway structure. Even jet routes are predicated on NDB's in some places. In parts of the world where ADF is the main navigation tool for en route as well as terminal operations, many aircraft are equipped with dual sets, just as we have dual VOR's. Virtually all large airliners have dual ADF receivers.

Lack of experience with ADF procedures and perhaps incomplete or confusing training originally, makes many pilots reluctant to use NDB approaches. But these approaches are a valuable option, and when other equipment fails, the ADF is a good backup.

Of all the instrument pilot's skills, mastery of

the ADF may be the most mysterious and elusive. This innocent instrument, which simply points to the chosen station, is the one which most pilots have the most difficulty learning. Perhaps part of the problem is that even many flight instructors are not familiar enough with ADF to clearly present its peculiarities. The good news about ADF is that, once it is understood thoroughly, it is easy to use — perhaps even easier than VOR.

The Equipment

The **Automatic Direction Finder (ADF)** is a low frequency radio receiver, compatible with signals in the 200-1600 KHz frequency range. The 540-1650 KHz range contains the commercial A.M. broadcast stations, so, when flight conditions permit, the ADF can be used to listen to baseball scores, news, and rock and roll. The 190-535 KHz frequency range is assigned to the non-directional radio beacons (NDB).

The ADF has two antennas. Known as the loop and the sense antennas, They use the directional properties of low frequency radio waves (remember how a portable A.M. radio fades when you rotate it?) to determine the direction to the selected station.

A fairly recent development in ADF technology, now available in several makes of light airplane equipment, is called "synchronous" or "coherent detection."

Standard radio turning circuits work by blocking everything that comes in on the antenna, but leaving a narrow opening around the selected frequency through which the station can be received. This works fine except when there is a large amount of noise or interference; then, these nuisance signals leak in through the opening, sometimes drowning out the desired station completely. This interference can be cut down by narrowing the opening, but this also reduces the sensitivity of the receiver to desired signals.

In simple terms, a coherent detection system internally generates a signal on the same frequency as the desired station, and then searches through the material coming in on the antenna for the same thing. If it finds something, it "locks on" to it, and is then able to cut out almost everything else.

This enables the equipment to receive stations that would be "buried in the noise" for other ADF's, and permits greater success in resisting the attempts of electrically noisy thunderstorms to woo the ADF needle into pointing at them.

It also allows the use of very compact combined loop/sense antennas, which unfortunately often reduces the performance of the sets to that of conventional ADF's.

While commercial broadcast stations often offer the best reception on the ADF, they do not identify themselves frequently enough to be used legally for IFR navigation in these modern times.

(Broadcast stations were used for ADF approaches in the past. For example, United Airlines used to get into Visalia, California, using KVIS. They had an agreement with the station under which the UAL crew would radio their agent at Visalia, he would phone the radio station, and the announcer would break into the programming with, "Hello, United Flight . . . ., this is K-V-I-S, Visalia!")

Even today, commercial broadcast stations are excellent as VFR homing devices, and can often be used over hundreds of miles. Listings are available of the names and locations of all commercial broadcast stations in the country.*

The NDB transmits an amplitude modulated (A.M.) signal with an audible Morse code identifier. Some NDB's may also carry voice transmissions (weather, etc.) which override the identifying code. When using an NDB for navigation, always tune and identify the station carefully. With the older, continuous tuning scale sets, getting the station exactly can be quite a chore, and using the wrong station can have serious consequences, especially on an approach.

Low frequency signals are not limited to line-of-sight reception, as are VHF signals. Thus, if the transmitting power is high enough, the NDB signal is usable at low altitudes and great distances from the station.

---

*See *"ADF Directory & Manual"* by Skip Carden. Available at $10.00 from Aviation Book Co., 25133 Anza Dr., Santa Clarita, CA 91355.

NDB's are grouped in four classes. *HH* class beacons transmit with at least 2000 watts of power and have a range of at least 75 miles. They are normally used for long over water routes. *H* class beacons have a power output of from 50 to 1999 watts and a range up to 50 miles. *MH* class beacons are the most common in the continental United States; they have a power output of less than 50 watts, and a range of 25 miles.

Each of these classes broadcasts a continuous three letter Morse code identifier, which is interrupted when there is a voice transmission, such as a transcribed weather broadcast (TWEB) on the frequency. If the station has no voice capability, the class designator is given a final "W", e.g., class *MHW*. On government charts the frequency is underlined.

The last class of NDB is the *compass locator*, which has a power output of less than 25 watts and a range of 15 miles. Compass locators are part of instrument landing systems (ILS) and are usually collocated with the outer marker. The class designator is LOM (for Locator Outer Marker), and the identifier is the first two letters of the ILS identifier. For example, if the ILS is IJFK, the LOM identifier will be JF. Compass locators at the middle marker are known as locator middle markers (LMM's). Their identifier is the last two letters of the localizer identification — e.g., if the localizer is IJFK, the LMM would be FK. LMM's are being phased out by the FAA.

Any individual beacon may have a range significantly better or worse than these standards. Some NDB's in remote areas are so weak that they are hard to find on approach and hard to keep in range during the procedure turn. By contrast, some strong HH class beacons can be received reliably for hundreds of miles.

While not limited to line of sight transmission, low and medium frequency radio beacons do have drawbacks not shared with VHF stations.

Unless the alternator of an aircraft is properly shielded, it may disable the ADF. Improperly installed strobe light systems and bad ignition harnesses are other sources of ADF interference. A needle that points to the alternator is not very informative on a tight approach! If you suspect that your instrument is doing this,

consider turning off the alternator for the few minutes the approach is in progress.

Around sunrise and sunset, erratic ADF indications may be noticed at long distances from the station. This is due to the signal's being reflected by the ionosphere and may be reduced by flying at a higher altitude, or selecting a station with a lower frequency.

In mountainous areas, the signal can be reflected by irregular terrain or magnetic deposits, which cause erratic indications. A higher altitude or a stronger station are solutions to this problem.

The NDB signal can be bent in areas where it crosses a shoreline. This problem is more pronounced close to the shore and can be avoided by using a bearing as nearly as possible perpendicular to the shoreline.

Near thunderstorms, the ADF has a tendency to point towards lightning discharges and to give erratic indications owing to "precipitation static." The latter phenomenon tends to spoil the instrument's performance precisely when it is needed most, in bad weather. Precipitation static can be reduced by putting static dischargers on the trailing edges of the wings.

Especially at night, it is possible to receive signals from a distant station on the same frequency as the one in use. For this reason and because the ADF dial typically has no failure flag or indicator, some pilots continuously monitor the NDB identifier during an ADF approach.

The ADF should be tuned with the function switch in the *Receive* or *Antenna* position. When the identifier is clearly heard, switch to the *ADF* position and the needle should swing towards the station. Use the *Test* function to swing the needle away from the selected station and determine that it returns smartly to the proper position. During the preflight check, it is good practice to tune and identify a nearby NDB.

The *BFO* (beat frequency oscillator) position of the ADF function switch is used for tuning continuous wave (as opposed to A.M.) signals. This type of signal is not used in the United States.

The Poor Man's RMI
ADF is very simple. All it does is point to the

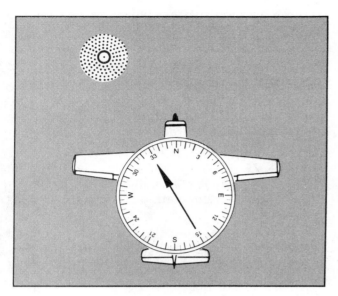

Figure 6-1

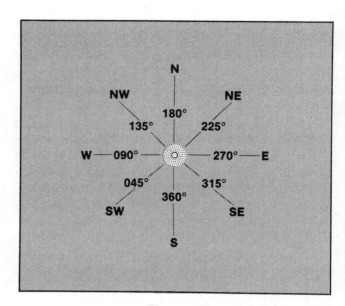

Figure 6-2

station. In figure 6-1, the NDB is in front of and to the left of the aircraft. In old fashioned terminology, its **relative bearing** is 330°. Since the airplane would turn 30° left to fly to the station, a more convenient expression of this is to say the station is 30° left of the nose. The concept of relative bearing is cumbersome, and it is usually more practical to express the NDB's position with respect to the airplane as a number of degrees left or right of the nose or tail.

An airplane's **magnetic bearing**, or more simply, **bearing**, is its direct course *to* the NDB. The eight cardinal bearings of an NDB are shown in figure 6-2.

Magnetic bearing is the basic information the pilot uses to visualize his position around an NDB. Notice the difference from VOR work. Bearings are courses *to* the NDB, while VOR radials are courses *from* the VOR. You can speak of bearings *from* an NDB (controllers sometimes do), but the preposition "from" must be stated. A bearing *from* the station is simply the reciprocal of the corresponding bearing *to* (figure 6-3).

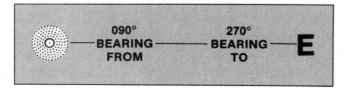

Figure 6-3

Where a published NDB bearing is used to define an intersection, it is invariably a bearing *to*. On an approach procedure where an inbound and an outbound bearing must be flown, both are published. The traditional way of determining your bearing to the NDB is the old formula:

Relative Bearing + Magnetic Heading =
Magnetic Bearing.

In figure 6-4, the relative bearing is 330°, and the magnetic heading is 240°:

330° + 240° = 570°

Subtracting 360° to get us back in the first turn around the compass:

570° - 360° = 210°,

we get a magnetic bearing to the station of 210°.

While this is a good method for working problems on written tests, it is hardly something you want to do in the cockpit, with or without a calculator. Look again at figure 6-4. Using our simplified phrasing, the station is 30° to the left of the nose. From the DG, we see that if the airplane turns thirty degrees left, it will be heading 210°. *Voila*, our magnetic bearing to the

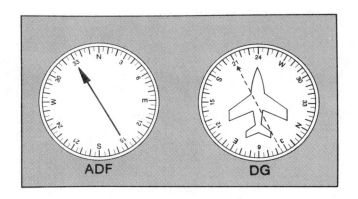

Figure 6-4

station, the same result with a lot less figuring.

Once you know your bearing to the station, visualize the ADF compass rose (figure 6-2) to determine your position. In the example, your bearing is 210°; therefore you are northeast of the NDB.

This process mentally superimposes the ADF needle on the DG so that you can read the bearing at the imaginary arrow head. The tail of the imaginary needle gives the bearing *from* the NDB. This method always works, and it eliminates arithmetic in the cockpit, a worthwhile goal.

The mental process just described is accomplished mechanically by the **radio magnetic indicator (RMI)**. The RMI has long been favored by airlines and the military and is occasionally seen in general aviation aircraft. It is a combination DG and ADF. As the airplane turns, the card turns, so that the heading is always read from the top of the dial, just as on a conventional DG. At the same time, the needle swings, continuously pointing towards the station and giving the aircraft's bearing to it. With an RMI, all navigation information is read directly from that instrument, and the pilot's job is considerably simplified. Most RMI's can be tuned to two facilities at once and can receive VOR as well as NDB stations.

Viewing the ADF as we have above, as the "poor man's RMI," eliminates the need for the confusing term "relative bearing," an expression that frequently leads to errors. When preparing for a flight test, however, you'll be wise to remember the definition of "relative bearing," as it appears occasionally among an examiner's oral questions. Relative bearing is merely the number to which the ADF needle points, on the ADF dial.

Since the bearing to the NDB is read directly from the DG, the DG must be set correctly. Check the DG against the magnetic compass before beginning any ADF work, and frequently while doing it. What if you lose the DG? Don't despair. Either rotate the ADF card, if it is movable, or rotate the DG card to agree with the heading you read off the compass. Don't forget to cover the DG once you're done with it, so you don't follow a dead instrument. While this procedure might be considered chancy in actual conditions, a partial panel approach is currently part of every instrument rating flight test, and you may be asked to do it.

The movable card ADF is a compromise between the RMI and the "poor man's RMI." This device has a knob for manually turning the ADF card to agree with the DG. Like many compromise solutions, it works better in theory than in practice. While it certainly does allow you to read your bearing directly from the ADF, it increases pilot workload rather than reducing it. On an approach, there are enough knobs to twist and things to remember without one more task after every heading change. Although it may be useful for identifying en route intersections, it is easier and safer to find your bearing during an approach by cross checking the ADF and DG, than to use a movable card ADF.

Intercepting a Specified Bearing

When radar-vectored to intercept a specific bearing of an NDB — as when vectored to an NDB final approach course — the element most likely to confuse the average instrument pilot is the concept of *intercepting* the final approach course. When intercepting a specified bearing, just how do you know when you are on course?

Most ADF navigation problems arise not in misreading position in relation to a station, but in relation to a specified course. To intercept a specific bearing of an NDB, the first step is to determine your intercept angle.

The **intercept angle** is the difference between your intercept heading and the course being intercepted. Determine it by counting degrees on the DG between the two numbers. When

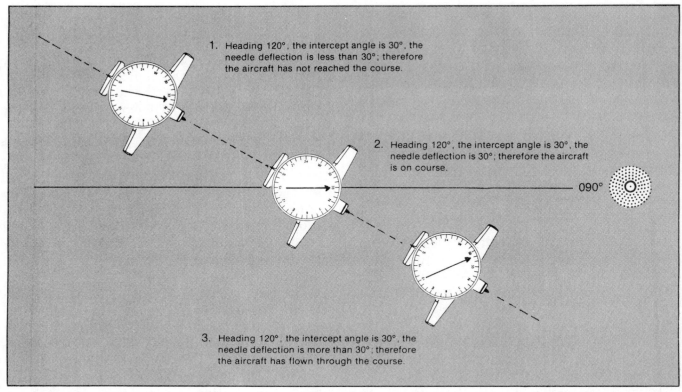

1. Heading 120°, the intercept angle is 30°, the needle deflection is less than 30°; therefore the aircraft has not reached the course.

2. Heading 120°, the intercept angle is 30°, the needle deflection is 30°; therefore the aircraft is on course.

090°

3. Heading 120°, the intercept angle is 30°, the needle deflection is more than 30°; therefore the aircraft has flown through the course.

Figure 6-5

flying a conventional procedure turn, the intercept angle with the final approach course is 45°. When radar vectored to an approach, the intercept angle is usually about 30° (figure 6-5).

Figure 6-6 shows the ADF and DG readings for the three aircraft positions in figure 6-5. At position 1, the ADF needle is 20° left of the nose, showing that the airplane would have to turn 20° left, to a heading of 100°, to point directly at the beacon. Superimposing the needle on the DG shows its bearing to the station is 100°; it is north of course. Similarly, superimposing the ADF needle on the DG at position 2 shows your bearing to the station is 90°; you are on course. *You are on course when the ADF needle deflection equals the angle of intercept.*

When intercepting any bearing, the needle will always move towards the back of the airplane, i.e. toward the bottom of the dial. Thus, when intercepting a bearing to fly inbound, if the needle deflection is greater than the angle of intercept, you have already flown through the course, as in figure 6-6, position 3. The needle will not move back towards the nose. Forgetting this, and consequently flying

well beyond the desired bearing, is a common error in ADF intercept work.

Intercepting an outbound bearing is similar to intercepting an inbound bearing, but there are important differences in the needle indications. Suppose you are approaching the beacon from the west, cleared to cross the fix and fly outbound on the 270° bearing *from* the station. Your job is to cross over the NDB, turn left approximately 210°, to a heading of 240°, for a 30° intercept angle with the 270° bearing from the station (figure 6-7).

Figure 6-8 shows the aircraft before intercepting, on course, and having passed through the course, while figure 6-9 shows the corresponding ADF and DG indications. Once again, the needle moves towards the back of the airplane and *you are on course when the needle deflection equals the angle of intercept*. In figure 6-9 position 2, mentally superimposing the ADF needle on the DG reveals that your bearing to the station is 90°, the course you are intercepting. If the needle is closer to the tail than 30°, you have flown through the course and forgotten to turn.

One goal of ADF practice is to recognize and

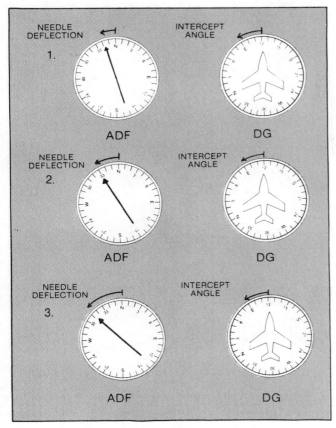

Figure 6-6

Figure 6-7

quickly interpret needle indications that are different from what you expect. For example, if you finished your turn to heading 240° and immediately saw the indication in figure 6-9 position 3, you should recognize you have flown a pattern such as that shown in figure 6-10, possibly because of a north wind.

Figure 6-11 shows two other unexpected needle indications that you might see after completing your turn to 240°. Can you see what might have gone wrong and where the airplane is?

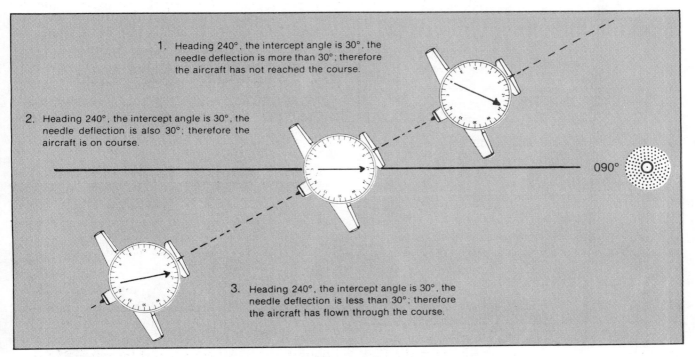

1. Heading 240°, the intercept angle is 30°, the needle deflection is more than 30°; therefore the aircraft has not reached the course.

2. Heading 240°, the intercept angle is 30°, the needle deflection is also 30°; therefore the aircraft is on course.

3. Heading 240°, the intercept angle is 30°, the needle deflection is less than 30°; therefore the aircraft has flown through the course.

090°

Figure 6-8

113

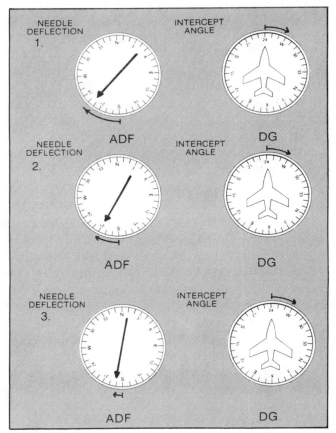

Figure 6-9

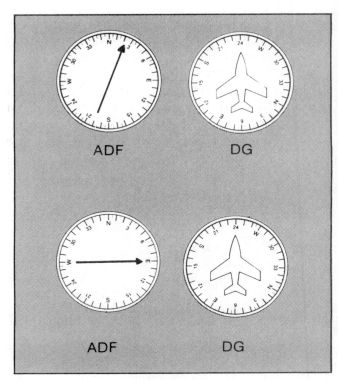

Figure 6-11

In the top illustration, the aircraft position is shown in figure 6-12. Either a west wind carried you well past the station as you turned, or owing to a cockpit distraction, you missed station passage and began the turn a few moments late.

Figure 6-13 shows the aircraft position corresponding to the second illustration. Here you had a combination of the problems illustrated in figures 6-10 and 6-12, i.e. a northwest wind and possibly a delayed pilot response to station passage.

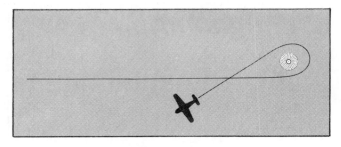

Figure 6-10

Figure 6-12

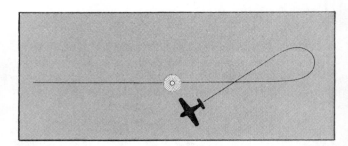

Figure 6-13

Tracking Inbound

To fly to an NDB, you could simply turn towards the station and, each time the wind caused you to drift, turn slightly to keep the needle on the nose of the airplane. This would certainly get you to the station, although by a curved path and not on the original bearing. You would reach the beacon heading into the wind (figure 6-14). This process is called homing, as opposed to tracking, and should be avoided during instrument flight.

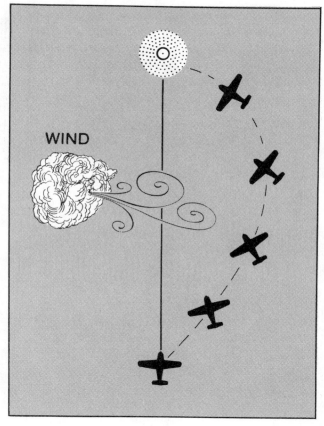

WIND

Figure 6-14

If homing were used on the final approach to Runway 18 at an airport with the NDB on the field, with a strong west wind blowing, the aircraft would reach the runway from the east instead of on course. In addition to requiring a possibly dangerous turn to line up with the runway, homing might take the aircraft out of the obstacle clearance area for the final descent.

To *track* an NDB course, we must determine the heading that will compensate for wind drift and keep the aircraft on the desired bearing. As in VOR tracking, we find this **reference heading** by bracketing.

The first approximation to the reference heading is the heading which agrees with the course (figure 6-15). Think of it as the first trial of a trial-and-error process — just to see what the wind will do to you. As wind drift occurs, the ADF needle will swing away from the nose *towards the course*. Notice that it also points towards the wind.

To correct, turn to intercept the course. If the correction equaled the off course indication, you would head directly towards the station and would not intercept the course before reaching it. You would be homing. Therefore, *the minimum intercept angle is the smallest angle which will cause the ADF needle to cross the nose.* A good rule of thumb is to double the off-course indication and turn that many degrees towards the needle. (In figure 6-15, the off course indication is 20° and the airplane turns 40°.)

If the intercept angle is big enough the needle will cross the nose and continue moving towards the wing.

The "double the angle" rule is just a rule of thumb which must occasionally be broken. While it does work in most cases, the rule is not a perfect method for all situations. It will fail when you are very close to the station or when the off course indication is very large. Close to the station, smaller corrections are called for, just as in VOR tracking, because the bearings are close together. Though you may find a large off course indication far from the station, you never want an intercept angle of more than 90°; usually, 60° is ample.

When the needle deflection equals the intercept angle, you are crossing the desired bearing, i.e., you have re-intercepted the course. Then turn back towards the original heading by half the intercept angle (20° in figure 6-15) and try this as your reference heading.

Additional corrections will be smaller and smaller in your series of trials and errors. If the needle moves towards the wing, the wind correction angle is too big and you are flying through the course. Turn back to the original heading and allow the airplane to drift back on course. Then try a smaller wind correction

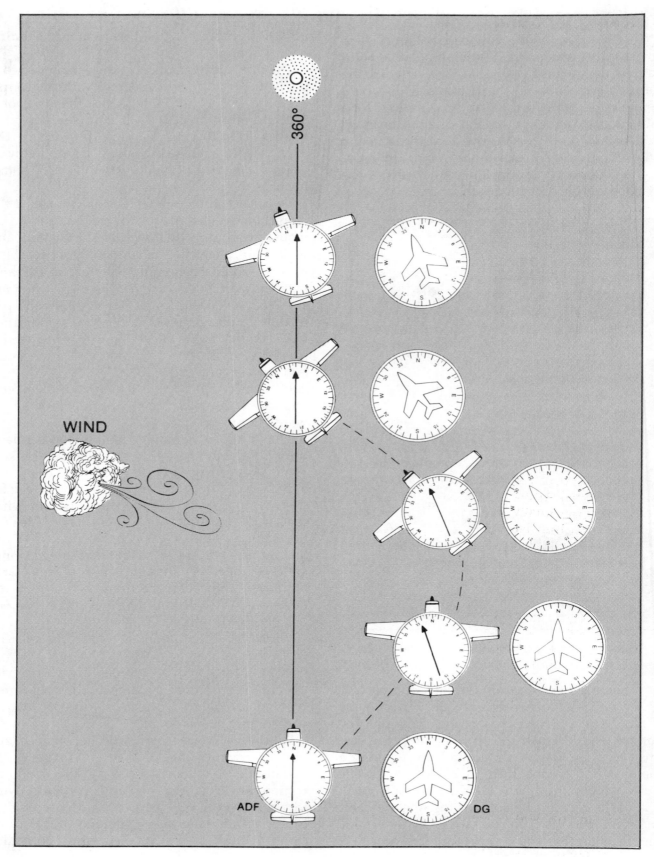

360°

WIND

ADF

DG

Figure 6-15

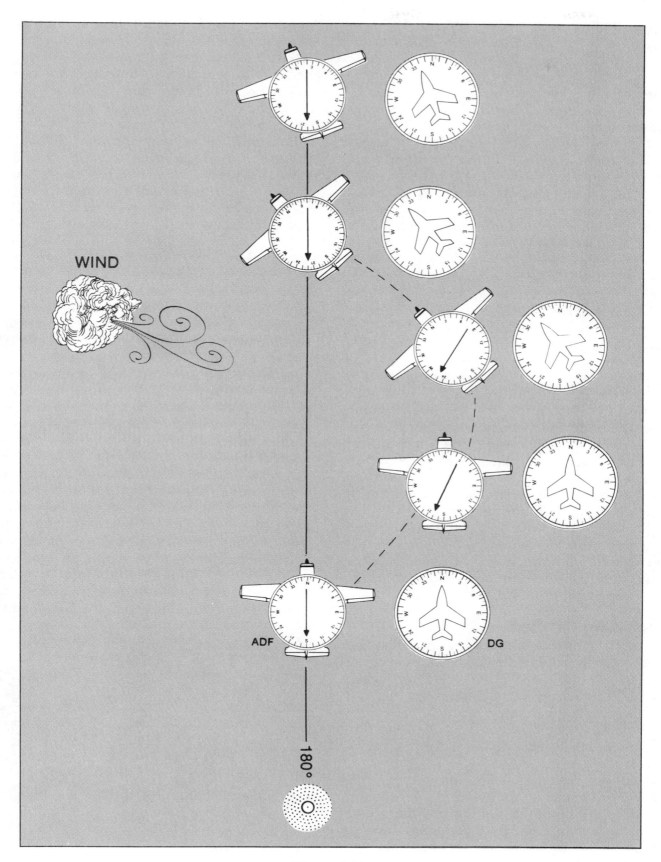

WIND

ADF

DG

180°

Figure 6-16

angle. If the needle moves towards the nose again, the wind correction angle is too small and you are being carried away from the course. Turn back to an intercept heading by doubling the needle deflection angle, until you re-intercept the course. In either case, turn in the direction of the needle's *trend*.

Continue the bracketing process with successively smaller corrections until you know exactly what the reference heading is. At each stage, holding heading exactly and making precise corrections is the key to success. Since navigation information comes from cross checking the ADF and DG, it is only as good as your heading which must be steady to be reliably informative. *If at any time you become unsure which side of the course you are on, turn to the heading that agrees with the course and the ADF will point to the course.*

As you near the station, the needle will move to one side. If you pass directly over the NDB, it will swing smartly to the tail, but if you miss by a short distance, the needle will dawdle as it drifts around. Resist the temptation to chase the needle. Once you realize you are close to station passage, hold the reference heading that has been working. Remember, "the wind doesn't change at the station." If you track outbound on the same course, the same reference heading will work. Station passage has occurred when the needle passes the wing.

If your tracking exercise is part of an approach and you begin descending at station passage, the reference heading may change, as the wind shifts during the descent. Be prepared to change your heading if necessary.

Tracking Outbound

Tracking outbound is similar in method to tracking inbound, but the needle indications are somewhat different (figure 6-16). Once again, let's begin tracking on the desired bearing, and on the heading that agrees with the course. Be sure the heading is correct. If you have just left the beacon, the needle will be on the tail regardless of the heading.

If the needle drifts off the tail, you are being carried off course by the wind. As in inbound tracking, the needle points towards the course line and towards the wind. As before, double the off course indication (waiting until the

needle is 5° or 10° off the tail) and turn that much towards the needle. Now here is the big difference between outbound and inbound tracking: as you turn to intercept, the needle will move towards the wing, *it will not cross the tail* as it did the nose during inbound tracking. (figure 6-16).

If the intercept angle is large enough, holding that intercept heading will cause the needle to move back towards the tail. When the deflection angle from the tail equals the intercept angle, you are on course but on a heading that will take you right through it. So turn halfway back to the heading that agrees with the course. The needle will then move back towards the tail. If this new heading is your reference heading, given the wind, the needle will maintain a steady position. As with inbound bracketing, if the needle continues to move, keep seeking the reference heading with successively smaller corrections.

If, at any time during the tracking process, you become unsure of your position, turn immediately to parallel the course. The needle will then point towards the course, whether you are tracking inbound or outbound, and you can re-intercept by doubling the angle and turning towards the needle.

A more sophisticated method of determining which side of the course you are on is to notice the position of the ADF needle, as superimposed on the DG, *in relation to the desired course*. If the needle is to the right of the desired course, the course is to your right and you may correct to the right. If it is to the left, fly left. In figure 6-17, you would fly left to intercept the 240° bearing, right to intercept the 180° bearing.

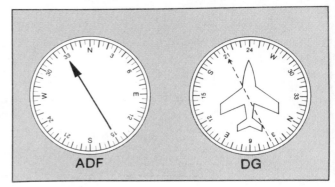

ADF   DG

Figure 6-17

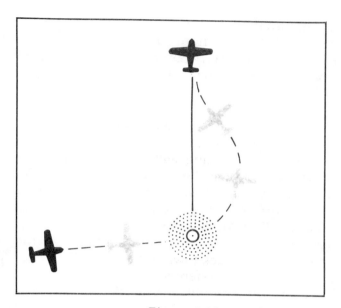

Figure 6-18

In tracking outbound, notice what happens when you cross the fix to turn outbound on a specified bearing. The needle points to the tail, regardless of your heading, and may give the false impression that you are on course. You are on course when the needle is on the tail only when you are also on the heading that agrees with the course. Remember, the needle points at the station. Your airplane's nose points at your heading. The right *combination* of heading (crab) and wind directon will keep the airplane planted on the course.

As you cross the NDB and turn to the outbound course, the needle will most likely be far from the tail. Do not make a large correction until you have flown at least a mile from the station and the needle has had a chance to swing around to the tail. If you make a large turn over the station, a 20° intercept heading is appropriate (figure 6-18). At station passage, the needle will be on the wing, even if you are directly over the fix.

The Procedure Turn

A procedure turn on an NDB bearing is the same as a procedure turn on a radial, but, of course, the needle indications are different (figure 6-19). There is never any "twisting," but remain in the habit of saying each of the five T's.

Begin by crossing the fix. Then track outbound two minutes, and make a 45° turn to the specified side. At this point, the ADF needle should be 45° off the tail and it will move towards the tail during the next minute. It should reach the 30° position from the tail — if it doesn't, you may be bucking a headwind and would be advised to go outbound a little longer to avoid flying through the inbound course during your 180° turn. If the ADF gets closer than 30° to the tail, the chances are that your leg after the 180° turn will be a little longer than usual.

After the 180° turn, the needle should be close

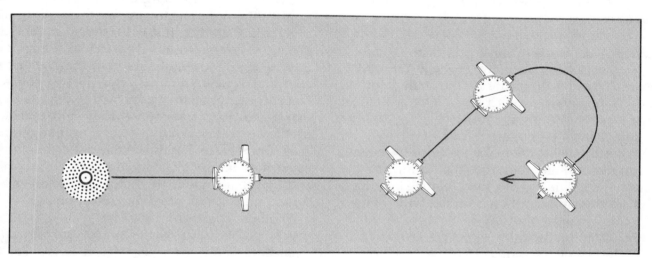

Figure 6-19

to the nose, moving towards the wing. Since your angle of intercept with the inbound course is now 45°, you should turn inbound when the needle reaches the 45° position (lead the turn slightly).

Once you have learned the needle indications at each point of the maneuver, introduce a wind factor and study the behavior of the needle in such conditions. When you understand what the ADF gauge is telling you, you will be able to appreciate the similarities between VOR and ADF procedure turns.

To The CFII

The comments in Chapter 5 regarding the objectives of orientation training apply equally to VOR and ADF work. The student must learn to *visualize* his position; these chapters are designed to develop mental habits, not airplane control. Have him be constantly aware of his position, frequently pointing to the course with his hand and describing his position in terms of compass direction — not left and right. During training and practice minimize straight and level flight, especially on the simulator. Do as many exercises as possible in the available time. Emphasize understanding of position.

It is important that the student *master* this material now. If he doesn't, the rest of the course will be difficult and chaotic — as will his attempts at radio navigation. Remember the building block theory of learning: you can't build a strong pyramid with a weak base.

Exercise on determining position

To develop the habit of checking the ADF against the DG, position the simulator at various positions around the NDB, asking at each spot, "What is your bearing to the station?" and "Where are you?"

Students commonly make the error of reading bearing to the station off the ADF, confusing the "magnetic bearing" with the "relative bearing." To clear this up point to the station with a finger and then look at the DG to determine which way to fly to it. The number off the DG, naturally, is the correct bearing.

Another common error is to know the bearing to the station but misjudge his position by 180°. He might think, for example, that if his bearing

is 045° then he is northeast of the station. Emphasize the difference between VOR radials and NDB bearings. VOR radials point outward from the station, the ADF needle points *at* and *to* the station.

Exercise on intercepting specified bearings.

The goal is to have the student quickly and accurately determine the intercept angle and to recognize when he is on course. It is another instance where simulator work directed by an experienced instructor can get the skills accross many times faster than is possible in the airplane.

Exercise on tracking inbound.

Before practicing inbound tracking, have the student home on the station first. Use a maximum crosswind on the simulator and observe that the "airplane" reaches the beacon heading into the wind. If you have a plotter, this can be an especially dramatic demonstration. Notice that if you were flying an approach and the runway lay underneath the course you were supposed to be flying, the homing method would eliminate your chances of landing and increase your chances of hitting something other than the runway.

Have the student point his arm to the station as he turns, and visualize why the needle behaves as it does. Suppose the needle is 10° right of the nose and he knows he is supposed to turn 20° to the right. Students commonly make the error of remembering that the needle was 10° right, seeing it 10° left at the end of the turn and concluding that they are on course. Not surprisingly, when they turn to the heading that agrees with the course, they find that the needle doesn't return to the zero position on the ADF. Emphasize that the needle deflection must equal the *intercept angle* to show him on course and that this angle is the number of degrees he turned *since he was paralleling* the course.

Another common error is to believe the needle points towards the course on the ADF regardless of the heading, which is not so. It always points to the *station*. In particular, after the intercept heading is established, the needle points away from the course itself. If the needle is mentally superimposed on the DG, it does point to the course *on the DG.*

Under pressure, even a pilot who understands ADF tracking will mistakenly turn to put the needle on the nose, thinking that means he is on course. The only remedy I know for such occasional lapses is to intersperse practice with practice and more practice.

Don't ask your student to fly outbound on bearings "to." Talk about bearings "from," but remember to mention the preposition. Controllers sometimes omit the "from" when talking about an outbound bearing. Explain that if he suspects an ATC clearance like this, he should request clarification.

ADF Quiz

1. What are the four different classes of NDBs and their nominal range?
2. What are the two types of antenna an ADF uses?
3. How should you check the ADF radio for proper operation before takeoff?
4. Will low altitude affect the reception of an NDB?
5. What other types of phenomenon affect NDB reception?
6. Define bearing.
7. What is the intercept angle and how is it determined?
8. Why should homing be avoided during IFR flight?
9. To track an NDB course, what must be determined first?
10. What is an RMI?
11. On what side of an NDB is the 240° bearing to the station located?
12. Your Heading is 330°. The ADF needle is pointing 30° to the right of your nose. What is your position in reference to the eight cardinal points?
13. Your heading is 040°. The ADF needle is 20° to the right of your tail. What is your approximate position in relation to the eight cardinal points?
14. What are the steps for making a procedure turn on an NDB bearing?

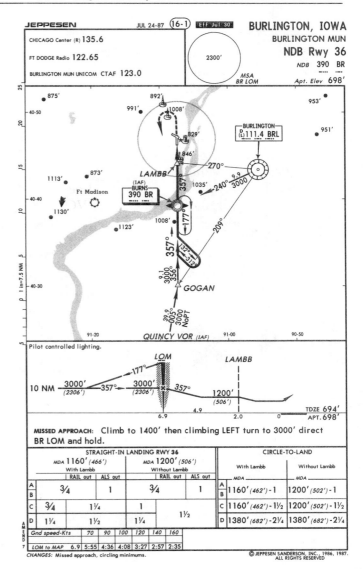

Figure 6-20

You are planning an NDB Runway 36 approach to Burlington Municipal Airport, Burlington, Iowa. (Figure 6-20.) You are cleared to the Burlington VORTAC at 5000' and cleared for the approach. Center advises you to contact Burlington Unicom for advisories.

15. What is the nominal power and range of the Burns non-directional beacon?
16. - 20. In these questions, an ADF and a DG are shown as they would appear at a certain stage of the approach (figures 6-21 and 6-22). In each case, state where you are on the approach.

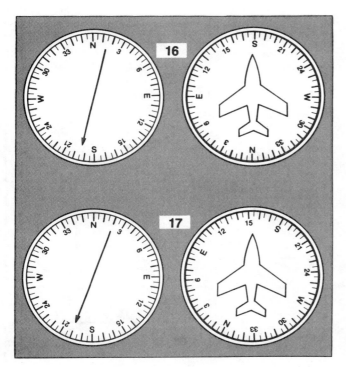

Figure 6-21

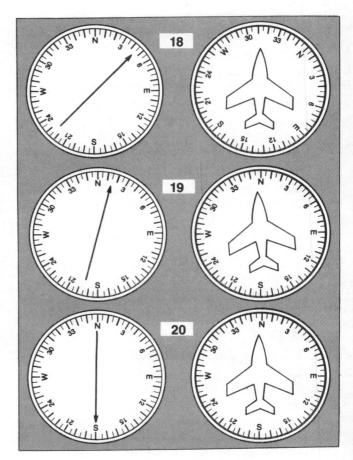

Figure 6-22

CHAPTER SEVEN

HOLDING

My student, Bill, was flying as we approached the VOR from the west to hold northeast. There was a strong northwest wind and we were south of the airway most of the time; the CDI was left of center. As we passed abeam of the VORTAC, the flag changed to FROM, we turned to the reciprocal of the holding course, and Bill dialed the inbound course. Naturally, the left crosswind carried us further from the course.

At the end of a minute we turned left 180° and took up the inbound heading to complete our parallel entry, but were still on the non-holding side, as was shown by a right needle. Naturally, the wind continued to carry us further onto the non-holding side and as the needle reached full scale, I wondered if we were still within protected airspace.

For traffic separation, ATC reserves an area of protected airspace around any holding aircraft, from which all other IFR traffic is banned. The amount of airspace protected for a holding pattern increases with altitude, but in a one minute holding pattern at a VOR at any altitude, the airplane will be within the protected area as long as the CDI is deflected less than full scale.

We passed the fix again and turned right. The flag changed back to TO, but the needle stayed to the right. **We were still on the non-holding side**. The correct action would have been to correct towards the course and make the inbound turn to the left, trying to intercept. Unfortunately, Bill failed to recognize the meaning of the right needle, became disoriented,

and turned "inbound" to the right, carrying us further to the non-holding side.

It was a practice flight in VFR conditions, and we were not on a clearance, so I refrained from criticizing and waited to see what would develop. Each outbound turn was compressed by the northwest headwind, and each inbound turn was extended by the tailwind, carrying us further and further from the protected area. The resulting pattern is shown in figure 7-1. I believe this is what radar controllers call "spaghetti." An embarrassing picture that, in real weather, would be far from safe.

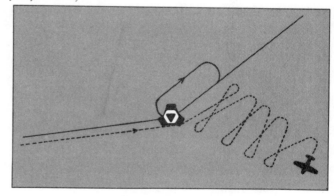

Figure 7-1

The exercise continued for several circuits, about 20 minutes, before I discontinued it. I realized in retrospect that it had been a waste of valuable training time. It also showed an error in course organization: understanding of orientation and wind effects should *have been thoroughly covered on the simulator before venturing into the airplane.*

A few months later, well after Bill had obtained his rating, I went on a short refresher flight with him and had the pleasure of seeing him expertly handle an almost identical situation. We were approaching the Hartford VORTAC at 6000 feet in a rough cumulus overcast when the radio crackled and Bradley Approach unexpectedly came on with a holding clearance. Victor 3 doglegged at Hartford from the 078° inbound course to the 057° outbound, and we had not received a clearance beyond Hartford. (a situation very similar to figure 7-1). The ride was bumpy inside the clouds, and Bill held a 10° correction against the blustery northwest wind. A rear seat passenger was slightly airsick, and we were anxious to reach Worcester, our destination. The last thing we needed was an en route hold.

"Skylane three four five papa fox, hold northeast of Hartford on the 057° radial, one minute legs, right turns." The DME showed 10 miles from Hartford, which, at 120 knots, meant five minutes. The controller had given us the minimum advance warning specified in his handbook.

"Hold northeast of Hartford on the 057° radial," Bill acknowledged, "one minute legs, right turns, five papa fox." Then, concerned at the lack of an expect further clearance time he prompted, "Say again the EFC time?"

The EFC time gives you an idea of how long you will have to wait, and more importantly, tells you when to leave the hold in the event of communications failure. If your comm radios do quit, ATC expects you to leave the hold at the EFC time.

There was a pause before the controller obliged. "Five papa fox, there will be a thirty minute delay due to traffic. Expect further clearance at 1930."

Bill jotted down the EFC time and groaned at the delay. Glancing at the en route chart he saw that the hold was not published, and so he penciled it onto the chart. It was on our course from the VORTAC and would necessitate, he saw, a parallel entry. Leaving the hold would mean turning outbound in the pattern and re-intercepting the airway. I wondered why ATC had chosen this rather awkward procedure.

As we reached the VORTAC we turned outbound to a 047° heading, keeping the same wind correction. Bill punched his stopwatch for the one minute leg, reset the OBS for the 237° inbound course, and reduced power to the approach speed setting. Later, to

conserve fuel, he would slow the airplane even further. In compliance with AIM procedures he reported, "Three four five papa fox, entered the hold at zero two."

The CDI settled about half scale right, showing the wind correction angle was adequate. During any parallel entry, the first outbound leg is flown on the non-holding side of the course where less protected airspace is reserved for the holding aircraft. At six thousand feet approximately 4.5 nautical miles were reserved for us on the holding side and 2.9 nautical miles on the non-holding side. In general, the protected area is about 50 percent wider on the holding side of the course.

At the end of one minute, Bill turned left again and watched the needle swing left as we crossed the course and return to center as we intercepted inbound. He held a 247° heading to compensate for wind.

Our inbound leg was exactly a minute. Evidently the wind at our altitude was directly on the wing. As we turned outbound, he took up a 037° heading, using the rule that the outbound correction should be double the inbound.

It must have been a textbook wind, because the inbound turn put us exactly on course and once again the 247° heading held the course. It is unusual to get a hold down pat in less than two or three circuits, and Bill must have felt a bit smug. Of course, as he may have privately admitted, it is easier to correct for a direct crosswind than for a quartering one.

With the headings and times under control, Bill decided to reduce the airspeed to save more fuel. The most fuel-efficient airspeed is about 75% of the airplane's best glide speed, or 75% of 80 knots in the Skylane. But at such a slow speed, the nose would be very high, the controls would be mushy and the ride rather uncomfortable. Bill opted to slow only to 80, and gradually reduced power as he raised the nose for the slower speed.

We were fortunately carrying plenty of fuel, so we had no anxiety about a fuel shortage owing to the hold. However, on some closely figured IFR flights, a thirty minute hold could leave a flight dangerously low if there were a missed approach at the destination and a stack of airplanes waiting for an approach at the alternate. In some cases, when the weather is very bad, an airplane would be well advised to decline a hold and divert to another airport if possible.

With the reduced airspeed, the inbound leg was ten seconds too long, but Bill realized that the one-for-one relationship between inbound and outbound times would return once the airspeed stabilized. On the outbound leg he used the 037° heading for one minute but, to his dismay, saw the CDI swinging to the right as we turned inbound. At the slower speed, larger wind corrections were required.

It took another two circuits to discover that a 15° wind correction worked inbound, with a 25° correction outbound. We orbited the hold five times before receiving our clearance to continue. The ride was bumpy and uncomfortable, and rain drummed on the fuselage. The one small consolation was that our times and angles were accurate so that we painted a consistent, egg shaped pattern on Bradley radar.

Nevertheless, I was relieved when our clearance came, eight minutes before the EFC time. "Cessna three four five papa fox is cleared to the Worcester airport via Victor 3, Whamy, direct." Bill read back the clearance, thanked the man, and we turned on our way.

This story has several elements that the instrument student might keep in mind as a morale booster.

First, in falling into his "spaghetti" pattern during training, Bill was like a great many students. Used to flying VOR to VOR under VFR, where holds and intricate maneuvers solely by instruments aren't part of the picture, he had never had to visualize his airplane's position in such a complex situation. He simply did not have VOR orientation as straight in his mind as he thought he did. Remedying that is, of course, basic to instrument training. Using a simulator and working problem after problem, he quickly learned to interpret the needle — which was par for the course.

Second, holding may be introduced as an unexpected challenge or "pain" in an otherwise routine flight, but that need not daunt you. Especially where the skies are "crowded," holding is part of the routine and can be handled comfortably as such if the pilot knows what he is doing.

Finally, while holding may be a nuisance if you are anxious to get somewhere, it need never be boring — and it won't be if the wind is making its presence felt. As Bill learned during his spaghetti flight, striving for precise holding patterns, and making sure you're correct, is not the mere preoccupation of the pedant but a critical matter of safety. Holding is a device for keeping airplanes separated when they can't see each other. It's the equivalent of a stoplight, and allowing oneself to drift into unprotected airspace is like letting one's car roll hazardously into a crowded intersection through a red light. Holding patterns can become monotonous, but they are never automatic. Holding: we don't have to love it, but we sure do need it.

Holding Pattern Terminology

Here are some definitions used in holding pattern work (figure 7-2):
—The **holding fix** can be a VOR, intersection, NDB, OM or DME fix.
—The **outbound turn** is begun at the fix. All turns in a holding pattern are made at standard rate.
—The **holding course** is the course on which the inbound leg is flown. *Always fly towards the fix on the course.*
—The **inbound leg** is one minute long (one and a half minutes above 14,000 feet MSL), unless otherwise specified in a clearance as a different time interval or a DME distance. The airplane should be *on course* throughout this leg.
—The **outbound leg** is adjusted in length to compensate for the wind so that the inbound leg is one minute long. The outbound heading is also adjusted so that the airplane completes the **inbound turn** just as it intercepts the holding course.
—**Abeam** is the position opposite the fix where timing of the outbound leg begins.
—The **holding side** of the course is the side where the hold is accomplished. There is more protected airspace allocated to the hold on the holding side.
—The **non-holding side** is the "other" side of the course. You shouldn't be there.
—A **standard** hold is one in which all turns are to the right.
—In a **non-standard** hold the turns are to the left. Again, all turns are standard rate.
—**Maximum legal holding speed** is 175 knots indicated airspeed for propeller driven aircraft. As a practical matter, holding speed is a compromise between minimum fuel burn and acceptable controllability. For training purposes we use our approach level power setting, with gear and flaps up.

Holding at a VOR

When holding at a VOR, always set the OBS to the *inbound* course. Then, in a standard hold,

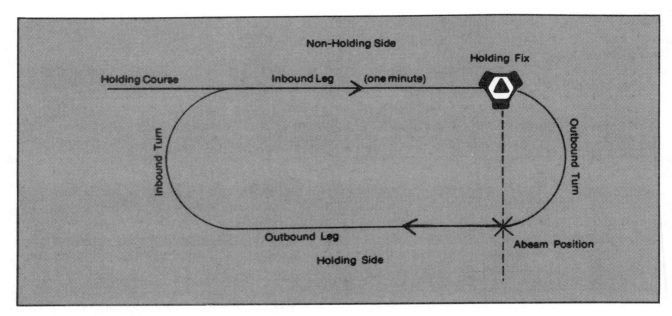

Figure 7-2

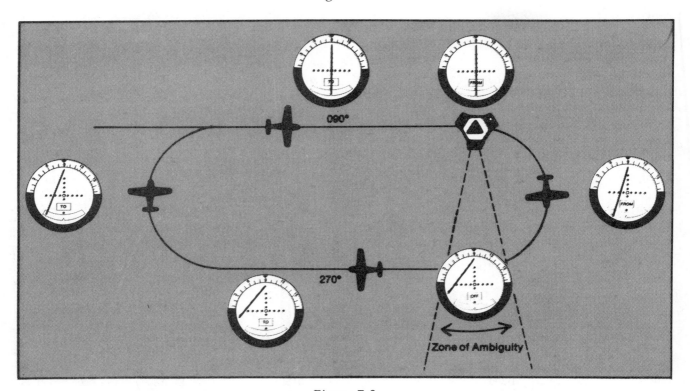

Figure 7-3

the flag and needle indications are as follows (figure 7-3):

Inbound leg: TO flag, centered needle.

Station passage: The needle may waver as you approach the fix. Don't chase the needle; hold the heading that kept you on course during the inbound leg. Station passage has occurred when a definite FROM reading is obtained.

Outbound turn: During the outbound turn the needle swings to the left.

Abeam: The abeam position is the center of the zone of ambiguity. The exact indication

126

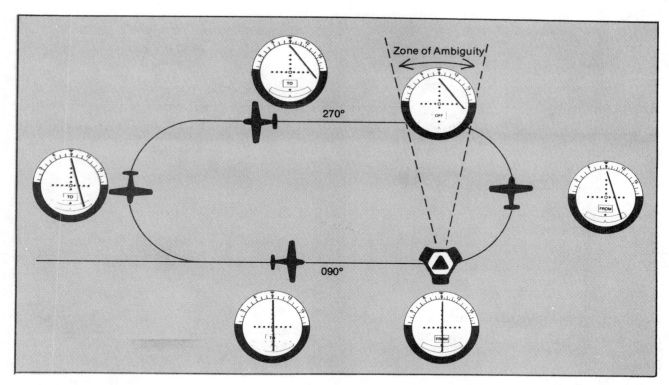

Figure 7-4

must be determined experimentally as it is a characteristic of your particular instrument.

Outbound leg: TO indication, full left needle. If the needle moves toward the center, you are flying too close to the inbound course. Adjust your heading to the left.

Inbound turn: The needle should swing towards center during this turn, reaching the center just as the heading reaches the inbound course. If you get to within 30° of the inbound heading during the turn and the needle has not left the peg, level the wings and wait for it to move. Resume turning as the needle swings, judging the turn to reach the inbound heading as it centers. If the needle swings early in the turn and crosses center before you reach the heading, you have flown through the inbound course. Continue turning to re-intercept from the non-holding side. Usually a 20° or 30° intercept works well. Adjust the outbound heading as necessary on the next circuit.

In a non-standard holding pattern the needle indications are reversed (figure 7-4).

Entries

The maneuvering required to enter a holding pattern depends on the direction from which the airplane arrives at the fix. There are three

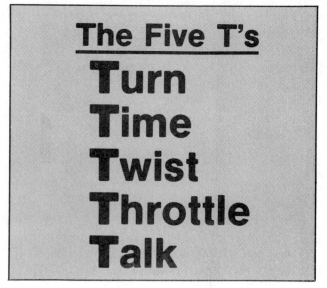

Figure 7-5

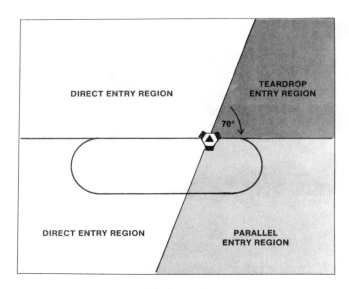

Figure 7-6

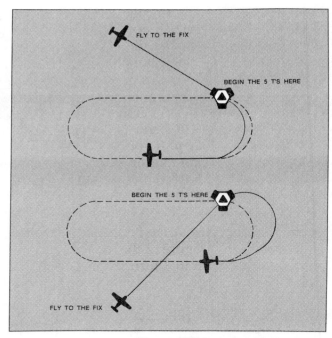

Figure 7-7

basic entry types and each begins with the same basic step: *Fly to the fix*. At the fix, begin the Five T's (figure 7-5). As in procedure turn work, the Five T's greatly simplify the entry process. From there on, the procedure varies depending on the direction of arrival at the fix (figure 7-6). If you arrive from the side of the fix where the holding course lies, a direct entry is called for.

1. The *direct entry* (figure 7-7). Let's assume you approach the fix from the general direction in which the holding course lies. After reaching the fix the steps are:

Turn right, at standard rate, to the outbound course (left if it is a non-standard hold);

Time. Begin timing one minute when the turn is completed;

Twist the OBS to select the *inbound* course;

Throttle to slow to holding speed. In a very fast airplane, you may prefer to slow down before reaching the fix, to simplify the entry maneuver. If you receive a holding clearance well in advance, request a speed reduction then and there. You will save fuel by flying more slowly and may use up enough time to eliminate the need for the hold;

Talk to report entering the hold.

The airplane is now outbound on the holding side of the course. At the end of one minute:

Turn right (left if a non-standard pattern) and intercept the inbound course;

Time the inbound leg. The inbound time may be longer than normal on this first circuit, since

you were slowing down on the outbound leg and the average outbound speed was higher than it will be later.

Twist, throttle, talk: These steps will not have to be repeated as long as you are in the hold at a constant altitude. However, it is a good idea to say them each time you cross the fix and each time you complete the inbound turn. Part of the work here is to build habits that won't desert you, even in a crisis.

Regardless of the type of entry, the Five T's are used in the same way for each holding pattern entry.

Become proficient at direct entries. Constantly ask yourself questions such as "Which side of the course am I on?" demanding answers such as "holding" or "non-holding," or compass directions, *not* left or right. Pointing to the proper spot on the chart can be used to reinforce visualization. Be sure you realize the significance of needle indications inbound and outbound. Sometimes beginners have trouble remembering whether to dial the inbound or outbound course when entering the hold. They have trouble dialing the inbound as they are turning to the outbound, reciprocal heading. You *always* dial the *inbound* course; there are no exceptions.

The direct entry is usually covered rather quickly. You will practice approaching the fix from several points in the direct entry region, from the holding and non-holding side. In marginal cases, a direct entry can require as much as a 250° turn to the outbound. Of course, in that case, you can choose a parallel entry which would mean only a 110° turn.

2. *The Teardrop Entry.* If you approach the fix from the opposite side and on the non-holding side, an immediate turn to the outbound course would put you too close to the holding course, so that on turning inbound, you would fly through it and have to re-intercept from the non-holding side (figure 7-8). To avoid this problem, make the initial turn to a heading 30° towards the holding side.

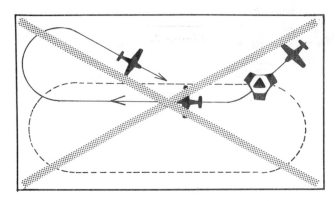

Figure 7-8

To determine the proper teardrop heading, note which side of the course the holding pattern is on, using one of the eight cardinal points. Then just turn to a heading 30° from the outbound course in that direction. For example, if you want to hold on the 270° radial with right turns, the holding pattern is south of the holding course. Therefore the teardrop heading is 30° south of 270°, or 240°. Determine and turn to this heading mechanically, by looking at the DG. Do not use mental arithmetic.

At the end of one minute, turn inbound and intercept the inbound course (figure 7-9). If the initial outbound leg of a teardrop entry is extended beyond one minute, you will find yourself too far from the inbound course. Watch the VOR needle during the inbound turn, and if

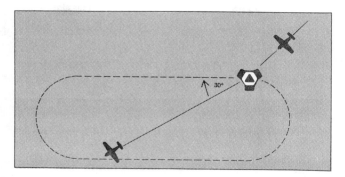

Figure 7-9

you get within 30° of the inbound heading before the needle leaves the peg, roll level until the needle moves. Then continue the turn to intercept as it centers. Consciousness of the needle during the turn is part of correct visualization.

3. *The Parallel Entry.* If you approach the fix from the opposite side, and on the holding side, turn *left* (right for a non-standard pattern) to the outbound course after you cross the fix. Hold this heading, paralleling the outbound course on the non-holding side. After one minute, turn *left* (for a standard hold) again, cross the course and re-intercept from the holding side. A good intercept angle is given by a heading 30° past the inbound course (figure 7-10).

In making a parallel entry, do not track outbound on the holding course; parallel it on the non-holding side. The CDI should be deflected to the right in a standard hold at a VOR. When you turn inbound, the CDI should cross to the left side. Do not fly direct to the VOR. Use a 30° intercept heading to get on course before reaching the station.

Compensating For The Wind

With few airplanes on his scope, the approach controller was relaxed and chatty. His vector to the airport had included a hefty wind correction, but we reported turning another 10 degrees into the wind. "Skyhawk four five nine one golf" he said, "you evidently see the airport, report right downwind for Runway 33."

My student, who had a quick wit, answered him: "Roger, Approach, nine one golf can land on 33 but it would be just as easy to back it in to Runway 15."

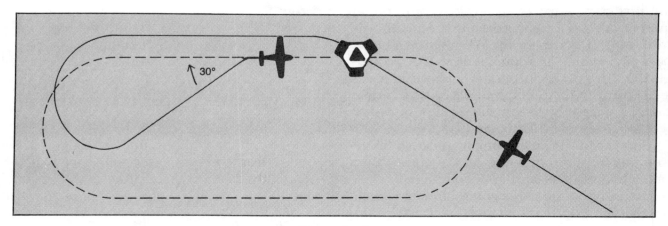

Figure 7-10

The controller laughed as he told us, "Sorry, nine one golf, 33 is the active runway. Contact the tower now, 119.6."

It was one of those cold blustery winter days with a strong northwest wind and noticeable turbulence to about 3000 feet. Our compensation for the strong wind and bumpiness was the virtually unlimited visibility.

We had practiced holding at a VOR and flying conditions were, to say the least, interesting. The published hold was southeast of the station with the inbound leg heading northwest, directly into the wind. It blew so strongly that we had been unable to achieve the standard one minute inbound leg length. Even by eliminating the outbound leg completely and making a 360° turn inbound as soon as we reached the VOR, our inbound segment was an excessive three minutes. Holding northwest of the fix had proved possible but difficult, requiring a *six minute* outbound leg to lengthen the inbound segment to one minute.

The wind at our altitude must have been nearly 50 knots, and, on the way back to the airport, we slowed the airplane to minimum controllable airspeed. Pointed into the wind, we had the interesting experience of observing a zero groundspeed. It is not often you get to "hover" in a Skyhawk.

Wind effect on an airplane is often confusing, even to experienced pilots, and even the difference between airspeed and groundspeed can be a particularly difficult concept.

We can think of the air we fly in as an ocean that may or may not be moving with respect to the ground. Currents within the air mass affect the airplane's position over the ground, but not its airspeed or position in relation to other airborne objects.

Wind is movement of the air mass in relation to the ground, and the airplane knows nothing about movement over the ground. Except that windy days are frequently more turbulent, we notice no difference in performance or safety in flight between windy and calm days. We hesitate to fly in high winds only because of the difficulty of taxiing, taking off and landing.

An analogy can be drawn between an airplane flying in a moving air mass and a motor boat navigating in a current. Imagine the boat on a river with a current equal to the boat's own speed. Headed upstream, the boat will not move relative to the riverbank, while headed downstream, it will appear to zoom along at twice its normal rate. The upstream case is analogous to our Skyhawk in slow flight bucking a 50 knot headwind.

Pointed upstream or downstream, the boat is using the same power and is moving at the same "water speed." Only if it has a destination and a schedule will its "groundspeed" be important. If it touches the riverbank its direction of travel will be critical. Angled upstream it will contact the shore softly, angled downstream it will crash while going at double its normal speed, illustrating why we prefer to land into the wind.

Here is a more complex illustration of the effects of the wind. Assume the wind is out of the west. An aircraft flies over the airport and releases a balloon with just enough bouyancy to exactly hold altitude. The aircraft then flies north for 15 minutes, makes a 180° turn and flies south for fifteen minutes. Where is the aircraft and where is the balloon?

The balloon and the aircraft are both suspended within the same air mass. Since the aircraft flew directly away from the balloon and then directly back towards it, the two are both over the same spot. Since the air mass is moving over the ground from the west, both are east of the airport.

So far, we have talked primarily about the effect of the wind on aircraft performance and position *within the air mass*. But the wind also has a very important effect on our cross country flying.

A variant of Murphy's Law states that "the wind is always against you." Although we have all occasionally enjoyed the exhilaration of a monstrous tailwind, over a lifetime of flying cross country, the net effect of the wind will be to slow you down. Assuming you will have headwinds and tailwinds over equal numbers of miles, you will fly many more hours with the wind on the nose.

Imagine a round trip from "point A" to "point B" and return. The distance is 100 nautical miles and your airspeed is 100 knots. In the absence of wind, the 200 mile trip would take two hours.

Now suppose there is a 20 knot wind blowing from "A" to "B". Your groundspeed on the leg from "A" to "B" is 120 knots, so you complete the 100 mile trip in 50 minutes. On the return leg your groundspeed is only 80 knots, so the trip takes one hour and 15 minutes, for a total flight time of two hours and five minutes! The wind has more time to work against you as a headwind than to help you as a tailwind.

Most winds are not directly on the nose or the tail but at some angle to the route of flight. If it comes from the half circle behind us, we are thankful for the extra groundspeed; if it comes from in front, we shake our heads and mutter. And with good reason, because a crosswind from ahead of the wingtip slows us down *more* than a quartering tailwind of the same magnitude and angle to the course speeds us up. (Get out your computer if you don't believe this.)

The explanation is that a certain *percentage of your groundspeed* is lost in counteracting the crosswind component to keep you on course. With a quartering tailwind, the groundspeed is higher to begin with, so more knots are lost in maintaining the crab.

A direct crosswind reduces groundspeed because some thrust must be used to crab into the wind. In fact, even a wind slightly behind the wing will have a negative effect on forward groundspeed if it is strong enough in relation to the airspeed.

But back to holds. If the wind is parallel to the holding course, either inbound or outbound, it is merely necessary to adjust the length of the outbound leg to achieve an inbound leg of exactly one minute. This is done by timing both the inbound and outbound legs and making pro-

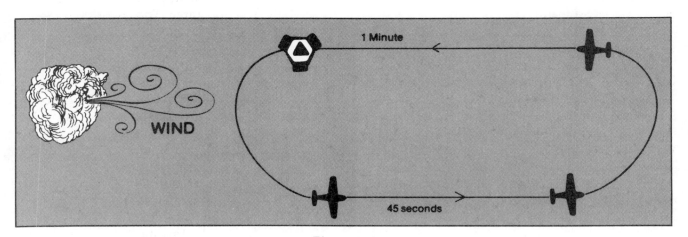

Figure 7-11

gressive adjustments until the correct outbound time is determined (figure 7-11).

If there is a direct crosswind, it is necessary to determine the wind correction angle to stay on course inbound. The outbound heading adjustment will be approximately *double* the inbound correction (figure 7-12).

This is another instance where thinking in terms of compass directions is much simpler than using "left" and "right." The inbound and outbound wind corrections will both be to the same compass direction, to the north for example. However, if the inbound correction is to the *left*, the outbound correction will be to the *right*, and vice versa. Since "left" means a smaller numeric heading and "right" means a greater numeric heading, you will soon be involved in mental arithmetic — something to be avoided in the cockpit. Compass directions are much more expedient.

Naturally, in most real life holding situations, there will be a headwind or tailwind *and* a crosswind component, so the pilot will have to determine the proper outbound time and proper

wind correction angles, inbound and outbound. On a fairly windy day, it is reasonable to take three or four turns in the hold to become properly established.

The Holding Clearance

While most holding patterns that you will be assigned are published on a chart or approach plate, occasionally you will receive an unpublished hold, and it is necessary to extract the information you need from the holding clearance. The clearance has a specific format:

1. The word **hold**;
2. A **direction** you are expected to hold from the fix;
3. The name of the **fix**;
4. A **course**;
5. **Leg length**, in minutes or miles;
6. The **direction** of the turns; if not stated, assume right turns;
7. **Expect further clearance (EFC)** time. This tells you when to leave the holding pattern if you lose communication capability while in the hold and allows you to evaluate your

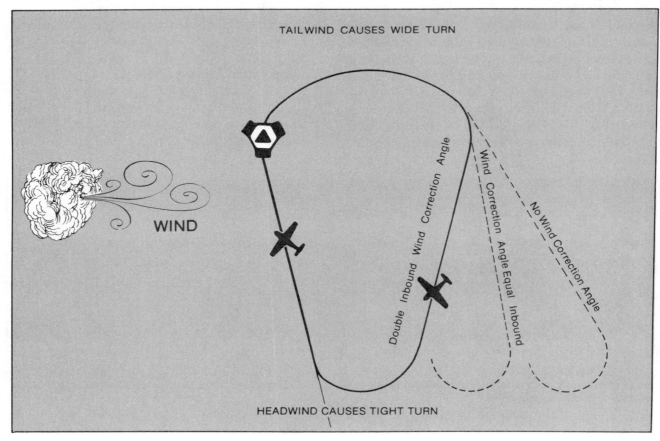

TAILWIND CAUSES WIDE TURN

WIND

Double Inbound Wind Correction Angle

Wind Correction Angle Equal Inbound

No Wind Correction Angle

HEADWIND CAUSES TIGHT TURN

Figure 7-12

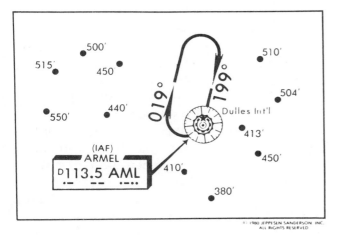

Figure 7-13

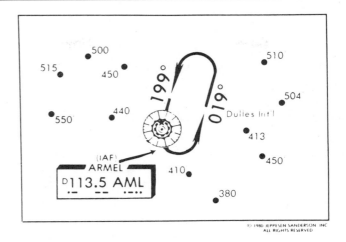

Figure 7-14

fuel situation. In the event of lost communications, leave the hold at the EFC time.

An example of a holding clearance, with the specified pattern shown in figure 7-13: "Hold north of Armel on the 019° radial, one minute legs, expect further clearance at 1700." (Times are given in UTC.)

Notice that the direction specifies the side of the fix where the course lies and is actually redundant. It is included in the clearance for emphasis to make sure no pilot mistakenly holds on the wrong side of the fix. It does not concern which side of the holding course is the holding side; that is determined by the direction of turn. The clearance for a hold at Armel on the other side of the same course would be given as follows: "Hold north of Armel on the 019° radial, left turns, one minute legs, expect further clearance at 1700" (figure 7-14).

Since timing the hold legs adds to your mental chores, a leg length in miles simplifies the holding procedure. When issued an en route holding clearance, you may request the privilege of flying an inbound leg that is a distance, rather than a time (assuming you are DME equipped, of course).

To properly interpret and comply with spoken holding clearances a definite procedure is helpful. Here is a suggested method:

a. Draw the fix.
b. Draw the course, with an arrow pointing inbound to the fix.
c. Draw the direction of turn.
d. Indicate the airplane's position in relation to the fix and visualize the entry. If a teardrop entry is required, determine the initial heading.

Consider this example: the aircraft is south of

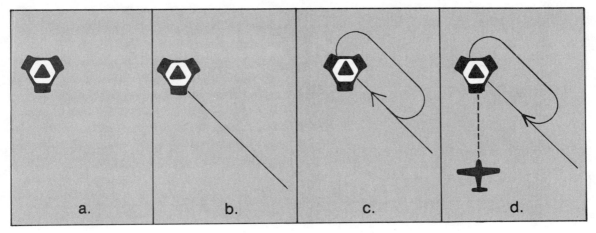

Figure 7-15

the VOR. Your clearance is: "Hold southeast of the VOR on the 130° radial, one minute legs, EFC at 1730." This clearance calls for a direct entry (figure 7-15).

Holding At Other Types of Fixes

If the holding fix is an intersection, some peculiarities distinguish the procedure from a hold at a VOR.

As at a VOR, the OBS should be set to the inbound course; that is, the inbound course *to the intersection*. In some cases, the inbound course to the intersection will be the outbound course from the VOR, so that the number one VOR instrument will have a FROM indication throughout the hold. Since you never cross the VOR, the flag indication will be the same throughout the holding pattern.

Unless the radials defining the intersection are nearly at right angles, there is no reliable way to determine the abeam position. Therefore, the outbound timing is begun when you

roll wings level on the outbound heading (figure 7-16).

Because of the distance from the VOR, the outbound needle indication may not be a full-scale deflection. Remember, a full-scale deflection means at least 10° off course.

With dual omnis, intersection holding is not complicated. However, with only one, you must switch back and forth between the two stations several times, since you use one station for course guidance and the other to determine station passage. In this case, requesting two minute legs will lighten your workload. Even better alternatives are requesting a leg length in miles, if you are DME equipped, a hold at a station instead of the intersection, or a sequence of vectors instead of a hold. When you have had an equipment failure, ATC will provide help, if you ask for it.

If you are holding at an intersection with only one omni, a common error is switching radios too frequently. Once you have determined your

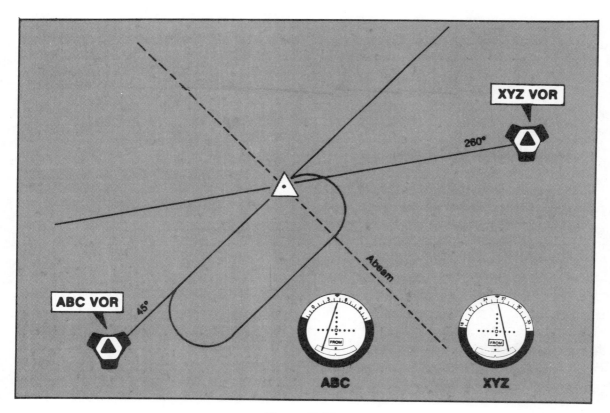

Figure 7-16

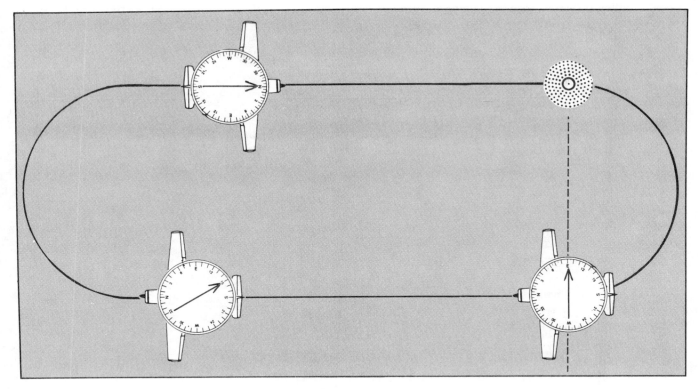

Figure 7-17

inbound reference heading, you can select the cross radial station while awaiting station passage and rely on heading control to keep you on course. Too frequent switching easily leads to confusion. Remember, each time you switch, you must change frequencies *and* OBS settings. It is all too easy to select the wrong OBS setting with the right frequency.

When holding at an NDB (figure 7-17), you have certain instrument indications to rely on.

Inbound leg: Track to the station as you normally track an NDB bearing.

Station passage: This is considered to occur when the swinging needle passes either wing. The faster the needle swings, the closer the flight path was to the station.

Outbound turn: During the outbound turn, the needle swings to the rear of the airplane and then moves back towards the front as the turn is completed, usually stopping somewhere in front of the wing.

Abeam: The abeam position is reached when the airplane is on the outbound heading and the needle is off the wing. Note that ADF indications are unreliable when the airplane is

banked, because the bank angle of the loop antenna adds a component to the bearing from the airplane to the station. Look at the indicator after the wings are level, then adjust as necessary.

Outbound leg: The needle swings to the right, towards the rear of the airplane. In "no-wind conditions", the needle is approximately 30° off the tail at the end of the outbound leg.

Inbound turn: As the heading approaches the inbound course, the needle swings towards the nose. If the DG and ADF reach the tops of their respective cards simultaneously, you will roll out exactly on course. If, after the wings are level, the needle is not on the nose, make a turn to intercept and track the inbound bearing normally (figures 7-18 and 7-19).

The Teardrop Entry: Cross the fix and choose the teardrop heading as in a hold at a VOR. *The needle will initially be on the tail.* The needle is on the tail any time you fly directly away from an NDB (figure 7-20).

The Parallel Entry: After initially crossing the fix, you will be on the non-holding side. The

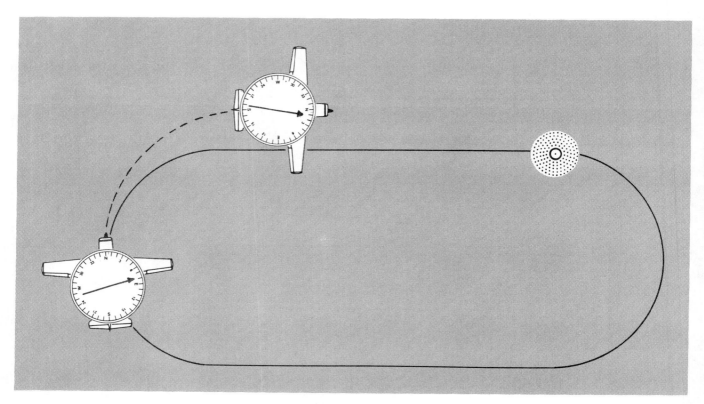

Figure 7-18

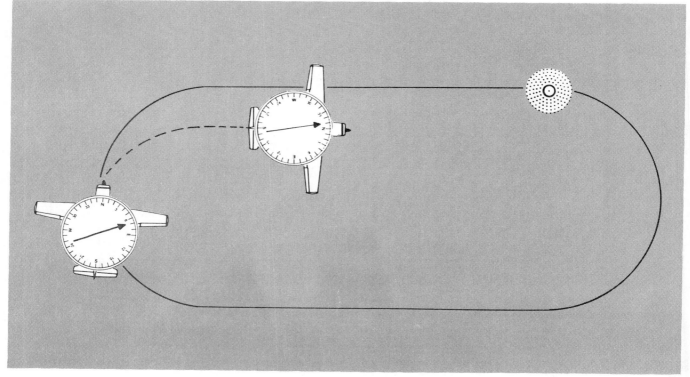

Figure 7-19

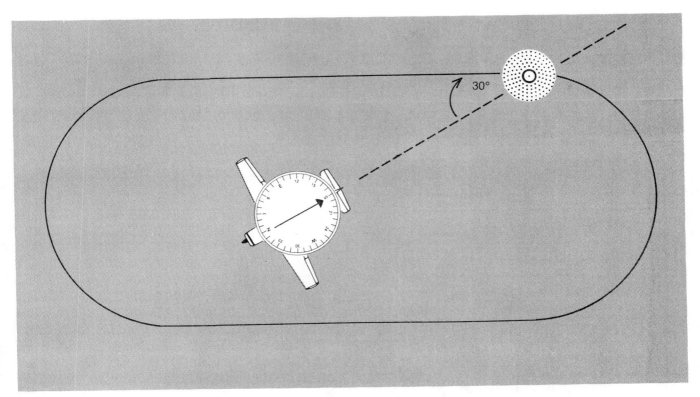

Figure 7-20

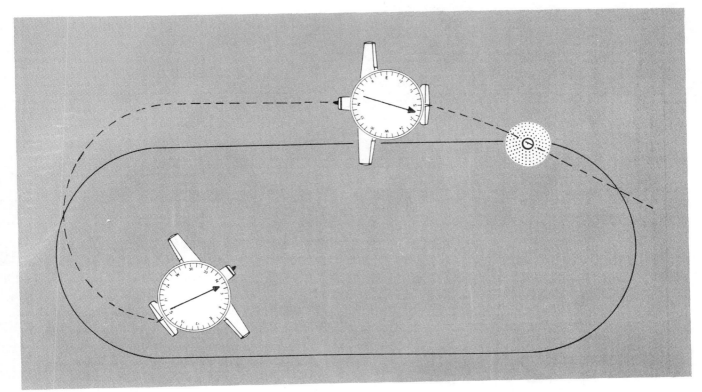

Figure 7-21

needle will be to the left of the tail (to the right of the tail in a non-standard hold). As you turn inbound, you will cross the course. Establish a 30° intercept angle by continuing the turn 30° beyond the inbound heading (figure 7-21). Notice that the ADF gives you more information than the VOR display in the corresponding situation. If, for example, the ADF needle were *on* the nose, or worse, to the left, you would know immediately that you would not intercept before reaching the station and could turn to a sharper intercept angle.

When holding at a LOM, the pilot has all the information provided by the NDB, plus the accuracy of the localizer on the inbound course. However, if there is no compass locator at the outer marker site, a hold is still possible.

Simply turn outbound when the marker beacon is received, start timing when the wings are level, and turn inbound after one minute to intercept the localizer (figure 7-22).

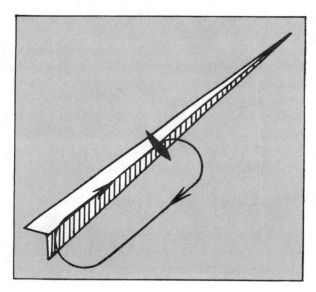

Figure 7-22

To The CFII

Correct needle interpretation and visualization of position are the goals of this section of the course. The same techniques used in the previous two chapters can be employed here. Repeatedly verify that your student knows where he is (compass directions or holding/non-holding side, *not* left and right) and that his

attention is focused on the proper instrument. A surprisingly common student error is losing track of whether he is inbound or outbound. Constantly emphasize use of the Five T's. Once again, a student who becomes "lost" in the airplane was taken off the simulator prematurely.

When the direct entry is down pat, introduce wind into the simulator. Experiment with various winds parallel to, across, and at an angle to the course. Give the student the experience of timing each leg and determining the crosswind correction for each type of wind. Concentrate at this stage on getting each pattern down pat, making as many circuits of the pattern as necessary.

Progress to the teardrop and parallel entries. Position the student in one of the regions around the fix, and have him fly towards it, visualizing the entry on the way. Give him ten miles at first, then shorten it to five. Once he has made several correct entries, it is not necessary to actually fly each one. As soon as he announces the correct entry, move him to another spot and start again. The simulator is a tremendous time saver here. Remember, correct visualization is the goal.

We recommend visualization for determining the entry, because all the various tricks for determining it rely on mechanical memory aids which, if forgotten, leave the pilot with no way to tell what to do. The best aid is to have him sketch the entry on his chart or kneepad to help the visualization process.

Cover holding clearances and unpublished holds. Carefully explain the format of a holding clearance so that he will know what to expect and will recognize if one part is missing. Read him official-sounding holding clearances and have him draw the hold and determine the entry while he is en route to the fix. Give him 10 miles at first, then five. This is yet another example of the power of the simulator to reduce training time. Thorough coverage of holding clearances and unpublished holds would take days in the airplane; you can do it in an hour or two on the simulator.

Having argued against mechanical aids, I now offer one for your instructional use. When you

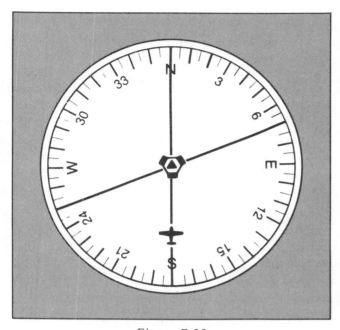

Figure 7-23

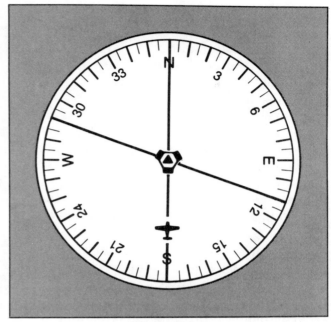

Figure 7-24

want to assign a teardrop entry, say, you may be interested in the following gimmick to quickly determine the proper holding clearance. First, clear him direct to the fix, and when he is on his heading, look at the DG (figure 7-23). Imagine two lines crossed on the face of the dial as shown, the fix at the center and the airplane at the bottom of the DG. Then any standard hold on a radial in the upper right segment of the gauge will need a teardrop entry. Likewise the upper left contains all the standard holds with parallel entries, and the two bottom segments contain all the direct entries. For a non-standard hold, the diagonal line rises the other way (figure 7-24).

Cover intersection holds. In clearing the student to an intersection, have him intercept one of the radials from an unknown position and determine for himself whether to turn towards or away from the VOR. This reinforces previous orientation work.

Once he is en route to the intersection on a radial, his entry determination is easier than at a VOR. At a VOR, there are 720 possible holding patterns (a standard and non-standard pattern on each radial), but at an intersection of two courses, there are only eight. In real life, the hold is usually on the radial on which he approaches the fix, either a simple direct entry or his choice of teardrop or parallel. Most pilots prefer teardrop over parallel, because it gets them on course farther from the fix.

In training, you may also give him some intersection holds on the crossing radial to stretch his visualization abilities.

If the simulator has only one VOR display, all intersection work is done in an equipment failure mode, i.e. as though his second VOR had failed. Explain carefully the difference between dual and single omni intersection holds. A common error in single omni work is to switch back and forth between stations too frequently. Demonstrate that once he knows his reference heading, he will stay on course by holding it. This is especially true if the intersection is far from the station. In that case, it is more important to accurately notice passage of the crossing radial.

In covering ADF holds, emphasize the expected needle indication at each point in the procedure. In the real world, unpublished ADF holds are rare. However, mention that if he does receive a clearance for an unpublished ADF hold, he must be sure to notice whether the stated course is an inbound or outbound bearing.

Holding Quiz

1. What is a standard hold?
2. What is the maximum holding speed for a propeller-driven aircraft?
3. What is an EFC time and what does it mean?
4. Define holding side and non-holding side of the course.
5. What are the three types of holding entries?
6. What indicates station passage at a VOR. At an NDB?
7. Draw the correct holding pattern for the following clearance: N1234 hold southwest of the XYZ/VOR on the 250° radial, EFC at 1435Z.
8. What assistance could you request of ATC when holding at an intersection with one omni?
9. What is the normal inbound leg length in a hold, up to and including 14,000 feet MSL? Above 14,000 feet MSL?

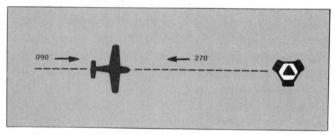

Figure 7-25

10. You are in a standard hold at a VOR. With the OBS properly set, what needle indication should you have on the outbound leg?

In the following questions, assume you are inbound to the Madison VORTAC on the 270° radial with a heading of 090° (figure 7-25). You unexpectedly receive a holding clearance and, glancing at the chart, realize it is an unpublished hold. For each of the following clearances,
(1) Draw the hold;
(2) Determine the recommended entry;
(3) State the heading and direction of turn crossing Madison.

11. "Hold west of Madison on the 255° radial, right turns, one minute legs, expect further clearance at 1800."
12. "Hold northwest of Madison on the 300° radial, left turns, one minute legs, expect further clearance at 1800."
13. "Hold south of Madison on the 180° radial, right turns, one minute legs."
14. "Hold northeast of Madison on the 060° radial, left turns, one minute legs, expect further clearance at 1800."
15. "Hold northeast of Madison on the 060° radial, one minute legs, expect further clearance at 1800."
16. "Hold southeast of Madison on the 130° radial, right turns, one minute legs, expect further clearance at 1800."
17. "Hold southeast of Madison on the 130° radial, left turns, one minute legs, expect further clearance at 1800."
18. "Hold northwest of Madison on the 340° radial, right turns, one minute legs, expect further clearance at 1800."
19. "Hold east of Madison on the 090° radial, right turns, one minute legs, expect further clearance at 1800."
20. "Hold southeast of Madison on the 160° radial, right turns, one minute legs, expect further clearance at 1800."

CHAPTER EIGHT

NONPRECISION APPROACHES

The Fairbury, Nebraska, Municipal Airport offered a meager choice of approaches, the NDB-17 and the NDB-A, both of which were predicated on the on-field MH class radio beacon. The NDB-17 approach had an MDA 700 feet above the terrain, the bottom of the transition area, and a visibility requirement of 1 mile. The approach would not get us in unless the weather at the field was basic VFR ("one mile and clear of clouds" in uncontrolled air space). But with our en route flight in solid IFR conditions, it did offer us a chance to find the airport.

The transition for the NDB 17 from Odell intersection to the IAF defined by the beacon was a course of 292° for 13.1 miles at 3100 feet (figure 8-1). At the intersection, we could just hear the NDB's identifier, and the needle swung sluggishly on the dial, pointing in the general direction to the fix. Had it been a transition from a VOR, we could have flown outbound on a radial, but from the intersection, there was only the NDB bearing to guide us. An MH class beacon officially has a range of 25 nautical miles, but we knew from experience that many local NDBs are often not up to spec. The Fairbury beacon was just adequate to allow us to navigate the transition.

We departed Odell and the needle indications became crisper. With the speaker selected and the volume up, we heard the NDB identifier become stronger as we proceeded. There was a strong north wind, so we held a 10° right wind correction to stay on course. The needle locked into position, 10° left of the nose, showing us ex-

actly on course. I reduced power and began the descent to 3100 feet.

Small turns left and right bracketed our reference heading and resulted in smart and appropriate needle excursions. The needle swung to the tail just as we reached 3100 feet.

I began the procedure turn outbound leg on the 345° bearing from the station and, because of the north wind, decided to fly outbound for a full 3 minutes. For the initial leg of the course reversal, I used a heading of 310° rather than the published 300°. After 1 minute on this heading, I turned through north to a heading of 110°, again compensating for wind. On this heading, I would intercept the inbound course when the needle reached 55 to the right of the nose.

After less than 30 seconds on the 110° heading, the needle reached 55° right of the nose and I turned to the inbound course of 165°. The needle stopped right on the nose.

Since I knew we were close to the field and had a tailwind to boot, I brought the throttle back to 1200 RPM, our nonprecision descent setting, for a 1000-foot per minute descent to the circling MDA of 2180 feet.

As we passed 2400 feet, we popped out the bottom of the flat stratus overcast and saw the airport, directly in front but nearly under the airplane. I leveled at 2200 feet, 700 feet above the field, and turned slightly right to enter a left downwind for Runway 35. As we entered the pattern, slightly below pattern altitude, we monitored unicom and watched for VFR traffic in the area.

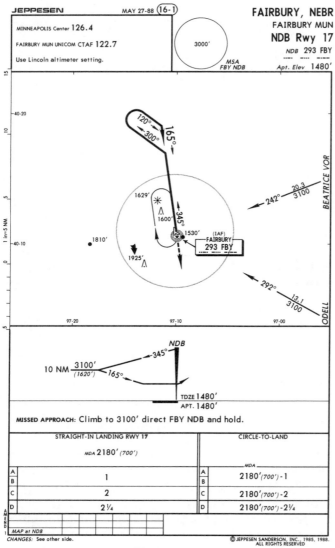

Figure 8-1

Two minutes later, we were on the ground.

Such approaches are not only common, but commonly simple to fly, even when equipment deficiencies, such as weak beacons, crop up. The NDB approach provides a simple and effective way of finding the airport, when weather conditions would otherwise make it impossible.

When your knowledge of radio navigation, en route charts, and ATC procedures has brought you to within striking distance of your destination airport, it is the instrument approach procedure that will bring you down safely to an altitude below the cloud bases from which a normal landing can be made.

An instrument approach requires flying specified courses and altitudes for particular lengths of time with the radios correctly set up, and ATC re-

porting chores properly handled. The Five T's is, again, a time-tested technique for ensuring that all these tasks are performed at the right time and in the right order of priority. It should be used without fail every time you make a turn and every time you cross a fix. Learning to adhere to this rule may be the single most important lesson for the instrument pilot in training.

There are two broad categories of instrument approach, precision and nonprecision. While very important, the difference between them lies only in the conduct of the final approach to the airport—a precision approach provides electronic descent guidance, and a nonprecision approach does not. Up to the FAF, the general considerations about segments, fixes, altitudes, and procedure turns apply equally to precision and nonprecision approaches.

It is commonly thought that the ILS, with its precise course guidance and great accuracy, is the most difficult of all approaches. In fact, nonprecision approaches present a greater challenge. They combine the skills demanded by all your previous aircraft control and visualization work. They require the pilot to perform an involved sequence of tasks, each at the right time and in the proper sequence. Good cockpit organization, a good understanding of approach procedures and faithful adherence to the Five T's are the keys to success on nonprecision approaches.

The most common nonprecision approaches are VOR and NDB. VOR procedures are available at many airports, large and small, and may be predicated on (T) class VORs or on en route facilities. NDB procedures may be based on compass locators, or another class of NDB.

Neatness Counts

Cockpit organization is critical. The instrument pilot, on top of all his other attributes, must be a good bookkeeper. Prior to takeoff, not only should the en route charts for the flight be out of the binder and folded to the route prior to takeoff, but the approach plates for the destination should be on the clipboard. Chapter Four contains other suggestions for the clipboard organization.

For the approach, a yoke clip is helpful, because it allows the pilot to glance at the plate without lowering his head to look in his lap, which saves motion and is a hedge against vertigo.

As we have seen earlier, a stop watch is very helpful, and a digital stopwatch is more convenient than a conventional one. The numbers should be as big as possible. If you use the stopwatch feature on your ultra-modern calculator-equipped, dual time zone, chronographic, Pac-Man wrist watch, twist the watch to the side of your wrist so you can see it easily. If you opt for a separate stopwatch, it can be backed with velcro and stuck onto the center of the yoke, unless the approach plate in your yoke clip would conceal it there. In that case, the top of one of the yoke grips or an open spot on the panel would be good places for the watch. Hanging it around your neck doesn't work, because it is too hard to see.

In studying an approach, it is helpful to make notes on the approach plate. Use a yellow highlighter or a pencil to mark the minimums for your category aircraft, the time to the MAP and the missed approach instructions. If you prefer not to write on the plate itself, Jeppesen offers plastic chart protectors that protect frequently used plates and also allow pencil notes to be easily erased. It should go without saying that all your charts, especially the approach plates, should be current, with all up-to-date revisions in place, and arranged in proper order for easy access should you need to change your route, destination or approach.

"Cleared for the Approach"

This clearance authorizes you to fly the procedure indicated on the approach plate and to descend to the published altitudes. You may not descend during an approach until you have received an approach clearance and are on a published route. The published route may be any approach segment, transition, or airway. If it is an airway, you may descend to the MEA, or the MOCA if within 22 nautical miles of the VOR, but be sure this altitude is higher than the transition or initial approach altitude. Otherwise, you will find yourself climbing later on. When flying "direct" to an approach fix, you may not descend, even if you are cleared for the approach, until you are on a published route. The importance of understanding and complying with this rule is underscored by the fact that the regulation was established and clarified as the result of an airliner's crash into a hilltop on an approach to Dulles Air-

port near Washington, D.C.

Minimum Safe Altitudes (MSA) do not apply to an approach; they are for emergencies only. MSAs are shown in the 25 nautical mile circle at the top of the approach plate (figure 8-2). The notation indicating a radio fix, such as MSA LLX NDB indicates the center of the circle. The approach plate also indicates significant obstructions. On a Jeppesen plate, the highest obstruction is shown by a curving black arrow.

Figure 8-3 illustrates the **segments** of a typical approach. The names and arrangement of the segments do not depend on the type of approach we assume it to be.

An approach may have as many as four segments and one or more published **transitions** from the en route environment. Each segment and transition is a clearly defined course, with a beginning and an end, and a published minimum altitude. The pilot has certain tasks to accomplish during each segment, and understanding the various segments of a particular approach is important in planning how to fly the approach.

The plan view (figure 8-2) shows transitions from three en route fixes to the Lyndonville NDB. Transitions are also called **feeder routes** or **terminal routes**. Assuming that he has received an approach clearance, the pilot may descend to the altitude published on the plan view for the transition he is on.

The **initial approach fix**, marked (IAF) on the plan view, is the Lyndonville NDB and is considered the point where the approach begins. There may be more than one IAF.

The **initial segment** begins at the IAF and is the "procedure turn outbound" segment of this approach. The initial segment includes the entire procedure turn and ends when the airplane is established inbound to the fix. During this segment, the pilot should slow the airplane to the approach speed and descend to the published altitude of 4300 feet (see profile view).

This particular approach, like most approaches, has no **intermediate fix**. The **intermediate segment** begins when the aircraft has turned inbound on the 023° bearing and ends at the NDB. It is the "procedure turn inbound" segment of the approach and a busy time for the pilot. During this segment, he completes the final landing checklist and memorizes the missed approach in-

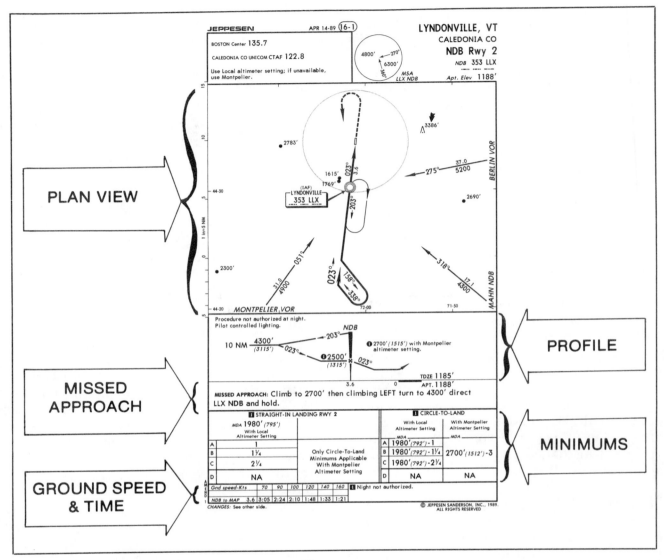

Figure 8-2

structions (see the missed approach section of the approach plate). Since the altitude specified for this segment is lower than that for the initial segment, the pilot should descend, in this case, to 2500 feet (see profile).

The **final approach fix (FAF)** is the Lyndonville NDB and is identified by the Maltese cross on the profile view. The FAF marks the beginning of the final letdown to the airport. When the airplane is not in radar contact, the FAF inbound must be reported to ATC. On this approach, the FAF and IAF are collocated, but such is not the case for all approaches.

The **final approach segment** is the course from the FAF to the missed approach point. During this segment, the final descent to minimums is made. Since this is a nonprecision approach (i.e., there is no electronic descent guidance) the pilot simply descends to the **minimum descent altitude (MDA)** of 1980 feet (see minimums box) and levels off, carefully tracking the 023° bearing from the NDB, until he reaches the **missed approach point (MAP)**. On this approach, the MAP is 3.6 miles from the NDB and is identified by timing the final approach segment (see time and ground-speed box).

Segments of the Approach

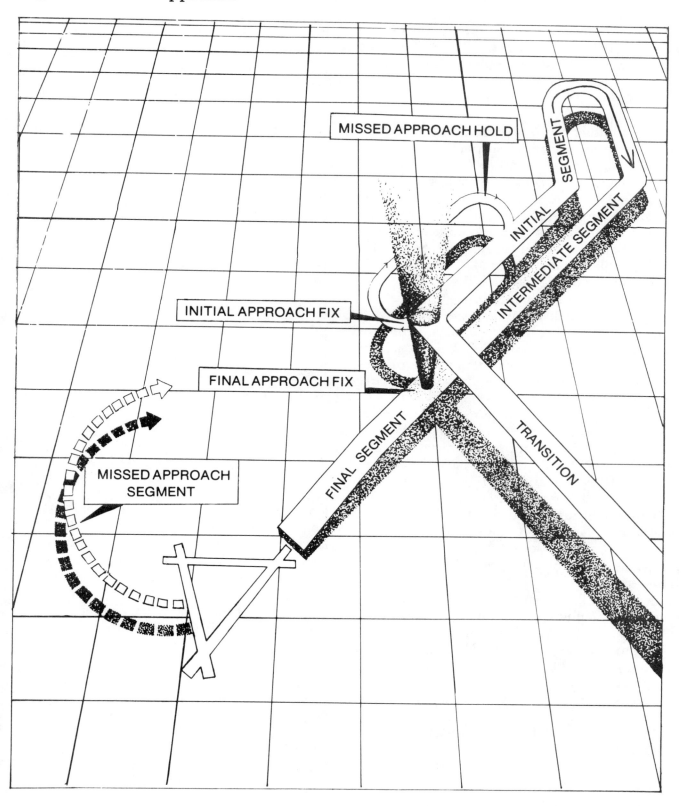

MISSED APPROACH HOLD

INITIAL SEGMENT

INTERMEDIATE SEGMENT

INITIAL APPROACH FIX

FINAL APPROACH FIX

TRANSITION

FINAL SEGMENT

MISSED APPROACH SEGMENT

Figure 8-3

The large numbers in the minimums box give MDA above sea level (MSL). In the straight-in landing section, the parenthetical number is the **height above touchdown (HAT)**. Adding this number to the **touchdown zone elevation (TDZE)** shown in the profile gives the MDA (795 + 1185 = 1980). The TDZE is the highest point in the first 3000 feet of the runway.

The parenthetical numbers in the circle-to-land section are **height above airport (HAA)**. This, plus the airport elevation (the highest point on any usable runway), equals the circling MDA (792 + 1188 = 1980), which happens to be the same as the straight-in MDA in this case. In other words, straight-in minimums are based on height above the touchdown zone, and circling MDAs depend on height above field elevation.

Assuming you do not see the runway, the **missed approach segment** begins at the MAP. It is crucial to immediately initiate a safe climb away from the terrain. You should not have to refer to the approach plate for the missed approach instructions at this time, but should have memorized at least the initial heading or course and the altitude limit before beginning the final approach. While a missed approach requires an ATC report, the first priority is to climb away from the ground and begin the missed approach procedure. Talking is the last of the Five T's and the radio call can safely wait a moment or two. It is important to be able to keep your scan solely on the instruments as you transition from glancing toward the ground to full in-cockpit concentration—with no distractions, such as looking at the plate or picking up a microphone. Disorientation can wreak havoc here.

In figure 8-2, the missed approach segment consists of climbing straight ahead to 2700 feet, then making a climbing left turn to 4300 feet and flying direct to the Lyndonville NDB. At the NDB, enter the published hold (see plan view and missed approach section of approach plate).

If you see the runway, you can land.

Straight-in and Circle-to-Land

With the airplane barreling down final, you have one eye on the clock, one eye on the altimeter, one eye on your attitude indicator, and both eyes on your navigation instruments. While carefully tracking the final approach course, mentally

prepared for a missed approach, you must also plan your course of action should the airport materialize out of the murk.

A **straight-in landing** is a landing on the runway named in the title of the approach. In the approach excerpted in figure 8-4, a straight-in landing can be made on Runway 35. Landing on any other runway would be a **circle-to-land** maneuver. Notice the 120-foot difference between straight-in and circling minimums for the localizer approach. The pilot must have clearly in mind which runway he plans to use, in order to choose the appropriate MDA.

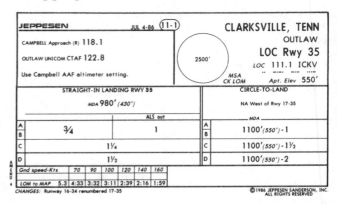

Figure 8-4

If straight-in minimums are to be authorized, the final approach course must be aligned within 30° of the runway heading. If the approach is not aligned within 30° of any runway (or, in FAA parlance, if there are other "operational considerations," such as an approach where the MDA leaves you so high at the MAP that you couldn't count on landing straight in) only circling minimums will be authorized. There will be no lower MDA if you are landing on the easiest runway to get to, even if the final track is within 30° of the runway heading. In such a case, the approach will be designated with a letter, rather than a runway number (figures 8-9, 8-10, 8-11).

To reduce the chances of having to make a missed approach, your circling maneuver should be carefully planned. The cardinal rule is keep the runway in sight at all times. If you lose visual contact for any reason other than the normal banking of the airplane, you must immediately initiate a missed approach. Since a circling maneuver may be conducted with low visibility (most procedures specify a 1-mile minimum) develop the habit of keeping the aircraft close to the airport. It is better to risk a visual go-around than to extend the downwind and risk losing sight of an unfamiliar airport. Some pilots prefer circling patterns that make all turns to the left, so the runway stays on the pilot's side.

There are no required patterns for the circling maneuver; you may fly right over the center of the airport if you want to. Usually, when the airport appears, you should take the shortest path to the base or downwind for the landing runway. There are exceptions to this; notice in figure 8-4 that the circling maneuver is not authorized west of runway 17-35. When practical, left traffic is preferable, since this keeps the airport on the pilot's side. Figure 8-5 shows several acceptable patterns for the circle-to-land maneuver.

A few guidelines for enhancing the safety of the circling maneuver are:

Altitude: Remain at the circling minimums as long as possible. In many general aviation airplanes, and at most airports, the MDA can be maintained until the aircraft is on final for the runway. This provides at least 300 feet of obstacle clearance and is usually low enough to allow a comfortable final approach to the runway. Landing flaps should be applied as the final descent is begun. During circling approaches, try to hold the MDA exactly. Climbing 50 or 100 feet could mean re-entering the clouds.

Figure 8-6 illustrates the importance of being aware of what altimeter setting you are given. On this approach, the MDA depends on whether or not you have the local altimeter setting. Notice the enormous difference this makes in the applicable MDA. The controller will always clearly state the origin of the altimeter setting he gives you; it is your job to note what he says. In cases where the local altimeter setting must be obtained from Unicom, you may want to leave the ATC frequency as soon as possible to request it. Especially where the terrain is hilly, this precaution is vital for protection.

Bank Angle: The bank angle should not exceed 30 even in visual conditions. Steep turns close to the ground are not advisable in the best of circumstances; during a circling approach in poor visibility, there is the additional risk of suddenly re-entering the clouds.

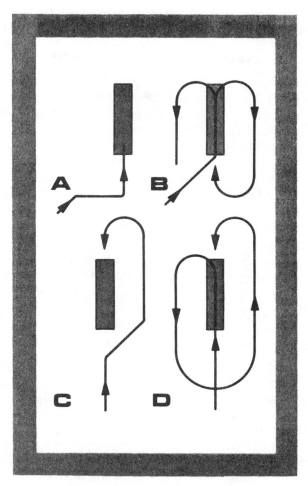

Figure 8-5

Heading: Check the DG on downwind to be sure you are in the pattern for the proper runway. You would not be the first pilot who circled to land in low weather and lined up with the wrong strip of concrete.

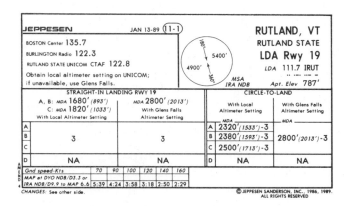

Figure 8-6

Airspeed: The approach category (see minimums section on any approach plate) is determined by the characteristics of the particular aircraft. The category is based only on airspeed, although formerly it depended on airspeed and weight. The following table defines the various approach categories. V_{so} represents the stall speed in the landing configuration at maximum certificated landing weight.

Category	1.3 V_{so}
A	less than 91 knots;
B	91-120 knots;
C	121-140 knots;
D	141-165 knots;
E	includes only certain military aircraft with 1.3 V_{so} 166 knots or more.

Circle-to-land minimums provide 300 feet of obstacle clearance within the circling approach area, the size of which depends on the aircraft category, as shown in the following table:

Aircraft Category	Radius (Miles)
A	1.3
B	1.5
C	1.7
D	2.3
E	4.5

The circling area is not simply a circle, but is constructed by drawing an arc with the appropriate radius from the threshold of each runway and joining adjacent arcs with tangent lines. A typical circling area is shown in figure 8-7.

Piston-powered general aviation aircraft usually fall into category A, and thus may use the lowest minimums printed in each approach situation. However, when an aircraft is circling to land, an unusually high speed will take it farther from the airport and possibly out of the obstacle clearance area. To guard against this, use category B minimums if circling at more than 95 knots and category C minimums above 125 knots, regardless of actual aircraft category.

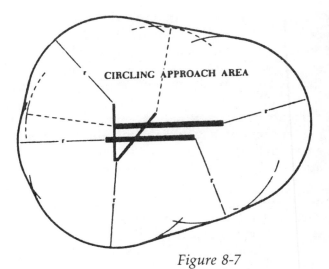

Figure 8-7

Missed Approach: If you lose visual contact with the airport during a circling approach, prudence (and FAR 91.175) requires an immediate missed approach. An occasional problem arises in knowing which way to turn when this happens. Once the circling maneuver is begun, the procedure on the plate may no longer apply, since it assumes that the missed approach begins from the MAP. For example, in figure 8-2, the published procedure calls for a straight climb to 2700 feet from the MAP, followed by a climbing left turn. If the pilot were circling on the west side of the airport when visual contact was lost, a left turn would be a turn away from the protected circling area. It would be safer to turn right towards the center of the protected area.

For maximum safety, a missed approach from a circling maneuver should always turn towards the landing runway, regardless of the turn depicted on the approach plate (figure 8-8).

Traffic: At a field without Class E designated to the surface, circling presents an additional problem. Below 700 feet AGL, you are in uncontrolled airspace where VFR minimums are "one mile and clear of clouds." There just might be a VFR airplane practicing touch-and-goes in the pattern, and you are both legal. Vigilance, and broadcasting your position and intentions on the common traffic advisory frequency (CTAF) are your only defenses against this danger. The CTAF is the FSS frequency or Unicom at a non-tower field, the tower frequency at a controlled field when the tower is closed, or 122.9 if the airport has no tower, FSS, or Unicom.

Approach Architecture

An approach may not have a full complement of fixes, segments, and transitions. The approach to Lyndonville (figure 8-2) is a typical nonprecision approach, but there are other approach designs that occur quite frequently. Perhaps the simplest variation of the procedure-turn approach is the design with the fix on the airport, such as at Fairbury, Nebraska (figure 8-1). On this approach, no inbound timing is required. There is no intermediate or final fix and no intermediate segment. The final segment and the descent to the MDA begin at the completion of the procedure turn. The MAP is the fix itself.

A more complex variant of the Lyndonville type of approach is shown in figure 8-9. This procedure has a turn at the FAF, so the pilot is particularly busy. The Five T's, therefore, become: (1) turn to the new heading; (2) start the watch; (3) twist the OBS setting to the new course; (4) throttle back to descend; (5) report as requested. Additionally, there is a steep final approach segment, so that a rapid descent rate is needed to get from 1600 feet to the pertinent MDA in time. On this approach, the pilot's best organizational and air-

craft control skills are tested.

Figure 8-10 shows an approach at the other extreme of complexity. It has no initial or intermediate fix and no initial or intermediate segment. ATC simply vectors the airplane onto the final approach course. The profile view note states that this approach can only be conducted with radar assistance.

The FAF on a VOR approach need not necessarily be the VOR itself. It may also be defined by an intersection or a DME fix. In figure 8-11, either method may be used to identify Kirdo.

Some nonprecision approaches have a visual descent point (VDP) on the final approach segment. Indicated by a "V" on the profile view of the procedure (figure 8-12), it is defined as the point where a normal 3° approach path to the runway would intersect the MDA. It may be identified by a crossing radial, a DME distance or a marker beacon, and if you are equipped to identify it, regulations prohibit descending below the MDA before reaching this point.

In some cases, the final approach segment is divided into parts, with different altitudes, separated by **step-down fixes**. A step-down fix may be an intersection or DME fix as in figure 8-13, or a marker beacon as in figure 8-16. A pilot equipped to identify the step-down fix may descend to lower minimums. In figure 8-13, a note in the profile view requires either dual VORs or DME to identify the step-down fix, Curro intersection. If you have one or the other, your MDA is 400 feet lower than if you have neither. If you are not equipped to identify a step-down fix, make certain that you descend only to the proper minimums for your airplane. Remember, minimums are established for sound safety reasons.

There are many odd variations to instrument approaches, and the pilot must learn to read the approach plate quickly and accurately to determine for himself what is required. Studying the approach plate in advance, while planning the flight or while en route, is always important.

The Final Descent on a Nonprecision Approach

A nonprecision approach does not provide glide slope information. The pilot simply descends to the MDA, levels off, and continues at that altitude until reaching the MAP. The MAP

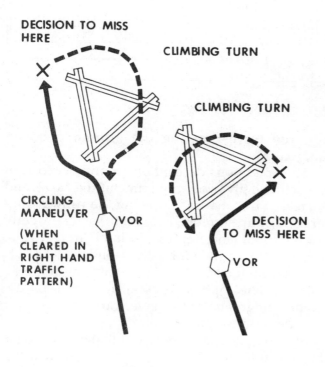

Figure 8-8

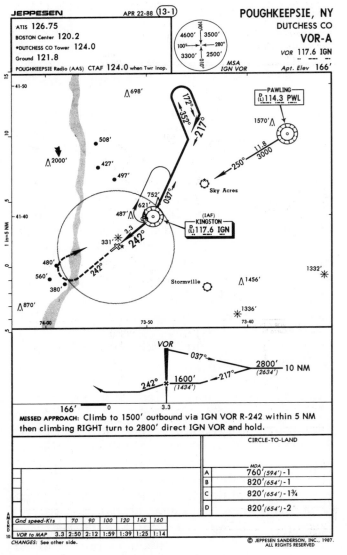

Figure 8-9

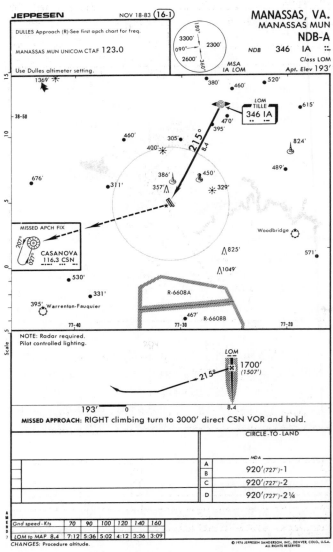

Figure 8-10

may be a DME fix (figure 8-12) or the navaid itself (figure 8-13), or it may be determined by time and groundspeed (figures 8-2, 8-4, 8-9, 8-10).

During a timed approach, you will estimate your groundspeed based on the indicated airspeed (or true airspeed if operating at high density altitude) and the known wind. At many airports, ATC will provide a recent weather report for that or a nearby field. In the absence of such a report, you may be able to get the wind on the local advisory frequency (Unicom). For a headwind or tailwind, estimate the groundspeed by subtracting or adding the speed of the wind to your airspeed. If the wind is quartering, use half its value. The effect of a direct crosswind can be

ignored for estimating the groundspeed on approach.

An expeditious descent on a nonprecision approach will give you more time at the MDA and increase your chances of seeing the runway (figure 8-14). Furthermore, in order to set up properly for a normal landing, it is desirable to reach the MDA at least a mile (i.e., 40 seconds at 90 or 100 knots) from the MAP, and preferably more. To do this on some approaches, your nonprecision descent configuration must give you a 1000-foot per minute descent rate.

In some cases, a more leisurely descent would bring you to the MAP before you've reached the MDA, increasing the chance of not breaking out

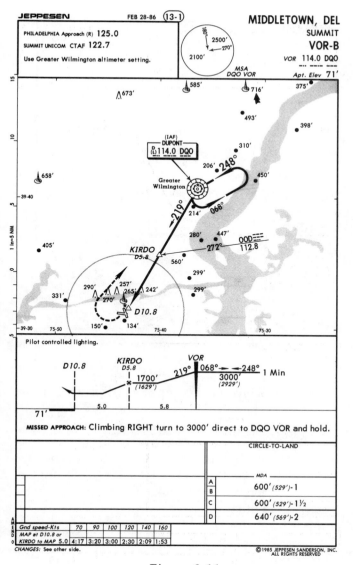

Figure 8-11

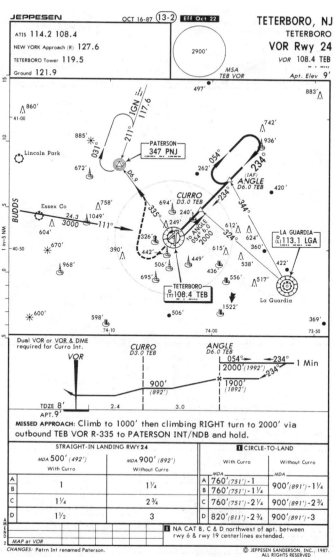

Figure 8-13

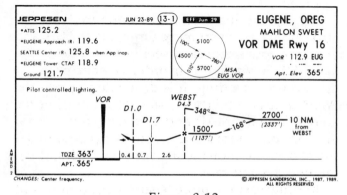

Figure 8-12

of the clouds. Even if you did break out, you might be too high above the airport to make a safe, controlled landing. During a nonprecision descent, be sure to control your airspeed accurately. If the airspeed is allowed to increase, your timing accuracy will be spoiled.

Other Nonprecision Approaches

VOR DME. DME comes in handy on some VOR approaches, even though the approach may be conducted without it. In figure 8-13, DME is not required, but it can be used to identify the Angle FAF and the Curro step-down fix. Even if you have dual VORs, using the DME is simpler, since it makes it unnecessary to set, and then change,

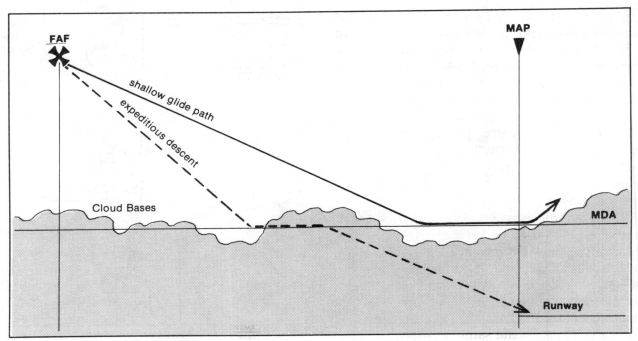

Figure 8-14

the number two OBS.

Approaches specified as VOR DME (figure 8-12) procedures may not be used by aircraft without DME. A typical VOR DME approach is similar to an ordinary VOR approach, with courses defined by radials, but it requires DME to identify one or more fixes. In some cases, an initial, intermediate, or even the final segment may be based on a DME arc (see discussion of DME arcs later in this chapter).

In addition to all the possible variations of VOR and NDB approaches, there are several other, less common, types of non precision approach. They include localizer (LOC), back course (BC), simplified directional facility (SDF), localizer type directional aid (LDA), airport surveillance radar (ASR) and area navigation (RNAV) procedures. See Chapter 10 for a discussion of RNAV.

A *localizer (LOC)* approach provides very accurate course guidance to the threshold of a runway. With a LOC frequency in the navigation receiver, the CDI is approximately four times as sensitive as when tracking a VOR course. The width of a LOC course is from 3° to 6°, approximately 700 feet at the runway threshold. The OBS is disconnected when a localizer is tuned in; the OBS then has no function, except possibly to remind the pilot of the course.

Since a localizer is a component of the ILS, most ILS approach plates have LOC, or glide slope out, minimums published in the minimums box (figure 8-15). In some cases, the LOC approach is published on a separate plate. In the event that your glide slope receiver fails or the glide slope is out of service, you can make a LOC approach by referring to the time and groundspeed box and by timing from the FAF. The technique of flying the localizer is included in our discussion of the ILS in Chapter Nine.

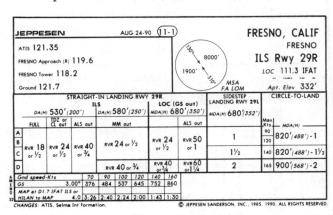

Figure 8-15

The localizer transmits another signal in the direction away from the airport. It is known as a **back course (BC)**, and at some airports there are separate LOC (BC) approach procedures. The CDI reacts to the localizer the same way regardless of whether the aircraft is on the front course or back course, so when flying a BC approach, you must make course corrections away from the needle. Since the transmitter is at the approach end of the runway when viewed from a BC approach, the CDI is much more sensitive as you get close to the airport than on a normal localizer approach. When flying a BC approach, ignore any glide slope indications you may receive. A BC approach is a nonprecision procedure.

A *localizer type directional aid (LDA)* is a localizer that is not aligned with a runway. The localizer transmitter may even be at a different airport. The Burbank, California, ILS localizer, for example, happens to cross nearby Van Nuys airport, and is the basis for the LDA-C approach to Van Nuys.

An LDA provides the same accuracy but does not bring the aircraft down the extended center line of the runway, as does a localizer. There may be straight-in minimums authorized if the LDA is aligned within 30° of the runway (figure 8-16).

The *simplified directional facility (SDF)* is humorously known as the "poor man's localizer," because it uses a simple, one or two element antenna and is much less expensive to install than a conventional localizer system. To make installation of the transmitter easier, the course centerline is often not aligned with the runway, although it crosses close to the approach end. It never has a glide slope, and the identifier is not preceded by "I" as is a localizer. It is flown like a localizer, but the course width is either 6° or 12°, wider than a standard localizer (figure 8-18).

Airport surveillance radar (ASR) approaches are available at some terminals. The controller uses a special large scale display on the radar screen to accurately vector the airplane to the threshold of the runway. The pilot is continuously informed of his distance from the runway and his position in relation to the course centerline. He is informed when to descend to the MDA. If, on the final segment of an ASR approach, the pilot receives no communications for 15 seconds, the rules require a missed approach.

At fields where there are published ASR approaches (Jeppesen publishes separate plates for ASR approaches), controllers are required to

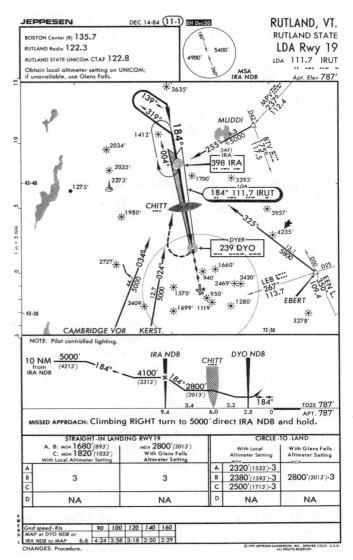

Figure 8-16

maintain ASR currency, so they are often willing to provide practice for a pilot, when their workload is not too heavy.

Visual and Contact Approaches. These approaches are meant to save time. Instead of executing a full instrument procedure or flying a circuitous series of vectors, the pilot simply flies to the airport and enters the pattern. The time saved is usually 10 or 15 minutes.

A visual approach clearance may be issued by the controller or requested by the pilot when the aircraft is in VFR conditions and can remain so throughout the remainder of the descent and landing. The pilot must maintain VFR and safe separation from any aircraft he is instructed to follow. Aircraft may be vectored for a visual approach when the ceiling is 500 feet above the controller's minimum vectoring altitude.

A pilot may refuse a visual approach if he prefers to conduct an instrument approach for practice or for any other reason, including unfamiliarity with the area.

A contact approach may be conducted even when the weather is less than VFR. It requires only "one mile and clear of clouds," and it must be requested by the pilot. During a contact approach, ATC will provide IFR separation, but the pilot is responsible for obstacle clearance. If he cannot maintain cloud clearance, or the visibility falls below 1 mile, the pilot must immediately advise ATC and alternate instructions will be issued.

Full and Straight-in Approaches

An approach that includes a procedure turn is called a **full approach**. There are several technicalities to understand regarding procedure turns.

A procedure turn is any maneuver used to reverse direction and establish the airplane inbound on the intermediate approach segment or final approach course. If a conventional turn is shown on the approach plate, the turn must be accomplished within the specified distance (usually 10 nautical miles), at or above the specified altitude, and on the specified side of the course. Distance and altitude information are obtained from the profile view on the approach plate (figure 8-16).

The outbound distance flown before the turn is started is at the pilot's discretion, as long as the turn is completed within the required distance from the fix. Two minutes is usually sufficient for all the necessary tasks and provides enough time inbound to become established on course and descend as necessary before getting back to the navaid. With a headwind or in turbulent conditions, the pilot may choose to lengthen this time. If the outbound leg is flown with a tailwind, the time may be shortened.

At the end of the outbound leg, make a 45 turn to the indicated side, and fly this heading for 1 minute. The proper course is always shown on the approach plate. At the end of a minute, make a 180° turn back towards the approach course, in the direction opposite the first turn, and hold the new heading until interception is accomplished. The turn onto the approach course is another 45°.

The conventional 45°-180°-45° procedure turn usually shown on approach plates may be flown as depicted, or it may be altered by the pilot to allow for wind or personal preference. Some alternate procedure turn patterns are shown in figure 8-17. Notice that there is no choice about the side of the course on which the turn is made.

The upper illustration shows a turn that might be used if there were a north wind. It consists of a 90° turn into the wind followed by a 270° turn in the other direction to intercept the course.

The second pattern might be used if there were a south wind. It uses only a 30° turn to diverge from the course, making it easier to re-intercept into the wind when the 1-minute leg is completed.

The third pattern can be used when the pilot has started a conventional 45° turn but sees that, because of bad navigating or a north wind component, he is not far enough from the inbound course. Even if he were inadvertently south of course, he could still re-intercept by making his second turn in the same direction as the first.

Some approach procedures prescribe a teardrop pattern instead of a conventional procedure turn. This maneuver is mandatory and must be flown as shown (figure 8-18).

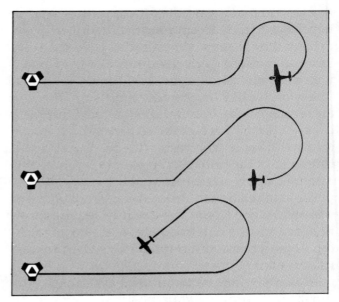

Figure 8-17

Figure 8-11 shows a VOR approach in which a holding pattern replaces the procedure turn. The holding pattern is also mandatory, and the pilot is expected to make the appropriate entry to the depicted pattern, according to his direction of arrival at the fix. The minimum number of turns in the hold is one, including the entry. That is, you must cross the fix twice, once outbound and once inbound. The length of the holding pattern leg is usually 1 minute and is shown in the profile view. If more time is needed to get established inbound at the proper altitude, the pilot should advise ATC that he wishes to make another circuit in the hold. The length of the holding pattern legs should not be extended.

Notice that figure 8-11 shows yet another structure that is different from those we have seen. The VOR is the IAF, and the holding pattern is the initial segment. At the completion of the hold, the aircraft is back at the VOR, which is now the intermediate fix and the beginning of the intermediate segment. The FAF, Kirdo Intersection, is not collocated with the IAF.

As previously mentioned, a full approach is one that includes a procedure turn. If, in some way, the procedure turn can be eliminated, it becomes a **straight-in approach**. Do not confuse a straight-in approach with a straight-in landing. An approach executed straight-in may be followed either by a straight-in landing or a circling maneuver.

There are four ways the procedure turn may be eliminated from an approach, as follows:

1. *Radar Vectors.* When radar vectored to an approach, you receive a sequence of headings to intercept the **final approach course** within 10 miles of the FAF on the outbound side. The final approach course is defined as the final approach segment extended past the FAF away from the airport. It usually coincides with the intermediate segment of the published procedure. When issuing the approach clearance, the controller includes your distance from the FAF, so that you know you are within the distance required for a descent to the intermediate segment altitude, once the course is intercepted. No procedure turn is expected.

When you are vectored for an approach, you must keep track of your position. To be as far ahead of the airplane as possible, set the radios for

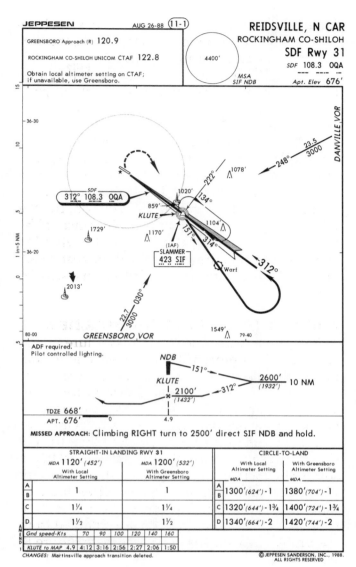

Figure 8-18

the approach as soon as the vectors begin and you are relieved of responsibility for navigating. Remember to identify the approach navaids. Complete the landing checklist before intercepting the final approach course, and if you are in any doubt about your position, do it sooner rather than later. Arriving at the FAF with an incomplete radio set-up, the mixture lean, the fuel on the wrong tank, and the airspeed too high, can be unnerving and dangerous.

Altitude awareness is important when you are being vectored for an approach. Occasionally a busy controller, or one accustomed to 3000-foot per minute descents from jets and turboprops, will keep you too long at too high an altitude for

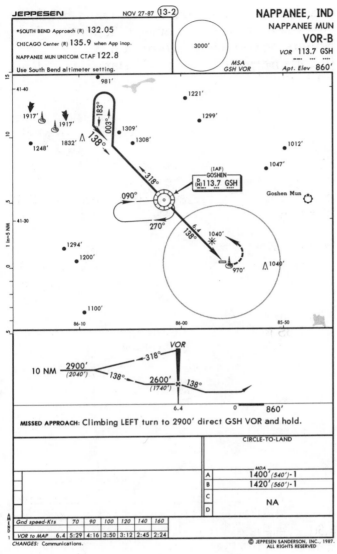

Figure 8-19

4. *DME Arc.* DME arcs are usually labeled "NoPT," but even if they are not, you are not expected to make a procedure turn after following a DME arc to intercept a final approach course.

An Actual Approach

Let's go through a typical nonprecision approach as you would study and fly it in actual conditions.

Assume that you are flying Piper Arrow N9876G, planning to land at Nappanee, Indiana. Figure 8-19 shows the plate for the VOR-B approach to Nappanee. Assume, also, that you receive the following weather information and clearance from South Bend Approach Control: "Cherokee nine eight seven six golf, no weather or runway information available for Nappanee; South Bend weather is 600 overcast, 2 miles in light rain and fog, wind 270° at 10, altimeter 29.98. You are cleared to the Goshen VOR via direct, cleared for the VOR-B approach to Nappanee Municipal, maintain 4000 until Goshen, report Goshen outbound."

"Roger, seven six golf, cleared for the approach, maintain 4000 until Goshen, will report Goshen outbound."

You descend to 4000 and, still at your cruise airspeed of 130 knots, track inbound to the VOR. Reaching the VOR is your first use of the Five T's: **Turn**—to the outbound course of 318°. **Time**—start your stopwatch for a 2-minute outbound segment. **Twist**—the OBS to the outbound course. **Throttle**—reduce power to slow to an approach speed of 100 knots. Since you have approach clearance, descend to the charted altitude of 2900 feet. **Talk**—to report Goshen outbound as instructed.

South Bend Approach, seven six golf, Goshen outbound."

During the procedure turn outbound (the initial segment of the approach), you concentrate on accurate tracking and leveling off slightly above 2900 feet (approach altitudes should be viewed as minimum altitudes; prefer to be a little high rather than a foot low).

Complete your landing checklist during this segment. Fuel is on the proper tank, and the fuel pump is on. Gear is down as you reach your gear speed of 129 knots, indicated airspeed (KIAS). Mixture is rich. Advancing the propeller with the

you to descend comfortably for the approach. If this situation develops, request a lower altitude.

2. *NoPT Transition.* When a feeder route is closely aligned with the final approach course and its altitude is low enough to permit a comfortable descent to minimums, it may be labeled "NoPT". In this case, no procedure turn is expected or required.

3. *Approach from a Hold.* If you are holding on the final approach course when cleared for the approach, you may go straight in; there is no need to reach the fix, turn outbound, and execute the procedure turn. This is true unless the profile view contains a note prohibiting a straight-in approach.

present power setting would cause it to go to redline RPM, so you delay the last item of the landing checklist.

On the initial segment of the approach, you also take the opportunity to review the approach plate, which you previously studied before takeoff, and burn the pertinent information into your memory.

The frequency box informs you that you should be talking to South Bend Approach, and you are. (It would help to have highlighted the frequency on the plate.) You received the South Bend altimeter setting with your last weather information, so your altimeter will read correctly on approach. You verify that you are flying the correct approach to the correct airport.

You see that the procedure turn will be conducted on the northeast side of your course and, from the profile view, that you will descend to 2600 feet once established inbound on the 138° inbound course (the inbound segment).

After crossing the VOR again, you may descend to the MDA of 1420 feet. (You should memorize this number, although you have already highlighted it on the approach plate with a yellow marker.) With a power-off stall speed in the landing configuration of 55 KIAS, your Arrow is actually a category "A" airplane, but you plan to enter the pattern and circle at a speed greater than 5 knots above the upper limit for the category (91 knots), so you must use category "B" minimums. At your approach speed of 100 knots, you will fly 3 minutes and 50 seconds between the FAF and the MAP, and the time, already highlighted on the plate, is also carefully etched in your memory.

With the South Bend weather reported at 600 feet, you may or may not see the airport on this approach. Another piece of information to memorize carefully is the first part of the MAP—a climbing left turn to 2900 feet back to the VOR station. You mentally note that the missed approach heading you will turn to before twisting the OBS to fly direct is approximately 290°. You mark this number in pencil on your chart, and you also memorize it.

During the initial segment, your head bobs up and down a bit as you divide your attention among the flight gauges, the clock and the approach plate. By the end of 2 minutes, you are established on course at the proper altitude and

have the rest of the approach committed to memory. You have also determined that the west wind requires a 5 southwest correction angle.

You turn right heading 003°, start the watch for a 1-minute leg, and twist in the inbound course of 138°. At this stage, there is no throttling or talking, and you mentally say "no throttle, no talk." On this leg, the CDI leaves the center for the right side of the dial.

One minute passes, and you make a left one-eighty to heading 183° and wait for the CDI to come off the peg. In about 30 seconds, the CDI starts moving and you begin your turn back to 143°, the inbound course plus your wind correction.

There is no timing on this segment; you merely wait for station passage, but, as you habitually say "time" to yourself, you check that the stopwatch is reset to "0" and ready to time the final segment. The OBS is already set to the inbound course, as you say "twist," you double check it. Throttle back to descend to 2600 feet. You are now "procedure turn inbound" but were instructed to report the FAF, so talking waits.

You approach the VOR with the needle centered, but it begins to wobble, presaging station passage. You ignore its fluctuations and hold the heading until the flag flips to FROM.

You begin the Five T's yet again. There is no turn, since the final approach course goes straight over the FAF. You start the stopwatch to time your 3:50. There is no twisting. You reduce the power to descend to 1450 feet (1420 plus a margin for error—it is often useful to round off the MDAs to the next higher multiple of 50 or 100 feet so that, if a gust costs you some altitude, you are still above minimums). Finally, you report final fix inbound.

"Roger, seven six golf, you can contact the advisory frequency now. Report on the ground by telephone or the missed approach on this frequency." You have already set your other radio to the unicom frequency, so you are ready to switch over.

Your 1200-foot descent takes slightly over a minute, and you reach the MDA with about two and a half minutes to go. Unicom advises that they are indeed using Runway 27, as you expected, and there is no reported traffic. The ground is visible, but the visibility is poor, and you don't see the airport immediately. Then it appears, straight ahead and about a mile away. You alter course slightly to cross the runway midfield and enter left downwind for Runway 27.

The DME Arc

"Cessna seven nine one yankee sierra, cleared for the VOR-DME Runway One-Two approach at Burlington via the one-nine-two radial and the 21 DME arc, maintain four thousand until established on the arc" (figure 8-20).

This is a simple and straightforward approach clearance, but such words strike fear in the hearts of many instrument pilots. Although it is fairly

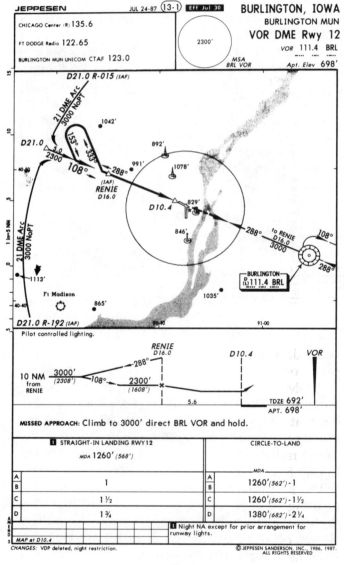

Figure 8-20

common as an initial approach segment, many pilots have had little experience with the DME arc and tend to view it as a sinister mystery. In fact, it is a useful maneuver and not at all mysterious.

Arcs are well worth practicing, not only because we must occasionally fly them, but because they are excellent exercises in the basic skills of visualizing position, heading and wind. Flying an arc means mentally picturing your position and distance from the station and the changing effect of the wind on the required heading. A Saturday afternoon practicing DME arcs not only helps to maintain your legal IFR currency, but also provides valuable experience.

It is easy to make up challenging and instructive DME arc exercises. Fly clockwise around a VORTAC on the 10 DME arc, make a 180° turn and fly counterclockwise on the 11 DME arc to a particular radial. Intercept the radial and track it inbound to intercept the 7 DME arc. Any combination of such exercises is good for sharpening proficiency and visualization skills.

DME arcs are used as initial segments of some VOR DME approaches, as shown in figure 8-20. A pilot approaching Burlington Municipal from the north, west or south, intercepts the arc, tracks it to the 288° radial and proceeds inbound to the airport. (Checking the low altitude en route chart, we see that the 015° and 192° radials define Victor airways; they form IAFs where they intercept the arc. Additional airways cross the arc on the 241°, 282°, and 322° radials.) An alternative would be to fly all the way to the VOR, track outbound on the 288° radial and execute a procedure turn. The arc is obviously more efficient.

DME arcs are also used as initial segments of ILS and localizer approaches, with the arc based on a nearby VORTAC (figure 8-21). At Pellston, the 158° and 176° radials are depicted for the benefit of the pilot equipped with only one nav radio. These **lead radials** alert him that it is time to turn inbound and switch over to the localizer.

Although most DME arcs are initial segments, the *United States Standard for Terminal Instrument Procedures* (TERPS) manual allows the use of DME arcs for the intermediate, final, and missed approach segments as well. In figure 8-22, the pilot arriving at Sloaf would follow the 14.7 DME arc all the way to the runway, descending at two step-

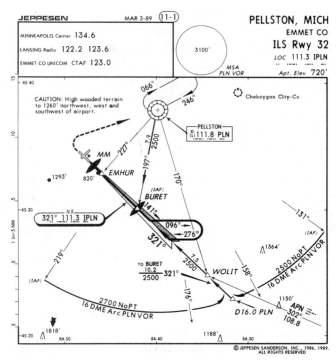

Figure 8-21

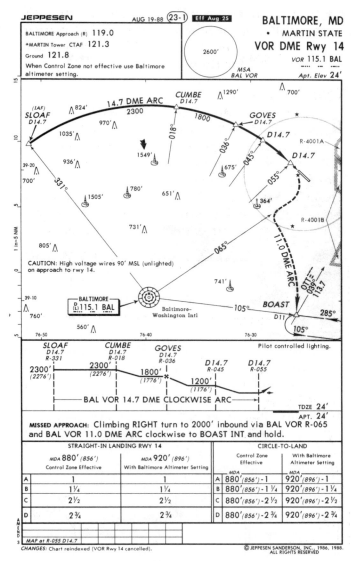

Figure 8-22

down fixes and the FAF, all of which are defined by crossing radials. The MAP is also defined by a crossing radial, and the missed approach procedure calls for intercepting another DME arc and tracking it to the holding fix. While this type of approach is rare, it is interesting and under lines the fact that the "complete" instrument pilot should have the DME arc in his bag of tricks.

It may reflect the average pilot's lack of familiarity with DME arcs that the FAA provides more obstacle clearance when the final approach segment is formed by one. For a straight final approach segment, the primary obstacle clearance area is 2 to 5 miles wide and provides 250 feet of clearance. When the final segment is an arc, it is 8 miles wide and gives 500 feet of clearance.

Flying a large curved arc as depicted on the typical approach plate is practically impossible. It would require both an infinitesimal bank angle and much more accurate rate of turn information than is provided by currently available instruments. For example, the 14.7 DME arc from Sloaf to the MAP (figure 8-22) is a distance of 22 miles. At 100 knots groundspeed, this would take 13 minutes, during which the heading would have to change 84°. The required rate of turn would be slightly more than one tenth of one degree per

second. I know of no way to fly with such precision.

A DME arc is actually flown as a sequence of **tangents** to the depicted circle. (You may remember that a tangent is a line that touches a circle at exactly one point.) Each tangent is perpendicular to the radial that touches the circle at that point (figure 8-23).

The shorter the tangents, the more often the heading is changed and the more nearly your flight path will approximate the actual curved arc shown on the plate. It would be ideal to change your heading every degree around the arc but also extremely difficult. For practical purposes, it is acceptable to change your heading every 10°, so

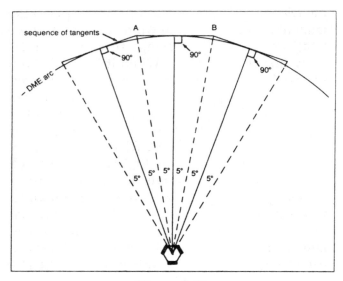

Figure 8-23

that in completing a full circle you actually fly a 36-sided polygon.

How closely this technique approximates the desired flight path depends on the size of the arc being flown. The larger the arc, the larger the error. However, the error will always be one tenth of a mile or less, if the arc's radius is not more than the FAA's maximum 30 miles. In figure 8-23, the maximum distance between the arc and the actual course flown occurs at points A and B.

The size of the arc also determines the difficulty of flying it accurately. The smaller the arc, the shorter is each straight course segment and the greater are the coordination and proficiency needed. The FAA designs approaches with arcs from 7 to 30 miles in radius. For various sizes, the following is a brief listing of the length of a 10° segment:

Arc Radius	Segment Length
7	1.2 nm
10	1.8 nm
15	2.6 nm
20	3.5 nm
25	4.7 nm
30	5.3 nm

In flying a DME arc, the first problem is to intercept it accurately. Typically, you will be flying inbound to the VORTAC on a particular radial with a clearance to intercept the arc.

Let's return to the clearance at the beginning of this section. The approach is shown in figure 8-20 and excerpted in figure 8-24. You are approaching the BRL VORTAC on the 192° radial (Victor-63) to intercept the 21 DME arc. Your OBS is set to 012°, and the DME is clicking down: 22, 21.9, 21.8, 21.7.... With a groundspeed of about 100 knots, begin a standard rate turn onto the arc about one half mile before reaching it. Turn to a heading at 90 to the course you are on, namely 282°. Since an inbound course to the VOR is always perpendicular to the tangent where it crosses the arc, this heading will put you exactly on course. During the turn, monitor the DME. If, as you approach your heading, you are still outside the arc, roll out of the turn early, heading 312°, a 30° intercept to join the tangent. If the turn carries you through the arc, continue turning to 252°, again a 30° intercept, to get on course from the inside.

At the completion of the turn, you are northwest of the 192° radial and ready to change the OBS setting. Since you are planning to turn inbound on the 288° radial, it would be convenient to use radials ending in "8" while flying the arc. Select the 198° radial and adjust your heading to 288°.

Once on the arc, fly each course segment perpendicular to the radial you are crossing. Since you are planning to fly each tangent across a 10° arc, it should extend from 5° before the selected radial to 5° beyond it. In our example, you would fly heading 288° until you are 5° past the 198° radial. But how do you know when you are 5° past it?

The CDI shows 10° off course as a full-scale deflection; it indicates 5 from the radial as a half-scale deflection. With the 198° selected, the needle will be half scale to the left as you cross the 203° radial. At that point, turn 10° right to heading 298°, and select 208° in the OBS. The CDI will initially be half scale to the right, moving left as you approach and cross the radial. When it reaches half scale left, turn again, this time to 308°, and select 218° in the OBS. Repeat this process of "turn 10, twist 10" until you approach the 288° radial.

The heading perpendicular to the radial you are crossing is called the **tangent heading**. It equals the tangent course, and, in "no-wind conditions," it will keep you close to the arc. Unfortunately, since "no-wind conditions" are rare, we must also plan a wind correction angle.

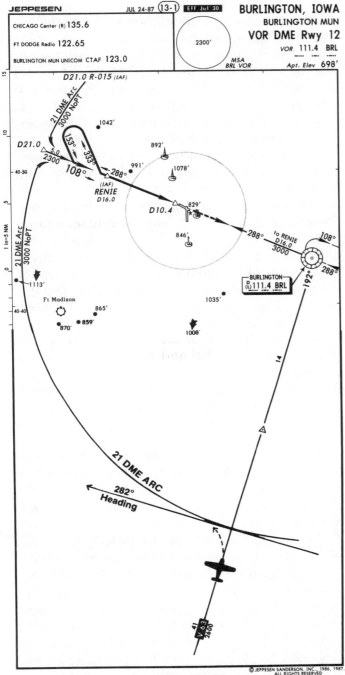

Figure 8-24

the DME returns to 21, turn 5° back towards the tangent heading as a trial wind correction. If the DME continues decreasing, turn another 10° away from the VORTAC. When it is steady, you are paralleling the tangent. Turn 10° more to intercept, then back towards the tangent heading half the total number of degrees used to intercept.

If the DME increases to 21.1, you are outside the arc. Turn 10° towards the VORTAC. If it does not return to 21.0, turn another 10°. It is more difficult to intercept the arc from outside than from inside, because you are flying away from, rather than towards it. Again, take a moment to visualize this. Once the arc is intercepted, turn back towards the tangent heading by half the number of degrees used to intercept. Repeat this process to bracket your arc segment.

The wind correction angle will change slightly and regularly from one segment to the next as the wind's effect on the airplane changes. At some point, it will be a direct crosswind, requiring a maximum correction, while 90° further around the arc, it will be a direct headwind, requiring no correction at all. On a windy day, the wind correction angle may vary from zero to 30° or 40°.

If many corrections are made, it can be difficult to keep track of the proper heading. Since arithmetic has no place in an IFR cockpit, we need a mechanical aid to figure it each time we turn. Comparing the OBS and DG is a good method. Since the tangent heading is perpendicular to the OBS setting, we can read it directly off the DG by putting the OBS setting on the wingtip. From this point, wind correction and intercept headings are easily chosen by turning 10° towards or away from the station.

How accurately can you fly a DME arc? With a good digital DME, the tangent heading will keep you within one tenth of a mile of the arc on a calm day. Except in the windiest conditions, a reasonable standard of accuracy is to stay within two tenths of a mile.

Confusion may occur as you intercept the 288° radial. As the needle centers, turn inbound to heading 108° and twist the OBS to the same setting. Do not make the common mistake of turning to the heading in the OBS, and flying away from the station. Once established on the 288° radial, make a straight-in approach to the airport. There is never a procedure turn from a DME arc, even

The wind correction technique is fairly simple. If the DME reads 20.9, you are inside the arc. By simply holding your heading, changing the OBS each 10° as explained above, you will eventually re-intercept it. Take a moment to visualize this. It explains why it is easier, on a very windy day, to fly slightly inside the arc than right on it.

To intercept more quickly and fly the arc more precisely, turn 10° away from the VORTAC. When if the arc is not labeled "NoPT." You'd better contact Burlington Radio now for airport advisories.

To The CFII

In this section of the course, cover all the approach plate symbols, including the obscure ones, and discuss how to study an approach plate. Emphasize the systematic study of the plate, the importance of being familiar with it before the flight begins, and the value of being able to extract necessary information quickly and accurately.

Some instructors delight in handing a student an unfamiliar plate ten miles from the initial approach fix and demanding that he fly the approach. This might realistically occur to a pilot on rare occasions, but it has very little training value. Giving a student a task for which he is not prepared and watching him botch it up erodes his confidence, reduces his respect for you, and ultimately lengthens his training. It is far better to teach him thoroughly how to do things correctly and to add little by little to the tasks you give him, so each one represents a slight stretch, not an impossible challenge.

Make sure the student understands the significance, not just the meaning, of each symbol on the approach plate. Jeppesen's documentation is excellent, and it is worthwhile to go through it with him so that he knows exactly how to look up an unfamiliar symbol. Knowing where to look for any piece of information can be more valuable than memorizing as much as you can.

Cover approach clearances, including their meaning and exact phrasing. Since communications are frequently difficult for new instrument pilots, knowing what to expect will help him interpret half understood clearances. Give him clearances repeatedly until he can say them back accurately. Your ability to realistically simulate ATC is valuable here. If your student has particular trouble with approach clearances, try having him make some up and read them to you. Often this exercise gets them over their fear of the "officialese."

Nonprecision approaches require no new skills; just the integration of previously learned material. Most errors will be in organization. Failure to use the Five T's is the most common,

and often causes trouble, especially in crossing the final approach fix. To work on this in a simulator, use an approach such as the Poughkeepsie VOR-A (figure 8-9). As soon as he crosses the FAF and correctly executes the Five T's, blip him back outside the fix, onto the intermediate segment, and let him do it again. This technique lets him practice the difficult part of the maneuver many times in a few minutes, rather than the few times an hour possible in an airplane.

Complete as much as possible of the orientation and procedure work on the simulator. Simulating ATC is a good skill for you to employ, to give the student a true impression of just how busy he will be. Break in with weather, unexpected clearances and traffic advisories at inopportune moments, and teach him the magic words "stand by."

When he handles communicating well, try this type of sample dialog to muddy the waters:

Student (reporting FAF to the tower): "Nine One Golf VOR inbound."

You: "Six Seven Lima cleared to land."

Student: "Nine One Golf VOR inbound."

You: "Aircraft calling tower, say again your call sign."

Student: "Cessna Two Three Nine One Golf, *VOR inbound.*"

You: "Apache Five Papa Lima, cleared for takeoff. . . ."

You get the idea. It is especially revealing if he makes the common mistake of reporting before starting the watch or reducing power. Emphasize the importance of the Five T's and of "aviating" and "navigating" before "communicating."

To give vectors for an NDB or VOR approach, use a collocated NDB and VOR if possible. This gives you continuous azimuth and distance information and you will quickly learn to vector him accurately, even if your simulator has no plotter.

Don't go to the airplane prematurely. If he gets disoriented in the airplane, you goofed.

Nonprecision Approach Quiz

1. You are cleared for an approach. When may you descend from your last assigned altitude?
2. What is the radius of the MSA circle on your approach plate?
3. When should the MSA be used and how much obstacle clearance do they provide?
4. What are the segments of a typical approach and where does each one begin?
5. Define MDA.
6. Define HAA. Where is it found?
7. Define HAT. Where is it found?
8. What is the cardinal rule for a circle-to-land maneuver?
9. What action should you take if you lose sight of the airport during a circle-to-land maneuver?
10. What is a VDP?
11. What is a step-down fix?
12. List the various types of nonprecision approach.
13. Define "straight-in approach."
14. Define "straight-in landing."
15. Define "full approach."
16. What are the four ways to eliminate a procedure turn?
17. What is the difference between a precision and a nonprecision approach?
18. What is the maximum radius of a DME arc?
19. What is a tangent heading?
20. What are the differences between a visual and a contact approach?

CHAPTER NINE

PRECISION APPROACHES

On top, at two thousand feet, we were enjoying beautiful sunshine. The dense cloud layer below us stretched to the horizon in every direction, like a movie maker's conception of heaven. Even a weather-savvy pilot could entertain idle thoughts of stepping out and walking on it. We imagined our earthbound friends below stumbling around in the murk of the low pressure system.

The destination weather was as reported 200 and an eighth. We had already missed one approach, and I pondered the alternatives as approach control gave us vectors for another try.

"Piper two two three one yankee, you are five miles from the outer marker, turn right heading two-one-zero, cleared for the ILS 24 at Suffolk County Airport, maintain two thousand until established on the localizer."

"Right to two-one-zero, cleared for the ILS, maintain two thousand until established, three one yankee."

"Three one yankee, contact Suffolk County Tower now, one two five point three."

"One two five point three, three one yankee.

"Suffolk Tower, two two three one yankee is with you at two thousand."

"Three one yankee, cleared to land Runway 24, report on the ground or missed approach. And three one yankee, be advised that Suffolk weather is now 200 and a half. Wind is calm."

Irrationally, the magic words "200 and a half"

bolstered my optimism. Like many veterans of years of hangar flying, I attach a delicious sense of romance to shooting approaches to "two-hundred-and-a-half." Actually, with the tower at least a mile and a half from the middle marker, where the visibility counts, the reported visibility has no close relationship to what the pilot will see at decision height. With the visibility hovering around minimums, the difference between a half and a quarter mile, between a landing and a missed approach, can be a few stray wisps of fog drifting across the approach lights.

As the localizer needle left the peg, I checked the DG against the mag compass one last time before beginning a right turn towards the inbound course. I was steady on a heading of 240°, and the needle was stationary, about two dots off center. "Wind calm. Two four zero is the reference heading," I said out loud, to rivet it in my memory.

A little rudder pressure and a 5° left turn started the needle creeping towards center. As it centered, a turn back to 240° stopped its movement. My job now was simply to hold heading exactly. Any movement of the localizer needle would signal a change in the reference heading and the need for a slight correction.

According to the approach plate, I could now descend to 1500 feet, but I chose to remain above the clouds as long as possible and descend only when the glide slope came alive.

As the needle moved down, I reduced the throttle to the approach descent power setting and lowered the *nose half a dot on the attitude indicator. I would fly the approach at 90 knots, making slight glide slope corrections on the attitude indicator and adjusting the power if the airspeed varied more than four knots. Since I had been level at 90 knots, no trim adjustment was necessary.*

We slipped into the clouds at 1800 feet and continued descending to what I hoped would be a landing. My companion, Jean, a cooperative and cheerful veteran passenger, observed the "no talking on approach" rule and sat alertly forward, looking for the approach lights. She had seen a car on the airport highway as we made our earlier go-around and now was determined to see the lights.

The approach went smoothly. Passing 1000 feet, light turbulence developed, and the localizer needle drifted slightly to the left. A 4° turn re-centered it and a new heading of 238° held it steady. Even with light winds, surface friction caused a slight change in the reference heading.

Passing 300 feet, 33 feet above DH, the localizer was a dot off, and I turned slightly left again, just as Jean exclaimed, "There they are!"

Sure enough, I saw what was obviously the beginning of the approach light system, flashing strobes and all, but canted at a crazy angle. It took a moment to realize that we were in a course correction and banked slightly left. The lights were the only ground reference, and they appeared to be sloping downward from above us. Interestingly, less than a 10° bank had caused this illusion.

Leveling the wings on the attitude indicator, checking the altimeter, and verifying the lights were still in sight and level as they should be, I decided to continue the approach. More lights, and then the threshold slid beneath the wheels. Forty seconds later, we were on the ground, engulfed in fog, reporting to the tower.

"Two two three one yankee on the ground."

"Roger, three one yankee. If you can find the center taxiway, turn right, taxi to the ramp."

Once again, what had seemed to be an adventure — especially when I was a student and then a new instrument pilot, had turned out to be essentially routine. The thrill of doing it successfully was still there, but so was the confidence borne of practiced skill, experience and faith in the procedures.

Precision approaches provide descent as well as course guidance. They require that the pilot develop the skill to control his glide path according to needle indications in the cockpit or verbal instructions from a controller on the ground.

The missed approach point on a precision approach occurs when the airplane, descending on the glide slope, reaches the **decision height**. At this altitude the pilot must either make visual contact with the runway (or lights or markings associated with the runway) or execute a missed approach. There is no leveling off at decision height; one must either continue visually to a landing or immediately start the missed approach.

The *microwave landing system (MLS)* has recently come out of the experimental phase. Installations are being made by the FAA and state aviation departments for general use at public airports, but there are still very few in commission. Long range plans call for the MLS to eventually replace the ILS as the standard landing system in the United States and also for international civil aviation.

In light airplanes, the MLS is flown with left-right and up-down indicators, but a special MLS receiver is required. In addition to DME, airborne MLS installations may provide such special features as variable glide slope angle and curved approach paths.

Precision approach radar (PAR) is available at only a handful of civil airports. Called Ground Controlled Approach (GCA) by the Navy, it exists at most military bases but is not available for civilian use except for practice approaches and emergencies. If a GCA exists, it is noted under the facility name on the communications panel of the Jeppesen low altitude en route chart.

The PAR approach uses a special precision radar, independent of the airport surveillance equipment, that scans only a narrow area of the final approach path. The controller uses a two part radar screen, one part showing the airplane's horizontal position in relation to the final approach course and one showng its vertical position in relation to the glide slope. The controller talks continuously to the pilot on final, giving him verbal course and glide slope instructions and providing an extremely accurate instrument letdown. Since this system requires one controller's full attention for each airplane on final approach, and the FAA lacks

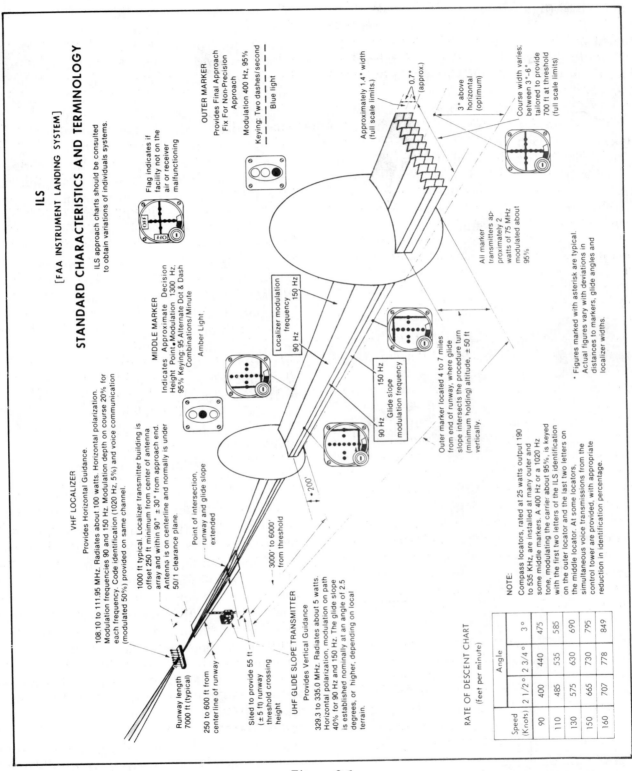

Figure 9-1

this amount of manpower, civilian use of PAR has declined. PAR approaches are shown on their own plates in the Jeppesen chart system.

For most practical purposes, when civilian lightplane pilots speak of a precision approach they are referring to the **instrument landing** system (ILS) (figure 9-1).

The ILS is the queen of instrument approaches. It allows you to land safely in weather that would be unthinkable if only nonprecision procedures were available. To the uninitiated, its accuracy seems almost supernatural. As if its extreme accuracy were not impressive enough, the ILS is one of the easiest instrument approaches to fly correctly.

The typical ILS consists of five parts (figures 9-1 and 9-2). The **localizer** transmitter provides lateral guidance and is usually located at the far end of the runway, so that its course overlies the centerline. The **glide slope** transmitter sits

about 1,000 feet from the runway threshold, abeam the fixed distance marker, so that the **threshold crossing height (TCH)** of the glide slope is approximately 50 feet (see figure 9-2 profile) and an aircraft flying the glide slope, and not altering its descent angle after passing the glide slope transmitter, will touch down on the fixed distance marker. The **outer marker** is roughly five miles from the runway, approximately where an aircraft at the intermediate approach altitude will intercept the glide slope. The **middle marker** is approximately one-half mile from the threshold, about where an airplane on the glide slope reaches decision height. There may be a low power NDB, known as a **compass locator**, at the outer or middle marker. These are then called the **locator outer marker (LOM)** or **locator middle marker (LMM)**. An **approach lighting system (ALS)** is usually associated with an ILS. These systems offer a large array of brilliant lighting as far as half a mile from the runway. They can be seen by the pilot in all but the worst of weather.

The decision height on the typical ILS is 200 feet above the touchdown zone. A Category II ILS offers a decision height of 150 or 100 feet above the touchdown zone but is usable only by specially certified aircraft and crew.

The Localizer

The localizer (LOC) transmitter sits beyond the far end of the ILS runway at most airports so its course overlies the centerline. It may look like a row of big red mushrooms across the runway end, a row of elongated plastic pods on poles, arrays of short lengths of pipe, or stretches of cyclone fence with various devices attached to their faces. The signal is broadcast on one of 40 designated frequencies in the 108.1 - 111.95 MHz range, the same range as terminal VOR's. Localizer frequencies are always on "odd tenth" channels (108.1, 108.15, 108.3, 108.35, etc.).

The Morse Code identifier is four letters, the first of which is always an "I" (figure 9-2). ATC can talk on these frequencies, so if your communications receiver fails it might pay to keep the volume up; you can respond with the ident button on your transponder. Localizer frequen-

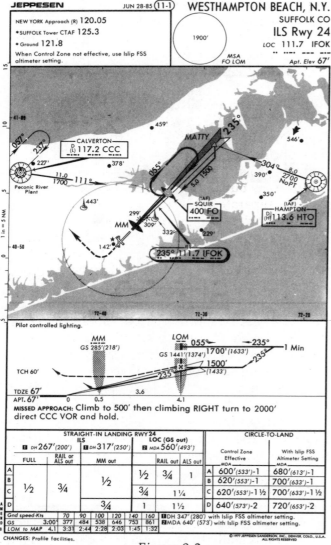

Figure 9-2

cies are received by the same nav equipment as VOR signals and although different circuits are used internally to decode the course signal, the CDI reacts to them similarly. The OBS is inoperative when the instrument is tuned to a LOC frequency.

Localizer width varies from 3° to 6°, depending on the distance of the transmitter from the landing threshold. The exact width is chosen to produce a signal 700 feet wide at the threshold. A full scale needle deflection indicates 1.5° to 3° off course, which means that the localizer is approximately four times as sensitive as a VOR signal. On an instrument with five dots each side of center, one dot represents approximately 300 feet at the outer marker, and 100 feet at the middle marker.

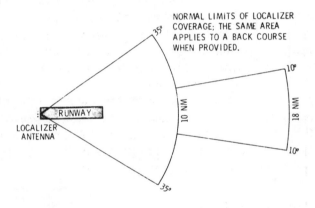

NORMAL LIMITS OF LOCALIZER COVERAGE; THE SAME AREA APPLIES TO A BACK COURSE WHEN PROVIDED.

RUNWAY

LOCALIZER ANTENNA

10°
10°
35°
35°
10 NM
18 NM

Figure 9-3

Off course indications are usable within 10° of the course centerline as far as 18 miles from the transmitter, and within 35° of the centerline within 10 miles of the transmitter (figure 9-3). Needle readings may be unreliable more than 35° from the course and sometimes cause confusion during vectors for an ILS, especially downwind abeam the airport.

The localizer is aligned to within 3° of the runway centerline and is normally lined up exactly. If it is angled one or two degrees from the runway, it is shown on the approach plate plan view as an "offset localizer" and a note is printed on the profile view (figure 9-4). In figure 9-4 the localizer course is 060°, while the runway heading is actually 059° (the runway heading is shown on the airport diagram below the runway number).

The localizer back course is transmitted away from the airport directly opposite the ILS. It should not be used for navigation, unless there is a published procedure for doing so.

The Glide Slope

The glide slope transmitting antenna is located about 1,000 feet from the runway threshold, abeam the fixed distance marker. It is about twenty feet high and is usually next to a small red and white shack. An aircraft following the glide slope to a landing would theoretically touch down on the fixed distance marker, the largest pair of white marks on the runway, 1000 feet from the threshold. However, the glide slope is *not* usable to touchdown. It may become unusable anywhere below decision height, but in any case, it "flares out" somewhere between 18 and 27 feet above the runway, and generates confused signals once you are past the antenna site.

Glide slopes are broadcast on UHF frequencies in the 330 MHz range, and aircraft using them must have a UHF glide slope receiver. The frequencies are paired with localizer frequencies and are *automatically* selected when the localizer is tuned in, but the glide slope signal is picked up by a separate receiver which may be part of the panel unit or may be installed behind the instrument panel or in the tail of the airplane.

The glide slope signal is 1.4° wide and is normally transmitted at an angle 3° above the horizontal. It coincides with the glide path provided by VASI lights. At the outer marker, the glide slope height is approximately 50 feet per dot; by the middle marker it narrows to a mere 8 feet per dot. It is normally usable to within a wingspan of the runway.

There are additional signals known as "false glide slopes" at altitudes above the proper glide slope. The glide slope transmitter may also emit signals in the opposite direction, towards the localizer back course, which may activate the glide slope needle during a back course approach. These signals should be ignored entirely.

In some cases ILS DME is provided. If your DME is manually tuned, you will have to set it to the LOC frequency. The DME ground beacon is located at the glide slope transmitter site,

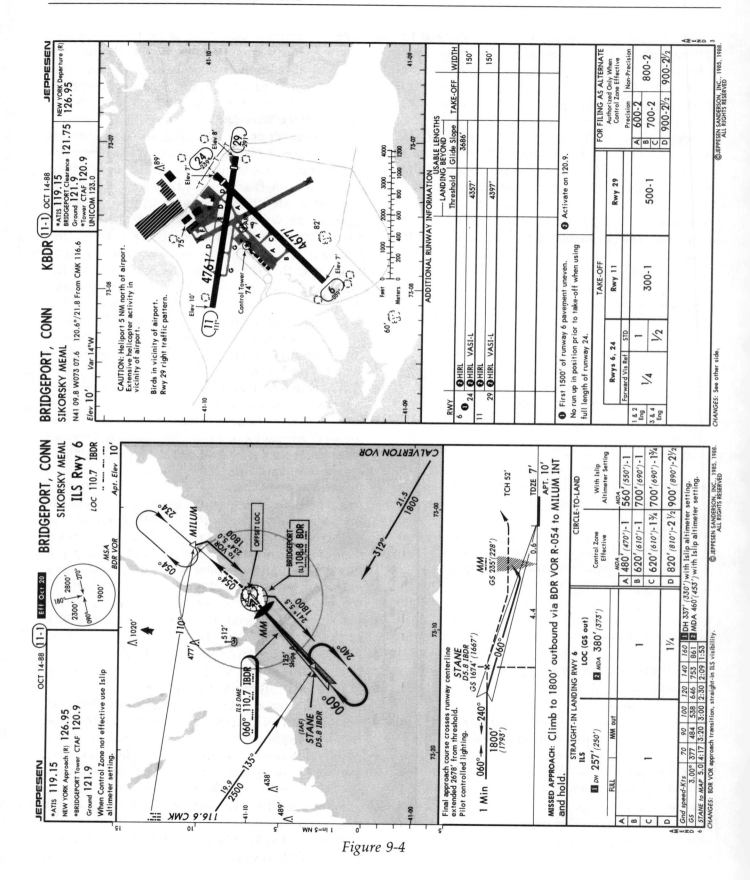

Figure 9-4

effectively providing distance to touchdown information.

Large and turbine powered aircraft are required by FAR 91.129 to remain at or above the glide slope on an approach to an ILS runway. All aircraft must remain on or above a VASI glide path, when available. While not mandatory, it is common sense for any pilot to fly at or above the glide slope on an ILS. Because of its accuracy, the ILS does not provide as much terrain clearance as other types of approach and to go below it is courting danger. On a bumpy day, it is wise to create a margin of safety by flying a dot high.

The missed approach point (MAP) on a precision approach is reached when the aircraft on the glide slope comes to **Decision Height (DH)** — there is no leveling off. The pilot sees the DH only once — as he reaches it and starts the missed approach climb or as he passes through it on the way to the runway. Happily, ILS approaches are so accurate and so easy to fly, that they are completed successfully far more often than not.

Other Equipment

A cardinal rule of instrument flying is to stay ahead of every situation. "Getting behind the airplane" can be blamed for most mishaps and near mishaps, not to mention failed checkrides. On an ILS, set up as much equipment as possible as early as possible in the approach. There may be as many as *seven* radios involved. A simple mental checklist is provided by the radios themselves: you may need to tune each and every one! Here is what you would do to prepare for the ILS 24 at Suffolk County (figure 9-2):

#1 com: Set to 120.05 to call approach;

#2 com: Preset to 125.3, anticipating handoff to tower;

#1 nav: Localizer (111.7) tuned and *identified*; OBS set to 235° as a memory aid;

#2 nav: Calverton VOR (117.2) tuned and *identified* in anticipation of a missed approach; OBS set to 300°, the approximate course to CCC;

ADF: Squir compass locator (400 KHz) tuned and *identified*;

Markers: On and tested.

DME: There is no ILS DME on this approach, but if there were, you would be sure the DME was slaved to the number one nav. If your DME is manually tuned, you would have to select the localizer frequency in the DME itself.

The Squir radio beacon, like most beacons at outer marker sites, is a *compass locator* or class LOM (locator outer marker) NDB. Its power output is less than 25 watts, and its range is nominally 15 miles. However, the range of individual beacons may be more or less than the rated 15 miles and may even vary from one direction to another. Like all LOM's, Squir broadcasts the first two letters, not counting the leading "I", of the associated localizer identifier (FO).

LOM's permit flying direct to the outer marker from any point on the chart. In a non-radar environment they allow flexibility in routing and can often save minutes from a flight. They are also a valuable aid to orientation when radar is available.

The **marker beacon** receiver is a single frequency radio permanently tuned to 75 MHz. All marker beacons in the ATC system, Outer, Middle, Inner, Fan, and Back Course, transmit on this frequency. There is usually a test switch for the marker beacon lights. The audio portion can be "tested" if your departure takes you out over a middle or outer marker. Marker beacons should be turned on and tested before each IFR flight. The high-low sensitivity switch should be in the *low* position, unless you are suspicious of the receiver. High sensitivity means reception over a greater area and less precise position identification.

CDI behavior (on a standard VOR display — not an HSI) is not affected by aircraft heading, and correct interpretation depends only on the direction you are flying. With a right needle, you are left of course, if your heading agrees with the localizer front course. However, when flying *outbound from* the runway on the front course or *inbound to* the runway on the back course, a right needle means right of course, and you must make corrections away from the needle.

In effect, the CDI behaves with the localizer as with a VOR. If you fly a course TO a VOR, you fly to the needle and continue to do so flying FROM the station after passage. Similarly, if you fly inbound on the localizer and continue over the airport and outbound on the back course, the needle interpretation will not change: corrections will all be made towards the CDI. Flying *inbound* on the *back* course and continuing outbound on the front course, all corrections will be away from the needle.

On some nav instruments, the CDI's arc is divided into yellow and blue halves, reflecting an older method of interpreting the needle, which was to remember that it points to the color where the airplane is. The needle on the

blue side meant the airplane was on the shaded side of the localizer; the yellow side was the unshaded part. Notice that a localizer is shaded on the right (facing the airport), while a back course is shaded on the left (figure 9-5).

Some CDI displays and some auto pilots have a "back course select" switch to reverse the needle indications and allow normal needle interpretations when inbound on a back course or outbound on a front course. If your display has such a function, make sure *well before the approach* that the switch is set correctly.

The two marker beacons on a standard ILS provide range information, but neither is actually required for the conduct of the approach. The Outer Marker (OM) is located at approximately the point where the glide slope intersects the intermediate approach altitude. However, the OM should not be treated as the final approach fix. Descent begins at glide slope interception, usually outside the marker, as on the ILS 24 at Suffolk County. On this approach, the marker is crossed at 1441 feet on the glide slope (figure 9-2, profile). If it occurs inside the marker, *interception* is still the signal to begin descent.

The OM is identified by a flashing blue light and an audio signal emitting 120 *dashes* per minute. There is no change in landing minima if the OM is out of service.

The MM is positioned approximately where the aircraft reaches decision height, about 3500 feet from the runway threshold. It should not be used to identify the missed approach point — it merely provides backup information. The MM is identified by alternate dots and dashes (·–·–·–) at the rate of 95 of each per minute.

If the decision height is 200 feet above touchdown, it increases by 50 feet with the MM out of service unless an allowable substitute (a LMM or precision radar) is available (see minima box figure 9-2). This applies whether the inoperative component is on the ground or in the airplane.

With no MM installed, the decision height is 250 feet above touchdown rather than 200. A few ILS's have 250 feet minima owing to other design considerations, such as a required climb gradient for the missed approach segment or poor ground station performance due to reflections from terrain or buildings. If the DH is 250 feet, there is no penalty for an inoperative MM.

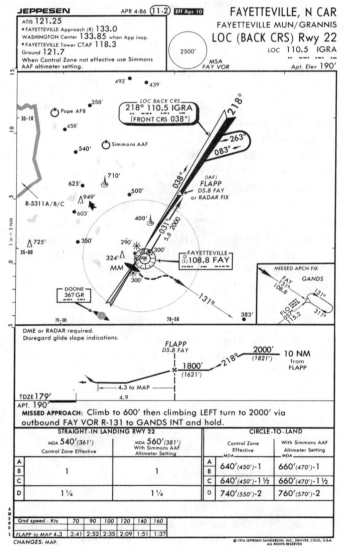

Figure 9-5

The final component usually associated with an ILS is the *approach light system* (ALS). The ALS is one of the most welcome sights to a pilot on a tight approach. On an ILS to minimums he sees the approach lights before he sees the runway and it is on that basis that he decides to continue below minimums and land. Approach lights, especially large systems such as the ALSF-I and ALSF-II, which are installed at the approach end of Category II runways, can be mind boggling, especially when combined with touchdown zone lighting and runway centerline lights. On a clear night they can be blinding from miles away from the airport, and by the same token, can be seen through awfully heavy murk. Some clear night, ask the approach controller to turn them up all the way for you. The display is truly amazing.

For the relatively small role they play, approach light systems add a surprising amount to the body of aviation acronyms. Here is a partial list (see also figure 9-6):

ALS	Approach Light System
HIALS	High Intensity ALS
MIALS	Medium Intensity ALS
MALS	MIALS
SFL	Sequenced Flashing Lights
F	SFL
RAIL	Runway Alignment Indicator Lights
ALSF-I	ALS with SFL
ALSF-II	ALS with SFL
SALS	Short ALS
SALSF	Short ALS with SFL
SSALS	Simplified Short ALS
SSALF	Simplified Short ALS with SFL
SSALR	Simplified Short ALS with RAIL
MALSF	Medium Intensity ALS with SFL
MALSR	Medium Intensity ALS with RAIL
ODALS	Omni-Directional ALS

It is *not* necessary to memorize all the approach light system names or abbreviations. Just notice that they nearly all contain the letters "AL" for approach lights. In the minima box on the approach plate, they are referred to merely as ALS (figure 9-2), regardless of type, while the exact information is included on the airport diagram.

The difference between RAIL and Sequenced

Flashers is that the former are positioned beyond the main part of the ALS, while the latter are within it (figure 9-6). They are both known to pilots as the "rabbit," after the artificial critter that leads the greyhounds around the track at dog races. Visibility requirements are increased when the ALS is out of service.

In low weather, the approach light system often determines whether or not a landing can be made, as it is usually the first sight the pilot gets of the ground. FAR 91.175 gives a good practical yardstick for deciding whether to continue a descent below the DH. It requires that at least one of the following be clearly visible to the pilot:

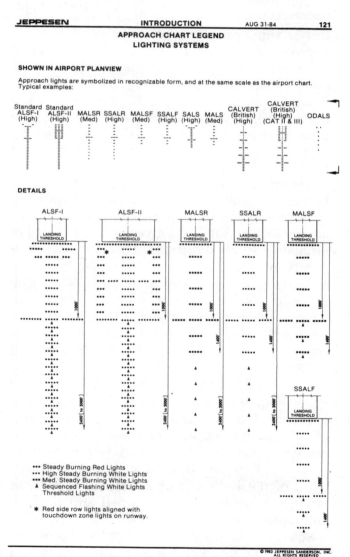

Figure 9-6

The ALS;

The threshold, threshold markings or lights;

Runway end identifier lights (REIL, not RAIL!);

VASI;

The touchdown zone, touchdown zone markings or lights;

The runway, runway markings or lights.

FAR 91.175 also requires at least the flight visibility specified by the procedure being flown. If the ALS or RAIL is out of service, visibility minimums increase (figure 9-2). For commercial operators under Parts 135 or 121 of the FAR's, this is significant, as they may not begin the approach if the field is reporting below landing minimums. For private operators there is no such restriction. The approach may be *tried* even if reported conditions are 0-0. As a practical matter, if the approach lights can be seen through the windshield, and not merely out the side window, you probably have the required landing visibility.

Reported visibility is the greatest distance that can be seen through half the horizon circle from the observation point. When conditions are varying rapidly, it is given as the average of visibilities in all directions. Since the observation point is usually the tower, which is at least a mile from your position at decision height, the reported visibility is not a good indicator of what you can expect to see at the end of your approach. This is especially true when it is changing rapidly, as for example, in thin and drifting fog.

The white light on the marker beacon panel has several uses. It will flash in conjunction with a series of audio dots (. . . . .) at the rate of 360 per minute as you pass over an inner marker. Inner markers are installed at decision height on Category II ILS approaches. A refinement of the ordinary, or category I ILS, these facilities allow specially equipped and certified aircraft to descend to even lower minimums.

Some localizer back course (BC) approaches include a BC marker which flashes white and transmits pairs of audio dots (.. .. .. ..).

Fan markers (FM) still exist in some places,

usually as part of a nonprecision approach. They are identified by a flashing white light and a repeating dot-dash-dot signal (.—. .—.). If two fan markers are close together, one may be identified by dash-dot-dash (—.— —.—) to avoid confusion.

Technique

There is an important difference between *procedure* and *technique*.

An ILS is a charted procedure for approaching an airport. When assigned an approach, you are required by FAR Part 91 to fly the courses and altitudes on the approach plate. A radar controller would be surprised and probably irate to see you doing something different from the published procedure.

Technique is a method of completing the approach, and allows a fair amount of discretion. You set the radios, lower the landing gear, and memorize the decision height when you like. You fly the approach at any reasonable airspeed, and you organize your instrument scan to suit yourself. These are parts of your technique and are up to you.

Pilots enjoy arguing the merits of their own techniques. In addressing the ILS, we hasten to mention that there is often more than one good technique to conduct a particular procedure. Those recommended here are not chiseled in stone, but they do work nicely.

Learning to track an ILS need not take the weeks it so often does. Properly taught, a student can learn it quickly and painlessly. With a good briefing and attention to scan, many students fly a satisfactory approach on the very first try.

The ILS is an application of basic attitude flying. As we discussed in Chapter 3, we divide the instruments into control and performance groups, according to their function. The attitude indicator and tachometer (or manifold pressure gauge) are control instruments, while the airspeed indicator, altimeter, turn coordinator, DG, and VSI are the performance group. For the ILS, the localizer and glide slope needles are additional *performance* instruments.

A key principle in developing a scan pattern is that you must look at a control instrument when making a control input. If you are adjusting the power, look at the power indicator to be sure you set it to the desired value. For any pitch or bank change, look at the attitude indicator.

The performance instruments are used to judge the control inputs. The airspeed indicator evaluates your power setting, the DG shows whether you are holding the desired heading, and the nav needles reveal the overall efficacy of your control movements.

Let's assume you are being radar vectored for the ILS approach to Runway 9 in your Turbo Arrow N57299. There is a compass locator at the outer marker, and you have arrived in the terminal area from the east. You will be vectored in a large pattern with downwind, base, and final legs.

"Two niner niner, fly heading two-seven-zero, descend and maintain two thousand."

The CDI is unreliable as you pass abeam the airport; the localizer signal is guaranteed usable only within 35° of the final approach course. The ADF indicates whether you are north or south of the airport, and we'll assume you are vectored around to the south, as in figure 9-7.

As the ADF needle passes the wing, showing you abeam of the outer marker, slow to your approach speed of 100 knots. If you had not already been cleared to the intermediate segment altitude of 2000 feet, you would suspect approach has forgotten you, and it would be wise to query the controller.

As the airplane is slowed opposite the outer marker, complete the landing checklist: mixture, fuel selector, and shoulder belts. Postpone advancing the prop control to avoid a blast of noise at redline RPM. If you fly the approach with partial flaps, lower them here.

When to drop the gear is a subject of controversy. Some pilots slow down with the wheels in the wells and lower them at glide slope interception. For many airplanes, this starts a 500 feet per minute descent with no airspeed change and is quicker and easier than making a power adjustment. It also allows a slightly more fuel efficient operation during the early parts of the approach, while actually getting through them at a higher overall speed.

This gear management technique is efficient

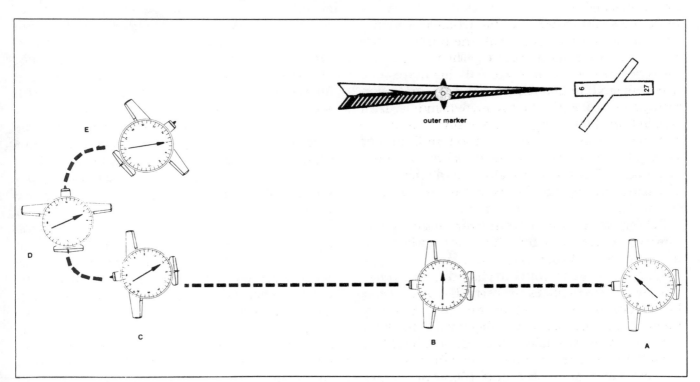

Figure 9-7

and widely used, especially by professional pilots. It also has notable drawbacks.

Slowing a fast airplane to approach speed with the gear up is time consuming and must be started well in advance. One technique is to reduce the power below the required setting and then increase it again when the desired airspeed is reached. This slows the airplane down more quickly but increases pilot workload and may overcool the engine, with resulting long term damage.

This technique also means memorizing two additional power settings, since you still need a gear down approach configuration for leveling off on a nonprecision approach, as well as a gear up approach descent configuration for descending during initial and intermediate approach phases. The latter configuration is especially hard on the engine in cold weather.

The main disadvantage of keeping the gear up until final is that it increases the chance of a wheels up landing, which, unlikely as it may seem, is possible when some distraction makes the pilot vary his normal routine. Difficulty in communicating, a minor equipment failure, or turbulence can result in a departure from habit and an embarrassing, expensive, dangerous incident. Lowering the gear earlier during a less busy portion of the approach allows more time to check and notice a possible gear extension malfunction and provides more time to deal with such a failure.

A good technique, especially for low time or marginally current instrument pilots in high performance airplanes, is to include lowering the gear in performing the rest of the landing checklist, opposite the outer marker. The airplane slows down more easily and can be trimmed once and for all to the approach configuration. Additional gear checks can be programmed into your routine at the outer marker and over the threshold, to further reduce chances of forgetting it.

The first turn towards the final approach course frequently comes when the ADF needle is 30° off the tail (figure 9-7).

"Two niner niner, turn right heading three-three-zero."

This is the beginning of the "base leg" portion of the approach, which usually consists of one or two vectors. This is the ideal time to memorize critical details of the procedure: the ILS course, the decision height, and at least the first part of the missed approach (i.e., climb to what altitude and turn to what heading). Make a last check of the frequencies. The tower frequency is in the second radio, so you don't have to fumble with the selector when handed off, probably just as you intercept the glide slope.

"Two niner niner, turn right heading zero-two-zero."

You can anticipate the approach clearance with the next vector. The final vector usually gives a 30° intercept with the localizer.

"Five seven two niner niner, you are six miles from the outer marker; turn right heading zero-six-zero, cleared for the ILS Runway Niner, maintain two thousand until intercepting the localizer."

The CDI is pegged left. The ADF can be used to verify that you will intercept outside the marker. On your 30° intercept heading, the needle should be slightly right of the nose, moving towards the wing (figure 9-7). If it were straight up, you would be flying directly towards the LOM, and if it were to the left, you would intercept *inside* the marker. Once cleared for the approach, you need no further clearance to alter your heading as necessary to ensure intercepting outside the marker. Since you will occasionally receive bad vectors, it is good technique to be aware of what the ADF tells you. Intercepting at or inside the marker makes it difficult to complete a good approach.

Assuming your intercept course is good, hold your heading until the CDI comes alive. As the aircraft starts to intercept the localizer, the CDI will move from full-scale deflection towards the center. As soon as the needle moves, begin turning the airplane towards the final course (assuming you have received approach clearance). When the CDI stops moving, stop turning. The DG now shows the first approximation to the **reference heading**. If the needle moves slightly, turn 5° towards the movement. Continue bracketing with smaller turns until it stops completely. *When the needle stops, centered or not, you have found the reference heading.* Note it to the nearest degree and say it aloud as a memory aid.

As long as the CDI is stationary, you are a constant number of degrees off course. Since the localizer narrows towards the runway, you are actually getting closer to its center line. The important step at this point is to note the DG and mentally record the reference heading.

The reference heading compensates for the wind and lets you parallel the localizer. It may equal the course shown on the approach plate, or, owing to wind or DG precession, it may be somewhat different. If the needle were centered, the reference heading would keep you on the centerline.

Once you know the reference heading, it is a simple matter to center the needle. Turn 5° towards the needle (10° if deflection is more than half scale, but this is the maximum turn on an ILS once you have intercepted the localizer) and, as the needle centers, turn back to the reference heading.

It is crucial while flying the ILS to make all turns with reference to specific headings on the DG and to start and end all turns with reference to the attitude indicator. Minor corrections on the localizer are made with 2° or 3° heading changes.

As you descend on the glide slope, the wind may shift, and the reference heading may change. This will be apparent as a correction towards the needle stops it but does not bring it in. The new heading is now the reference heading, and further corrections should be made in relation to it. If the needle is moving slowly toward the center, be patient. The needle becomes increasingly sensitive, so that if you impatiently increase your cut towards the needle, you may suddenly find it whipping through the center of the dial and out to the other side.

On an ILS, begin the final descent at glide slope interception, *not* at the outer marker. Glide slope interception is usually slightly outside the marker.

As the glide slope needle centers, reduce the power to the approach descent setting. Since no airspeed change is involved, no trim adjustment is likely to be necessary. Advance the prop control, and check the landing gear as down. Your report to the tower waits until these flying duties are completed. Do not consult the approach plate again, but make the first verbal announcement, something like, "Sixteen hundred feet to decision height." Do not skip this, even when alone in the cockpit. In this case, talking to yourself is a sign of sanity.

Fly the ILS at a specific indicated airspeed. The rate of descent depends on the inclination of the glide slope and on groundspeed. Rates are given for various groundspeeds in the time and distance table at the lower left of the Jeppesen approach plate. With an approach speed of 90 or 100 knots and a normal 3° glide slope the rate is approximately 500 feet per minute. In the bracketing process, this is the first approximation to your **reference descent rate**.

On a day with a strong headwind, your reduced groundspeed will require a smaller than normal rate of descent and, therefore, a higher than normal power setting for the approach descent configuration. If there is a strong tailwind, you will need a lower than normal power setting.

Once the power has been set, make glide path corrections with small pitch changes. The particular descent rate that will keep the aircraft on the glide slope with the existing wind and power conditions, the reference descent rate, must be determined by bracketing on the VSI just as you bracket the reference heading on the DG. Make pitch changes with reference to the artificial horizon and evaluate them on the VSI. (See Figure 9-8.)

Airspeed excursions of more than a knot or two are undesirable (the instrument flight test guide allows a ten knot variation) and will not occur if pitch corrections are made promptly. If you are very high or low, the necessary pitch change may affect the airspeed so much that a power adjustment is also needed. A good rule of thumb is to adjust the power one inch of manifold pressure (or 100 RPM, as the case may be) if a half-scale deflection occurs. Correcting with pitch alone would cause too much of an airspeed change.

On a tight approach, the transition from instrument flight to a visual landing can be difficult. Keep the altimeter in the instrument scan and periodically call out the number of feet remaining to decision height. At the altitude where you expect to break out, incorporate an

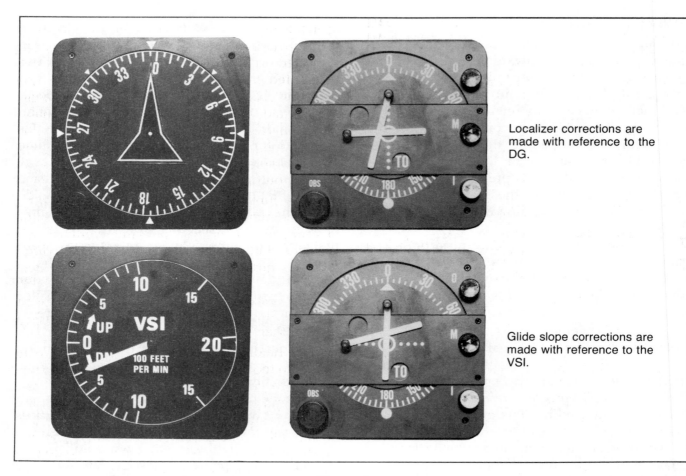

Localizer corrections are made with reference to the DG.

Glide slope corrections are made with reference to the VSI.

Figure 9-8

occasional glance out the windshield into your scan. Do not fixate on the murk outside the cockpit! Another pilot or an experienced passenger can help by looking for the lights as you concentrate on the gauges. If you happen to be in a heading correction when the lights are sighted, the aircraft's bank can make them appear canted or even above you. If you make visual contact and then lose it below decision height, *begin the missed approach immediately*.

Crossing the threshold to your triumphant landing, check for gear down one last time.

The Missed Approach

As we approached the Dunca compass locator, via the terminal route from Barnes VOR (figure 9-9), approach control gave us: "Worcester weather is 400 overcast, one half mile in light rain and fog, wind 090° at 10, altimeter 29.85. Be advised that the Crow Hill radio beacon is out of service. In the event of a

missed approach, climb to 1500 feet then turn right direct Dunca, climb and maintain 2900, hold as published. Cleared for the ILS 11 approach, contact tower now 120.5." My student, Steve, acknowledged the long clearance, including the special missed approach instructions, and switched to the tower, "Worcester Tower, Mooney three four nine one golf is with you."

The tower replied, "Roger nine one golf, Worcester weather is 400 overcast, one mile in light rain and fog, wind 090° at 10, altimeter 29.85; report Dunca inbound." The visibility had improved slightly at the tower, since the last time he reported to approach. The ILS only requires one half mile visibility and the report indicated we should get in.

But at Worcester Municipal, the tower is a mile from the approach end of Runway 11. Decision height is just inside the middle marker, another half mile out. We would be a mile and a

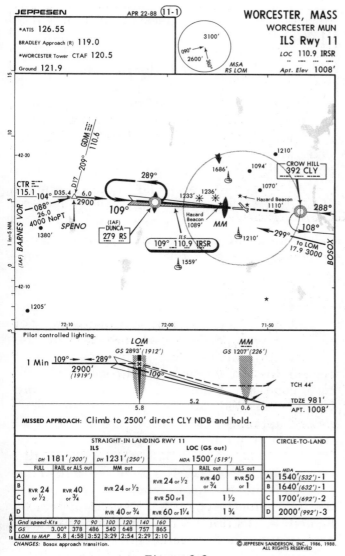

Figure 9-9

glanced to the windshield. I noticed signs of nervousness as we passed the altitude where he expected to see the lights and returned disappointed to the gauges. We both knew that with the ceiling 400 and the visibility one mile, we should see the RAIL (or rabbit as pilots affectionately know it) already. His localizer and glide slope performance deteriorated slightly as he interspersed his instrument scan with glances out the front of the airplane.

"One hundred feet above decision height," and I reminded him again to return to the instruments. I peered out the front of the airplane, but the inside of the soft gray cloud was no different than from a thousand feet higher.

As we reached the decision height he looked out one more time and announced, "Missed approach."

Then he did two things I have seen too many pilots do too frequently: he picked up the microphone to report the missed approach to the tower and put his head down to read the procedure off the approach plate.

The altimeter dropped sickeningly as we continued our descent. "Fly the airplane first!" I barked, resisting the temptation to take over immediately. What if I hadn't been there?

A cliche says that the only really dangerous thing in aviation is hitting the ground. Missed approach points (MAP) are very close to the ground, and this should be the primary fact in your mind when you realize that a missed approach is in order.

An instrument approach procedure may have as many as four segments: the initial, intermediate, final, and missed approach. Not every approach has all four, *but every one does have a missed approach.* Because an unexpected missed approach is rare, many pilots do not adequately plan for it. When it does occur, they find themselves dangerously unprepared, as Steve did at Worcester. Even though you may not fly it, study and plan the missed approach as if you expect to.

The main goal at the MAP is to get away from the terrain. Step one is always to "Fly the airplane."

Steve relinquished the microphone, applied climb power and allowed the nose to rise to our

half from the tower and with reported visibility close to minimums, I wasn't convinced our flight visibility would be a mile. A visibility report from a mile and a half away doesn't tell you much.

We intercepted the glide slope at the charted 2900 feet, started down and dutifully reported inbound. Steve flew the needles well, keeping them squared over the doughnut, and made the appropriate litany of calls: "One thousand feet from decision height; five hundred feet from decision height; four hundred feet from decision height, we should see it any minute," he said.

"Continue flying and calling out," I cautioned. "Three hundred feet from DH."

"Two hundred feet above," he said and

initial climb attitude. In our non-turbocharged Mooney, this meant full throttle.

Since our approach airspeed was the same as our climb speed, no airspeed change was necessary at the MAP and therefore no trimming was required. The pitch settled at the correct attitude and the airspeed remained constant without Steve's touching the trim.

He checked the VSI for a positive rate of climb and confirmed the climb airspeed on the airspeed indicator. If the airspeed had been a bit off, he would have adjusted the pitch attitude.

The gear was down, and we had used 10° approach flaps. With the climb established, Steve cleaned up the airplane.

To summarize, the goal at the MAP is to separate yourself from the terrain as expeditiously as possible: apply climb power immediately, then raise the nose, check for a positive rate of climb on the VSI, monitor the climb airspeed on the airspeed indicator, and finally clean up the airplane.

Most missed approaches involve a climbing left or right turn and then a hold back at the final approach fix. Some, like our unpublished missed approach procedure at Worcester, require a straight climb to a certain altitude before the turn, in order to clear obstacles which may lie on both sides. In such cases a premature turn would put you uncomfortably close to the terrain.

Memorize the first part of the missed approach procedure during the intermediate approach segment. You already use that segment of the approach, just prior to the final approach fix, to memorize the decision height or the minimum descent altitude and time on a nonprecision approach. Also memorize the direction of turn and the altitude, if any, to climb to before turning on the missed approach procedure. It helps to say to yourself, perhaps aloud, "Okay, on missed approach, I will . . . ."

Whatever you do, at the MAP, don't put your head down to study the approach plate. If you do forget the turn direction, climb straight ahead; at least you will be climbing over the airport and within the area protected for the circle-to-land maneuver . . . . for a few seconds.

If the missed approach fix is an NDB, as at Worcester, simply glance at the ADF indicator to see how many degrees of turn in which direction will be required to put the needle on the nose, make the turn in the proper direction and check the ADF needle for the proper result.

If the fix is a VOR, or if a specific course must be intercepted as part of the procedure, memorize the appropriate *heading* during the intermediate segment. Notice that if the hold is at the final approach fix, it is directly behind you at the missed approach point, and the turn will be simply 180° plus 20° or 30° (as in our experience at Worcester, figure 9-9). You shouldn't need to check the approach plate or center the VOR needle to figure out the heading; memorize it before starting down final. If you're just going back to the fix, it's behind you.

With the heading memorized, setting the OBS can wait. It is not advisable during a turn. In fact you shouldn't do anything while turning: not twist the OBS, copy a clearance, talk on the radio, change frequencies, or anything else. Just concentrate on continuing the standard rate turn, especially a climbing turn, which is more diffcult. This is particularly critical during a missed approach, close to the ground. It is all too easy to roll out of the turn or start descending while you are otherwise occupied, and run into an obstacle outside the protected area in the process. With the turn completed you can set the OBS and report the missed approach. Remember that the missed approach is a mandatory reporting point.

As in all instrument work, a successful missed approach means doing things one step at a time and in an organized way. Plan exactly what you are going to do and do it exactly the way you planned it. Remember the old salesman's motto, "Plan your work and work your plan."

The hold entry for our special missed approach procedure at Worcester was a teardrop. If the procedure called for a left turn instead of right or if the hold was right turns, it would be parallel. The entry to such a hold is rarely direct, as the holding pattern is usually on the final approach course on the outbound side of the fix. The entry heading is usually the reciprocal of the final approach course, or 30° off it.

Once in the holding pattern, what will you do next? What are the choices after a missed approach? The most frequent answer is, "I'll go to my alternate."

This is a good choice, if the alternate is not too far away and there are no better alternatives. However, in some areas of the country it is actually unlikely, and here's why: You've just made a missed approach in weather below minimums. With the weather so bad, if you are not in a coastal region, it is probably low over a wide area and was probably forecast to be so. To be legal, your alternate must have forecast at least 600 and two. "Chance of," "variable to" or "occasionally" anything less makes it unacceptable. With such bad conditions locally, the chances are that the alternate you picked is far away and probably not where you want to go.

In bad weather, the limiting factor on a particular trip may be the availability of a legal alternate within the range of the aircraft. This is especially true of light singles with less speed and less fuel capacity. In IFR training work, we will sometimes make a half hour cross country flight. The trip is so short because we need four hours of fuel on board to reach the nearest legal alternate.

So going to the alternate is probably not what you will do. We do not file alternates because ATC, playing Big Brother, insists that we plan ourselves an out. It is so they know what to expect in the event our radios quit. If the radios keep humming, you may choose not to use the alternate.

You probably will do one of three things:

1. Ceilings are often ragged and visibilities variable. Suppose you flew down to minimums without seeing anything, applied climb power, raised the nose, checked the VSI and airspeed indicator for proper readings, cleaned up the airplane, and, as you settled into the climb, your passenger saw the approach lights out the side window. It happens. You would probably try the approach again.

You might try it two or three times, provided you have plenty of fuel and don't get nervous. One of the things we must take into consideration is internal factors. The way we feel, the way we are thinking, the way our judgment is holding up, are very important. If you feel fine and have plenty of fuel, it's all right to shoot several approaches to the same field. If the repetition starts to make you uneasy and you

begin to worry about it, your performance will deteriorate, and your chances of getting into that airport will decrease. Unfortunately, one's own mental attitude, judgment, and level of fatigue are some of the hardest factors to be objective about.

A variation of this strategy is to try a different approach to the same field. The missed approach point for another runway may be as much as three miles away — far enough for a difference in visibility that could mean seeing the airport even with the same minimums. Just be sure to consider the speed and direction of the wind in your planning. An approach to the opposite runway will mean a downwind landing. Be sure the wind isn't too strong and the runway is long enough.

2. Another option is to hold. If the weather is expected to improve shortly, you can hold for a while, as long as your fuel is adequate, and try the approach again later. For this decision, you would need a thorough weather briefing and a good understanding of local conditions. And be sure you have enough gas left to get to your filed alternate if necessary.

3. Another choice is to try another field, not necessarily your alternate. The controller knows where they are getting in nearby and will tell you if you ask. Go there; it may be a lot closer than your filed alternate.

With these alternatives, a missed approach does not have to be a crisis. It may be infrequent, but with proper planning it need not be a cause for alarm. Just be sure that one of your options *works*, before you run out of fuel.

To The CFII

Twenty minutes of effective ground school on the ILS can be more productive than 20 practice approaches. Teach the student the exact scan for the ILS. Discuss pitch and power again. One or two practice approaches on the simulator are plenty; just enough to let him try the scan you have taught him. In the airplane, demonstrate one approach, describing your scan as you go. Then let him do one, directing his eyes constantly. With your direction, he should fly a good approach the first time. Then back off and let him direct his own scan. Offer any criticisms and directions in terms of his scan pattern.

Most common faults on the ILS can be traced to scan errors.

Flying "vertical S's" through the glide slope is caused by making pitch corrections with reference to the glide slope needle or chasing the VSI. With the airplane level or even climbing, the needle centers from above, leaving the airplane in a nose high attitude, and continues towards the bottom of the dial. Lowering the nose to correct, you plunge through the glide slope, and the process starts again. You also get wild airspeed variations. To cure this, have the student make pitch corrections on the attitude indicator. When the glide slope needle centers, have him return to the reference descent rate, again by using the attitude indicator.

Flying "S" turns through the localizer is caused by looking at the CDI when making heading changes. Turning until the needle centers can result in 30° or 40° heading "corrections," instead of the 5° you want. By the time the student starts turning back towards the proper heading, he is well on the other side of course.

The cure is small heading changes to specific values left or right of the reference heading. A good technique is to have the student say aloud the heading to which he is turning, before blindly banking the airplane. One or two degree heading changes are made almost entirely with rudder pressure. He should level the wings to hold the heading for several seconds until he sees the effect of his correction. When the needle centers, he should turn back to the reference heading. Usually, 5° or less is a large enough correction. With a half scale deflection, he may use a 10° cut towards the course, except when very close to decision height.

Difficulty holding heading is caused by omitting the attitude indicator from the scan. If the wings are level in coordinated flight, the heading will not change.

Precision Approaches — Quiz One

(Figure 9-10)

You are at 4000 feet, approaching Goshen VOR from the west in Cessna Skylane N6893F.

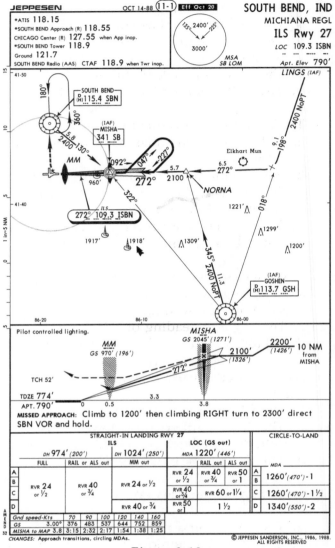

Figure 9-10

South Bend Approach advises, "Niner three fox, South Bend weather is five hundred overcast, one mile in light rain and fog. Radar is out of service. Expect ILS Two-Seven approach."

Your DME reads nine miles from Goshen and the ADF shows you due south of Misha when you receive the clearance: "Cessna six eight niner three foxtrot proceed direct Misha; cleared for the ILS Runway two-seven Approach."

1. You:
    a. Must remain at 4000 feet until Misha;
    b. May descend to 3000 feet immediately;
    c. May descend to 2900 feet immediately;
    d. May descend to 2400 feet immediately.

2. After crossing Misha you expect to see:
   a. The CDI to the left as you turn inbound;
   b. The CDI to the left as you turn outbound;
   c. The glide slope needle full up;
   d. The ADF pointing to the left of the tail.

3. Track the localizer outbound:
   a. Unless ATC instructs you to proceed straight-in;
   b. For two minutes;
   c. To complete the procedure turn within ten miles of the airport;
   d. To complete the procedure turn within ten miles of Misha.

4. You may descend below 2200 feet:
   a. Established outbound on the localizer;
   b. Turning to a heading of 047°;
   c. Turning to a heading of 227°;
   d. Established inbound on the localizer.

5. As you intercept the localizer on the heading 227°:
   a. The CDI swings from right to center;
   b. The ADF needle is 45° left of the nose;
   c. Your relative bearing to Misha is 45°;
   d. The CDI reaches full scale left deflection.

6. You may begin descent from 2100 feet when:
   a. The outer marker light flashes blue;
   b. You hear the audio signal of the outer marker;
   c. You intercept the glide slope outside the outer marker;
   d. The ADF needle swings to the tail.

7. Your groundspeed is 100 knots. The missed approach begins at:
   a. The middle marker;
   b. 974 feet AGL on the glide slope;
   c. 974 feet MSL on the glide slope;
   d. 2 minutes 17 seconds past the outer marker.

8. You must add 50 feet to decision height if:
   a. The OM is out of service;
   b. The MM is out of service;
   c. Radar is out of service;
   d. All of the above.

9. If the localizer were out of service you could:
   a. Use LOC minimums;
   b. Request an NDB approach;
   c. Fly the glide slope and the ADF;
   d. Descend to 1024 feet MSL.

10. Staying on the glide slope, your height over the threshold would be:
    a. 200 feet;
    b. 973 feet;
    c. 52 feet;
    d. 774 feet.

Precision Approaches — Quiz Two

You are planning the ILS Rwy 32 approach to Muskegon, Michigan (figure 9-11).

1. Referring to the minimums section of the approach plate, what does "RVR 40 or 3/4" mean?

2. As you prepare for the approach, the weather is reported 100 overcast, RVR 1000. Can you legally start the approach?

3. You intercept the glide slope at the charted altitude of 2000 feet. According to the profile view, your altitude as you pass the outer marker is 1874 feet MSL. What is indicated by the "(1247')" shown at the OM?

4. The middle marker is out of service. Do you have to modify your conduct of the approach?

5. You are cleared to land. With the weather reported as in question 2, could you legally land?

6. As you reach decision height, you clearly see the ground, including a road and some buildings that you know are near the end of Runway 32. Can you legally continue descending?

7. Referring to the profile view, there are three elevations associated with the airport. Give the meaning of each: TCH 39', TDZE 627', and APT. 628'.

8. You reach decision height, see the runway, and continue your descent towards a landing. Suddenly, the visibility drops and you lose sight of the ground. Is an immediate missed approach required?

9. What is the missed approach procedure?

10. The missed approach fix, Whall intersection, is shown on the inset map. Approximately how far is Whall from the airport?

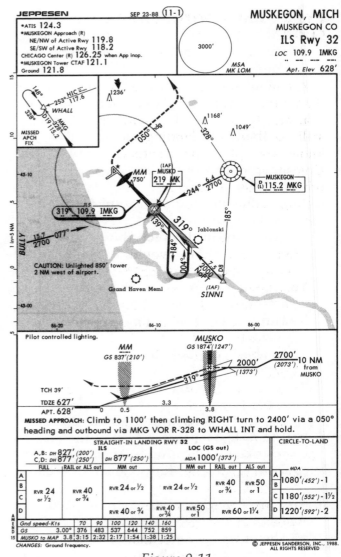

Figure 9-11

Precision Approaches — Quiz Three

(Figure 9-12)

You are planning the ILS 9 approach to Oneida County airport in Rhinelander, Wisconsin. You are flying a single engine airplane with a stall speed in the landing configuration of 50 knots and plan the approach at 100 knots. Unicom is not in operation and you have no other means of obtaining the local altimeter setting. Your glide slope receiver is not working.

1. What is meant by "control zone not effective," and how would you obtain the Wausau altimeter setting? *See note below.

2. Assume you are approaching the localizer on the 13 DME arc. What is the purpose of the 255° and 274° radials depicted on the approach plate?

3. Can this approach be conducted without DME?

4. Can this approach be conducted without marker beacons?

5. Can this approach be conducted without DME or marker beacons?

6. When flying the teardrop procedure from the Rhinelander VOR, how far outbound would you fly, and to what heading would you turn to intercept the localizer?

7. You might prefer to track outbound on the localizer to the outer marker and execute a normal procedure turn instead of flying the charted teardrop pattern. Would this be legal?

8. To what altitude would you descend after passing ARSHA?

9. Where is the missed approach point and how would you identify it?

10. You are planning to circle at 100 knots to land on Runway 27. At what altitude would you circle?

*NOTE: The "Control Zone" has been replaced by Class E airspace designated to the surface. Until the Standard for Terminal Instrument Approach Procedures (TERP's) is revised by a rule making action, the terms Control Zone effective or not effective, will continue to be used on the approach charts.

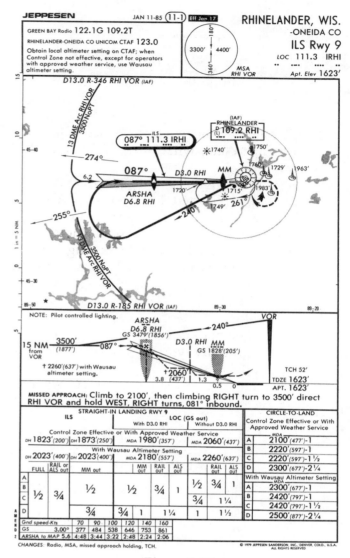

Figure 9-12

CHAPTER TEN

AREA NAVIGATION (RNAV)

Takeoff from Baltimore-Washington International was smooth. The quite ordinary routing to Greater Pittsburgh airport had been approved—Direct Wooley, Victor 214 to Martinsburg VOR, Victor 214 to Indian Head VOR, then Victor 274 to Nesto, a transition fix outside Greater Pittsburgh airport. I anticipated no problems as I switched frequencies from Baltimore Departure to Washington Center.

"Washington Center, Mooney four five eight five fox is with you, level at six thousand."

The radio crackled with the come-back, merely acknowledging my presence, "Roger, Mooney four five eight five fox, Baltimore altimeter is 29.95." The radio continued to spit out various directives, all aimed at other aircraft in the area.

I knew from experience not to bother Washington Center with my request. Using RNAV in a system not really built for it calls for some ingenuity. I'd wait until I was past Martinsburg VOR, coming up on Flint intersection. That was where Washington Center would hand my flight over to Cleveland Center, and I felt certain they would approve the route amendment I had in mind.

The call came when expected, "Mooney four five eight five fox, contact Cleveland Center on 124.4."

"Cleveland Center on 124.4, eight five fox," I responded. I made the switch with a short turn of the knob.

Keying the mike, I said, "Cleveland Center, Mooney four five eight five fox is with you, level at six thousand."

After the center controller responded, I keyed the mike again and made my request, "Cleveland Center, Mooney four five eight five fox. I'd like to amend my routing to direct Nesto."

It took a second or two for the controller to respond, "Mooney four five eight five fox. Approved as requested. Cleared direct Nesto."

I had already set up the waypoints to take me directly to the Nesto fix, so it was a matter of pushing a button and I was free, temporarily, from the rigid structure of airways and VORs.

Proceeding direct would save time and fuel. I had included the appropriate RNAV-capable suffix on my flight plan in anticipation that, somewhere, I'd find a controller willing to approve the direct routing. They don't have to approve it if they think it will interfere with other traffic. But, more often than not, I have been able to get my clearance amended in the air for an RNAV routing.

The rest of the flight proceeded normally. I occasionally used the groundspeed/distance feature on my RNAV unit to check my progress. Just before Nesto, I contacted Pittsburgh Approach for vectors to the ILS Runway 32. It would have been nice to shoot an RNAV approach, but Greater Pittsburgh doesn't have one, so the ILS had to do.

Navigating in the IFR environment is largely a matter of flying from one VOR to another. But, as every IFR pilot knows, VORs are scattered across the countryside in a somewhat random and arbitrary way. Rarely can an entire IFR flight go in a straight line from point A to point B. Although the VOR system is, at present, our most common means of navigating, it is not the most efficient. The seemingly endless series of doglegs and detours up and down the airways is costly in terms of time and fuel.

But how do you improve the present system of VOR navigation to increase its efficiency? One way is to add more VORs, and lots of them. Another is to move the VORs. But both these solutions, in the physical sense, are impractical. What is practical is to do both in the computer brain of a little black box coupled to your VOR/DME—an area navigation or RNAV unit.

There are several types of RNAV, but the most common are VOR/DME-based, and, increasing in popularity in recent years, LORAN-C. The VOR/DME RNAV, the type most pilots think of when RNAV is mentioned, is a **course line computer (CLC)**. It takes raw data from VOR/DME or VORTAC sites within range, processes it, and returns it to the pilot in the form of straight-line course information.

Exactly how the little box works is a matter of simple trigonometry. Any point within the service area of a VOR/DME or VORTAC can be defined in terms of a specific radial and distance. This being so, suppose you are at an airport 20 miles from a VOR/DME on the 180 radial (figure 10-1). Your destination is 20 miles from the same VOR/DME, but on the 270 radial. You now have two sides of a triangle, with known lengths and angles. With this information, it is simple to determine the length of the remaining side. The RNAV unit calculates a direct course between the two points, called **waypoints** in RNAV lingo. Its direction is with respect to magnetic north.

The beauty of RNAV is its ability to make any definable (in terms of radial and distance or, for LORAN-C, latitude and longitude) point a waypoint, giving you great navigational flexibility. Any IAF, FAF, MAP, intersection, airport, or even the edge of a restricted area can become a waypoint, as long is it lies within range of a VOR/DME. All this can be had with the push of a but-

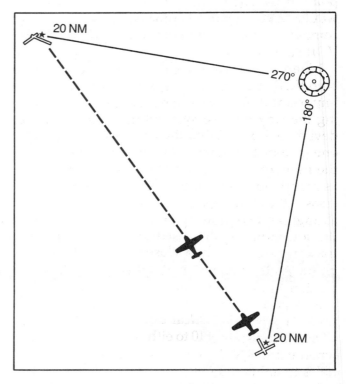

Figure 10-1

ton or turn of a knob, and some planning on your part.

The Equipment

VOR/DME RNAV units vary in size and complexity, ranging from simple single-waypoint units to sophisticated systems able to store up to 10 waypoints. Extra features such as time-to-way point, groundspeed, and parallel track are also available on some units. Those on the higher end of the complexity/cost scale are completely self-contained, eliminating the need for an existing VOR and DME installation.

Regardless of complexity, all VOR/DME RNAVs have certain basic components. An onboard computer comes first on the list. Second is some means to input the radial/distance information (or waypoint address; more on this later) for each waypoint, usually buttons or knobs. Third is a digital display that indicates distance information in nautical miles and bearing to the way point selected. The RNAV can be tied directly to the CDI, with the directional information from the computer translated electronically into visual course steering information. From your vantage point in the cockpit, you fly the CDI just as you would a VOR, but all information you receive comes from the position of the waypoint, not the VOR station.

When on course, the CDI remains centered in both VOR and RNAV navigation. But there is an important difference when it comes to interpreting the way the two systems indicate off-course deviation. With a VOR, the CDI needle swings to one side or the other, its movement dictated by the number of degrees off-course you are. Thus, as mentioned in Chapter Five, its sensitivity increases the closer you are to a VOR. This is known as **angular deviation**. With RNAV, the needle deflection indicates the distance from the desired track, regardless of how close you are to the waypoint. As long as you maintain the needle's deflection in one spot, you fly a perfectly parallel course at a constant distance from the desired track. This is called **linear deviation**. While most VORs have a scale of 10 to either side of the center, when using RNAV the scale indicates 5 nautical miles to either side.

Figure 10-2 illustrates the difference between angular and linear deviation. Both aircraft are flying the same course to the same VOR station. The one on the left, with VOR-only capability, indicates a full-scale deflection, 10°, at 60 miles from the station, which equals at least 10 miles off-course. At 30 miles from the station, he is 5 miles off-course as the intercept angle narrows. In the aircraft on the right, however, a full- scale deflection on the CDI indicates he is paralleling the desired track at a distance of 5 nautical miles. This remains constant, no matter what the distance from the waypoint. Every dot of deflection indicates a specific distance off-course.

Most RNAVs have a switch to increase the sensitivity without changing the accuracy, for use on approaches. Aptly called the approach mode switch, it changes the scale of the CDI, making it indicate between 1.25 and 2.5 nautical miles at full-scale deflection. This distance may vary depending on your equipment.

The one thing all VOR/DME RNAVs don't have in common is a blanket IFR-certification for en route and approach use. To be certified, the RNAV-equipped airplane must be flight tested. Specifications found in Advisory Circular (AC) 90-45 must be met and demonstrated, including

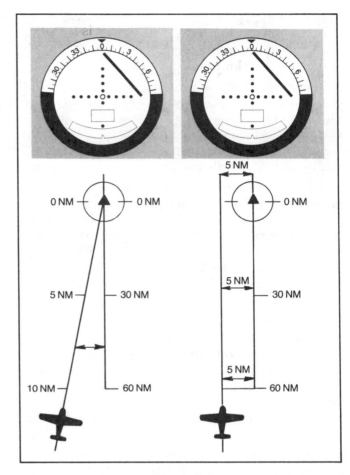

Figure 10-2

accuracy to within 0.4 nautical miles over the test area. Some RNAVs just don't make the grade; in which case you can still use your RNAV in instrument conditions, but only to monitor the performance of your other navigation equipment. You cannot depend on it for IFR navigation or file as RNAV capable. For the units that do meet certification requirements, no further test or check is ever needed, and use is restricted only to the limits of the equipment.

Using RNAV

Having the necessary charts is a prerequisite to your flight planning. RNAV charts, both en route and approach, are available from Jeppesen, (figures 10-3 and 10-4). These charts provide all the information you need for RNAV flight. The government does not publish RNAV en route charts, but does provide RNAV approach plates bound into the books along with the standard approaches (figure 10-5). There are some disadvantages to government RNAV charts. They sometimes do not publish the VOR/DME defining the procedure, leading a busy pilot to possibly enter the correct radial and distance information but fly the procedure using the wrong VOR/DME. And, if the VOR/DME is charted, they sometimes omit its identifier and frequency.

Once you have the charts, you and your IFR-certified RNAV are ready to work. You can begin by figuring the waypoint addresses for each waypoint along your route of flight. A waypoint address consists of the radial and the distance from the VOR/DME or VORTAC in nautical miles. An example of a waypoint address is: Eagle Lake 262050, meaning 50 nautical miles on the 262 radial of Eagle Lake VOR, near Houston, Texas. You continue this exercise until you reach your destination. (Figure 10-3 is an example of what your trip might look like when plotted on a RNAV chart.) One tip is to make your final waypoint the fix from which you will begin the instrument approach, just in case of a radio failure.

If you don't desire to do the waypoint address figuring yourself, and you're a Jeppesen subscriber, you'll receive a listing of almost every airport in the country and its waypoint address along with your subscription. If you use this list, keep in mind that it is based on the VOR/DME nearest to the airport. Some of the more sophisticated RNAVs can be preprogrammed with lists of canned waypoint addresses and VOR frequencies, with the RNAV unit going as far as tuning and changing waypoints automatically.

The flight planning over, its time to get yourself into the system. This is a bit harder to do. Despite the best intentions of the FAA, using RNAV in the system is still uncommon as only 15 percent of the general aviation fleet has RNAV capability. Controllers are apt to be somewhat uncooperative when dealing with an RNAV routing, especially when crossing from one center to another. Keep in mind that ATC's first job is to separate traffic, and they do this best when you're nicely situated on a known airway. However, don't give up on getting approval for direct RNAV routes and approaches; you just have to work at it a bit more than you would for other instrument procedures.

RNAV Clearance

The first requirement for obtaining an RNAV IFR clearance is the availability of radar coverage. Since much of the United States has radar coverage above 5,000 AGL, this usually means your route can be approved, if you file at a high enough altitude. If ATC cannot follow your flight from start to finish, you won't get the RNAV clearance. Even though ATC monitors the flight, navigation on the random RNAV route is your responsibility. This includes choosing the proper IFR altitude for terrain and obstacle clearance. Jeppesen RNAV charts help a bit by including a safe enroute altitude at each VOR call-out box, but this is only over the VOR itself—in between you're on your

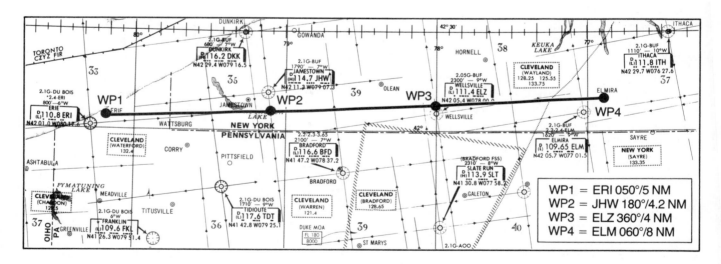

Figure 10-3

190

own. One way to check for obstacles is to review the VFR sectional charts along your route.

The one factor that can often prevent you from receiving your direct routing clearance is "compatibility with traffic volume and flow," meaning that approval of your route is solely at the discretion of ATC. So what can you do to improve the odds? First, follow their directions for filing:

1. File airport to airport prior to departure, and use the appropriate suffix (/C for RNAV and transponder, no altitude reporting; /R for RNAV and transponder with altitude reporting; /W for RNAV with no transponder).

2. Plan the random portion of the flight to be-

gin and end over appropriate arrival and departure transition fixes or other navigational aids. Use SID and STAR routes when available. File route structure transitions to and from the random portion of the flight.

3. Define the route by radial/distance waypoints with at least one waypoint in each ATC center that the route crosses. At least one waypoint in each center should be located within 200 nautical miles of the edge of the preceding center.

4. Plan waypoints where turns occur. Plan enough way points to ensure accurate navigation along the entire route. ATC may as-

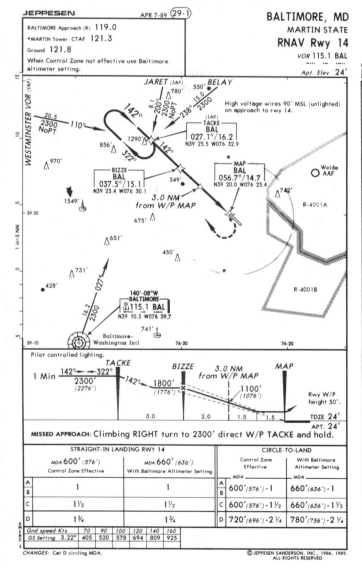

Figure 10-4

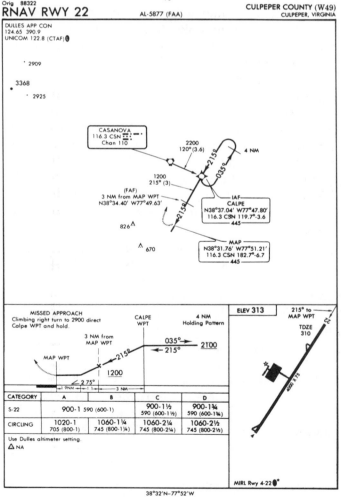

Figure 10-5

sist with navigation, if asked, but the primary responsibility is yours.

5. Plan the route to avoid all prohibited and restricted airspace by at least 3 nautical miles, unless permission has been obtained to operate in those areas and you advise ATC.

If the RNAV equipment on board is IFR certified to the specifications found in AC 90-45 you may legally use it for IFR navigation. But it is your responsibility to advise ATC if you cannot accept a particular RNAV clearance owing to equipment limitations.

An RNAV suffix on the flight plan merely tells ATC that you're RNAV equipped. They don't know whether you have a long-range navigation RNAV, like LORAN-C, or INS and OMEGA (which the airlines use), or just a short-range VOR/DME RNAV. If the first cleared waypoint is hundreds of miles ahead of you, far past the range of your equipment, speak up. You can quickly plot a few waypoints to get you there while the controller helps you on your way with the initial heading to the fix.

Other than the RNAV suffix and the routing, everything else about obtaining the clearance and the IFR flight is the same as with other types of navigation. On the phone with the briefer, be sure he knows you're filing an RNAV flight plan, then give him the routing direct from waypoint to waypoint. Be sure to use the identifier of each VOR, not its full name, then the numerical address of each waypoint, as that is the format entered into the ATC computer.

Do what you will, you still might not be cleared as filed. In this case, consider requesting an amendment once in the air; and, as you are handed off to each new sector or center, request a direct RNAV routing. The circumstances that lead to refusal while on the ground may have changed, so don't be surprised when the clearance is granted.

RNAV Approaches

With close to 6000 instrument approaches available in the United States, one would assume that RNAV approaches make up a good portion of them. Unfortunately, there are only 338 RNAV instrument approaches available, and only three airports (one in Washington and two in California) where RNAV is the sole approach. Figures 10-4 and 10-5 show typical RNAV approaches.

ATC has a tendency not to offer an RNAV approach, even if you have indicated on the flight plan that you carry the equipment. This lowers the probability of your becoming proficient at RNAV approaches. To counter this, take every opportunity to shoot an RNAV approach; request it from the controller whenever it is available at your destination airport. RNAV approaches are known to be workload intensive. Practicing them will help prepare you for the day when you might need to fly one.

An RNAV approach has the same features and characteristics as other nonprecision approaches. The difference is that waypoints replace other types of navaids and fixes. The average number of waypoints on a typical RNAV approach is between two and three, but there is an approach with as many as seven waypoints —Washington Dulles, RNAV Runway 1R. This makes it necessary to have an RNAV unit capable of holding three or more waypoints; attempting an approach with limited one-waypoint-at-time equipment would not be in your best interest. Needless to say, double checking the waypoint addresses is advisable. If you have the luxury of a co-pilot or an astute passenger with you, have him or her cross-check the waypoints addresses as well.

As you begin the published procedure turn, or are established inbound on the final approach course, switch your unit to the approach mode. With the sensitivity switch on, much smaller corrections are needed, as when flying a localizer.

Cross-checking your waypoints is a good idea once established inbound on the approach. If there is no turn at the FAF, you can do this by switching from the IAF to the MAP waypoint and back again, making sure the CDI remains centered. Also note whether the distance between these two waypoints is as shown on the published procedure. If anything looks out of whack, fly a missed approach and hold at a nearby VOR until you understand the problem.

MSAs are not indicated on RNAV approach procedures because they are not directly centered on a navaid. You can check the other approach plates for the airport to get the MSA information.

All the waypoints used on an RNAV approach are usually based on the same VOR/DME, but this isn't always the case. Some approaches use two different VOR/DMEs to establish waypoints on the approach, so be on your guard. The waypoints you are most likely to see on the approach plate are the FAF, the MAP, and the holding fix for the missed approach. Often the IAF and the missed approach holding fix are the same. Once you've reached the FAF, no more waypoint switching is necessary and you can begin your descent to a landing.

Because RNAV approaches are nonprecision, they have no descent guidance. You can, however, "make" your own glide slope if you have vertical navigation (VNAV) equipment. RNAV charts show an angle to use, generally between 2.5° and 3.5°, that enables VNAV to create an instant "glide slope." This descent path is purely advisory and is not a mandatory part of the approach. You should not fly it past the MDA, unless you have the field in sight. The point where the VNAV glide slope crosses the MDA is considered a VDP and the distance from the VDP to the MAP is usually published in the profile view.

RNAV approaches at some airports have lower minimums to a straight-in landing than the other available approaches. But while the minimums are lower, some RNAV approaches are quite complicated. If you plan to fly an unfamiliar RNAV approach with the weather at minimums, take the time to study the approach plate before you get in the airplane. With the proper equipment and some practice, flying VOR/DME RNAV approaches is just as easy and effective as any other nonprecision approach.

Limitations of VOR/DME RNAV

The limitations of VOR/DME RNAV are essentially that of VOR- only navigation, restricted range and scalloping. VOR/DME and VORTAC signals are limited to line-of-sight, and if you lose the signal, you lose the waypoint. VOR/DME RNAV is basically a short-range navigational tool.

The other problem, scalloping, occurs when the VOR equipment picks up reflected or secondary signals from another VOR. This causes the needle to begin a side-to-side movement, and can lead to wandering, especially if you're coupled into an autopilot. Generally, these are minor annoyances and can be easily dealt with. Waypoints can be strung together in such a way as to avoid loss of signal, and scalloping can be stopped through a little extra scanning. Never

leave the navigating to the equipment alone. That's why you are there.

LORAN-C

Much has been written about long-range navigation, version C (better known as LORAN-C) in recent years, mostly touting its extraordinary accuracy over long distances. And accurate it is —it can leave other types of navigation trying to play catchup. Recent improvements in LORAN-C development have made it the preferred form of VFR navigation for many pilots. Unfortunately, its use in the IFR environment is limited principally to the en route segments of a flight, and only if the unit is IFR certified.

The earliest form, LORAN-A, was developed during World War II and was used strictly as a marine navigational system. It was extremely limited in range and prone to errors. In the 1950s, LORAN-C was developed and, with the coming of the computer chip, it moved off the water and into airplanes. A third type, LORAN- D, is used by the military and provides even more accuracy than the C version—plus or minus 600 feet—but it has limited range.

LORAN-C uses low frequency (100 KHz) radio signals broadcast from land-based stations worldwide. These low frequency signals follow the curvature of the earth (unlike VOR/DME signals, which are line-of-sight), thereby providing very long range coverage, as much as 2,000 miles when over water. Although the aviation world has adopted LORAN-C for general use, the U.S. Coast Guard is still responsible for the operation and upkeep of the nine chains (groups of transmitting stations) located in the United States. Figure 10-6 shows a sample chain.

LORAN-C picks up the pulsed signals from three transmitting stations. It translates these signals into latitude and longitude coordinates representing the aircraft's present position over the Earth's surface. It is necessary to program the LORAN computer before takeoff with the latitude and longitude of the departure airport. Latitude and longitude are used in the same way as radial and distance are used with VOR/DME RNAV to determine waypoints. After that, the system automatically tracks your position.

LORAN-C can be a useful addition to your set of navigational tools. Its relatively low cost brings it within reach of the average aircraft owner, and it takes up less panel space than VOR/DME RNAV system. It has a much larger waypoint memory—up to 500 user-programmable waypoints. Entire routes can be programmed into the computer, enabling you to fly waypoint to way point without additional data input. And it provides a wealth of navigational information with the push of a button. Features can include desired and actual track, distance to the desired track, distance from origination point and to destination, wind, ETE, ETA, bearing and distance to the nearest airport/navaid, and fuel flow information. Some manufacturers even offer "canned" data bases containing over 10,000 preprogrammed waypoints for airports, TCAs, and restricted areas—all ready for you to insert into the computer.

Limitations of LORAN

The biggest drawback to LORAN-C has been its limited use in the IFR environment. To use a LORAN-C under instrument flight rules it must be IFR certified. If you want to set up a random routing, you must follow the same rules as with

VOR/DME RNAV. However, a random route flown at Flight Level 390 and above is less restrictive. The difference is the deletion of the requirement to file at least one waypoint per center and the requirement to define waypoints by degree-distance from the navigational aid. IFR certification - and not all units can be certified - primarily covers enroute and terminal use. Instrument approaches using LORAN-C have limited approval based on more restrictive certification. Although currently quite constrained, LORAN-C for approach use should quickly gain increased approval.

Additionally, LORAN-C is not as "user-friendly" as the VOR/DME RNAV. Its greater complexity makes it a virtual requirement to carry the operating manual with you. It is also prone to electronic interference caused by weather, signal propagation, tracking errors, cycle errors, and other anomalies. Transmitting stations go down for maintenance frequently.

Most LORAN-C units are not IFR certified. And so, in a strictly IFR sense, LORAN-C is mainly used at the present time as a cross-check to your other forms of navigation. But, in this regard, it is quite an excellent piece of equipment, and many pilots wouldn't fly without one.

The Future of RNAV

Like it or not, RNAV will eventually completely change air navigation. And, in many ways, the revolution has already begun. It will continue into the next century with the advent of a global navigation satellite network called NAVSTAR/Global Positioning System (GPS).

NAVSTAR/GPS, when completed sometime in the 1990s, will consist of 18 satellites, with 3 satellites to be used as spares, orbiting the Earth at evenly spaced and synchronized intervals two times per day. From their position in high orbit (10,900 nautical miles above the Earth's surface) they will provide complete three-dimensional (latitude, longitude, and altitude) navigational coverage for the entire globe. Both military and civil aviation will use the system.

Like a DME, the system operates by transmitting signals to a receiver and measuring the amount of time it takes to travel there and back, then multiplies the time by the speed of light. The result is a **line of position**. It uses three such

Figure 10-6

measure ments to determine position in the three dimensions. The main difference between DME and the NAVSTAR/GPS is that DME is initiated by an interrogation from the user, and NAVSTAR/GPS operates continuously without need of interrogation.

Thinking of what this could mean to you as an IFR pilot might send a thrill up your spine. NAVSTAR/GPS will allow you to know your position anywhere in the world in three dimensions at an accuracy unparalleled up to the present—to within 150 **feet**. NAVSTAR/GPS is a 24-hour a day, 365 days a year, rain or shine system. It is not subject to atmospheric or solar disturbances. Receivers will probably cost close to what a VOR/DME unit costs today and features might include flight following and position reporting, aircraft conflict alert and resolution, and precision approach guidance.

The potential exists for NAVSTAR/GPS to totally eclipse our present forms of navigation. VOR/DME, NDB, and ILS, would become secondary, back-up systems to the primary NAVSTAR/GPS navigational system. With this system in place, the future IFR navigational environment could be a much easier place to be.

RNAV Quiz

1. What is RNAV?
2. What does a course line computer (CLC) do?
3. Define waypoint and waypoint address.
4. What are the three basic components in a VOR/DME RNAV?
5. What is the first requirement for obtaining an RNAV clearance?
6. When planning your RNAV route, where must the random routing portion fall?
7. What are the suffixes for RNAV capability?
8. How do you define your random routing?
9. What is the requirement for location of waypoints?
10. Is IFR certification of the RNAV unit necessary for you to file IFR?
11. What are the waypoints you are most likely to see on a published RNAV approach?
12. Do RNAV approaches have glide slopes?
13. Are MSAs indicated on the RNAV approach plate?
14. What are the limitations to VOR/DME RNAV?
15. What is the maximum distance a waypoint can be from its originating VOR/DME?
16. Define LORAN-C.
17. What type of radio signals are used for LORAN-C?
18. What defines a LORAN-C waypoint?
19. Is it legal to use your VFR LORAN-C when filing IFR?
20. What is the NAVSTAR/GPS?

CHAPTER ELEVEN

EMERGENCIES

Instrument flying can throw you a curve, an unexpected challenge that you didn't anticipate or plan for. It might be a full blown emergency or the failure of a minor piece of equipment. I have seen pilots become upset, fixate, and nearly lose control of the airplane over something as small as an inoperative clock or EGT gauge. Airplane owners, who are responsible for paying repair bills, seem especially prone to getting in trouble over such things. They forget that in all flying, you must discipline yourself to fly the airplane first. If you want to tap the clock and curse the mechanic, fine, but such attention is still only one element of your total scan.

At the other end of the spectrum is the bona fide emergency: communications failure, gyro failure, electrical failure, or engine failure. Such events test the mettle of every pilot.

Are You Ready?

Being well prepared to meet unexpected situations is really part of currency. You may fly comfortably every day, never think about emergencies, and believe you are doing fine. You may frequently and skillfully file flight plans, copy clearances and even shoot approaches to minimums. But that only means that you are prepared when things go right.

You would be "conditionally proficient." A conditionally proficient pilot is like conditionally unstable air, which has the potential for convective activity if disturbed, but will remain stable if left alone. The conditionally proficient pilot will be okay if nothing goes wrong, but if something does slip, if he has not planned for emergencies he probably won't react well.

In a way, we pilots are generally less prepared for emergencies today than we were years ago. The systems we use are much more reliable than formerly. Engines rarely fail, and we are used to relying on ATC to a great extent for our navigation and separation. We don't think of the consequences of a certain piece of equipment failing at a particular moment. On a trip, how often do you think about what you would do if you were to lose your radios *now*? Or if the engine were to quit *now*? Or if you were to have a total electrical failure *now*?

When flying IFR, it doesn't always take a serious emergency to throw a pilot off his stride. In the busy routine of the instrument cockpit, any departure from the expected can be disconcerting. Your ability to meet emergencies depends on how well you have planned and practiced for the unexpected.

Once I took a training flight with an experienced instrument pilot who at the time was technically current. He had scheduled the training day specifically for the experience of flying in particularly low weather. I had expected the exercise to be routine.

The trip began at Teterboro, New Jersey. Alan had filed an IFR flight plan to Bradley Field, in Hartford, Connecticut. After preflighting and starting the airplane, he called Clearance Delivery, "Teterboro Clearance, Bonanza two four five six fox." As he unkeyed the mike, the clearance came back: "Novembertwofourfivesixfoxis clearedtothedestinationairport; Afterdeparture RunwaySixturnlefttheadingzerofourzerountil leavingfifteenhundred, thenturnleftheading threezerozero. . . . ," etc.

Although he had been ready to copy, Alan missed a good part of the departure instructions. "Heck," he said, "they read it as though they were being paid by the word." He picked up the mike and with a slight twinkle in his eye transmitted, "You can repeat that, please, about fourteen times, or say it again once more slowly." The controller was slower the second time.

Before taxiing, we studied the complex departure instructions and set up the nav radios. They were: "After departure Runway Six turn left heading zero four zero until leaving fifteen hundred, then turn left heading three zero zero, radar vectors to the Sparta one five zero radial, via the one five zero radial to Sparta VORTAC." Teterboro was 400 overcast, and the last thing we wanted was to be studying the clearance and setting the radios just as we entered the clouds. It took several minutes on the ramp before we had clearly visualized the post-takeoff procedure.

Shortly after reaching our cruising altitude of 5000 feet, Alan was cleared on course, and he put the autopilot in the tracking mode. With a sigh he sat back, folded his arms, and began a leisurely scan of the instruments.

He soon noticed that something was not quite right. The CDI moved to the right, but the heading had not changed. Soon we had a nearly full scale deflection.

Then a very interesting thing happened. Alan tapped the autopilot and stared at it angrily. He also inadvertently touched the yoke, and the V-tail Bonanza rolled into a slight left bank. He set the number two VOR to our present course and switched the nav select switch to the number two position. Without his noticing, the left bank steepened slightly and the airplane began losing altitude. "The damn radio shop," he muttered, "they swore they had it fixed this time." As he glared at the VOR display and tapped the autopilot again, the bank steepened further and the rate of descent increased. I noticed a buildup of wind noise over the cockpit. Alan continued to stare at the nav instruments. The airspeed increased by 25 knots, and the bank reached 30°. Finally, I cautioned him, "Check your flight instruments." In a moment Alan recovered from the unusual attitude and regained the lost altitude. Had someone not been with him, would he have roused himself in time? How many "unexplained" accidents are caused by similar distractions?

Unable to cure the autopilot, we agreed he had better hand-fly the rest of the trip. In the hectic minutes later in the flight, the absence of the autopilot added a great deal to his work load.

Communications failure is an emergency situation that every basic instrument student is briefed on, but as we had seen on the Teterboro ramp, communications that are working can cause problems of their own. Now, as we approached Bradley, cleared direct to the Hartford VOR, a similar situation developed, but one more serious because we were no longer comfortably on the ground but hand-flying in heavy rain.

The radio crackled, and we heard: "Bonanza two four five six fox, an amendment to your route: cleared to Briss intersection via direct Bridgeport, the Bridgeport 014° radial to Judds, and the Carmel 058° radial. Hold east of Briss on the Hartford 293° radial left turns one minute legs expect further clearance at one eight three zero. Descend and maintain three thousand. Bradley weather is 400 overcast, 2 miles in light rain and fog. Wind 050° at one five gusting two five, altimeter 29.88. Bradley radar is out of service. Runway 6 localizer is out of service. Expect NDB Runway 6 approach. Contact approach now 125.65."

Alan wasn't holding a pencil when the call came, and he missed most of it. He had never heard of these intersections and didn't know the frequencies of the VOR's in question. Nor did he have the NDB approach plate out, and he couldn't visualize the parallel entry to the holding pattern. Furthermore, he needed to change communications frequencies and start a descent. Having missed the weather, he didn't know if the field was below minimums. "Suddenly," he said, "I feel very nervous."

Was this an emergency? Hardly. But such a situation would test the preparedness of many pilots.

Alan's response was excellent. Carefully continuing to monitor his flight instruments, he requested a repeat of the clearance. With that in hand, he checked the frequency for the Bridgeport VOR, tuned it in, and turned towards the station. On course, he reduced the power to begin a descent from 5000 to 3000 feet, located the Judds and Briss intersections on his area chart and drew the required holding pattern. By the time we reached Bridgeport and turned outbound on the 014° radial, we were at the proper altitude. He had determined the hold entry and was able to take a minute to pull the NDB approach plate out of the Jepp book.

Thirty minutes later, we discussed the flight in the airport coffee shop. Alan felt the way to prevent autopilot failure from becoming a major problem is simple: maintain your confidence and proficiency during all phases of flight. The autopilot should be an *aid* on the long stretches of a flight, not a crutch you can't do without. Your routine for staying current should include practice at hand flying the airplane in all situations, especially when the cockpit load increases. It is particularly valuable to switch off the autopilot when you are nearing the terminal area, planning the approach, and the communications pick up. After all, the autopilot is a black box, and, like any other device, it can quit.

Especially if you fly a clean airplane with a rapid roll rate, it is surprisingly easy to induce unusual attitudes when you start fumbling through your approach plates, copying the weather and memorizing key facts about the approach, not to mention fooling with a recalcitrant autopilot. The first item on any equipment failure checklist should be, "Fly the airplane."

Don't use the autopilot during any part of the approach. Most of us general aviation pilots have enough trouble staying current anyway, so take every opportunity to practice your procedures.

What are some of the other "little" emergencies that can develop?

For an approach to minimums, are you fully prepared? Did you get a thorough briefing? Do you know the missed approach procedure? Practice approaches should always be flown to minimums, and simulated missed approaches are good practice, too. Nevertheless, an actual approach to minimums in weather can put a psychological strain on a pilot who doesn't do it very often. Remember that the greatest proportion of IFR accidents involve an airplane on approach descending below minimums.

An unexpected diversion following a missed approach can present a challenge. During instrument practice, it is helpful to occasionally fly an unfamiliar approach with very little lead time to study the chart. If you are truly current on approach plate interpretation, you should be able to read the crucial information in the few miles before reaching the initial fix.

Now let's look at some "big" emergencies.

Engine Failure

Above a rural area of New Jersey — farm country with nothing around but big open fields — the engine failed in a single engine airplane. The pilot elected to try to glide to an airport about three miles away. He didn't make it, and all three people on board were killed.

This pilot was not mentally prepared for such an emergency. Since he evidently thought he could get to the airport, he was clearly not prepared to judge his glide distance accurately. He was not prepared to make an off-airport landing, even though he was surrounded by attractive fields. On your long cross-country trips, spend a little time imagining what you would do if your engine quit, *now*. In your recreational flying, practice gliding to forced landings and spiraling down over small fields. Get into the *habit* of coping with an engine failure.

How an engine failure can bring out one's qualities as a pilot was demonstrated when it happened to an instructor friend of mine.

Anger was evident in Tom's features and in the abruptness of his movements as he entered our offices. His complexion was ruddier than usual, and his normally cool blue eyes seemed to glare like a bull's. He stamped around the office, banging the furniture and leaving things out of place in his wake.

"What's with you?" I wanted to know.

"Engine failure," he said briskly and off-handedly, as though "engine failure" were an every day occurence.

It took most of the afternoon before I heard the full story of Tom's emergency. It was simple but dramatic.

His student was flying the Skyhawk as they climbed away from the airport towards South Bay. Tom divided his attention between looking for traffic, periodically leaning forward to peer around the student's hood, and checking the instrument panel. "Climb and maintain three thousand five hundred," he instructed. "Fly heading one eight zero. Climb at eighty. Your key performance instrument in a climb is the airspeed indicator."

Suddenly, as Tom's eyes scanned the panel, they lit on the startling and terrifying sight of the oil pressure needle resting quietly on zero. The engine droned on normally, but the silent little gauge set off a screaming in his brain.

The instrument pilot's eyes must constantly move, cross checking the flight instruments, the navigation equipment and the engine gauges. Under the heavy workload of an IFR flight, pilots most often omit the engine gauges, and usually with impunity. But many failures are foretold by an instrument indication that can buy the pilot valuable time. The pressure and temperature gauges, the ammeter, and the suction gauge can give advance warning of impending emergencies.

Below them, the waters of the bay twinkled in the sunlight. The adjacent beaches were eerily serene. "I have the airplane," Tom announced. He knocked off the student's hood, began a turn back towards land and reduced the power to a low cruise setting. Their altitude was 2000 feet.

"I didn't know," he later explained, "whether it was an oil leak or a bad gauge. If it was the engine, I wanted to keep the remaining oil as long as possible."

The engine sound and oil temperature were normal. The aircraft was eight miles from the

airport and cruising well at the reduced airspeed. Pointed towards the airport they had left five minutes earlier, Tom called approach.

"Approach, seven eight six five echo. We're returning to the airport — we appear to have lost our oil pressure."

"Roger, six five echo," was the reply, "do you wish to declare an emergency?"

"Negative, not at this time."

"Roger, six five echo, please keep me informed," said approach.

Now the engine was beginning to show the first signs of roughness — "as if something were not *quite* right with it," said Tom afterward. "I was overwhelmed with the desire to get back to the field quickly, and I increased the power. The roughness did not get worse right away, but I noticed an increase in the oil temperature, suggesting we were nearly out of oil."

The wind was strong out of the south, and they would have to enter downwind for Runway 15. The wind was too strong for a downwind landing. "We were four miles from the airport. I didn't trust the engine, and I was afraid the turn to final would be hairy — if we made it that far."

There was an abandoned 1200 foot long dirt runway below them. As the engine roughness increased, Tom committed himself to landing at the old airport. Circling to the left, the Skyhawk descended into a downwind leg. The engine noise was increasing, and the cockpit vibrated with its uneven rumbling. To save what oil was left and lose altitude for the pattern, Tom brought the throttle nearly back to idle. On base, they were still high for the short runway, so he closed the throttle completely and applied full flaps.

Still high turning final, Tom tried a severe side slip to lose altitude. The Skyhawk is placarded against slipping with full flaps, but Tom had no confidence in their chances of a go-around. The descent rate increased.

They landed halfway down the dirt strip and with hard braking stopped before the end. By this time, the engine was squealing alarmingly, a grating sound of metal against metal, like a fingernail on a blackboard. To save it, Tom shut it down immediately. Later, the mechanics found the engine to be out of oil and impossible to start. Making the larger airport, or even a go-around where they were, would have been impossible.

For days after the incident, Tom's emotions ran the gamut of rage, fear, relief, and thoughtful reflection. His timely noticing of the oil pressure gauge had undoubtedly saved their lives. We talked about the importance of the engine gauges in the instrument pilot's scan. How often in their routine scanning of the panel should the eyes light on them? "How often do you check the oil pressure?" I asked Tom.

"I don't really know," he said, "but evidently, often enough."

What had Tom done to be prepared for the emergency? First, he regularly included the engine gauges in his instrument scan so that he was alerted to the problem early. In his own training and in his work with students, he had planned for engine failure, frequently going through the mental exercise of deciding just what he would do if it happened. He practiced forced landings and was familiar with the glide characteristics of his airplane. And he was prepared and willing to abandon his initial decision and land short of the first chosen spot.

This incident occurred in VFR conditions, but even in the soup, there *are* things you can do. Right away, trim for the best glide speed and prepare for a forced landing. Buckle all shoulder belts and instruct your passengers to assume a crouch position as the landing approaches. Tell your front seat passenger to remove his shoe and jam it in the door shortly before touchdown to guard against the possibility that the door will buckle on impact and trap the occupants in the airplane. A Jeppesen manual is another possible door wedge. Turn into the wind, away from high terrain, or parallel to the valleys in mountainous country. When the engine driven vacuum pump fails you will have only partial panel, so cover the attitude indicator to avoid the temptation to follow its indications. Turn off the fuel supply, lean the mixture, turn off the mags, and perform any other items on the forced landing checklist (which, incidentally, you should study from time to time).

Prepare yourself mentally to *land the airplane*. A controlled landing on any surface, even treetops, water, or busy city streets, is preferable to an uncontrolled crash. There are many true stories of heroic pilots refusing to the last second to give up their responsibilities and thus bringing survivors out of desperate circumstances.

Communications Failure

"Lance six seven eight papa fox, maintain 5000, contact Fort Worth Center now, on 127.7."

Tim Tonkin and I had departed Lubbock, Texas, for Waco and were joining Victor 102 when Lubbock Approach issued the handoff to Fort Worth Center. We had entered solid IFR at 400 feet, but it was a friendly kind of IFR day. Inside the clouds, it was bright enough to require sunglasses, and we imagined the tops were just above us, although pilot reports said they were way up in the jet routes. The outside air temperature was in the 40's. The ride was very smooth. There was no turbulence anywhere in Texas, and we had no concerns about icing. The clouds that day hid no invisible hazards but seemed to protect us like a great mass of warm cotton.

I acknowledged the handoff and tuned the number two radio to 127.7. Flicking the transmit switch to the second position, I reported, "Fort Worth Center, Lance six seven eight papa fox is with you at five thousand."

No response.

I double checked the transmit switch and volume knob before broadcasting again. Still no answer. The speaker didn't even crackle. Turning the squelch up all the way, I realized that either the radio or the speaker was not working.

Carefully jotting down the approach control frequency from the number one radio, I tuned number one to 127.7, flicked the transmit switch up and tried the squelch. Nothing. Whatever the problem was, it evidently affected both radios.

As a busy CFII, I have taught communcations failure procedures hundreds of times. And Tim, who owns and operates Riteway Radio, in Waco, has a thorough understanding of the problems that beset modern avionics. "Well," I joked grimly, "it couldn't happen to two nicer guys."

"Try the nav audio," Tim suggested.

I turned up the volume on both navs and for

good measure, on the ADF as well. As I flicked the audio panel switches to the "speaker" position, the silence from the overhead speaker became increasingly oppressive. "Definitely something wrong with the speaker," I muttered.

"It could be a transmitter short," Tim said, "A keyed mike will mute the audio function."

I jiggled the mike key. "Seems okay," I said.

"A short in the mike jack or the wire would have the same effect," Tim said, "and is also harmful to the radios. Most aircraft radios are designed to transmit about a minute at a time before excessive heat develops. If the mike is keyed or the system is shorted for 20 or 30 minutes, power is used all that time and damage to the radios is likely.

"A worn jack could also disable the system. We can check for this by unplugging the mike. I have even seen cases where a pilot believed he had a radio failure when the standby mike, plugged in the auxiliary jack on the right side of the cockpit, caused a short."

The plug was tight in the jack, but I unplugged it to be sure the jack or a bad wire wasn't the culprit. There was still no sound from the speaker.

"How could the speaker quit so suddenly?" I asked.

"It's not unusual," Tim answered. "An internal part called the voice coil may have broken. If that happens, perfectly good speakers can quit suddenly, the result of fatigue caused by use and old age. On a turbulent day, we might occasionally hear static and scraps of words as the rough air caused the broken coil to intermittently make contact.

"Another type of speaker failure is when sound distortion gradually builds up over time. It usually results from moisture leaking in and causing the speaker material to soften. In such cases, the speaker doesn't quit suddenly, but the quality deteriorates to the point where most transmissions are unreadable.

"Fortunately, the speaker and headset run on completely different systems, so let's just plug in your headset, and we'll probably have our communications back."

At that moment, something flashed before my mind's eye. I have given many a lecture on the necessity of carrying a spare mike, a headset, and even a battery powered backup comm radio on every flight. "You'd feel pretty foolish," I would admonish my students, "when you can't use your eight thousand dollars worth of radios because of a bad $40 mike, or because the speaker died and you didn't have a headset." Now, sitting in the clouds with no radio reception and with my headset on the table by the front door of my house, I knew exactly how foolish they would feel.

"Fly the airplane," I ordered myself, snapping out of my sudden embarrassment. Thanks to my negligence, we were in a potentially serious situation, but I forced my mind to turn to the task of planning the rest of the flight.

To confirm our predicament, I quickly ran my hands and eyes over the volume controls, audio panel switches, frequency selectors, master switch, avionics master switch, and circuit breaker panel. The bad news was that everything was on, but nothing was sounding. The good news was that the ammeter showed the alternator working normally; at least we were in no danger of a total electrical failure.

Under the circumstances, I saw no point in trying various frequencies, not even the emergency channel, 121.5. However, I did leave the volume controls on "loud," in case our speaker miraculously returned to life. I left the nav radios turned up as well, knowing that ATC, through Flight Service, could try to reach us on a VOR frequency.

"Since the radios quit together," said Tim, "we have to assume that only the speaker is out. The radios have separate antennas, and we know they are not iced up. For the radios to die separately and simultaneously is very unlikely, so the transmitters are probably still working."

I reconnected the mike and broadcast a message in the blind, using 127.7, our last assigned frequency. I decided to use the center frequencies on the en route chart for the rest of the flight and those on the approach plate once in the terminal area. "Fort Worth Center," I said, "Lance six seven eight papa fox has lost radio reception. Everything else is working normally, including the electrical system. We intend to continue the flight to Waco as planned and will report our position and intentions every fifteen minutes."

"Since you may have conflicted with another airplane's message, I suggest you repeat that," Tim said. "If you did step on another transmission, the controller would have heard only a squeal and may not even know who called him. On the other hand, we don't want to make too many calls. There have been instances of a center frequency being virtually monopolized by a panicky pilot in this situation repeatedly trying his radio."

I repeated the message while Tim switched the transponder to 7600. "7600 tells them that the emergency is only a radio failure," he said. "To get attention we used to squawk on 7700 for one minute prior to using 7600, but that is no longer necessary."

Flying IFR with no communications created an eerie feeling. We are so used to reporting, requesting, copying and complying that the experience of making our own decisions, without assistance or interference, made us a little uneasy. However, it was far from a crisis.

The pilot has three basic tasks: to fly the airplane, to navigate, and to communicate. The first is absolutely critical, and the second is important. The third is also important, but only as the basis of IFR separation, keeping blind flying airplanes from colliding. Perhaps our comm failure inconvenienced controllers and other pilots, but we continued our flight, following the simple comm failure procedures of FAR 91.185. **Keeping us separated would not be difficult for ATC.** After all, they still had us on radar. A comm failure need not precipitate a crisis.

"I'm still blushing over forgetting my headset," I said to Tim, "but I'm glad you're here. Your radio expertise is really helpful."

"I promise I won't tell," he smiled. "I only wish the transmitter had failed instead of the receiver. If we could hear, the flight could continue almost normally. When a controller has trouble reaching an airplane, his first reaction is to say 'ident if you hear me.' If the aircraft is listening, he asks simple questions and they ident for yes, do nothing for no.

"But you know," he added, "I'm glad I'm not the pilot here. I haven't studied comm failure procedures in quite a while."

"If we encountered VFR conditions, it would be very simple," I said, "We'd maintain VFR and land as soon as conveniently possible. One phone call to ATC, and the whole thing would be over. Unfortunately, we're in the middle of thousands of cubic miles of cloud; I don't expect to see any VFR."

"So we just follow our assigned route?" Tim

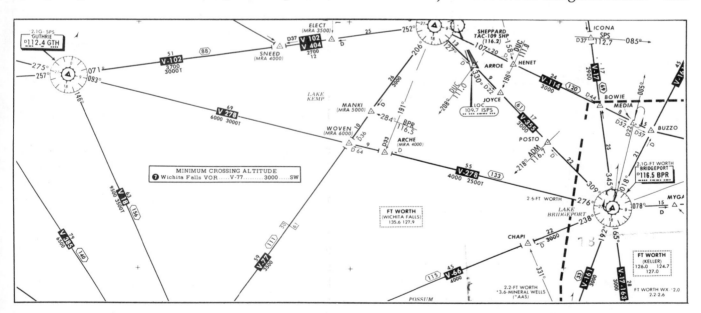

Figure 11-1

asked.

"Yes. It's Victor 102 to Guthrie VORTAC, Victor 278 to Bridgeport, and Victor 17 to Waco VORTAC (figure 11-1). If we had no assigned route and no 'expected' route, we would use what we filed on our flight plan. That's one reason I always have a copy of the flight plan on my knee board. I also have a copy of the last weather briefing I got, so we have some information, although it will be hours old when we reach Waco."

Tim was studying the en route chart. "We're at the minimum en route altitude now," he said, "but past Guthrie it goes up to 6000. Will we climb to the MEA?"

"Yes," I said, "we'll stay at our last assigned altitude, or the MEA, *whichever is higher*. Notice that halfway from Guthrie to Bridgeport the MEA drops to 4000. What do you think we'll do then?"

"Down to 4000?" said Tim.

"No," I said, "our last assigned altitude was 5000, so that's as low as we'll go until we're ready to start the approach."

Fixes slipped by quickly, and the flight proceeded well. It was a smooth and comfortable ride, and we soon found ourselves chatting casually about our predicament, enjoying the day and, to some extent, our freedom from the radio. Our groundspeed was higher than planned, and I suspected we would reach Waco ahead of schedule.

At Guthrie we climbed to 6000, and 78 miles later, when the MEA dropped to 4000, we descended to 5000. I reported each time to Fort Worth Center, using 127.9 and 135.6, the closest frequencies shown on the en route chart. At Bridgeport, as we turned south on Victor 17, I reported on 126.0.

As we approached the Waco VORTAC, Tim studied the approach plates. "Which approach do you think they're using?" he asked.

"We have our choice of approaches," I said, "From our ETA until 30 minutes later, the airport will be closed for us. The last forecast I have for Waco, from just before takeoff, called for light northwest winds and a 500 foot ceiling. We'll shoot the ILS 19. It might mean a downwind landing, but it is their only ILS and we *don't* want to make a missed approach."

We had lifted off at 2:15 P.M., according to the note I had made on my route log just before taxiing onto the active. I estimated the Coffi LOM (figure 11-2) at 4 o'clock. Since our flight planned estimated time en route was an even two hours, we were 15 minutes early.

As we crossed Waco, I slowed the airplane down and turned outbound on the 051° radial at 5000 feet. Checking the plate Tim said, "Shouldn't you descend to 2500?"

"With the radios out," I said, "we must maintain the last assigned altitude until the initial approach fix, *and* until our ETA. We're 15 minutes early, so we'll have to hold at Coffi at 5000 feet until 4:15."

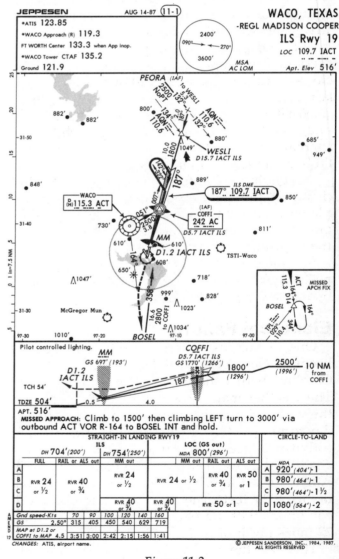

Figure 11-2

"There is no hold shown at Coffi," said Tim, "and the en route chart shows one at the VOR. Perhaps we should hold over the VOR."

"The regulation is slightly unclear," I said, "but the *Airman's Information Manual* spells it out. We hold at the initial approach fix, on the same side of the approach course as the procedure turn, in this case the west side. Incidentally, we have our choice of the IAF's on the plate. The airspace is cleared for us at each one. We'll use Coffi, since it is most convenient."

We made a parallel entry to the unpublished hold and started watching the minutes click away. The northwest wind required a one and a half minute outbound leg to achieve a one minute inbound on the localizer. Four-fifteen arrived as we turned inbound on our fourth circuit, and I reduced the power to begin our descent. The altimeter read 4200 feet as we crossed the beacon and turned outbound for the last time.

"We'll intercept the glide slope at 1800 feet," I said, "and fly a darn careful approach." Our alternate was San Antonio, 150 miles away, and I'd had enough no-radio flying for one day.

Descending at 700 feet per minute in the fifth circuit of the hold, we reached 1800 feet as planned and intercepted the glide slope just outside the marker. Minutes later we were on the ground.

Several days afterward, I received an unexpected gift from Tim Tonkin's Riteway Radio: a brand new top quality headset.

Electrical Failure

One of our instructors set out from Poughkeepsie, New York to Raleigh-Durham, North Carolina, with a student and the student's wife. The weather map showed a front coming from the west, with deteriorating weather and thunderstorms. West of their route there were turbulence, heavy rain, thunderstorms, and 0-0 conditions at some airports. To the east was the Atlantic coast and better weather with ceilings up to 1000 feet. The trip began in solid IFR conditions with no particular problems — until 22 miles north of Richmond.

Then all the electrical equipment suddenly and simultaneously failed. Because the auto pilot was engaged, the airplane started rolling

into a steep left bank. The navigation needles went dead, the lights went out, and the turn coordinator began spinning down. The communication radios failed completely, and the transponder stopped blinking. It was eerie.

Electrical failures usually occur gradually. After an alternator failure, the equipment runs for a time on the battery, and the ammeter shows that a problem has occurred. A center needle type ammeter shows a slight discharge rate and a left needle type drops to zero. In such case, steps can be taken to conserve electricity for the approach.

In this case, it was learned later, the failure resulted from voltage spike from an incorrectly installed alternator. There was nothing that could be done to save electricity — it was all gone. This crew had no means of navigating or communicating. In fact they almost didn't keep flying until Bill disconnected the autopilot and they recovered from the bank they were in.

With the airplane under control (remember: whatever happens, fly the airplane first) it became a matter of planning. They knew the front was coming from the southwest, so they took a heading of about 060°, towards the higher ceilings, better weather, and also towards the coast. They decided to fly at a VFR altitude, reasoning that in such terrible weather, they would be less likely to encounter other traffic. Bill wrote down the time when they made the turn and their last known position. For the rest of the flight he used dead reckoning to keep running track of their estimated location.

Bill's log of the times when the tanks had been switched, which he had kept routinely even before the electrical failure, became even more important than it is normally. With no electricity, the electric fuel gauges rested quietly on zero — giving no information at all.

Several difficulties arose during the more than one hour they flew the new heading, still in the clouds. The clouds were uneven, giving rise to optical illusions. Once they thought they saw the coastline beneath them, and resisted descending only because Bill's dead reckoning showed them some fifty miles from the ocean. Minutes later they realized they had been looking at a lower cloud formation, not the ground. While the pilots concentrated on flying and navigating as best they could, the lady in back had no such distraction and tended to become a bit nervous. Providing reassurance became one of their tasks.

Bill had a Washington sectional in his flight bag, and, after an hour, he was able to figure that they were over an area where the highest obstruction was 1500 feet. Gingerly, they began a slow descent. Passing two thousand, they began to see holes to the ground. Bill recognized a river from the sectional, and they continued descending. Sure enough, they broke out at 1200 feet with ground clearance to spare. The visibility below the clouds was good, and half an hour later, they were on the ground calling ATC by telephone.

What had Bill done to prepare for an unexpected total loss of electrical power? His preparation for this emergency had started a long time ago.

He had *thought* about electrical failures and realized that the autopilot would have to be disengaged.

He had *considered* what altitude he would use to minimize the chance of a mid-air in the clouds — he didn't invent the VFR altitude tactic on the spot.

He also realized that in order to know where he was, he had to begin dead reckoning immediately.

He had developed the *habit* of keeping VFR charts in his flight bag on *all* flights.

Finally, he had a thorough weather briefing and knew the big picture of the weather, not just reports and forecasts for selected stations. He knew there was bad weather to the west, and improvment to the east.

And he knew that, as a last resort, he could dead reckon out over the ocean and descend almost to sea level without fear of hitting anything. In the worst case, with the clouds right on the water, he could still descend safely, fly west and probably land on a beach.

These were all considerations that had gone into Bill's planning for that IFR flight; in fact, they were contingency plans for every flight.

Electrical failure can occur suddenly, as in Bill's experience, or owing to an electrical fire. The fire-in-flight checklist, like all the emergency checklists, should be studied carefully in the comfort of your living room, and your actions should be carefully visualized. You can't expect to search for and read these checklists in an emergency, when you have everything but time, but should be studied and understood as part of flight preparation. After your next flight, bring the owner's manual home and go through the fire in flight checklist, slowly, and imagine yourself performing each action on the list. Think about the logic of the checklist so that even if you forget the exact order and details, you will retain the concepts and perform well under pressure.

Most electrical failures occur slowly, starting with a failed alternator. If this happens and the ammeter is a regular part of your scan, there may be an hour of electrical current left in the battery, provided you cut your electrical usage to a minimum. Your goal then becomes to conserve electricity and terminate the flight as soon as possible.

You will need some electricity to make any kind of instrument approach, even ASR. If possible, turn off the master switch as this is the only way of shutting off some current users such as electric fuel and temperature gauges, and the gear up light. In some airplanes it will also stop the gear motor which runs periodically to maintain the hydraulic pressure that holds the wheels up. Dangling gear will cause some drag and slow you down, but we're assuming you are short of electricity, not gas.

Assuming that the master switch must remain on, here are some tips for conserving electricity:

Transmitting uses much more current than receiving communications, but both are a drain on the battery. After an electrical failure, make one transmission to report your predicament, then turn the radios off except when you need assistance.

Turn off the transponder; it contains a powerful, high electrical consumption transmitter. The radar controller may be able to see you as a primary target without it. Even if he can't, you are better off saving the electricity it uses until you are in the terminal area where radar can help you get on the ground.

Pitot heat is one of the most costly electrical users, but at the first signs of a lost airspeed indicator, you may have to turn it on.

Lights are a drain. Always carry a flashlight at night and use it exclusively in an electrical failure. The rotating beacon is a particularly heavy electrical drain, with the nav lights close behind.

When being vectored, turn off the nav radios. For a long en route leg, if high terrrain is not a danger, dead reckon. The current you save is more valuable than the few miles you may drift off course. Get to an airport with ASR, if possible.

In some airplanes it is possible to turn off the electric turn coordinator, either with the master or a separate switch. If it is, and your artificial horizon is working, do it.

Fly to the ocean or the "nearest VFR." You will be grateful you remembered to ask where the nearest VFR was located during your weather briefing. If you must descend unassisted, do it before you run out of gas. You will need fuel to maneuver once you break out of the clouds and also to keep the attitude indicator working.

We all hope this kind of incident never happens to us, but if it does the outcome will be much better if we are adequately prepared.

Vacuum Failure

We have been harping on preparedness as the best defense against any unexpected circumstance. Plan for the unexpected, and when it occurs, you will be ready. In no type of IFR emergency is this more true than in a vacuum failure. As every pilot who has had partial panel training knows, the airplane *can* be flown without the vacuum instruments, but it takes a good scan and a light touch.

Although most modern airplanes have vacuum driven attitude indicators and directional gyros, and electrically driven turn instruments, there are exceptions. Many HSI's, for example, are all-electric and some attitude indicators are electric as well. Be sure you know *for certain* what systems drive what instruments in your cockpit. This is very important for analyzing situations where the instruments appear to behave strangely and for anticipating what other problems may develop.

During instrument training, simulated gyro failures occur abruptly. The instructor covers the attitude indicator and DG with a couple of opaque disks and says, "Okay, let's try some partial panel." Partial panel usually refers to the three pressure instruments and the electric turn coordinator, the instruments that would remain after a vacuum system failure.

Real life failures occur much more insidiously. DG precession increases. The attitude indicator becomes sluggish and may come to rest in a slightly banked attitude, contradicting the indication on the turn coordinator. The pilot may become confused and have trouble telling which instrument is faulty. A glance at the suction gauge may reveal a vacuum failure, but it may not. Force yourself to keep the airplane from turning by referring to the turn coordinator, and carefully watch the vacuum instruments. If the attitude indicator dips to one side or the DG turns, you know you have a vacuum failure.

Once you determine that your vacuum instruments have failed, you can apply your partial panel skills. Since it is practically impossible to consciously delete the attitude indicator from your scan, cover it with a business card to avoid being tricked by its false indications.

Partial panel flight technique is covered in Chapter Three.

Once you have recognized vacuum failure, and the flight is under control, notify ATC. In a radar environment, they can be of special assistance. *No-gyro* vectors may be issued on pilot request. The controller will instruct, "turn left" or "turn right," and when he observes that your aircraft is flying in the proper direction he will say "stop turn," freeing you of the need to time your turns. You are expected to make all turns at standard rate.

At an airport with an ASR approach, you can request a no-gyro approach. The procedure is the same except that on final, turns are made at half standard rate. Practice no-gyro approaches are available at fields with ASR procedures.

A gyro failure is a genuine emergency. Even if you are proficient enough to continue the flight on partial panel and fly an impeccable approach (few pilots are), the remote chance of a turn coordinator failure is too serious to risk. Get on the ground as soon as you can.

Low Fuel

Naturally, you conscientiously plan your flights so that you are never low on fuel. However, if everything always went according to plan, there would be no need for a chapter on emergencies.

In a low fuel situation you may give the controller a "minimum fuel advisory," indicating that you are low on gas and cannot accept any "undue" delay. This is not equivalent to declaring an emergency, and does not afford you traffic priority. It merely informs the controller of your low fuel status and, hopefully, reduces your chances of delay. When he hands you off, he is expected to pass this information to the next controller.

Thunderstorms and Ice

The best advice about thunderstorms is: **avoid them**. Kenneth Wilk, the director of the Severe Weather Research Center in Kansas City, has said that after twenty years of studying thunderstorms he is still increasingly impressed with their ferocity and danger to airplanes. Research cannot improve our ability to fly in thunderstorms. Research can only provide more sophisticated ways of avoiding them.

Chapter Four discusses forecasts, radar summaries, and PIREPS, as they apply to thunderstorm avoidance. In areas and at times of the year when thunderstorms exist, use these aids diligently to give the killer storms a wide berth.

Airborne and ground based radar are defenses against thunderstorms, but ATC radar is not completely reliable. It is designed to filter out many precipitation returns. There have even been cases of pilots being vectored directly into thunderstorms.

The 3M Stormscope offers an alternative means of thunderstorm avoidance. The Stormscope registers electrical discharge, not precipitation, as does radar. Electrical discharge is caused by wind shear, that is, by adjacent masses of air moving in radically different directions, and therefore is a direct indicator of turbulence.

Just as strong turbulence can exist without much rain, heavy rain is sometimes unaccompanied by turbulence. Stormscope equipped pilots in light airplanes can sometimes penetrate heavy showers around which large jets, with radar only, divert.

Air mass thunderstorms can be seen in clear weather. Avoid them by at least 20 miles. Even though it may appear clear beneath a storm, don't try flying under it. Some of the worst turbulence can be beneath the storm, along with severe updrafts that can suck a small airplane up into the middle of it. Beneath the "anvil" portion of the storm is the worst area for hail. Don't risk flying in this area.

Embedded thunderstorms are the most dangerous type for IFR pilots because they are invisible. Apparently benign cloud masses can conceal strong embedded thunderstorms. If you should penetrate one by accident, fly attitude, according to your gyro instruments, and slow to maneuvering speed, not on the airspeed indicator, but by setting the power. The airspeed indicator, altimeter and VSI become completely unreliable in a thunderstorm because of the radical pressure differences that exist. Don't try to hold altitude, and don't turn back. Thunderstorms do have other sides, and there is more danger in the banking required to turn back than in trying to make it through to the other side.

The best advice about thunderstorms also applies to ice: avoid it.

While ice is surely to be avoided, you would never fly in the winter in some parts of the country if you believed the forecast every time it said, "CHC OF ICG ICIP" (chance of icing in clouds and precipitation). This warning is routinely attached to many winter area forecasts by defensive government forecasters. The key to successfully negotiating icing situations is to plan yourself an out: climb above the tops or into air that is so cold that icing is unlikely. Descend below the freezing level or below the cloud bases. Avoid freezing rain which is the worst ice maker of all. If you do inadvertently enter an area of ice and none of these options is available, make a 180° turn and fly right back out of it.

Just as embedded thunderstorms are a good reason to postpone a flight, so are widespread icing conditions. If there are low ceilings, high tops, few light aircraft flying, and reports of icing encounters; stay home.

Since the purpose of obtaining the instrument rating is to be able to fly in weather, you must understand weather conditions. A thorough briefing for every flight is the first prerequisite. The second is a solid base of weather knowledge. This book cannot cover all the weather wisdom the IFR pilot needs, so continue your study with some of the excellent weather references in the bibliography. And, of course, there is no substitute for experience.

The key to dealing with unexpected situations — whether they are "curves" thrown to you by weather or equipment or ATC — is to eliminate the surprise element. Expect the unexpected. Use your practice time and your study time to consider possible emergencies and carefully visualize your response to every conceivable situation.

CHAPTER TWELVE

THE FLIGHT TEST AND AFTER

Once, only once, have I made the mistake of riding along on a student's instrument flight test. Frank Daniels, a good friend and one of the most genial examiners I know, invited me along as an extra pair of eyes in the crowded sky over Bradley International Airport. Little did I expect the ordeal that lay ahead as I climbed into the Skyhawk and my student, Jim Oglethorpe, taxied out with Frank in the right seat.

Helpless in the back, I worked and sweated, anticipating every maneuver and mentally screaming directions to my student. My muscles tensed, as I leaned into each turn and crushed my foot against an imaginary rudder pedal; my hands made tiny, twitchy pitch corrections, for I was painfully aware of every little error. Each frequency change was a nightmare. Convinced that Jim had forgotten to make it, I miserably gave up his chances of passing until, each time, he casually made the switch at the last possible moment and I collapsed like a mound of warm jelly.

Jim's airwork went well, although the unusual attitudes were a little hair-raising from my vantage point. Jim and I had practiced partial panel turns, and his use of compass and clock were impressive. Frank also had him do an imminent stall under the hood.

The VOR and ADF approaches were also acceptable, and I began to believe that Jim was passing. Finally, Frank instructed him to fly southwest and call Bradley Approach for an ILS to Runway 6. "Full approach," he specified (figure 12-1).

Exhausted by then, I hardly dared hope that Jim could still handle the intricacies of a full ILS. I was transforming myself from an instructor full of confi-dence in my teaching skills, the course I was teaching and this quite adequate student, into a mother hen who was afraid of her chicks getting lost among foxes. I sagged slightly in the uncomfortable back seat and tried to concentrate on looking for traffic. As Jim began preparing for the approach, I realized that he might well be coping better than I. I watched with approval as he set up each radio for the ILS 6 and made a preliminary study of the approach plate, thereby improving his chances of staying ahead of the situation.

"Bradley Approach, Cessna six nine eight one hotel."

"Eight one hotel, Bradley."

"Eight one hotel, ten south of Bradley, request a full ILS."

"Eight one hotel, squawk zero four zero zero and ident; say altitude and type Cessna."

"Cessna 172 at two thousand five hundred, eight one hotel," was Jim's reply. My hours playing ATC in simulated communications were paying off as he responded to the controller's rapid fire instructions.

"Eight one hotel, radar contact eleven miles south of Bradley; fly heading two seven zero, vectors for the ILS Runway Six; descend and maintain two thousand. Verify this will be a full stop."

Here was a slightly unusual situation, and Jim rose to the occasion. "Affirmative on the full stop landing, but we want a full approach, eight one hotel," he responded.

"Unable full approach at this time, due to numerous traffic on the approach," said the controller.

There was silence in the cockpit as Jim turned to 270 and began descent to 2000 feet.

FAR 91.123 requires compliance with ATC clearances, but it also seems to encourage friendly negotiation. It says that a pilot may not deviate from a clearance, "except in an emergency, unless he obtains an amended clearance." But how best to "obtain an amended clearance?"

Not surprisingly, the same principles apply here as in other human interactions. Controllers put their pants on only one leg at a time. They like to avoid trouble, and they have good days and bad days just like everyone else. You should treat them as you would like to be treated.

Clarity is important. Plan your transmissions to be easily understood. Be concise and specific. If the controller knows what you want, you are more likely to get it.

Courtesy is helpful. Controllers are there to be used, but they don't like to be abused any more than the rest of us. I have often heard a pleasant manner win a favor when shrill demands were ineffective.

Persistence is another virtue. If a request is turned down, request clarification, then make the request again. If what you want is reasonable, the radar man may eventually find it easier to say yes.

Perhaps Jim was thinking of these same things as he made his next call, "Bradley Approach, eight one hotel."

"Eight one hotel, go ahead."

"Sir, this is a flight test. Is there any way you could work in a full approach?"

"Eight one hotel, proceed direct Chupp; cleared for the ILS Runway Six; maintain three thousand until advised. Report procedure turn inbound."

Jim gave a quick "Thank you, sir," started the climb, and brought the ADF needle to the nose with a right turn to 350. We would fly the procedure turn at 3000 feet, while vectored traffic shot the approach safely beneath us.

It was a calm day, and the ADF needle solidly held the nose. Heading and altitude were steady, and Jim appeared to have the approach well under control. Soon the needle crept slightly to the right, suggesting that we were nearing the station. Jim saw it too, and as it reached 5 right, he turned the airplane ten degrees in the same direction! I was in a turmoil. "STATION PASSAGE..." I mentally shrieked at him, "Don't make corrections for station passage! The wind does not change at the station!"

Despite the right turn, the needle swung further right, and Jim evidently realized what was happening. As it continued towards the right wing, he turned back

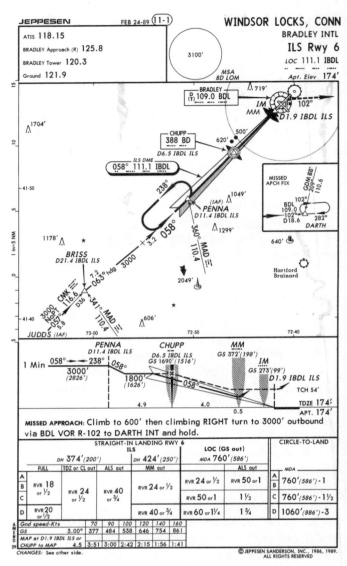

Figure 12-1

to 350.

The needle orbited past the right wing, the OM light flashed blue, and the audio signal invaded the cockpit. With no marker beacon volume control in the minimally equipped aircraft, the signal was unpleasantly loud. As he began his turn to 238, Jim shrugged disgustedly and flicked the marker receiver off.

The ADF needle continued its swing to the right and came to rest 10° left of the tail as Jim leveled the wings heading 238°. The localizer needle was pegged on the right, showing us northwest of the course. Wings level, Jim hit the stop watch he had velcro-fastened to the center of the yoke, waved his hand at the panel as he mentally checked his radio settings, reduced the throttle to 2000 RPM for a 90-knot approach speed and murmured to himself, "No report required." Frank nodded approval at his systematic use of the "Five T's." With the T's completed, Jim pressed left rudder and turned 5 away from the needle to re-intercept the localizer course.

We tracked the localizer outbound for slightly over three minutes. As the number two CDI centered (did it swing in from left or right?), he turned to 268° for a teardrop entry to the hold. While a parallel entry would have been equally correct, the teardrop was preferable in getting the aircraft on course sooner. After 1 minute on the 268° heading, Jim began a left turn.

He leveled the wings heading 058° as the localizer needle centered, but it began moving back towards the right. There was evidently a southeast crosswind. A 5° right turn, and it stopped moving, two dots off center. "Reference heading 063°," Jim muttered, as the second needle centered, marking the Madison VOR 360 defining radial over Penna. Jim took the mike and called, "Eight one hotel, procedure turn inbound."

"Eight one hotel, you are five miles from Chupp, cleared for the ILS Runway Six approach, your altitude restriction is canceled, contact tower one two zero point three at the marker."

With a quick, "Cleared for the approach, eight one hotel, tower at the marker," Jim put down the mike and reduced the throttle to 1600 RPM for a 90-knot descent to 1800 feet. A 5° right turn brought the needle back to center, and he returned to the reference heading of 063°. At 1800 feet, he raised the nose and returned to a power setting of 2000 RPM. Jim flipped the radio selection switch, preparing for the call to the tower.

Soon the glide slope needle came alive. As it centered, Jim reduced the power to 1600 RPM and began his descent on the glide slope. As the ADF swung to the tail, he reported, "Bradley Tower, eight one hotel is with you."

"Roger, eight one hotel, cleared to land straight-in Runway Six."

Jim flew the approach beautifully. I imagined his eyes on the nav head verifying course and glide slope alignment, darting to the DG to check heading, back to the nav head, and to the AI for a slight pitch correction. The needles were steady as he set pitch attitudes on the AI and the heading on the DG. Our comfortable, stable progress would have been impossible if he were chasing the needles.

Our rate of descent was between 400 and 500 feet per minute, with the airspeed steady at 90 knots. His pitch attitude was about one half dot below the horizon and was working nicely.

It was a smooth evening with a light crosswind from the southeast. A 063° heading held the localizer steady down to 1000 feet, at which point it began wandering to the left. The wind seemed to have shifted left slightly as the surface friction became significant. Jim centered the needle by turning to 058° and held it steady with a new reference heading of 060°.

Apparently, he did not notice that the marker beacons were still off. He didn't miss the OM signal. I began to worry and could only hope he would remember before reaching the MM.

I was fidgeting terribly in the back, half afraid that my nervousness would affect Jim's performance and half hoping he was sufficiently clairvoyant to get my telepathic signal to turn on his markers before 424 feet, the DH with the MM out. He had done well so far and I didn't want him to fail the flight test for such a minor error. It was a lovely evening, the ALSF-II was on, and the visibility was good. I would usually have enjoyed the ride and the view, but all my concentration was riveted on the marker beacon switch.

Once again, as though he were purposely trying to turn my hair gray, Jim avoided disaster at the last possible moment. As he flicked on the marker switch, the MM was just beginning to flash. Frank reached over and took off Jim's hood. We passed the middle and then the inner marker and glided to an uneventful landing on Runway 6.

My student had passed the test.

Tips on Flight Test Preparation

It is widely believed, with some justification, that the instrument rating is the most difficult of all ratings to obtain. Tougher than the private or the multi, it requires a lot of specialized knowledge and the ability to fly with precision. No wonder that the instrument flight test is viewed with trepidation by most applicants for the IFR ticket.

Knowledge of the exam format can go a long way to ease the anxiety that comes with the flight test. An official description of the flight test, along with acceptable performance guidelines, is given in the FAA's Instrument Rating, Practical Test Standards booklet (FAA-S-8081-A, AVN-130 03/89).

Most flight tests are given by FAA designated examiners. These individuals are not employed by the FAA, but are independent business people appointed by the local FAA office to administer tests and issue certificates and ratings. Many are associated with a flight school or charter operation and give flight tests as a sideline. A few make their entire living giving flight tests. Designees charge the applicant directly for their examining services and most require full payment before the flight test begins.

Although appointed and regulated by the FAA's General Aviation or Flight Standards District Offices (GADOs or FSDOs), examiners have a great deal of flexibility in how the flight test is administered. While following the broad outline of the Practical Test Standards, there is plenty of room for judgment in how the test is designed, how long it takes, and how the applicant is judged. With this in mind, what follows is a description of a typical or "average" instrument flight test.

There are two main parts of the instrument flight test—the oral exam and the flight test. The oral exam is typically one hour and 30 minutes long. Unlike the instrument written exam, the oral tends to emphasize the practical, real-world knowledge that you will need to fly instruments in the ATC system.

The oral typically begins with the planning of a cross-country flight. The examiner will expect to see you obtain a weather briefing, select a route, and correctly fill in a flight plan form. He may or may not ask you to actually file the flight plan with Flight Service.

With the flight planning out of the way, specific questions follow. The range of possible subjects is great, but some popular ones are:

1. **Weight and balance.** This could vary from a simple "you and me and full fuel in the airplane, do a weight and balance," to a complicated, "Take off with minimum legal fuel, calculate the fuel burn on the cross-country you just planned, and figure the weight and balance for landing at the end of the trip with our skis and snowmobiles in the back."

2. **Communications failure.** These questions frequently involve the specific application of FAR 91.185 to hypothetical comm failures on the cross-country trip you just planned.

3. **Chart symbols.** The only way to answer these questions is to thoroughly understand all the symbols and abbreviations on the IFR charts. While the written exam focused on understand-

ing government charts, the flight examiner will quiz you on whatever type you bring to the flight test. Most instrument pilots use Jeppesen charts.

4. **Regulations.** These questions can cover anything from required equipment checks to alternate airport weather requirements. It is a good idea to review thoroughly just prior to the flight test. A good performance on the oral will bolster your confidence and will give the examiner a good feeling about your abilities, even before he sees you fly.

The flight portion of the exam also averages, typically, 1 hour and 30 minutes. It frequently begins with an IFR takeoff for the beginning of your planned cross-country flight. Once the examiner has seen you handle ATC communications and properly enter the en route airway structure, he will have you cancel IFR. Flight tests are rarely conducted in IFR conditions. Even in Districts where it is permitted by the FAA District Office, most examiners are reluctant to give the test in less than VFR weather.

The balance of the flight test consists of two parts—airwork and approaches. The airwork phase may include some steep turns, stalls, and partial panel unusual attitude recoveries. There may also be a holding pattern.

The approaches include one each VOR, NDB, and ILS approach. One of the nonprecision approaches is usually conducted with the AI and DG covered.

Success on the instrument flight test depends primarily on your ability to do and understand the things taught in your instrument course. That is, you must be able to fly the airplane on instruments, visualize your position in relation to stations and courses, and understand and interact with the ATC system. A fair check ride does not bombard the applicant with every possible emergency—it tests his ability to function safely as a pilot under IFR conditions.

The most common reason for failure of the instrument flight test is the common disease called checkride-itis. Sweaty palms, tightness in the throat, and disorganized thoughts are symptoms of this illness. They can interfere with a pilot's functioning and cause mistakes that he would not make in a less anxiety-laden situation. For many pilots, a flight test provokes more nervousness than flying a tough approach in minimum weather.

Meeting the examiner prior to the flight test is one way to alleviate this problem. Feeling comfortable with him as an individual can go a long way towards easing your mind on flight test day.

Many examiners recognize the anxiety problem on flight tests and make an effort to put the applicant at ease. If sharing a friendly cup of coffee together is part of his routine, remember to use the rest room before heading to the airplane.

Speaking to the examiner several days before the flight test can put your mind at rest. He may tell you what he expects—usually simply a safe and competent performance of the maneuvers specified in the Practical Test Standards. He may tell you whether or not you will be expected to do all the radio work during this ride (this varies among examiners). He may even tell you the sequence he uses on his flight tests—which approaches you'll be expected to fly and how long the test can be expected to last. But don't press too hard—he may take offense if he feels you are trying to get an "easy" ride.

Once in the airplane, don't hurry. Perform your normal routine methodically and at your normal speed. Pay special attention to your checklist; it contains all the items that any nervousness might cause you to forget.

If you make a mistake on the flight test, acknowledge it, correct it, and forget about it. You haven't failed the flight test until the examiner says so. If you get off course on an approach (e.g., if you get a full-scale deflection on the ILS) declare a missed approach and begin the appropriate missed approach procedure. Many examiners will consider this a sign of good judgment, the hallmark of a safe pilot, and will not discontinue the ride.

Be very careful of minimum altitudes. It is preferable to be 50 feet above your MDA, rather than a foot below it. A few feet high is safe, but a foot low could be a disqualifying error.

If you fly well on instruments and are able to visualize your position, the only reason for a failure would be an out-and-out mistake. For example, you might select the wrong radial or descend below a minimum altitude, owing to nervousness. In this case, you may be allowed to complete the flight test and still receive a pink slip at the end. On your retest, you will only be required to demonstrate the maneuver that was unsatisfactory on the first ride—not retake the entire exam.

The majority of those who take the instrument flight test, pass it on the first attempt. Barring any unusual problems, you should be among them. Good luck!

Maintaining Instrument Currency

I wonder how many rated readers are legally instrument current?

The currency regulation says:

[61.57 (e)] Instrument—(1) Recent IFR experience. No pilot may act as pilot in command under IFR, nor in weather conditions less than the minimums prescribed for VFR, unless he has, within the past 6 calendar months—

(i) In the case of an aircraft other than a glider, logged at least 6 hours of instrument time under actual or simulated IFR conditions, at least 3 of which were in flight in the category of aircraft involved, including at least six instrument approaches, or passed an instrument competency check in the category of aircraft involved.

(2) Instrument competency check. A pilot who does not meet the recent instrument experience requirements of subparagraph (1) of this paragraph during the prescribed time or 6 calendar months thereafter may not serve as pilot in command under IFR, nor in weather conditions less than the minimums prescribed for VFR, until he passes an instrument competency check in the category of aircraft involved, given by an FAA inspector, a member of an armed force of the United States authorized to conduct flight tests, an FAA-approved check pilot, or a certificated instrument flight instructor. The Administrator may authorize the conduct of part or all of this check in a pilot ground trainer equipped for instruments or an aircraft simulator.

Certain aspects of the currency rule occasionally cause confusion. Only half the required 6 hours, and none of the approaches, must be in the airplane. In fact, 3 of the hours, and all the approaches, can be on a ground trainer as long as the training device has been approved by the FAA. If you happen to hold airplane and helicopter ratings on your pilot certificate, then 3 hours in each within the last 6 calendar months will make you current in both, as long as you have also logged the required six approaches.

What time can be logged as instrument time? This is answered by [61.51 (c)(4)], which reads, in part, as follows:

"Instrument flight time. A pilot may log as instrument flight time only that time during which he operates the aircraft solely by reference to instruments, under actual or simulated instrument flight conditions....."

The key phrase is "controlling the aircraft solely by reference to instruments." Time in the clouds, on a very dark night with no ground lights and no horizon and in extremely hazy conditions over water might all qualify as instrument time. Note that time "on top," when you are navigating on instruments but controlling the airplane with reference to the excellent horizon formed by the level undercast, does not qualify as instrument time.

Flight time under the hood also qualifies as instrument time, and you need not have an instructor along. You do need a safety pilot to watch for traffic, and his name must be included in your logbook entry. The safety pilot need not sign your book. The only requirement is that the safety pilot be qualified to fly the airplane. Usually, this just means that he holds a private pilot certificate, rated for single-engine, land. If your bird has retractable gear or more than 200 horsepower, he also needs a high performance sign-off.

If your instrument currency should lapse, you have another 6 calendar months to meet the requirements of FAR 61.57, only now, of course, you cannot do it by filing and flying in the clouds. You must use a safety pilot and practice in VFR conditions under the hood until you are again legally current.

If 6 months elapse since you were last current, you must pass an instrument competency check. This can be administered by a "double-I," designated examiner, or by the FAA.

How easy it is for you to stay current depends primarily on how much you fly. For the businessman pilot who flies regularly, and more or less regardless of the weather, IFR time tends to average about 10% of the total. If you fly less than 60 hours every 6 months, tend to postpone trips when the weather is IFR, or live in Arizona, you will probably find it hard to stay legally current.

And remember that legal currency does not imply proficiency. Even if you are legally current, your proficiency depends on how you use the rating.

The instrument rating is a credential that allows a wide range of activities. You can use it to take off zero-zero from a tiny grass field and fly for hours in the clouds in heavy rain and turbulence while you pick your way through thunderstorms, and then shoot a tough approach to minimums, breaking out of the murk at 200 and a half. You can also, consequently, grow very old very quickly.

Most general aviation pilots don't use the rating for such purposes. A more common use is to take off with a 1000- or 2000-foot ceiling, penetrate the overcast and get on top at 4000 or 6000 or 8000 feet. You fly in smooth air and enjoy the sunshine for a while and then shoot an approach to break out at 1000 feet or higher. Going up and down through that overcast is a useful privilege. That same hypothetical flight, conducted below the ceiling (it would have been VFR, remember) would have been nerve wracking owing to terrain and poor visibility. It also would have been uncomfortable, because it is a lot bumpier below the clouds.

Is the pilot who flies a little "easy" IFR qualified for trips in hard, strain-filled IFR?

Probably not, even if he is legally current. Your level of proficiency depends on how much effort you are willing to put into maintaining it.

There is a cliche that says you will never be more proficient than on the day you passed your check ride, because you will never put as much effort into sharpening your IFR skills. If you want to use the rating for serious IFR traveling, this shouldn't be true. But it is hard to stay current, and you have to work at it. What can you do to stay proficient?

The experience of flying IFR within the ATC system will do a lot to improve your proficiency and confidence. One of the biggest problems experienced by "sometime" IFR pilots is confusion in dealing with ATC communications.

You can do a lot for yourself by filing IFR every time you go on a trip, even when the weather is CAVU ("ceiling and visibility unlimited"). Dealing with ATC, handling navigation problems, reading the chart, keeping a route log, planning the approach, and flying the airplane, imagining that you are in the clouds, is valuable experience. And if you get overloaded, you can always say the magic words, "Cancel my IFR."

If there is a high ceiling with low tops you can still request an altitude that will put you in the clouds. Now, flying on the gauges, you are doing everything you will ever have to do during the en route phase of flight. If you tire of being in the soup, simply request a different altitude.

At your destination, shoot an instrument approach. Even in the clearest weather, it is perfectly all right to refuse a visual, and you will almost always get the approach you request. Remember to scan for traffic. Without a safety pilot, it is illegal and dangerous to wear the hood. Afterwards, take a few minutes to review and critique your performance.

If you do have a safety pilot on board, take the opportunity to wear the hood. During the en route part of the trip, fly the airways partial panel for a while.

Another thing you can do to stay current and proficient is to practice regularly. What gets rusty when you don't fly enough? Let's break IFR work down into its component skills.

The first thing you lose is your scan and the habits required to fly the airplane precisely. Therefore, you should practice flying the aircraft while not worrying about navigating, communicating, or shooting approaches. Nothing will go well for you if you are not sharp at basic aircraft control. The more complex the airplane, the more difficult are the basic maneuvers and the faster you will lose your proficiency at them. You therefore need to devote some time on the basics in your practice sessions, all the more if you fly heavier metal. Even if you fly instruments regularly, you will benefit from an occasional session of basic airwork.

The next thing that gets rusty is your ability to visualize your position on the chart and to follow complicated procedures. Holding patterns and approaches need to be practiced.

When you practice approaches, don't just fly the ILS, which is the easiest approach, and the one you probably use the most. Nonprecision approaches, especially ADF, are more difficult and therefore need more work.

It is helpful to have another instrument pilot as your safety pilot—if you can arrange to practice occasionally with another rated pilot, you can help each other immensely. Take turns flying and issuing practice clearances, giving each other holding patterns and navigation problems around an NDB or VOR. Both roles will benefit each of you; every instructor knows that we learn something most thoroughly when teaching it to someone else.

The most important thing you can do to stay current and proficient is to take refresher training once or twice a year, like professional pilots do.

Regular proficiency training helps you stay sharp, checks you for bad habits, and helps you prepare for emergencies. The airlines recognize this proven fact, as do charter operators, corporate flight departments, the FAA, the insurance companies and all professional pilots. In the United States, companies and individuals spend hundreds of millions of dollars a year on recurrent pilot training. Even though they may fly almost daily, the pros take recurrent training every six months. Refresher training is even more essential for pilots who do not fly as much. Let's face it, if you are operating under IFR, it is in everyone's interest that you be current and proficient.

If a pilot "has been flying for years, and never had a problem," it may be because the equipment, the weather and the system have never thrown him a nasty curve. Many general aviation pilots are recognizing this fact and are taking recurrent training courses at least once a year.

Effective recurrent training checks your skills and knowledge piece by piece. Then it leads you to new levels of proficiency, introducing advanced procedures and building more accuracy. A good proficiency course will start by reviewing all the basics, and end with a good dose of practice emergencies.

Selecting a proficiency course involves many of the same issues you considered in choosing your initial instrument training program (see Chapter One). Among other things, you should ask, "Is there an established course curriculum, and is it flexible enough to accommodate my needs and ability level?" A reasonable length for your annual proficiency course is two or three eight hour days, including ground school, simulator work, and flight.

By flying IFR in the system frequently, practicing regularly, and taking an annual refresher course, you can maintain your instrument proficiency at any level you desire.

Answers to Quizzes

Chapter Two— The Flight Instruments

These answers apply to most light airplanes.

1. The vacuum system. (Some AIs are electric.)
2. It should become erect and stable within approximately 2 minutes (to a maximum of 5 minutes, recommended by the FAA). Adjust it to the proper position. During taxi, applying the brakes should cause noticeable pitch down, but turning should not reveal indications of bank.
3. No. The AI only shows the airplane's attitude in relation to the horizon.
4. The vacuum system. (Some DGs are electric.)
5. In modern light airplanes, both turn indicators and turn coordinators are electrically driven gyros.
6. (1) The exaggerated reaction caused by the canted gimbal axis only occurs when the airplane is changing bank angle, not in a constant bank. (2) Although the turn symbol suggests a banking airplane, it does not necessarily mean the airplane is in a bank.
7. a. The ball moves toward the inside of a turn.
   b. The ball moves toward the outside of a turn.
8. Check your owner's manual.
9. Only the airspeed indicator.
10. Only the DG and the AI.
11. Every 10 or 15 minutes in cruise—more frequently in a hold. Before beginning any approach and once or twice during the approach.
12. Check your owner's manual.
13. The barometric pressure at the field has changed.
14. Indicated altitude is that shown on the altimeter; True altitude is height above MSL; Absolute altitude is height above terrain; Pressure altitude is height above the pressure plane where the pressure is 29.92 in. Hg.; Density altitude is pressure altitude corrected for nonstandard temperature.
15. When first initiating a climb or descent, the needle will indicate a trend (up or down). It only provides an accurate rate when in a sustained constant-rate climb or descent and when in smooth air during level flight.
16. Indicated airspeed is the airspeed read off the airspeed indicator, calibrated airspeed is indicated airspeed corrected for position error. True airspeed is calibrated airspeed corrected for density altitude.
17. The compass tries to align itself vertically as well as horizontally along the Earth's magnetic lines of force.
18. Tachometer and manifold/tachometer combination.
19. A center needle ammeter should read a fraction of a needle width to the "+" side of center. If it reads to the "-" side, the battery is being drained and you should reduce the electrical load. The reading on a left needle instrument (load meter) depends on the load on the system. If it drops suddenly without cause, suspect an alternator problem.
20. 130 knots.

Chapter Three— Attitude Instrument Flying

1. Airspeed.
2. AI, power indicator.

3. Airspeed indicator, altimeter, VSI, DG, turn coordinator (or turn indicator).
4. Fixating and omitting.
5. Climbing, level cruise, cruise descent, approach level, approach descent, nonprecision descent.
6. Pitch.
7. Lower the nose on the AI, leading the desired altitude by 50 feet; wait for the airspeed to build to proper value before reducing power with reference to the power instrument.
8. Correct with pitch alone. For larger corrections, make a power change as well.
9. AI, DG, AI, VSI, altimeter.
10. Apply climb power, raise the nose with reference to the AI, double check the AI, cross check for decreasing airspeed and increasing altitude.
11. Reduce power and pitch attitude simultaneously.
12. Raise the nose on the AI when 50 feet above the desired altitude and increase power with reference to the power instrument.
13. Build-up of airspeed.
14. Three degrees per second. A complete 360 turn takes 2 minutes.
15. Calibrate the turn instrument by making a level 360 turn with the instrument showing the exact standard rate. Time the turn.
16. Turn needle or turn coordinator.
17. The three pressure instruments and electric turn coordinator.
18. The aircraft, if trimmed correctly and if it is not banked, will recover on its own from extreme pitch attitudes. The alternating and decreasing nose up and nose down attitudes are called a phugoid oscillation.
19. Add power, lower the nose to the horizon, level the wings.
20. Reduce power, level the wings, raise the nose to the horizon.

Chapter Four— Flight Planning

1. Weather radar displays precipitation and is useful in determining the location, intensity, and movement of showers and storms. There is often a correlation between precipitation and cloud cover and turbulence.
2. No. Of the six basic instruments, only the VSI is not required for IFR flight.
3. Within the preceding 24 calendar months.
4. It must have been tested within the previous 30 days. This test must be noted on a "permanent record" and can be logged by the pilot.
5. The airspace at and above 18,000 feet where all traffic is controlled and under IFR.
6. A cylinder of airspace, within a radius of 5 statute miles from the center of an airport with an operating control tower, and extending upward to, but not including, 3000 feet above the surface.
7. A = airworthiness certificate;
   R = registration;
   R = radio station license;
   O = operating limitations;
   W = weight and balance data, including installed equipment list.
8. Six, six, and six. Six hours of instrument flight, including six approaches, within the last six calendar months.
9. 10,000 feet MSL, unless within 2500 feet of the surface (as in mountainous regions).
10. It guarantees a usable signal from at least one of the VORs defining the airway segment to which it applies. It also guarantees 1000 feet of obstacle clearance (2000 feet in designated mountainous areas) over the entire width of the airway.
11. It is the lowest altitude along an airway at which a usable signal is guaranteed from the off airway fix defining that intersection.
12. The crew must use oxygen if they are above 12,500 feet MSL for more than 30 minutes; they must use it all the time above 14,000 feet MSL; it must be provided for the passengers above 15,000 feet MSL.
13. In the *Airport/Facilities Directory* or the front of the *Jeppesen Airway Manual*.
14. Enough to fly to the destination, then to the alternate, and then for an additional 45 minutes at normal cruise power.
15. 1, 2, 3: When, for the period from 1 hour before to 1 hour after your estimated time of arrival, the destination is forecasting at least a 2,000 foot ceiling and 3 miles visibility.

16. Alternate minimums are published for each airport—many airports are not authorized for use as an alternate. Standard alternate minimums are as follows: If you plan to use a precision approach at the alternate, it must forecast at least a 600-foot ceiling and 2 miles visibility for your estimated time of arrival at the alternate. If you plan to use a nonprecision approach, it must forecast at least an 800-foot ceiling and 2 miles visibility for your estimated time of arrival at the alternate.

17. It tells ATC what to expect you to do in the event of communications failure.

18. It authorizes the recipient to fly at the specified altitude, to descend at his discretion to the MEA, and to fly the approach at his destination. If he reports descending out of an altitude, he may not return to it without further ATC approval.

19. /U.

20. A published procedure depicting standardized departure instructions from a particular airport. SIDs are designed to simplify the clearance delivery process.

Chapter Five—VOR

1. (T) VOR—25 NM
   (L) VOR—40 NM
   (H) VOR—40 NM; 100 NM above 14,500 feet and 130 NM above 18,000 feet.

2. No—only at VORTAC and VOR-DME sites.

3. The DME has its own identifier that broadcasts approximately twice a minute. It is higher pitched than the VOR identifier and broadcasts the same Morse code identifier.

4. You may have tuned in the wrong station, or the station may be undergoing maintenance and broadcasting an unreliable signal.

5. The voice identifier is sufficient.

6. Within the last 30 days.

7. VOT—the CDI should center within 4° of 360° FROM or 180° TO.

   Designated ground checkpoint—the CDI should center within 4° of the indicated course;

   Designated airborne checkpoint—the CDI should center within 6° of indicated course;

   "Homemade" airborne check—the checkpoint should be on a Victor airway at least 20 miles from the station—the CDI should center within 6° of the indicated course;

   Dual check—the two CDIs should center within 4° of each other;

   Radio shop check—performed and signed off by a radio shop.

8. "DEPS." The date, bearing error, place and signature. This information can be kept in any "permanent record."

9. A radial is an outbound course FROM a VOR.

10. The omni-bearing selector (OBS) is used to select a particular VOR course. The Course Deviation Indicator shows your angular deviation from the selected course.

11. The cone of confusion is the region directly above the station where radials are so close to each other that it is difficult to avoid crossing over many of them at once. The zone of ambiguity, on the other hand, is the region close to the line that separates the TO and FROM areas on the VOR, at which the VOR instrument will give an OFF or NAV indication.

12. The horizontal situation indicator (HSI) replaces both the DG and the VOR display. It also includes a glide slope indicator.

13. Center the CDI with a FROM and read your radial off the OBS.

14. a) Center the needle with a TO;
    b) Turn to the indicated course;
    c) Re-center the needle;
    d) Track the new indicated course.

15. a) Visualize your position in relation to the desired course;
    b) Turn to the one of the eight cardinal points that most nearly give you a 90° intercept;
    c) Select the reciprocal of the desired radial in the OBS;
    d) As the CDI comes off the peg, turn towards the station and track inbound.

16. OFF. You are in the zone of ambiguity.

17. The indications would not change. The VOR knows only your position—nothing about your heading.

18. See Answer Figure 1.

19. See Answer Figure 2.

20. Turn, Time, Twist, Throttle, Talk.

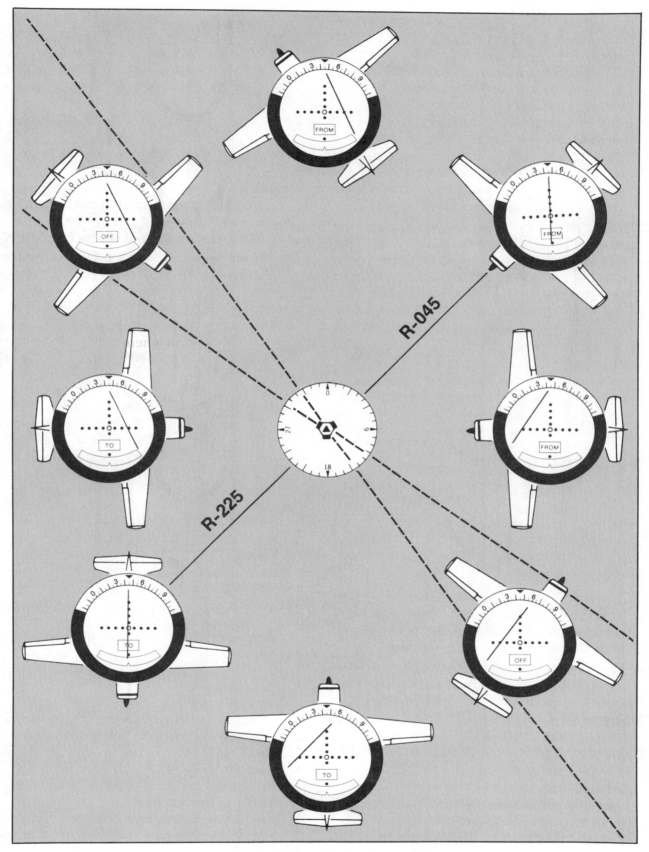

Answer Figure 1

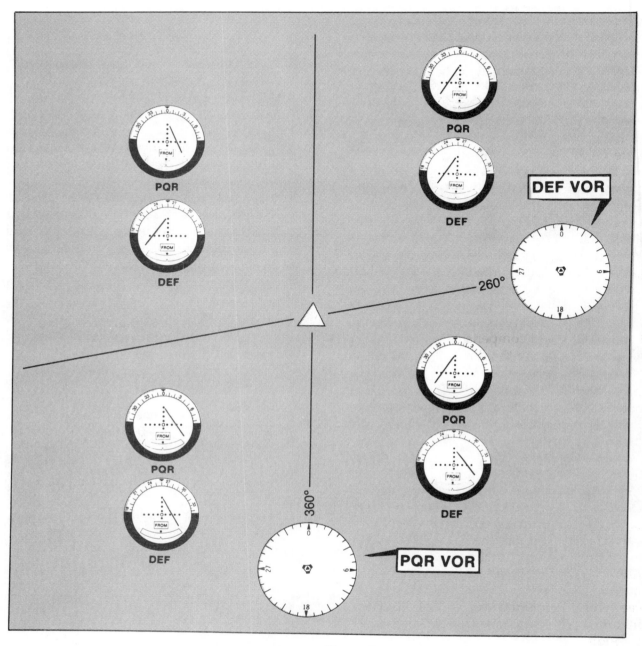

Answer Figure 2

Chapter Six—ADF

1. LOM—15 NM;
   MH —25 NM;
   H —50 NM;
   HH —75 NM.
2. Loop and sense antennas
3. Tune in a nearby NDB and listen for the identifier. Use the "Test" function switch to swing the needle away from the beacon and see that it returns to point in the proper direction when you return the switch to "ADF" position.
4. No, signals in this frequency range are not limited to line-of-sight.
5. Erroneous readings may occur when crossing mountainous terrain and shorelines; at sun-

rise, sunset and at night; when near thunderstorms; or may be due to poorly shielded aircraft alternators, improperly installed strobe lighting systems, and bad ignition harnesses.

6. The airplane's direct course to an NDB.

7. It is the difference between your intercept heading and the course being intercepted. Determine this by counting degrees on the DG between the two numbers. When flying a conventional procedure turn, the intercept angle with the final approach course is 45°. When vectored to the final approach course, it is usually 30°.

8. You would approach the airport from another angle instead of on course. This can put you outside the obstacle clearance area for final descent.

9. If the airplane drifts off course, determine the heading that will compensate for wind, and keep the aircraft on the desired bearing. This is called the reference heading.

10. It is a combination DG and ADF (sometimes both VOR and ADF), enabling the pilot to read all navigation information from one instrument.

11. Northeast.

12. South of the station.

13. North of the station.

14. Cross the fix and track outbound for two minutes. Turn 45° to the specified side, and time one minute. Turn 180° the direction opposite to the previous turn. At the completion of this turn, the needle should be close to the nose, moving toward the wing. Your angle of intercept with the inbound course is 45°, so turn inbound when the needle reaches the 45° position.

15. The Burns NDB is a compass locator: less than 25 watts of power, 15 NM range.

16. You have just turned outbound from the beacon and are slightly west of course.

17. You are still outbound from the beacon, you made a 20° correction towards the course and have just intercepted.

18. You are on the 312° leg of the procedure turn and have just intercepted the inbound course (45° intercept angle).

19. You delayed the inbound turn too long and are slightly west of course, inbound to the beacon.

20. You are inbound from the beacon to the airport, on course.

Chapter Seven—Holds

1. Any hold with right turns.

2. 175 Knots.

3. Expect further clearance time. It is the time you will leave the hold in the event of communications failure.

4. The holding side of the course is the side where the hold is accomplished. Airspace allocated to the hold is protected on this side. The non-holding side is the other side of the course where the hold should not occur.

5. Direct entry, teardrop entry, and parallel entry.

6. At a VOR, the TO-FROM flag changes to FROM. At an NDB, the needle passes the wing.

7. See Answer Figure 3.

8. Two minute legs, a DME distance-define leg length, an alternative hold at a station, or a sequence of vectors instead of a hold.

9. One minute. Above 14,000 feet MSL, one and a half minutes.

10. The CDI should be pegged to the left.

(In answers 11 through 20, refer to Answer Figure 4.)

11. Direct entry. Turn right to the outbound heading of 255°.

12. Direct entry. Turn left to the outbound heading of 300°.

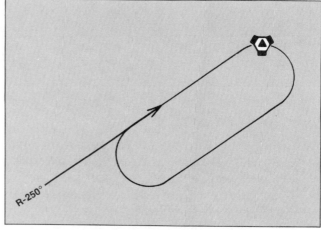

Answer Figure 3

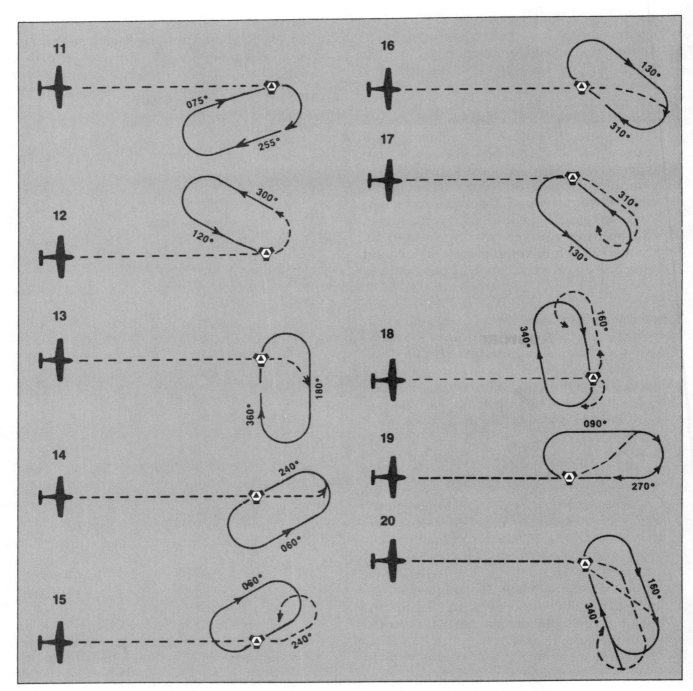

Answer Figure 4

13. Direct entry. Turn right to the outbound heading of 180°. The clearance does not include an EFC time, so be sure to ask for it.
14. Teardrop entry. Proceed straight across the fix on your heading of 090°.
15. The direction of turn is not specified, so assume a "standard" pattern, i.e. right turns.

Make a parallel entry by turning left to the outbound heading of 060°. After 1 minute, turn left again to intercept the inbound course.
16. Teardrop entry. Turn right 10° to heading 100°, 30° less than the outbound heading.
17. Parallel entry. Turn right to 130° for 1 minute,

then right again to intercept the inbound course.

18. Your choice of parallel or direct entry. Turn left for parallel, right for direct, to the outbound heading of 340° in either case.

19. Teardrop or parallel. For teardrop turn left 30° to heading 060°, for parallel proceed straight across the fix heading 090°. The teardrop will allow you to intercept the inbound course farther from the fix.

20. Teardrop or direct. Turn right to 160° for direct, 130° for teardrop. With the direct entry, your outbound leg will probably be close to the holding course, causing you to fly through it before completing the inbound turn.

Chapter Eight—
Nonprecision Approaches

1. When you are on a published route, including any terminal route or approach segment.
2. 25 nautical miles.
3. They are used only in emergencies, and provide 1000 feet of obstacle clearance.
4. Initial Segment: From the IAF, procedure turn outbound, to established inbound to the fix.
   Intermediate Segment: From when the aircraft turns inbound on the approach course to the final approach fix until reaching the NDB.
   Final Approach Segment: From the FAF to the MAP.
5. Minimum descent altitude. The lowest altitude to which you may descend on a nonprecision approach before making visual contact with the landing area.
6. Height above airport. In parentheses with the circling landing minimums.
7. Height above touchdown zone. In parentheses with the straight-in landing minimums.
8. Keep the runway in sight at all times.
9. Execute an immediate missed approach.
10. A visual descent point (VDP) is the point where a normal 3° approach path to the runway would intersect the MDA.
11. The final approach segment is divided into parts with different altitudes, separated by step-down fixes. These can be intersections or

DME fixes. Those with aircraft equipped to determine these fixes have lower minimums.

12. VOR, NDB, localizer (LOC), back course (BC), simplified directional facility (SDF), localizer type directional aid (LDA), airport surveillance radar (ASR), and area navigation (RNAV).
13. An approach with no procedure turn.
14. A landing on the runway named in the approach title.
15. An approach that includes a procedure turn.
16. 1) Radar vectors; 2) Approach from a hold; 3) NoPT transition; 4) DME arc.
17. A precision approach gives descent guidance. A nonprecision approach does not.
18. 30 miles.
19. A heading perpendicular to the radial you are crossing.
20. A contact approach must be requested by the pilot; a visual approach may be initiated by the controller. A visual approach requires VFR conditions; a contact approach requires only "one mile and clear of clouds."

Chapter Nine—
Precision Approaches

Quiz One

1. (a) There are two criteria for descent on approach: You must receive approach clearance and be on a published route. When flying "direct" to an approach fix, maintain your last assigned altitude until cleared lower. Of course, you can request such clearance.
   When issuing approach clearance via an unpublished route, the controller is required to give a minimum altitude for crossing the approach fix. However, in the real world, as in our example, this part of the clearance may be omitted. You must maintain the last assigned altitude. The MSA circle at the top of the plate is for emergency use only. You may not automatically descend to the MSA when cleared for approach.

2. (b) Execute a procedure turn except from a NoPT transition, a DME arc, radar vectors, or approach from a hold on the ap-

proach course. In this example, you must turn outbound and make a procedure turn.

As you cross to the north side of the course, the CDI would swing left, regardless of which way you turned. Aircraft heading has no effect on the CDI.

At 4000 feet you are well above the glide slope; the needle would be full down.

The ADF points to the LOM, to the right of the tail as you turn outbound.

3. (d) ATC issues clearances for authorized standard and special instrument approach procedures (IAPs) only. Expect a straight-in approach only in the four cases mentioned above. Moreover, from 4000 feet heading north over Misha, trying to intercept the localizer and glide slope inbound would be difficult and dangerous.

The procedure turn must be completed within "10 NM from LOM" (see profile view). In choosing the length of the outbound leg decide how much time you need on the inbound segment. Two minutes usually allows enough time inbound to get established and make any required descent, without the risk of exceeding the 10-mile limit. With a strong headwind outbound, increase the time, with a tailwind, shorten it.

4. (d) The two-step flight path in the profile view indicates the outbound and inbound altitudes. You may descend to 2100 feet when established on the inbound course. This descent is not mandatory. It is permissible to remain at 2200 feet until intercepting the glide slope, giving yourself slightly more time to become established and getting a little more practice on the glide slope.

5. (c) When north of the course, the CDI will be to the left, regardless of aircraft heading. As you intercept the localizer it will move towards center. With good technique, you will reach the inbound heading just as the needle centers.

On a heading of 227°, the ADF will point right of the nose. On interception, it will be 45° to the right, i.e., the relative bear-

ing will be 045°.

6. (c) Begin final descent when you intercept the glide slope. The profile view shows you will intercept a short distance outside the marker and cross it at 2045 feet MSL on the glide slope. On some ILSs, interception occurs inside the marker. In this case also, begin the descent at glide slope interception.

For the ILS approach, the LOM gives backup information only. This approach plate also shows localizer (glide slope out of service) and NDB approaches to Runway 27. The LOM is the FAF for these approaches.

7. (c) The MAP is at DH on the glide slope. In this case, DH is 974 feet MSL or 200 feet above TDZE. This is shown in the minimums box as DH 974' (200').

The time and groundspeed box is provided for the localizer and NDB approaches only. Some pilots also time an ILS from the OM as a backup, i.e., if the glide slope fails during approach they can turn it into a LOC procedure.

The MM gives backup information only. It is positioned approximately where the aircraft reaches DH on the glide slope, but not exactly. Its exact location depends on terrain and the availability of real estate, so consider it a reminder only.

8. (b) The DH increases by 50 feet if the MM is out of service. There is no penalty for an inoperative OM or radar. If the ALS or RAIL are out of service, the required visibility increases to 3/4 mile from 1/2 (see minima box). These increases in approach minima are standard for all ILSs.

Most ILSs have a DH 200 feet above TDZE. A few have 250 feet minima owing to the lack of a MM or other considerations in the design of the approach, such as required climb gradient for the missed approach segment. If the DH is 250 feet, there is no penalty for an inoperative MM.

9. (b) If the localizer is out of service, the approach is not authorized. You may request an NDB approach, or any other approach you like. The LOC procedure is for

glide slope out of service approaches.

10. (c) TCH is shown in the profile view to be 52 feet.

Quiz Two

1. "RVR 40" means runway visual range 4000 feet. RVR is determined by a transmissometer near the touchdown point and gives the pilot a good idea of what he can expect to see when he breaks out of the clouds. "3/4" is the corresponding visibility in miles.

2. A private operator, flying under Part 91, may legally try the approach regardless of the reported weather. Commercial operators may not begin the approach unless the field is reporting above minimums for that approach.

   The rule governing commercial operations makes sense from a safety standpoint. With the field reporting below minimums, and no good reason to doubt the report, trying the approach exposes you unnecessarily to a situation where a small error could be critical. "Good reasons" to doubt the weather report might include an old report, rapidly changing conditions, or marginal prevailing visibility reported from a tower more than a mile from the landing threshold.

3. The parenthetical number is altitude above the touchdown zone.

4. On this approach, which has a 250-foot AGL DH, there is no penalty for an inoperative MM. On approaches with a 200-foot AGL DH, DH increases to 250 feet AGL with the MM out.

5. You may land, according to FAR 91.175, only if the flight visibility is at least 1/2 of a mile (remember that the MM is out of service). Flight visibility is determined by the pilot in the cockpit. However, RVR usually corresponds closely to flight visibility and it would be unusual to find 1/2 mile flight visibility at DH with only 1000 feet RVR.

6. According to FAR 91.175, you may legally descend below DH only if you see one of the following:
   a. The approach light system;
   b. The threshold;
   c. The threshold markings;
   d. The threshold lights;
   e. The runway end identifier lights (REIL), i.e., the flashing strobes on either side of the runway end;
   f. The visual approach slope indicator (VASI);
   g. The touchdown zone or touchdown zone markings;
   h. The touchdown zone lights;
   i. The runway or runway markings;
   j. The runway lights.

7. TCH stands for threshold crossing height. It is the theoretical height of the glide slope antenna as the airplane crosses the threshold on the glide slope. It is of interest to pilots of large aircraft, whose main gear may extend considerably below their glide slope antenna. TDZE stands for touchdown zone elevation, and is the elevation of the highest point of the first 3000 feet of the landing runway.

   APT is the airport elevation and is the elevation of the highest point on any usable runway.

8. Yes. FAR 91.175 requires an immediate missed approach.

9. Climb straight ahead to 1100 feet. Then turn right to heading 050° as you continue climbing to 2400 feet. Intercept the Muskegon 328° radial and track it outbound to Whall intersection. Hold at Whall, maintaining 2400 feet.

10. The inset map is used to depict the missed approach hold when it lies beyond the normal limits of the approach plate. The symbol "D19" on the inset map indicates that Whall is 19 DME from Muskegon VOR. Whall appears to be a little closer to the airport than to the VOR.

Quiz Three

1. A control zone is effective when there is a certificated weather observer on duty and current weather information for the airport is available.

   Obtain the Wausau altimeter setting from Wausau Radio by calling on 122.1 and listening on the VOR frequency. Be sure the volume is turned up on the nav radio. The frequency box in the upper left shows that Wausau Radio "guards" 122.1 and transmits on 109.2.

2. 274° and 255° are shown to assist the pilot in

turning accurately onto the final approach course. They are especially useful if you have only one nav radio and must switch from the VOR to the localizer frequency as you intercept the final approach course.

3. Yes. Without DME you would fly to the VOR and execute the teardrop procedure.

4. Yes, as long as you have DME or can obtain a radar fix to identify the FAF.

5. Yes, if you can get a radar fix for the FAF.

6. The course reversal must be completed within 15 nautical miles (see profile view). You must go outbound far enough to intercept the localizer outside the outer marker. The best distance is between 10 and 14 miles, depending on airspeed, and can be determined with DME or by time and an estimate of groundspeed.
Intercepting the localizer is a problem in dead reckoning. Since the 240° radial is at almost a 30° angle to the localizer, each mile outbound takes you more than half a mile from the inbound course. The depicted turn is misleading since it gives the impression that a continuous standard rate turn would lead to course interception. In fact, such a turn, terminated with a 30° intercept angle, would result in interception inside the outer marker. Depending on wind and the distance flown outbound, the ideal intercept angle lies somewhere between 45° and 90°. The drawback to such large intercept angles is that when the localizer needle comes alive, it moves fast and you will almost certainly fly through the course and have to re-intercept from the north. This procedure would be simplified by the installation of a compass locator at the outer marker.

7. No. FAR 91.175 (a) requires that the published procedure be followed.

8. 2260 feet. See * note in profile view.

9. The MAP is at the runway threshold. It is identified by timing from the FAF. If your glide slope receiver were working, the MAP on the ILS would be at DH.

10. Even though you are flying a category A airplane, circling to land at a speed more than 5 knots above the upper limit of the category (91 knots) requires that you use category B minimums, in this case 2420 feet, since you have the

Wausau altimeter setting.

Chapter Ten—Area Navigation

1. RNAV is an acronym for area navigation. With RNAV equipment, you have the ability to plot your own random routings using existing VOR/DME or VORTAC stations.

2. A CLC takes raw data in the form of radial/distance information and translates it into straight-line course data.

3. A waypoint is a computer-generated point, similar to a checkpoint, established by the RNAV unit on the straight-line course.

4. 1. An onboard computer
2. Pushbuttons or knobs for input of data
3. A digital display

5. In order for you to obtain an RNAV clearance, radar coverage of the area you wish to fly through must be available.

6. The random portion of the flight must occur between arrival and departure transition fixes or other navigational aids.

7. /C for RNAV and transponder with no altitude reporting; /R for RNAV and transponder with altitude reporting; /W for RNAV with no transponder.

8. The random route must to defined by radial/distance waypoints.

9. At least one waypoint in each ATC center you cross. Also one waypoint in each center must fall within 200 nautical miles of the edge of the preceding center.

10. Yes, it is required that your RNAV be IFR-certified prior to using it for IFR navigation. If not so certified, it can be used as supplemental navigation only.

11. The IAF and MAP. The holding fix for the missed approach and the IAF may be one and the same.

12. No, they are nonprecision approaches and do not have glide slopes.

13. No. Always check other approaches into the same airport for this information.

14. The same as for standard VOR navigation: restricted range and scalloping.

15. Maximum distance can be as far as 200 miles away; however, this is only at extremely high

altitudes. You should not use this range when flight planning your route.

16. LORAN-C stands for long-range navigation. It uses radio signals transmitted by land-based stations to determine position in latitude and longitude coordinates.

17. Low frequency (100 KHz) pulsed signals.

18. Latitude and longitude.

19. No. It is illegal to use your VFR unit for IFR navigation. Some LORAN-C units have IFR certification, but this is for en route and terminal use only. There are no legal LORAN approaches at this time.

20. NAVSTAR/GPS is a global satellite navigation system expected to be complete in the 1990s. It will provide highly accurate navigation on three levels: latitude, longitude, and altitude.

OBSTACLE CLEARANCE
AND THE TERPS MANUAL

On a tight approach on a windy day, have you ever gotten a half-scale deflection and wondered whether you were still in the area of safe obstacle clearance? Just how much clearance is provided by each segment of the approach, and how far from the centerline does the protected area extend? It can be reassuring to know the answers to these questions.

The standards for designing instrument approach procedures are set out in the United States Standard For Terminal Instrument Procedures (TERPS) Manual. The TERPS Manual covers such matters as obstacle clearance, course alignment, and establishment of visibility minimums.

The TERPS Manual describes the methods used in designing civil and military instrument approaches everywhere within United States jurisdiction. Within the United States, the Regional FAA offices have the responsibility for designing civil instrument approaches. If you would like one at your local strip, you may file a request with the Regional Office. If the airport passes inspection (a paved runway is not required) and you can show that the public interest will be served, the FAA will go to work designing a procedure. If only one user would benefit, they will still design an approach, but at a price, and it will be an unpublished, private approach procedure, sort of like an unlisted phone number.

The TERPS Manual sets general criteria for instrument approaches and goes on to specifics for the case of each approach type (VOR, NDB, etc.).

An instrument approach procedure may have up to four segments, the initial, intermediate, final, and missed approach segments. There may also be initial, intermediate, and final approach fixes, and, of course, a missed approach point (MAP) at the beginning of the missed approach segment. An area of obstacle clearance for circling to land in visual conditions must also be defined. For the individual who designs approach procedures, the manual contains instructions such as, "...the final approach course should be identified first because it is the least flexible and most critical of all the segments. When the final approach has been determined, the other segments should be blended with it to produce an orderly maneuvering pattern which is responsive to the local traffic flow."

Detailed discussions are given of each approach segment. For example, nearly two pages are devoted to "Initial Approach Segment Based on a Procedure Turn." The designer is instructed to specify the fix, outbound and inbound courses, minimum altitudes, distance and direction of turn. He is also given course alignment, descent gradient and obstacle clearance criteria and told how large an area must be considered for obstacle clearance.

Two good argument stoppers are contained in this section. The designer is advised that the starting point and degree of turn are left up to the pilot, as long as he stays in the procedure turn area and above the prescribed altitude. He is also told that when no fix marks the beginning of the intermediate or final approach segment associated with the procedure turn, these segments begin on the inbound procedure turn course, at the maximum distance specified in the procedure.

Initial and intermediate segments of all instrument approaches are designed to the same standard, regardless of the type of facility. On the final approach segment, obstacle clearance criteria depend on the type of approach. Not surprisingly, the ILS requires the least obstacle clearance, while the on-airport NDB approach requires the most. Calculating the minimum altitude requires complex geometry and survey techniques. However, it is safe to generalize that for the various types of straight-in approaches, minimum obstacle clearance is as follows:

On-Airport VOR:	300 feet
Off-Airport VOR:	250 feet
On-Airport NDB:	350 feet
Off-Airport NDB:	300 feet
ILS	190 feet

In all cases, 300 feet of obstacle clearance must be provided for a circling approach. The area protected for a circling approach is described and illustrated in Chapter Eight.

The initial segment of any approach provides 1000 feet of obstacle clearance, 4 miles on either side of the course. On the intermediate segment, the protected area tapers uniformly from the initial segment to the width of the final approach course at the FAF. If the intermediate segment is in a procedure turn area, it is 8 miles wide at 10 miles from the FAF and tapers to the final approach course at the FAF. It provides at least 500 feet of obstacle clearance.

If a VOR approach has no FAF (i.e., the VOR is on the field) and there are no stepdown fixes, the final approach course provides 300 feet of obstacle clearance. The width of the obstacle clearance area is 2 miles at the VOR, widening uniformly to 6 miles at 10 miles from the facility (figure A-1). Figure A-1 also shows the area within 10° of course, well within the protected area. Remember that a full-scale needle deflection indicates 10° off course, so as long as your needle is not pegged,

you are within the obstacle clearance area.

If an approach with no FAF has a stepdown fix on the final approach course within 4 miles of the VOR, obstacle clearance may be reduced to 250 feet. In such cases, it is normally required that the aircraft be equipped to simultaneously receive the course and the crossing indication, i.e., it must have dual VORs or VOR and DME, as the case may be.

On a VOR approach with a FAF, obstacle clearance is at least 250 feet, but determining the obstacle clearance area is more complex. It is based on a trapezoid centered on the final approach course, which is 2 miles wide at the VOR and expands uniformly to 5 miles wide 30 miles from it. The obstacle clearance area is the portion of this trapezoid between the FAF and the MAP or runway. Because the obstacle clearance area is defined by the distance from the course, and the VOR display shows degrees off course, it is not always easy to determine whether you are in the obstacle clearance area.

The maximum distance a runway may be from the facility is 30 miles, and the maximum length of a final approach course is 10 miles. The number of degrees you may be off course and still remain in the obstacle clearance area depends on the length of the final approach course and the distance of the airport from the VOR.

Figure A-2 shows two extreme cases. In the first case, at left, the VOR is the FAF and the final approach course is less than 7 miles long. As in the case of no FAF, you would be within the obstacle clearance area unless the CDI were pegged.

In the second case, the airport is the maximum permissible distance, 30 miles, from the VOR, and the final approach course is 10 miles long. You would be within the obstacle clearance area if you were within 5° of course, that is, if the CDI were deflected no more than half scale.

It is clear from these examples that, in *most* cases, 250 or 300 feet of obstacle clearance is guaranteed on a VOR approach, even to the airplane whose CDI is nearly pegged. "Most" includes all approaches with no FAF, and those where the VOR itself is the FAF and the final approach segment is less than 7 miles long.

Protection from obstructions does not end abruptly at the edge of the obstacle clearance area. Rather, the *secondary obstacle clearance* area begins

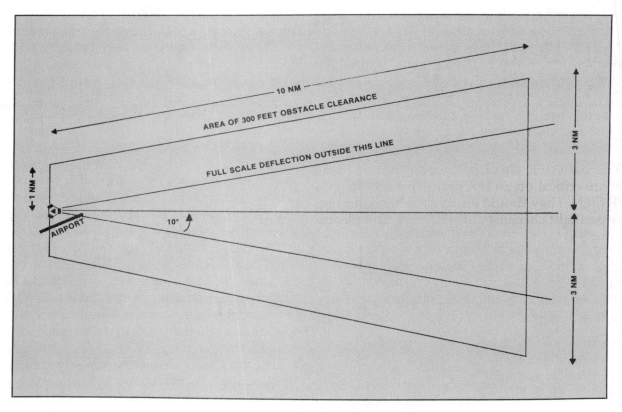

Figure A-1

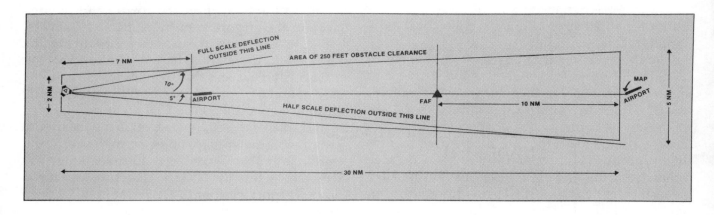

Figure A-2

at this point. Within the secondary area, obstacle clearance slopes gradually to zero from the amount offered in the primary area.

Any DME arc, even a final approach course, provides 500 feet of obstacle clearance, 4 miles either side of course.

The **TERPS** Manual also contains chapters on helicopter procedures, departure procedures, radar approaches, obstacle clearance on Victor Airways, and ALS. Information on holding pattern airspace is contained in another FAA publication, Holding Pattern Criteria (see bibliography).

THE BASIC
IFR CHECKLIST

The basic IFR checklist includes those items that are critical on an IFR flight and less so on a VFR flight. They should be inserted into your regular preflight checklist at the appropriate places. (figure B-1)

IFR CHECKLIST

1. Charts, plates, clipboard, pencils
2. Master radio switch - on
3. Copy ATIS
4. Altimeter
5. D/G - set
6. Attitude indicator - set
7. VSI - 0 rate
8. Pitot heat - check
9. Marker beacon - on and test
10. VORs - current test logged
11. ADF - test
12. Alternate static air - check
13. Clock - check and set (Time ck., gnd. cntl. or FSS)
14. Call for taxi and clearance
15. Check gyros during taxi
16. Radio - set as per clearance
17. When cleared onto runway:

    a. Txpdr. on
    b. Copy time
    c. Check DG

Figure B-1

ACRONYMS

AC	advisory circular
ADF	automatic direction finder
AGL	above ground level
AI	attitude indicator
AIRMET	meteorological advisories for light aircraft
ALS	approach lighting system
ALSF	ALS with sequenced flashing lights
AM	amplitude modulated
ARTCC	air route traffic control center
ASR	airport surveillance radar
ATC	air traffic control
ATIS	automatic terminal information service
ATP	airline transport pilot
BC	back course
BFO	beat frequency oscillator
BFR	biennial flight review
CAVU	ceiling and visibility unlimited
CDI	course deviation indicator
CFIA	certified flight instructor, airplane
CFII	certified flight instructor, instrument
CLC	course line computer
CTAF	common traffic advisory frequency
DG	directional gyro
DH	decision height
DME	distance measuring equipment
DUAT	Direct User Access Terminal
EFAS	en route flight advisory service
EFC	expect further clearance
ETA	estimated time of arrival
ETE	estimated time en route
F	sequenced flashing lights
FAA	Federal Aviation Administration

FAF	final approach fix
FAR	Federal Aviation Regulation
FBO	fixed base operator
FDC	flight data center
FM	fan marker
FO	localizer identifier
FSDO	Flight Standards District Office
FSS	flight service station
GADO	General Aviation District Office
GCA	ground controlled approach
GPS	Global Positioning System
HAA	height above airport
HAT	height above touchdown
Hg	mercury
HIALS	high intensity approach lighting system
HSI	horizontal situation indicator
IAF	initial approach fix
IAP	instrument approach procedure
ILS	instrument landing system
IMC	instrument meteorological conditions
in.	inches
IFR	instrument flight rules
KHz	KiloHertz
KIAS	indicated airspeed in knots
LDA	localizer type directional aid
LOC	localizer
LOM	locator, outer marker
LORAN	long-range aid to navigation
LMM	locator, middle marker
LRCO	limited remote communications outlet
MAA	maximum authorized altitude
MALS	medium intensity ALS
MALSF	medium intensity ALS with SFL

MALSR	medium intensity ALS with RAIL	SDF	simplified directional facility
MAP	missed approach point	SFL	sequenced flashing lights
MCA	minimum crossing altitude	SID	standard instrument departure
MDA	minimum descent altitude	SIGMET	significant meteorological information
MEA	minimum en route altitude	SSALF	simplified short ALS with SFL
MHz	MegaHertz	SSALR	simplified short ALS with RAIL
MIALS	medium intensity approach light system	SSALS	simplified short ALS
MLS	microwave landing system	SSALSR	simplified short ALS with RAIL
MM	middle marker	STAR	standard terminal arrival route
MOCA	minimum obstruction clearance altitude	TACAN	tactical air navigation
MRA	minimum reception altitude	TCH	threshold crossing height
MSA	minimum sector altitude	TDZE	touchdown zone elevation
MSL	mean sea level	TEC	tower en route control
NDB	non-directional radio beacon	TERPS	Terminal Instrument Procedures
NOTAM	Notice to Airmen	TPP	Terminal Procedure Publication
NWS	National Weather Service	TWEB	transcribed weather broadcast
OBS	omni-bearing selector	UHF	ultra high frequency
ODALS	omni-directional ALS	VASI	visual approach slope indicator
OM	outer marker	VFR	visual flight rules
PAR	precision approach radar	VNAV	vertical navigation
PIREP	pilot report	VDP	visual descent point
RAIL	runway alignment indicator lights	VOR	VHF omni-directional radio range
REIL	runway end identifier lights	VORTAC	combined VOR and TACAN system
RPM	revolutions per minute	VOT	VOR test facility
RMI	radio magnetic indicator	VSI	vertical speed indicator
RNAV	area navigation	VHF	very high frequency
SALS	short ALS	WP	waypoint
SALSF	short ALS with SFL	Z	Zulu (time)

SELECTED FEDERAL AVIATION REGULATIONS

FAR Part 61 — Certification: Pilots and Flight Instructors

(Excerpts)

§ 61.3 Requirements for certificates, rating, and authorizations.

(e) *Instrument rating.* No person may act as pilot in command of a civil aircraft under instrument flight rules, or in weather conditions less than the minimum prescribed for VFR flight unless—

(1) In the case of an airplane, he holds an instrument rating or an airline transport pilot certificate with an airplane category rating on it;

(2) In the case of a helicopter, he holds a helicopter instrument rating or an airline transport pilot certificate with a rotorcraft category and helicopter class rating not limited to VFR;

§ 61.51 Pilot logbooks.

(c) *Logging of pilot time.*

(4) *Instrument flight time.* A pilot may log as instrument flight time only that time during which he operates the aircraft solely by reference to instruments, under actual or simulated instrument flight conditions. Each entry must include the place and type of each instrument approach completed, and the name of the safety pilot for each simulated instrument flight. An instrument flight instructor may log as instrument time that time during which he acts as instrument flight instructor in actual instrument weather conditions.

§ 61.57 Recent flight experience: pilot in command.

(e) *Instrument.*

(1) *Recent IFR experience.* No pilot may act as pilot in command under IFR, nor in weather conditions less than the minimums prescribed for VFR, unless he has, within the past 6 months—

(i) In the case of an aircraft other than a glider, logged at least 6 hours of instrument time under actual or simulated IFR conditions, at least 3 of which were in flight in the category of aircraft involved, including at least 6 instrument approaches, or passed an instrument competency check in the category of aircraft involved.

(ii) In the case of a glider, logged at least 3 hours of instrument time, at least half of which were in a glider or an airplane. If a passenger is carried in the glider, at least 3 hours of instrument flight time must have been in gliders.

(2) *Instrument competency check.* A pilot who does not meet the recent instrument experience requirements of subparagraph (1) of this paragraph during the prescribed time or 6 months thereafter may not serve as pilot in command under IFR, nor in weather conditions less than the minimums prescribed for VFR, until he passes an instrument competency check in the category of aircraft involved, given by an FAA inspector, a member of an armed force in the United States authorized to conduct flight tests, an FAA-approved check pilot, or a certificated instrument flight instructor. The Administrator may authorize the conduct of part or all of this check in a pilot ground trainer equipped for instruments or an aircraft simulator.

§ 61.65 Instrument rating requirements.

(a) *General.* To be eligible for an instrument rating (airplane) or an instrument rating (helicopter), an applicant must—

(1) Hold at least a current private pilot certificate with an aircraft rating appropriate to

the instrument rating sought;]

(2) Be able tor ead, speak, and understand the English language; and

(3) Comply with the applicable requirements of this section.

(b) *Ground instruction.* An applicant for the written test for an instrument rating must have received ground instruction or have logged home study in at least the following areas of aeronautical knowledge appropriate to the rating sought.

(1) The regulations of this chapter that apply to flight under IFR conditions, the Airman's Information Manual, and the IFR air traffic system and procedures;

(2) Dead reckoning appropriate to IFR navigation, IFR navigation by radio aids using the VOR, ADF, and ILS systems, and the use of IFR charts and instrument approach plates;

(3) The procurement and use of aviation weather reports and forecasts, and the elements of forecasting weather trends on the basis of that information and personal observation of weather conditions; and

(4) The safe and efficient operation of airplanes or helicopters, as appropriate, under instrument weather conditions.

(c) *Flight instruction and skill—airplanes.* An applicant for the flight test for an instrument rating (airplane) must present a logbook record certified by an authorized flight instructor showing that he has received instrument flight instruction in an airplane in the following pilot operations, and has been found competent in each of them:

(1) Control and accurate maneuvering of an airplane solely by reference to instruments.

(2) IFR navigation by the use of the VOR and ADF systems, including compliance with air traffic control instructions and procedures.

(3) Instrument approaches to published minimums using the VOR, ADF, and ILS system (instruction in the use of the ADF and ILS may be received in an instrument ground trainer and instruction in the use of the ILS glide slope may be received in an airborne ILS simulator).

(4) Cross-country flying in simulated or actual IFR conditions, on Federal airways or as routed by ATC, including one such trip of at least 250 nautical miles, including VOR, ADF, and ILS approaches at different airports.

(5) Simulated emergencies, including the recovery from unusual attitudes, equipment or instrument malfunctions, loss of communications, and engine-out emergencies if a multiengine airplane is used, and missed approach procedure.

(d) *Instrument instruction and skill—(helicopter).* An applicant for the flight test for an instrument rating (helicopter) must present a logbook record

certified to by an authorized flight instructor showing that he has received instrument flight instruction in a helicopter in the following pilot operations, and has been found competent in each of them:

(1) The control and accurate maneuvering of a helicopter solely by reference to instruments.

(2) IFR navigation by the use of the VOR and ADF systems, including compliance with air traffic control instructions and procedures.

(3) Instrument approaches to published minimums using the VOR, ADF, and ILS systems (instructions in the use of the ADF and ILS may be received in an instrument ground trainer, and instruction in the use of the ILS glide slope may be received in an airborne ILS simulator).

(4) Cross-country flying under simulated or actual IFR conditions, on Federal airways or as routed by ATC, including one flight of at least 100 nautical miles, including VOR, ADF, and ILS approaches at different airports.

(5) Simulated IFR emergencies, including equipment malfunctions, missed approach procedures, and deviations to unplanned alternates.

(e) *Flight experience.* An applicant for an instrument rating must have at least the following flight time as a pilot:

[(1) A total of 125 hours of pilot flight time, of which 50 hours are as pilot in command in cross-country flight in a powered aircraft with other than a student pilot certificate. Each cross-country flight must have a landing at a point more than 50 nautical miles from the original departure point.]

(2) 40 hours of simulated or actual instrument time, of which not more than 20 hours may be instrument instruction by an authorized instructor in an instrument ground trainer acceptable to the Administrator.

(3) 15 hours of instrument flight instruction by an authorized flight instructor, including at least 5 hours in an airplane or a helicopter, as appropriate.

(f) *Written test.* An applicant for an instrument rating must pass a written test appropriate to the instrument rating sought on the subjects in which ground instruction is required by paragraph (b), of this section.

(g) *Practical test.* An applicant for an instrument rating must pass a flight test in an airplane or a helicopter, as appropriate. The test must include instrument flight procedures selected by the inspector or examiner conducting the test to determine the applicant's ability to perform competently the IFR operations on which instruction is required by paragraph (c) or (d) of this section.

§61.73 Military pilots or former military pilots: special rules.

(a) *General.* A rated military pilot or former rated military pilot who applies for a private or commercial pilot certificate, or an aircraft or instrument rating, is entitled to that certificate with appropriate ratings or to the addition of a rating on the pilot certificate he holds, if he meets the applicable requirements of this section.

(f) *Instrument rating.* An applicant for an airplane instrument rating or a helicopter instrument rating to be added on the pilot certificate he holds, or for which he has applied, is entitled to that rating if he has, within the 12 months preceding the month in which he applies, satisfactorily accomplished an instrument flight check of a U.S. Armed Force in an aircraft of the category for which he seeks the instrument rating and is authorized to conduct IFR flights on Federal airways.

(g) *Evidentiary documents.* The following documents are satisfactory evidence for the purposes indicated:

(1) To show that the applicant is a member of the armed forces, an official identification card issued to the applicant by an armed force may be used.

(2) To show the applicant's discharge or release from an armed force, or his former membership therein, an original or a copy of a certificate of discharge or release may be used.

(3) To show current or previous status as a rated military pilot on flying status with a U.S. Armed Force, one of the following may be used:

(i) An official U.S. Armed Force order to flight duty as a military pilot.

(ii) An official U.S. Armed Force form or logbook showing military pilot status.

(iii) An official order showing that the applicant graduated from a United States military pilot school and is rated as a military pilot.

(4) To show flight time in military aircraft as a member of a U.S. Armed Force, an appropriate U.S. Armed Force form or summary of it, or a certified United States military logbook may be used.

(5) To show pilot-in-command status, an official U.S. Armed Force record of a military checkout as pilot in command, may be used.

(6) To show instrument pilot qualification, a current instrument card issued by a U.S. Armed Force, or an official record of the satisfactory completion of an instrument flight check within the 12 months preceding the month of the application may be used. However, a Tactical (Pink) instrument card issued by the U.S. Army is not acceptable.

Subpart B—Flight Rules

GENERAL

§91.103 Preflight action.

Each pilot in command shall, before beginning a flight, become familiar with all available information concerning that flight. This information must include—

(a) For a flight under IFR or a flight not in the vicinity of an airport, weather reports and forecasts, fuel requirements, alternatives available if the planned flight cannot be completed, and any known traffic delays of which the pilot in command has been advised by ATC;

(b) For any flight, runway lengths at airports of intended use, and the following takeoff and landing distance information:

(1) For civil aircraft for which an approved Airplane or Rotorcraft Flight Manual containing takeoff and landing distance data is required, the takeoff and landing distance data contained therein; and

(2) For civil aircraft other than those specified in paragraph (b)(1) of this section, other reliable information appropriate to the aircraft, relating to aircraft performance under expected values of airport elevation and runway slope, aircraft gross weight, and wind and temperature.

§91.121 Altimeter settings.

(a) Each person operating an aircraft shall maintain the crusing altitude or flight level of that aircraft, as the case may be, by referenct to an altimeter that is set, when operating—

(1) Below 18,000 feet MSL, to—

(i) The current reported altimeter setting of a station along the route and within 100 nautical miles of the aircraft;

(ii) If there is no station within the area prescribed in paragraph (a)(1)(i) of this section, the current reported altimeter setting of an appropriate available station; or

(iii) In the case of an aircraft not equipped with a radio, the elevation of the departure airport or an appropriate altimeter setting available before departure; or

(2) At or above 18,000 feet MSL, to 29.92" Hg.

(b) The lowest usable flight level is determined by the atmospheric pressure in the area of operation as shown in the following table:

Current altimeter setting	Lowest usable flight level
29.92 (or higher)	180
29.91 through 29.42	185
29.41 through 28.92	190

FAR Part 91 — General Operating and Flight Rules
(Excerpts)

28.91 through 28.42 ------------------------------ 195
28.41 through 27.92 ------------------------------ 200
27.91 through 27.42 ------------------------------ 205
27.41 through 26.92 ------------------------------ 210

(c) To convert minimum altitude prescribed under §§91.119 and 91.177 to the minimum flight level, the pilot shall take the flight level equivalent of the minimum altitude in feet and add the appropriate number of feet specified below, according to the current reported altimeter setting:

Current altimeter setting	Adjustment factor
29.92 (or higher)----------------------------	None
29.91 through 29.42 ------------------------	500 feet
29.41 through 28.92 ------------------------	1,000 feet
28.91 through 28.42 ------------------------	1,500 feet
28.41 through 27.92 ------------------------	2,000 feet
27.91 through 27.42 ------------------------	2,500 feet
27.41 through 26.92 ------------------------	3,000 feet

§91.123 Compliance with ATC clearances and instructions.

(a) When an ATC clearance has been obtained, a pilot in command may not deviate from that clearance, except in an emergency, unless that pilot obtains an amended clearance. However, except in Class A airspace, this paragraph does not prohibit that pilot from canceling an IFR flight plan if the operation is being conducted in VFR weather conditions. When a pilot is uncertain of an ATC clearance, that pilot must immediately request clarification from ATC.

(b) Except in an emergency, no person may operate an aircraft contrary to an ATC instruction in an area in which air traffic control is exercised.

(c) Each pilot in command who, in an emergency, deviates from an ATC clearance or instruction shall notify ATC of that deviation as soon as possible.

(d) Each pilot in command who (though not deviating from a rule of this subpart) is given priority by ATC in an emergency, shall submit a detailed report of that emergency within 48 hours to the manager of that ATC facility, if requested by ATC.

(e) Unless otherwise authorized by ATC, no person operating an aircraft may operate that aircraft according to any clearance or instruction that has been issued to the pilot of another aircraft from radar air traffic control purposes.

§91.126 Operating on or in the vicinity of an airport in Class G airspace.

(a) *General.* Unless otherwise authorized or required, each person operating an aircraft on or in the vicinity of an airport in a Class G airspace area must comply with the requirements of this section.

(b) *Direction of turns.* When approaching to land at an airport in a Class G airspace area —

(1) Each pilot of an airplane must make all turns of that airplane to the left unless the airport displays approved light signals or visual markings indicating that turns should be made to the right, in which case the pilot must make all turns to the right; and

(2) Each pilot of a helicopter must avoid the flow of fixed-wing aircraft.

(c) *Flap settings.* Except when necessary for training or certification, the pilot in command of a civil turbojet-powered aircraft must use, as a final flap setting, the minimum certificated landing flap setting set forth in the approved performance information in the Airplane Flight Manual for the applicable conditions. However, each pilot in command has the final authority and responsibility for the safe operation of the pilot's airplane, and may use a different flap setting for that airplane if the pilot determines that it is necessary in the interest of safety.

§91.127 Operating on or in the vicinity of an airport in Class E airspace

(a) Unless otherwise required by part 93 of this chapter or unless otherwise authorized or required by the ATC facility having jurisdiction over the Class E airspace area, each person operating an aircraft on or in the vicinity of an airport in a Class E airspace area must comply with the requirements of §91.126.

(b) *Departures.* Each pilot of an aircraft must comply with any traffic patterns established for that airport in part 93 of this chapter.

§91.129 Operations in Class D airspace

(a) *General.* Unless otherwise authorized or required by the ATC having jurisdiction over the Class D airspace area, each person operating an aircraft in Class D airspace must comply with the applicable provisions of this section. In addition, each person must comply with §§91.126 and 91.127. For the purpose of this section, the primary airport is the airport for which the Class D airspace area is designated. A satellite airport is any other airport within the Class D airspace area.

(b) *Deviations.* An operator may deviate from any provision of this section under the provisions of an ATC authorization issued by the ATC facility having jurisdiction over the airspace concerned. ATC may authorize a deviation on a continuing basis or for an individual flight, as appropriate.

(c) *Communications.* Each person operating an aircraft in Class D airspace must meet the following two-way radio communications requirements:

(1) *Arrival or through flight.* Each person must establish two-way radio communications with the ATC facility (including foreign ATC in the case of foreign airspace designated in the United States) providing air traffic services prior to entering that airspace and thereafter maintain those communications while within that airspace.

(2) *Departing flight.* Each person—

(i) From the primary airport or satellite airport with an operating control tower must establish and maintain two-way radio communications with the control tower, and thereafter as instructed by ATC while operating in the Class D airspace area; or

(ii) From a satellite airport without an operating control tower, must establish and maintain two-way radio communications with the ATC facility having jurisdiction over the Class D airspace area as soon as practicable after departing.

(d) *Communications failure.* Each person who operates an aircraft in a Class D airspace area must maintain two-way radio communications with the ATC facility having jurisdiction over that area.

(1) If the aircraft radio fails in flight under IFR, the pilot must comply with §91.185 of the part.

(2) If the aircraft radio fails in flight under VFR, the pilot in command may operate that aircraft and land if—

(i) Weather conditions are at or above basic VFR weather minimums;

(ii) Visual contact with the tower is maintained; and

(iii) A clearance to land is received.

(e) *Minimal altitudes.* Each pilot of a large or turbine-powered airplane must—

(1) Unless otherwise required by the applicable distance from cloud criteria, enter the traffic pattern at an altitude of at least 1,500 feet above the elevation of the airport and maintain at least 1,500 feet until further descent is required for a safe landing;

(2) When approaching to land on a runway served by an instrument landing system (ILS), if the airplane is ILS-equipped, fly that airplane at an altitude at or above the glide slope between the outer marker (or point of interception of glide slope, if compliance with the applicable distance from clouds criteria requires interception closer in) and the middle marker; and

(3) When operating an airplane approaching to land on a runway served by a visual approach slope indicator, maintain an altitude at or above the glide slope until a lower altitude is necessary for safe landing.

Paragraphs (e)(2) and (e)(3) of this section do not prohibit normal bracketing maneuvers above or below the glide slope that are conducted for the purpose of remaining on the glide slope.

(f) *Approaches.* Except when conducting a circling approach under Part 97 of this chapter or unless otherwise required by ATC, each pilot must—

(1) Circle the airport to the left, if operating an airplane; or

(f) (2) Avoid the flow of fixed-wing aircraft, if operating a helicopter.

(g) *Departures.* No person may operate an aircraft departing from an airport except in compliance with the following:

(1) Each pilot must comply with any departure procedures established for that airport by the FAA.

(2) Unless otherwise required by the prescribed departure for that airport or the applicable distance from clouds criteria, each pilot of a turbine-powered airplane and each pilot of a large airplane must climb to an altitude of 1,500 feet above the surface as rapidly as practicable.

(h) *Noise abatement.* Where a formal runway use program has been established by the FAA, each pilot of a large or turbine-powered airplane assigned a noise abatement runway by ATC must use that runway. However, consistent with the final authority of the pilot in command concerning the safe operation of the aircraft as prescribed in §91.3(a). ATC may assign a different runway if required by the pilot in the interest of safety.

(i) *Takeoff, landing, taxi clearance.* No person may, at any airport with an operating control tower, operate an aircraft on a runway or taxiway, or take off or land an aircraft, unless an appropriate clearance is received from ATC. A clearance to "taxi to" any point other than an assigned takeoff runway is clearance to cross all runways that intersect the taxi route to that point.

§91.130 Operations in Class C Airspace

(a) *General.* Each aircraft operation in Class C airspace must be conducted in compliance with this section and §91.129. For the purpose of this section, the primary airport is the airport for which the Class C airspace area is designated. A satellite airport is any other airport within the Class C airspace area.

(b) *Traffic patterns.* No person may take off or land an aircraft at a satellite airport within a Class C airspace area except in compliance with FAA arrival and departure traffic patterns.

(c) *Communications.* Each person operating an aircraft in Class C airspace must meet the following two-way radio communications requirements:

(1) *Arrival or through flight.* Each person must establish two-way radio communications

with the ATC facility (including foreign ATC in the case of foreign airspace designated in the United States) providing air traffic services prior to entering that airspace and thereafter maintain those communications while within that airspace.

(2) *Departing flight.* Each person—

(i) From the primary airport or satellite airport with an operating control tower must establish and maintain two-way radio communications with the control tower, and thereafter as instructed by ATC while operating in the Class C airspace area; or

(ii) From a satellite airport without an operating control tower, must establish and maintain two-way radio communications with the ATC facility having jurisdiction over the Class C airspace area as soon as practicable after departing.

(d) *Equipment requirements.* Unless otherwise authorized by the ATC having jurisdiction over the Class C airspace area, no person may operate an aircraft within a Class C airspace area designated for an airport unless that aircraft is equipped with the applicable equipment specified in §91.215.

§91.131 Operations in Class B Airspace

(a) *Operating rules.* No person may operate an aircraft within a Class B airspace area except in compliance with §91.129 and the following rules:

(1) The operator must receive an ATC clearance from the ATC facility having jurisdiction for that area before operating an aircraft in that area.

(2) Unless otherwise authorized by ATC, each person operating a large turbine engine-powered airplane to or from a primary airport for which a Class B airspace area is designated must operate at or above the designated floors of the Class B airspace area while within the lateral limits of that area.

(3) Any person conducting pilot training operations at an airport within a Class B airspace must comply with any procedures established by ATC for such operations in that area.

(b) *Pilot requirements.*

(1) No person may take off or land a civil aircraft at an airport within a Class B airspace area or operate a civil aircraft within a Class B airspace area unless—

(i) The pilot in command holds at least a private pilot certificate; or

(ii) The aircraft is operated by a student pilot or recreational pilot who seeks private pilot certification and has met the requirements of §61.95 of this chapter.

(2) Notwithstanding the provisions of paragraph (b)(1)(ii) of this section, no person may take off or land a civil aircraft at those airports listed in section 4 of appendix D of this part unless the pilot in command holds at least a private pilot certificate.

(c) *Communications and navigation equipment requirements.* Unless otherwise authorized by ATC, no person may operate an aircraft within a Class B airspace unless that aircraft is equipped with—

(1) *For IFR operation.* An operable VOR or TACAN receiver; and

(2) *For all operations.* An operable two-way radio capable of communications with ATC on appropriate frequencies for that Class B airspace area.

(d) *Transponder requirements.* No person may operate an aircraft in a Class B airspace area unless the aircraft is equipped with the applicable operating transponder and automatic altitude reporting equipment specified in paragraph (a) of §91.215, except as provided in paragraph (d) of that section.

§91.133 Restricted and prohibited areas

(a) No person may operate an aircraft within a restricted area (designated in *part 73) contrary to the restrictions imposed, or within a prohibited area, unless that person has the permission of the using or controlling agency, as appropriate.

(b) Each person conducting, within a restricted area, an aircraft operation (approved by the using agency) that creates the same hazards as the operations for which the restricted area was designated may deviate from the rules of this subpart that are not compatible with his operation of the aircraft.

§91.135 Operations in Class A airspace

Except as provided in paragraph (d) of this section, each person operating an aircraft in Class A airspace must conduct that operation under instrument flight rules (IFR) and in compliance with the following:

(a) *Clearance.* Operations may be conducted only under an ATC clearance received prior to entering the airspace.

(b) *Communications.* Unless otherwise authorized by ATC, each aircraft operating in Class A airspace must be equipped with a two-way radio capable of communicating with ATC on a frequency assigned to ATC. Each pilot must maintain two-way radio communications with ATC while operating in Class A airspace.

(c) *Transponder requirement.* Unless otherwise authorized by ATC, no person may operate an aircraft within Class A airspace unless that aircraft is equipped with the applicable equipment specified in §92.215.

(d) *ATC authorizations.* An operator may deviate from any provision of this section under the provisions of an ATC authorization issued by the ATC facility have jurisdiction of the airspace concerned. In the case of an inoperative transponder, ATC may immediately approve an operation within a Class A airspace area allowing flight to continue, if desired, to the airport of ultimate destination, including any intermediate stops, or to proceed to a place where suitable repairs can be made, or both. Requests for deviation from any provision of this section must be submitted in writing, at least 4 days before the proposed operation. ATC may authorize a deviation on a continuing basis or for an individual flight.

INSTRUMENT FLIGHT RULES

§ 91.167 Fuel requirements for flight in IFR conditions.

(a) Except as provided in paragraph (b) of this section, no person may operate a civil aircraft in IFR conditions unless it carries enough fuel (considering weather reports and forecasts and weather conditions) to—

(1) Complete the flight to the first airport of intended landing;

(2) Fly from that airport to the alternate airport; and

(3) Fly after that for 45 minutes at normal cruising speed or, for helicopters, fly after that for 30 minutes at normal cruising speed.

(b) Paragraph (a) (2) of this section does not apply if—

(1) Part 97 of this chapter prescribes a standard instrument approach procedure for the first airport of intended landing; and

(2) For at least 1 hour before and 1 hour after the estimated time of arrival at the airport, the weather reports or forecasts or any combination of them indicate—

(i) The ceiling will be at least 2,000 feet above the airport elevation; and

(ii) Visibility will be at least 3 statute miles.

§ 91.169 IFR flight plan: Information required.

(a) *Information required.* Unless otherwise authorized by ATC, each person filing an IFR flight plan shall include in it the following information:

(1) Information required under § 91.153(a).

(2) An alternate airport, except as provided in paragraph (b) of this section.

(b) *Exceptions to applicability of paragraph (a) (2) of this section.* Paragraph (a) (2) of this section does not apply if Part 97 of this chapter prescribes a standard instrument approach procedure for the first airport of intended landing and, for at least 1 hour before and 1 hour after the estimated time of arrival, the weather reports or forecasts, or any combination of them, indicate—

(1) The ceiling will be at least 2,000 feet above the airport elevation; and

(2) The visibility will be at least 3 statute miles.

(c) *IFR alternate airport weather minimums.* Unless otherwise authorized by the Administrator, no person may include an alternate airport in an IFR flight plan unless current weather forecasts indicate that, at the estimated time of arrival at the alternate airport, the ceiling and visibility at that airport will be at or above the following alternate airport weather minimums:

(1) If an instrument approach procedure has been published in Part 97 of this chapter for that airport, the alternate airport minimums specified in that procedure or, if none are so specified, the following minimums:

(i) Precision approach procedure: Ceiling 600 feet and visibility 2 statute miles.

(ii) Non precision approach procedure: Ceiling 800 feet and visibility 2 statute miles.

(2) If no instrument approach procedure has been published in Part 97 of this chapter for that airport, the ceiling and visibility minimums are those allowing descent from the MEA, approach, and landing under basic VFR.

(d) *Cancellation.* When a flight plan has been activated, the pilot in command, upon canceling or completing the flight under the flight plan, shall notify an FAA Flight Service Station or ATC facility.

§ 91.171 VOR equipment check for IFR operations.

(a) No person may operate a civil aircraft under IFR using the VOR system of radio navigation unless the VOR equipment of that aircraft—

(1) Is maintained, checked, and inspected under an approved procedure; or

(2) Has been operationally checked within the preceding 30 days, and was found to be within the limits of the permissible indicated bearing error set forth in paragraph (b) or (c) of this section.

(b) Except as provided in paragraph (c) of this section, each person conducting a VOR check under paragraph (a) (2) of this section shall—

(1) Use, at the airport of intended departure, an FAA-operated or approved test signal or a test signal radiated by a certificated and appropriately rated radio repair station or, outside the United States, a test signal operated or approved by an appropriate authority to check the VOR equipment (the maximum permissible indicated bearing error is plus or minus 4 degrees); or

(2) Use, at the airport of intended departure, a point on the airport surface designated as a VOR system checkpoint by the Administrator, or, outside the United States, by an appropriate authority (the maximum permissible bearing error is plus or minus 4 degrees);

(3) If neither a test signal nor a designated checkpoint on the surface is available, use an airborne checkpoint designated by the Administrator or, outside the United States, by an appropriate authority (the maximum permissible bearing error is plus or minus 6 degrees); or

(4) If no check signal or point is available, while in flight—

(i) Select a VOR radial that lies along the centerline of an established VOR airway;

(ii) Select a prominent ground point along the selected radial preferably more than 20 nautical miles from the VOR ground facility and maneuver the aircraft directly over the point at a reasonably low altitude; and

(iii) Note the VOR bearing indicated by the receiver when over the ground point (the maximum permissible variation between the published radial and the indicated bearing is 6 degrees).

(c) If dual system VOR (units independent of each other except for the antenna) is installed in the aircraft, the person checking the equipment may check one system against the other in place of the check procedures specified in paragraph (b) of this section. Both systems shall be tuned to the same VOR ground facility and note the indicated bearings to that station. The maximum permissible variation between the two indicated bearings is 4 degrees.

(d) Each person making the VOR operational check, as specified in paragraph (b) or (c) of this section, shall enter the date, place, bearing error, and sign the aircraft log or other record. In addition, if a test signal radiated by a repair station, as specified in paragraph (b) (1) of this section, is used, an entry must be made in the aircraft log or other record by the repair station certificate holder or the certificate holder's representative certifying to the bearing transmitted by the repair station for the check and the date of transmission.

§ 91.173 ATC clearance and flight plan required.

No person may operate an aircraft in controlled airspace under IFR unless that person has—

(a) Filed an IFR flight plan; and

(b) Received an appropriate ATC clearance.

§ 91.175 Takeoff and landing under IFR.

(a) *Instrument approaches to civil airports.* Unless otherwise authorized by the Administrator, when an instrument letdown to a civil airport is necessary, each person operating an aircraft, except a military aircraft of the United States, shall use a standard instrument approach procedure prescribed for the airport in Part 97 of this chapter.

(b) *Authorized DH or MDA.* For the purpose of this section, when the approach procedure being used provides for and requires the use of a DH or MDA, the authorized DH or MDA is the highest of the following:

(1) The DH or MDA prescribed by the approach procedure.

(2) The DH or MDA prescribed for the pilot in command.

(3) The DH or MDA for which the aircraft is equipped.

(c) *Operation below DH or MDA.* Where a DH or MDA is applicable, no pilot may operate an aircraft, except a military aircraft of the United States, at any airport below the authorized MDA or continue an approach below the authorized DH unless—

(1) The aircraft is continuously in a position from which a descent to a landing on the intended runway can be made at a normal rate of descent using normal maneuvers, and for operations conducted under Part 121 or Part 135 unless that descent rate will allow touchdown to occur within the touchdown zone of the runway of intended landing;

(2) The flight visibility is not less than the visibility prescribed in the standard instrument approach being used; and

(3) Except for a Category II or Category III approach where any necessary visual reference requirements are specified by the Administrator, at least one of the following visual references for the intended runway is distinctly visible and identifiable to the pilot:

(i) The approach light system, except that the pilot may not descend below 100 feet above the touchdown zone elevation using the approach lights as a reference unless the red terminating bars or the red side row bars are also distinctly visible and identifiable.

(ii) The threshold.

(iii) The threshold markings.

(iv) The threshold lights.

(v) The runway end identifier lights.

(vi) The visual approach slope indicator.

(vii) The touchdown zone or touchdown zone markings.

(viii) The touchdown zone lights.

(ix) The runway or runway markings.

(x) The runway lights.

(d) *Landing.* No pilot operating an aircraft, except a military aircraft of the United States, may land that aircraft when the flight visibility is less than the visibility prescribed in the standard instrument approach procedure being used.

(e) *Missed approach procedures.* Each pilot operating an aircraft, except a military aircraft of the United States, shall immediately execute an appropriate missed approach procedure when either of the following conditions exist:

(1) Whenever the requirements of paragraph (c) of this section are not met at either of the following times:

(i) When the aircraft is being operated below MDA; or

(ii) Upon arrival at the missed approach point, including a DH where a DH is specified and its use is required, and at any time after that until touchdown.

(2) Whenever an identifiable part of the airport is not distinctly visible to the pilot during a circling maneuver at or above MDA, unless the inability to see an identifiable part of the airport results only from a normal bank of the aircraft during the circling approach.

(f) *Civil airport takeoff minimums.* Unless otherwise authorized by the Administrator, no pilot operating an aircraft under Part 121, 125, 127, 129, or 135 of this chapter may take off from a civil airport under IFR unless weather conditions are at or above the weather minimums for IFR takeoff prescribed for that airport under Part 97 of this chapter. If takeoff minimums are not prescribed under Part 97 of this chapter for a particular airport, the following minimums apply to takeoffs under IFR for aircraft operating under those parts:

(1) For aircraft, other than helicopters, having two engines or less—1 statute mile visibility.

(2) For aircraft having more than two engines—½ statute mile visibility.

(3) For helicopters—½ statute mile visibility.

(g) *Military airports.* Unless otherwise prescribed by the Administrator, each person operating a civil aircraft under IFR into or out of a military airport shall comply with the instrument approach procedures and the takeoff and landing minimum prescribed by the military authority having jurisdiction of that airport.

(h) *Comparable values of RVR and ground visibility.*

(1) Except for Category II or Category III minimums, if RVR minimums for takeoff or landing are prescribed in an instrument approach procedure, but RVR is not reported for the runway of intended operation, the RVR minimum shall be converted to ground visibility in accordance with the table in paragraph (h)(2) of this section and shall be the visibility minimum for takeoff or landing on that runway.

(2) RVR (feet)	Visibility (statute miles)
1,600	1/4
2,400	1/2
3,200	5/8
4,000	3/4
4,500	7/8
5,000	1
6,000	1 1/4

(i) *Operations on unpublished routes and use of radar in instrument approach procedures.* When radar is approved at certain locations for ATC purposes, it may be used not only for surveillance and precision radar approaches, as applicable, but also may be used in conjunction with instrument approach procedures predicted on other types of radio navigational aids. Radar vectors may be authorized to provide course guidance through the segments of an approach to the final course or fix. When operating on an unpublished route or while being radar vectored, the pilot, when an approach clearance is received, shall, in addition to complying with § 91.177, maintain the last altitude assigned to that pilot until the aircraft is established on a segment of a published route or instrument approach procedure unless a different altitude is assigned by ATC. After the aircraft is so established, published altitudes apply to descent within each succeeding route or approach segment unless a different altitude is assigned by ATC. Upon reaching the final approach course or fix, the pilot may either complete the instrument approach in accordance with a procedure approved for the facility or continue a surveillance or precision radar approach to a landing.

(j) *Limitation on procedure turns.* In the case of a radar vector to a final approach course or fix, a timed approach from a holding fix, or an approach for which the procedure specifies "No PT," no pilot may make a procedure turn unless cleared to do so by ATC.

(k) *ILS components.* The basic ground components of an ILS are the localizer, glide slope, outer marker, middle marker, and, when installed for use with Category II or Category III instrument approach procedures, an inner marker. A compass locator or precision radar may be substituted for the outer or middle marker. DME, VOR, or nondirectional beacon fixes authorized in the standard instrument approach procedure or surveillance radar may be substituted for the outer marker. Applicability of, and substitution for, the inner marker for Category II or III approaches is determined by the appropriate Part 97 approach procedure, letter of authorization, or operations specification pertinent to the operations.

§ 91.177   Minimum altitudes for IFR operations.

(a) *Operation of aircraft at minimum altitudes.* Except when necessary for takeoff or landing, no person may operate an aircraft under IFR below—

(1) The applicable minimum altitudes prescribed in Parts 95 and 97 of this chapter; or

(2) If no applicable minimum altitude is prescribed in those parts—

(i) In the case of operations over an area designated as a mountainous area in Part 95, an altitude of 2,000 feet above the highest obstacle within a horizontal distance of 4 nautical miles from the course to be flown; or

(ii) In any other case, an altitude of 1,000 feet above the highest obstacle within a horizontal distance of 4 nautical miles from the course to be flown.

However, if both a MEA and a MOCA are prescribed for a particular route or route segment, a person may operate an aircraft below the MEA down to, but not below, the MOCA, when within 22 nautical miles of the VOR concerned (based on the pilot's reasonable estimate of that distance).

(b) *Climb.* Climb to a higher minimum IFR altitude shall begin immediately after passing the point beyond which that minimum altitude applies, except that when ground obstructions intervene, the point beyond which the higher minimum altitude applies shall be crossed at or above the applicable MCA.

§ 91.179   IFR cruising altitude or flight level.

(a) *In controlled airspace*. Each person operating an aircraft under IFR in level cruising flight in controlled airspace shall maintain the altitude or flight level assigned that aircraft by ATC. However, if the ATC clearance assigns "VFR conditions on-top," that person shall maintain an altitude or flight level as prescribed by § 91.159.

(b) *In uncontrolled airspace*. Except while in a holding pattern of 2 minutes or less or while turning, each person operating an aircraft under IFR in level cruising flight in uncontrolled airspace shall maintain an appropriate altitude as follows:

(1) When operating below 18,000 feet MSL and—

(i) On a magnetic course of zero degrees through 179 degrees, any odd thousand foot MSL altitude (such as 3,000, 5,000, or 7,000); or

(ii) On a magnetic course of 180 degrees through 359 degrees, any even thousand foot MSL altitude (such as 2,000, 4,000, or 6,000).

(2) When operating at or above 18,000 feet MSL but below flight level 290, and—

(i) On a magnetic course of zero degrees through 179 degrees, any odd flight level (such as 190, 210, or 230); or

(ii) On a magnetic course of 180 degrees through 359 degrees, any even flight level (such as 180, 200, or 220).

(3) When operating at flight level 290 and above, and—

(i) On a magnetic course of zero degrees through 179 degrees, any flight level, at 4,000-foot intervals, beginning at and including flight level 290 (such as flight level 290, 330, or 370); or

(ii) On a magnetic course of 180 degrees through 359 degrees, any flight level, at 4,000-foot intervals, beginning at and including flight level 310 (such as flight level 310, 350, or 390).

§ 91.181   Course to be flown.

Unless otherwise authorized by ATC, no person may operate an aircraft within controlled airspace under IFR except as follows:

(a) On a Federal airway, along the centerline of that airway.

(b) On any other route, along the direct course between the navigational aids or fixes defining that route. However, this section does not prohibit maneuvering the aircraft to pass well clear of other air traffic or the maneuvering of the aircraft in VFR conditions to clear the intended flight path both before and during climb or descent.

§ 91.183   IFR radio communications.

The pilot in command of each aircraft operated under IFR in controlled airspace shall have a continuous watch maintained on the appropriate frequency and shall report by radio as soon as possible—

(a) The time and altitude of passing each designated reporting point, or the reporting points specified by ATC, except that while the aircraft is under radar control, only the passing of those reporting points specifically requested by ATC need be reported;

(b) Any unforecast weather conditions encountered; and

(c) Any other information relating to the safety of flight.

§ 91.185   IFR operations: Two-way radio communications failure.

(a) *General*. Unless otherwise authorized by ATC, each pilot who has two-way radio communications failure when operating under IFR shall comply with the rules of this section.

(b) *VFR conditions*. If the failure occurs in VFR conditions, or if VFR conditions are encountered after the failure, each pilot shall continue the flight under VFR and land as soon as practicable.

(c) *IFR conditions*. If the failure occurs in IFR conditions, or if paragraph (b) of this section cannot be complied with, each pilot shall continue the flight according to the following:

(1) *Route*.

(i) By the route assigned in the last ATC clearance received;

(ii) If being radar vectored, by the direct route from the point of radio failure to the fix, route, or airway specified in the vector clearance;

(iii) In the absence of an assigned route, by the route that ATC has advised may be expected in a further clearance; or

(iv) In the absence of an assigned route or a route that ATC has advised may be expected in a further clearance, by the route filed in the flight plan.

(2) *Altitude.* At the highest of the following altitudes or flight levels for the route segment being flown:

(i) The altitude or flight level assigned in the last ATC clearance received;

(ii) The minimum altitude (converted, if appropriate, to minimum flight level as prescribed in § 91.121(c)) for IFR operations; or

(iii) The altitude or flight level ATC has advised may be expected in a further clearance.

(3) *Leave clearance limit.*

(i) When the clearance limit is a fix from which an approach begins, commence descent or descent and approach as close as possible to the expect-further-clearance time if one has been received, or if one has not been received, as close as possible to the estimated time of arrival as calculated from the filed or amended (with ATC) estimated time en route.

(ii) If the clearance limit is not a fix from which an approach begins, leave the clearance limit at the expect-further-clearance time if one has been received, or if none has been received, upon arrival over the clearance limit, and proceed to a fix from which an approach begins and commence descent or descent and approach as close as possible to the estimated time of arrival as calculated from the filed or amended (with ATC) estimated time en route.

§ 91.187 Operation under IFR in controlled airspace: Malfunction reports.

(a) The pilot in command of each aircraft operated in controlled airspace under IFR shall report as soon as practical to ATC any malfunctions of navigational, approach, or communication equipment occurring in flight.

(b) In each report required by paragraph (a) of this section, the pilot in command shall include the—

(1) Aircraft identification;

(2) Equipment affected;

(3) Degree to which the capability of the pilot to operate under IFR in the ATC system is impaired; and

(4) Nature and extent of assistance desired from ATC.

Subpart C—Equipment, Instrument, and Certificate Requirements

§ 91.205 Powered civil aircraft with standard category U.S. airworthiness certificates: Instrument and equipment requirements.

(a) *General.* Except as provided in paragraphs (c)(3) and (e) of this section, no person may operate a powered civil aircraft with a standard category U.S. airworthiness certificate in any operation described in paragraphs (b) through (f) of this section unless that aircraft contains the instruments and equipment specified in those paragraphs (or FAA-approved equivalents) for that type of operation, and those instruments and items of equipment are in operable condition.

(b) *Visual-flight rules (day).* For VFR flight during the day, the following instruments and equipment are required:

(1) Airspeed indicator.

(2) Altimeter.

(3) Magnetic direction indicator.

(4) Tachometer for each engine.

(5) Oil pressure gauge for each engine using pressure system.

(6) Temperature gauge for each liquid-cooled engine.

(7) Oil temperature gauge for each air-cooled engine.

(8) Manifold pressure gauge for each altitude engine.

(9) Fuel gauge indicating the quantity of fuel in each tank.

(10) Landing gear position indicator, if the aircraft has a retractable landing gear.

(11) If the aircraft is operated for hire over water and beyond power-off gliding distance from shore, approved flotation gear readily available to each occupant and at least one pyrotechnic signaling device. As used in this section, "shore" means that area of the land adjacent to the water which is above the high water mark and excludes land areas which

are intermittently under water.

(12) Except as to airships, an approved safety belt with an approved metal-to-metal latching device for each occupant 2 years of age or older.

(13) For small civil airplanes manufactured after July 18, 1978, an approved shoulder harness for each front seat. The shoulder harness must be designed to protect the occupant from serious head injury when the occupant experiences the ultimate inertia forces specified in § 23.561(b) (2) of this chapter. Each shoulder harness installed at a flight crewmember station must permit the crewmember, when seated and with his safety belt and shoulder harness fastened, to perform all functions necessary for flight operations. For purposes of this paragraph—

(i) The date of manufacture of an airplane is the date the inspection acceptance records reflect that the airplane is complete and meets the FAA-approved type design data; and

(ii) A front seat is a seat located at a flight crewmember station or any seat located alongside such a seat.

(14) An emergency locator transmitter, if required by § 91.207.

(15) For normal, utility, and acrobatic category airplanes with a seating configuration, excluding pilot seats, of 9 or less, manufactured after December 12, 1986, a shoulder harness for—

(i) Each front seat that meets the requirements of § 23.785(g) and (h) of this chapter in effect on December 12, 1985;

(ii) Each additional seat that meets the requirements of § 23.785(g) of this chapter in effect on December 12, 1985.

(c) *Visual flight rules (night).* For VFR flight at night, the following instruments and equipment are required:

(1) Instruments and equipment specified in paragraph (b) of this section.

(2) Approved position lights.

(3) An approved aviation red or aviation white anticollision light system on all U.S.-registered civil aircraft. Anticollision light systems initially installed after August 11, 1971, on aircraft for which a type certificate was issued or applied for before August 11, 1971, must at least meet the anticollision light standards of Part 23, 25, 27, or 29 of this chapter, as applicable, that were in effect on August 10, 1971, except that the color may be either aviation red or aviation white. In the event of failure of any light of the anticollision light system, operations with the aircraft may be continued to a stop where repairs or replacement can be made.

(4) If the aircraft is operated for hire, one electric landing light.

(5) An adequate source of electrical energy for all installed electrical and radio equipment.

(6) One spare set of fuses, or three spare fuses of each kind required, that are accessible to the pilot in flight.

(d) *Instrument flight rules.* For IFR flight, the following instruments and equipment are required:

(1) Instruments and equipment specified in paragraph (b) of this section, and, for night flight, instruments and equipment specified in paragraph (c) of this section.

(2) Two-way radio communications system and navigational equipment appropriate to the ground facilities to be used.

(3) Gyroscopic rate-of-turn indicator, except on the following aircraft:

(i) Large airplanes with a third attitude instrument system usable through flight attitudes of 360 degrees of pitch and roll and installed in accordance with § 121.305(j) of this chapter; and

(ii) Rotorcraft with a third attitude instrument system usable through flight attitudes of ±80 degrees of pitch and ±120 degrees of roll and installed in accordance with § 29.1303(g) of this chapter.

(4) Slip-skid indicator.

(5) Sensitive altimeter adjustable for barometric pressure.

(6) A clock displaying hours, minutes, and seconds with a sweep-second pointer or digital presentation.

(7) Generator or alternator of adequate capacity.

(8) Gyroscopic pitch and bank indicator (artificial horizon).

(9) Gyroscopic direction indicator (directional gyro or equivalent).

(e) *Flight at and above 24,000 ft. MSL (FL 240).* If VOR navigational equipment is required under paragraph (d) (2) of this section, no person may operate a U.S.-registered civil aircraft within the 50 states and the District of Columbia at or above FL 240 unless that aircraft is equipped with approved distance measuring equipment (DME). When DME required by this paragraph fails at and above FL 240, the pilot in command of the aircraft shall notify ATC immediately, and then may continue operations at and above FL 240 to the next airport of intended landing at which repairs or replacement of the equipment can be made.

§ 91.211 Supplemental oxygen.

(a) *General.* No person may operate a civil aircraft of U.S. registry—

(1) At cabin pressure altitudes above 12,500 feet (MSL) up to and including 14,000 feet (MSL), unless the required minimum flight crew is provided with and uses supplemental oxygen for that part of the flight at those altitudes that is of more than 30 minutes duration;

(2) At cabin pressure altitudes above 14,000 feet (MSL) unless the required minimum flight crew is provided with and uses supplemental oxygen during the entire flight time at those altitudes; and

(3) At cabin pressure altitudes above 15,000 feet (MSL) unless each occupant of the aircraft is provided with supplemental oxygen.

(b) *Pressurized cabin aircraft.*

(1) No person may operate a civil aircraft of U.S. registry with a pressurized cabin—

(i) At flight altitudes above flight level 250 unless at least a 10-minute supply of supplemental oxygen, in addition to any oxygen required to satisfy paragraph (a) of this section, is available for each occupant of the aircraft for use in the event that a descent is necessitated by loss of cabin pressurization; and

(ii) At flight altitudes above flight level 350 unless one pilot at the controls of the airplane is wearing and using an oxygen mask that is secured and sealed and that either supplies oxygen at all times or automatically supplies oxygen whenever the cabin pressure altitude of the airplane exceeds 14,000 feet (MSL), except that the one pilot need not wear and use an oxygen mask while at or below flight level 410 if there are two pilots at the controls and each pilot has a quick-donning type of oxygen mask that can be placed on the face with one hand from the ready position within 5 seconds, supplying oxygen and properly secured and sealed.

(2) Notwithstanding paragraph (b)(1)(ii) of this section, if for any reason at any time it is necessary for one pilot to leave the controls of the aircraft when operating at flight altitudes above flight level 350, the remaining pilot at the controls shall put on and use an oxygen mask until the other pilot has returned to that crewmember's station.

§ 91.213 Inoperative instruments and equipment.

(a) Except as provided in paragraph (d) of this section, no person may take off an aircraft with inoperative instruments or equipment installed unless the following conditions are met:

(1) An approved Minimum Equipment List exists for that aircraft.

(2) The aircraft has within it a letter of authorization, issued by the FAA Flight Standards district office having jurisdiction over the area in which the operator is located, authorizing operation of the aircraft under the Minimum Equipment List. The letter of authorization may be obtained by written request of the airworthiness certificate holder. The Minimum Equipment List and the letter of authorization constitute a supplemental type certificate for the aircraft.

(3) The approved Minimum Equipment List must—

(i) Be prepared in accordance with the limitations specified in paragraph (b) of this section; and

(ii) Provide for the operation of the aircraft with the instruments and equipment in an inoperable condition.

(4) The aircraft records available to the pilot must include an entry describing the inoperable instruments and equipment.

(5) The aircraft is operated under all applicable conditions and limitations contained in the Minimum Equipment List and the letter authorizing the use of the list.

(b) The following instruments and equipment may not be included in a Minimum Equipment List:

(1) Instruments and equipment that are

either specifically or otherwise required by the airworthiness requirements under which the aircraft is type certificated and which are essential for safe operations under all operating conditions.

(2) Instruments and equipment required by an airworthiness directive to be in operable condition unless the airworthiness directive provides otherwise.

(3) Instruments and equipment required for specific operations by this part.

(c) A person authorized to use an approved Minimum Equipment List issued for a specific aircraft under Part 121, 125, or 135 of this chapter shall use that Minimum Equipment List in connection with operations conducted with that aircraft under this part without additional approval requirements.

(d) Except for operations conducted in accordance with paragraph (a) or (c) of this section, a person may takeoff an aircraft in operations conducted under this part with inoperative instruments and equipment without an approved Minimum Equipment List provided—

(1) The flight operation is conducted in a—

(i) Rotorcraft, nonturbine-powered airplane, glider, or lighter-than-air aircraft for which a master Minimum Equipment List has not been developed; or

(ii) Small rotorcraft, nonturbine-powered small airplane, glider, or lighter-than-air aircraft for which a master Minimum Equipment List has been developed; and

(2) The inoperative instruments and equipment are not—

(i) Part of the VFR-day type certification instruments and equipment prescribed in the applicable airworthiness regulations under which the aircraft was type certificated;

(ii) Indicated as required on the aircraft's equipment list, or on the Kinds of Operations Equipment List for the kind of flight operations being conducted;

(iii) Required by § 91.205 or any other rule of this part for the specific kind of flight operation being conducted; or

(iv) Required to be operational by an airworthiness directive; and

(3) The inoperative instruments and equipment are—

(i) Removed from the aircraft, the cockpit control placarded, and the maintenance recorded in accordance with § 43.9 of this chapter; or

(ii) Deactivated and placarded "Inoperative." If deactivation of the inoperative instrument or equipment involves maintenance, it must be accomplished and recorded in accordance with Part 43 of this chapter; and

(4) A determination is made by a pilot, who is certificated and appropriately rated under Part 61 of this chapter, or by a person, who is certificated and appropriately rated to perform maintenance on the aircraft, that the inoperative instrument or equipment does not constitute a hazard to the aircraft. An aircraft with inoperative instruments or equipment as provided in paragraph (d) of this section is considered to be in a properly altered condition acceptable to the Administrator.

(e) Notwithstanding any other provision of this section, an aircraft with inoperable instruments or equipment may be operated under a special flight permit issued in accordance with §§ 21.197 and 21.199 of this chapter.

§ 91.215 ATC transponder and altitude reporting equipment and use

(a) *All airspace: U.S.-registered civil aircraft.* For operations not conducted under part 121, 127, or 135 of this chapter, ATC transponder equipment installed must meet the performance and environmental requirements of any class of *TSO-C74b (Mode A) or any class of *TSO-C74c (Mode A with altitude reporting capability) as appropriate, or the appropriate class of *TSO-C112 (Mode S).

(b) *All airspace:* Unless otherwise authorized or directed by ATC, no person may operate an aircraft in the airspace described in paragraphs (b)(1) through (b)(5) of this section, unless that aircraft is equipped with an operable coded radar beacon transponder having either Mode 3/A 4096 code capability, replying to Mode 3/A interrogations with the code specified by ATC, or a Mode S capability, replying to Mode 3/A interrogations with the code specified by ATC and intermode and Mode S interrogations in accordance with the applicable provisions specified in *TSO C-112, and that aircraft is equipped with automatic pressure altitude reporting equipment having a Mode C capability that automatically replies to Mode C interrogations by transmitting pressure altitude information in 100-foot increments. This requirement applies—

(1) *All aircraft.* In Class A, Class B, and Class C airspace areas;

(2) *All aircraft.* In all airspace within 30 nautical miles of an airport listed in appendix D, section 1 of this part from the surface upward to 10,000 feet MSL;

(3) Notwithstanding paragraph (b)(2) of this section, any aircraft which was not originally certificated with an engine-driven electrical system or which has not subsequently been certified with such a system installed, balloon or glider may conduct operations in the airspace within 30 nautical miles of an airport listed in appendix D, section 1 of this part provided such operations are conducted—

(i) Outside any Class A, Class B, or Class C airspace area; and

(ii) Below the altitude of the ceiling of a Class B or Class C airspace area designated for an airport or 10,000 feet MSL, whichever is lower; and

(4) All aircraft in all airspace above the ceiling and within the lateral boundaries of a Class B or Class C airspace area designated for an airport upward to 10,000 feet MSL; and

(5) All aircraft except any aircraft which was not originally certificated with an engine-driven electrical system or which has not subsequently been certified with such a system installed, balloon, or glider—

(i) In all airspace of the 48 contiguous states and the District of Columbia at and above 10,000 feet MSL, excluding the airspace at and below 2,500 feet above the surface; and

(ii) In the airspace from the surface to 10,000 feet MSL within a 10-nautical-mile radius of any airport listed in appendix D, section 2 of this part, excluding the airspace below 1,200 feet outside of the lateral boundaries of the surface area of the airspace designated for that airport.

(c) *Transponder-on operation.* While in the airspace as specified in paragraph (b) of this section or in all controlled airspace, each person operating an aircraft equipped with an operable ATC transponder maintained in accordance with §91.413 of this part shall operate the transponder, including Mode C equipment if installed, and shall reply on the appropriate code or as assigned by ATC.

(d) *ATC authorized deviations.* Requests for ATC authorized deviations must be made to the ATC facility having jurisdiction over the concerned airspace within the time periods specified as follows:

(1) For operation of an aircraft with an operating transponder but without operating automatic pressure altitude reporting equipment having a Mode C capability, the request may be made at any time.

(2) For operation of an aircraft with an inoperative transponder to the airport of ultimate destination, including any intermediate stops, or to proceed to a place where suitable repairs can be made, or both, the request may be made at any time.

(3) For operation of an aircraft that is not equipped with a transponder, the request must be made at least one hour before the proposed operation.

Subpart E—Maintenance, Preventive Maintenance, and Alterations

§ 91.411 Altimeter system and altitude reporting equipment tests and inspections.

(a) No person may operate an airplane, or helicopter, in controlled airspace under IFR unless—

(1) Within the preceding 24 calendar months, each static pressure system, each altimeter instrument, and each automatic pressure altitude reporting system has been tested and inspected and found to comply with Appendix E of Part 43 of this chapter;

(2) Except for the use of system drain and alternate static pressure valves, following any opening and closing of the static pressure system, that system has been tested and inspected and found to comply with paragraph (a), Appendices E and F, of Part 43 of this chapter; and

(3) Following installation or maintenance on the automatic pressure altitude reporting system of the ATC transponder where data correspondence error could be introduced, the integrated system has been tested, inspected, and found to comply with paragraph (c), Appendix E, of Part 43 of this chapter.

(b) The tests required by paragraph (a) of this section must be conducted by—

(1) The manufacturer of the airplane, or helicopter, on which the tests and inspections are to be performed;

(2) A certificated repair station properly equipped to perform those functions and holding—

(i) An instrument rating, Class I;

(ii) A limited instrument rating appropriate to the make and model of appliance to be tested;

(iii) A limited rating appropriate to the test to be performed;

(iv) An airframe rating appropriate to the airplane, or helicopter, to be tested; or

(v) A limited rating for a manufacturer issued for the appliance in accordance with § 145.101(b) (4) of this chapter; or

(3) A certificated mechanic with an airframe rating (static pressure system tests and inspections only).

(c) Altimeter and altitude reporting equipment approved under Technical Standard Orders are considered to be tested and inspected as of the date of their manufacture.

(d) No person may operate an airplane, or helicopter, in controlled airspace under IFR at an altitude above the maximum altitude at which all altimeters and the automatic altitude reporting system of that airplane, or helicopter, have been tested.

§ 91.413 ATC transponder tests and inspections.

(a) No person may use an ATC transponder that is specified in § 91.215(a), § 121.345(c), § 127.123(b) or § 135.143(c) of this chapter unless, within the preceding 24 calendar months, the ATC transponder has been tested and inspected and found to comply with Appendix F of Part 43 of this chapter; and

(b) Following any installation or maintenance on an ATC transponder where data correspondence error could be introduced, the integrated system has been tested, inspected, and found to comply with paragraph (c), Appendix E, of Part 43 of this chapter.

(c) The tests and inspections specified in this section must be conducted by—

(1) A certificated repair station properly equipped to perform those functions and holding—

(i) A radio rating, Class III;

(ii) A limited radio rating appropriate to the make and model transponder to be tested;

(iii) A limited rating appropriate to the test to be performed;

(iv) A limited rating for a manufacturer issued for the transponder in accordance with § 145.101(b) (4) of this chapter; or

(2) A holder of a continuous airworthiness maintenance program as provided in Part 121, 127, or § 135.411(a) (2) of this chapter; or

(3) The manufacturer of the aircraft on which the transponder to be tested is installed, if the transponder was installed by that manufacturer.

GLOSSARY OF TERMS

Selected terms from the Pilot/Controller Glossary (FAA)

ABBREVIATED IFR FLIGHT PLANS— An authorization by ATC requiring pilots to submit only that information needed for the purpose of ATC. It includes only a small portion of the usual IFR flight plan information. In certain instances, this may be only aircraft identification, location, and pilot request. Other information may be requested if needed by ATC for separation/control purposes. It is frequently used by aircraft which are airborne and desire an instrument approach or by aircraft which are on the ground and desire a climb to VFR-on-top. (See VFR-ON-TOP) (Refer to AIM)

AIRCRAFT APPROACH CATEGORY— A grouping of aircraft based on a speed of 1.3 times the stall speed in the landing configuration at maximum gross landing weight. An aircraft shall fit in only one category. If it is necessary to maneuver at speeds in excess of the upper limit of a speed range for a category, the minimums for the next higher category should be used. For example, an aircraft which falls in Category A, but is circling to land at a speed in excess of 91 knots, should use the approach Category B minimums when circling to land. The categories are as follows:

1. Category A—Speed less than 91 knots.

2. Category B—Speed 91 knots or more but less than 121 knots.

3. Category C—Speed 121 knots or more but less than 141 knots.

4. Category D—Speed 141 knots or more but less than 166 knots.

5. Category E—Speed 166 knots or more. (Refer to FAR 1) (Refer to FAR 97)

AIRMAN'S METEOROLOGICAL INFORMATION— (See Airmet)

AIRMET [WA]— In-flight weather advisories issued only to amend the area forecast concerning weather phenomena which are of operational interest to all aircraft and potentially hazardous to aircraft having limited capability because of lack of equipment, instrumentation, or pilot qualifications. AIRMET's concern weather of less severity than that covered by SIGMET's or Convective SIGMET's. AIRMET's cover moderate icing, moderate turbulence, sustained winds of 30 knots or more at the surface, widespread areas of ceilings less than 1,000 feet and/or visibility less than 3 miles, and extensive mountain obscurement. (See AWW) (See SIGMET) (See Convective SIGMET) (See CWA) (Refer to AIM)

AIRPORT ADVISORY AREA— The area within ten miles of an airport without a control tower or where the tower is not in operation, and on which a Flight Service Station is located. (See Airport Advisory Service) (Refer to AIM)

AIRPORT ROTATING BEACON— A visual NAVAID operated at many airports. At civil airports, alternating white and green flashes indicate the location of the airport. At military airports, the beacons flash alternately white and green, but are differentiated from civil beacons by dualpeaked (two quick) white flashes between the green flashes. (See Special VFR Operations) (See Instrument Flight Rules) (Refer to AIM, Rotating Beacons)

AIR ROUTE SURVEILLANCE RADAR [ARSR]— Air route traffic control center (ARTCC) radar used primarily to detect and display an aircraft's position while en route between terminal areas. The ARSR enables controllers to provide radar air traffic control service when aircraft are within the ARSR coverage. In some instances, ARSR may enable an ARTCC to provide terminal radar services similar to but usually more limited than those provided by a radar approach control.

AIR ROUTE TRAFFIC CONTROL CENTER [ARTCC]—

A facility established to provide air traffic control service to aircraft operating on IFR flight plans within controlled airspace and principally during the en route phase of flight. When equipment capabilities and controller workload permit, certain advisory/assistance services may be provided to VFR aircraft. (See NAS Stage A) (See En Route Air Traffic Control Services) (Refer to AIM)

ALTITUDE RESTRICTION—

An altitude or altitudes, stated in the order flown, which are to be maintained until reaching a specific point or time. Altitude restrictions may be issued by ATC due to traffic, terrain, or other airspace considerations.

APPROACH CLEARANCE—

Authorization by ATC for a pilot to conduct an instrument approach. The type of instrument approach for which a clearance and other pertinent information is provided in the approach clearance when required. (See Instrument Approach Procedure) (See Cleared for Approach) (Refer to AIM) and FAR 91)

APPROACH GATE—

An imaginary point used within ATC as a basis for vectoring aircraft to the final approach course. The gate will be established along the final approach course 1 mile from the outer marker (or the fix used in lieu of the outer marker) on the side away from the airport for precision approaches and 1 mile from the final approach fix on the side away from the airport for nonprecision approaches. In either case when measured along the final approach course, the gate will be no closer than 5 miles from the landing threshold.

AREA NAVIGATION [RNAV]—

A method of navigation that permits aircraft operation on any desired course within the coverage of station-referenced navigation signals or within the limits of a self-contained system capability. Random area navigation routes are direct routes, based on area navigation capability, between waypoints defined in terms of latitude/longitude coordinates, degree/distance fixes, or offsets from published or established routes/airways at a specified distance and direction. The major types of equipment are:

1. VORTAC referenced or Course Line Computer [CLC] systems, which account for the greatest number of RNAV units in use. To function, the CLC must be within the service range of a VORTAC.

2. OMEGA/VLF, although two separate systems, can be considered as one operationally. A long-range navigation system based upon Very Low Frequency radio signals transmitted from a total of 17 stations worldwide.

3. Inertial [INS] systems, which are totally self-contained and require no information from external references. They provide aircraft position and navigation information in response to signals resulting from inertial effects on components within the system.

4. MLS Area Navigation [MLS/RNAV], which provides area navigation with reference to an MLS ground facility.

5. LORAN-C is a long-range radio navigation system that uses ground waves transmitted at low frequency to provide user position information at ranges of up to 600 to 1,200 nautical miles at both en route and approach altitudes. The usable signal coverage areas are determined by the signal-to-noise ratio, the envelope-to-cycle difference, and the geometric relationship between the positions of the user and the transmitting stations.

AUTOLAND APPROACH—

An autoland approach is a precision instrument approach to touchdown and, in some cases, through the landing rollout. An autoland approach is performed by the aircraft autopilot which is receiving position information and/or steering commands from onboard navigation equipment (See Coupled Approach)

Note: Autoland and coupled approaches are flown in VFR and IFR. It is common for carriers to require their crews to fly coupled approaches and autoland approaches (if certified) when the weather conditions are less than approximately 4,000 RVR.

AUTOMATIC DIRECTION FINDER [ADF]—

An aircraft radio navigation system which senses and indicates the direction to a L/MF nondirectional radio beacon [NDB] ground transmitter. Direction is indicated to the pilot as a magnetic bearing or as a relative bearing to the longitudinal axis of the aircraft depending on the type of indicator installed in the aircraft. In certain applications, such as military, ADF operations may be based on airborne and ground transmitters in the VHF/UHF frequency spectrum. (See Bearing) (See Nondirectional Beacon)

AZIMUTH (MLS)—

A magnetic bearing extending from an MLS navigation facility.

Note: azimuth bearings are described as magnetic and are referred to as "azimuth" in radio telephone communications.

CENTER WEATHER ADVISORY [CWA]—

An unscheduled weather advisory issued by Center Weather Service Unit meteorologists for ATC use to alert pilots of existing or anticipated adverse weather conditions within the next 2 hours. A CWA may modify or redefine a SIGMET. (See AWW) (See SIGMET) (See Convective SIGMET) (See AIRMET) (Refer to AIM)

CHARTED VISUAL FLIGHT PROCEDURE APPROACH [CVFP]—

An approach wherein a radar-controlled aircraft on an IFR flight plan, operating in VFR conditions and having an ATC authorization, may proceed to the airport of intended landing via visual landmarks and altitudes depicted on a charted visual flight procedure.

CIRCLE-TO-LAND MANEUVER—

A maneuver initiated by the pilot to align the aircraft with a runway for landing when a straight-in landing from an instrument approach is not possible or is not desirable. This maneuver is made only after ATC authorization has been obtained and the pilot has established required visual reference to the airport (See Circle to Runway) (See Landing Minimums) (Refer to AIM)

CIRCLE TO RUNWAY (RUNWAY NUMBER)—

Used by ATC to inform the pilot that he must circle to land because the runway in use is other than the runway aligned with the instrument approach procedure. When the direction of the circling maneuver in relation to the airport/runway is required, the controller will state the direction (eight cardinal compass points) and specify a left or right downwind or base leg as appropriate; e.g., "Cleared VOR Runway Three Six Approach circle to Runway Two Two," or "Circle northwest of the airport for a right downwind to Runway Two Two." (See Circle-to-Land Maneuver) (See Landing Minimums) (Refer to AIM)

COMPASS LOCATOR—

A low power, low or medium frequency [L/MF] radio beacon installed at the site of the outer or middle marker of an instrument landing system [ILS]. It can be used for navigation at distances of approximately 15 miles or as authorized in the approach procedure.

1. Outer Compass Locator [LOM]-A compass locator installed at the site of the outer marker of an instrument landing system. (See Outer Marker)

2. Middle Compass Locator [LMM]-A compass locator installed at the site of the middle marker of an instrument landing system. (See Middle Marker)

COMPOSITE FLIGHT PLAN—

A flight plan which specifies VFR operation for one portion of flight and IFR for another portion. It is used primarily in military operations. (Refer to AIM)

COMPOSITE ROUTE SYSTEM—

An organized oceanic route structure, incorporating reduced lateral spacing between routes, in which composite separation is authorized.

COMPOSITE SEPARATION—

A method of separating aircraft in a composite route system where, by management of route and altitude assignments, a combination of half the lateral minimum specified for the area concerned and half the vertical minimum is applied.

COMPULSORY REPORTING POINTS— Reporting points which must be reported to ATC. They are designated on aeronautical charts by solid triangles or filed in a flight plan as fixes selected to define direct routes. These points are geographical locations which are defined by navigation aids/fixes. Pilots should discontinue position reporting over compulsory reporting points when informed by ATC that their aircraft is in "radar contact."

CONFLICT ALERT— A function of certain air traffic control automated systems designed to alert radar controllers to existing or pending situations between tracked targets (known IFR or VFR aircraft) that require his immediate attention/action. (See Mode C Intruder Alert)

CONSOLAN— A low frequency, long-distance NAVAID used principally for transoceanic navigations.

CONTACT APPROACH— An approach wherein an aircraft on an IFR flight plan, having an air traffic control authorization, operating clear of clouds with at least 1 mile flight visibility and a reasonable expectation of continuing to the destination airport in those conditions, may deviate from the instrument approach procedure and proceed to the destination airport by visual reference to the surface. This approach will only be authorized when requested by the pilot and the reported ground visibility at the destination airport is at least 1 statute mile. (Refer to AIM)

CONTROLLED AIRSPACE— An airspace of defined dimensions within which air traffic control service is provided to IFR flights and to VFR flights in accordance with the airspace classification.
Note 1 – Controlled airspace is a generic term that covers Class A, Class B, Class C, Class D, and Class E airspace.
Note 2 – Controlled airspace is also that airspace within which all aircraft operators are subject to certain pilot qualifications, operating rules, and equipment requirements in FAR Part 91 (for specific operating requirements, please refer to FAR Part 91). For IFR operations in any class of controlled airspace, a pilot must file an IFR flight plan and receive an appropriate ATC clearance. Each Class B, Class C, and Class D airspace area designated for an airport contains at least one primary airport around which the airspace is designated (for specific designations and descriptions of the airspace classes, please refer to FAR Part 71).
Controlled airspace in the United States is designated as follows:
1. CLASS A: Generally, that airspace from 18,000 feet MSL up to and including FL600, including the airspace overlying the waters within 12 nautical miles of the coast of the 48 contiguous States and Alaska. Unless otherwise authorized, all persons must operate their aircraft under IFR.
2. CLASS B: Generally, that airspace from the surface to 10,000 feet FSL surrounding the nation's busiest airports in terms of airport operations or passenger enplanements. The configuration of each Class B airspace area is individually tailored and consists of a surface area and two or more layers (some Class B airspace areas resemble upside-down wedding cakes), and is designed to contain all published instrument procedures once an aircraft enters the airspace. An ATC clearance is required for all aircraft to operate in the area, and all aircraft that are so cleared receive separation services within the airspace. The cloud clearance requirement for VFR operations is "clear of clouds."
3. CLASS C: Generally, that airspace from the surface to 4,000 feet above the airport elevation (charted in MSL) surrounding those airports that have an operational control tower, are serviced by a radar approach control, and that have a certain number of IFR operations or passenger enplanements. Although the configuration of each Class C airspace area is individually tailored, the airspace usually consists of a surface area with a 5 nm radius, and an outer area with a 10 nm radius that extends from 1,200 feet to 4,000 feet above the airport elevation. Each person must establish two-way radio communications with the ATC facility providing air traffic services prior to entering the airspace and thereafter maintain those communications while within the airspace. VFR aircraft are only separated from IFR aircraft within the airspace.

4. CLASS D: Generally, that airspace from the surface to 2,500 feet above the airport elevation (charted in MSL) surrounding those airports that have an operational control tower. The configuration of each Class D airspace area is individually tailored and when instrument procedures are published, the airspace will normally be designed to contain the procedures. Arrival extensions for instrument approach procedures may be Class D or Class E airspace. Unless otherwise authorized, each person must establish two-way radio communications with the ATC facility providing air traffic services prior to entering the airspace and thereafter maintain those communications while in the airspace. No separation services are provided to VFR aircraft.

5. CLASS E: Generally, if the airspace is not Class A, Class B, Class C, or Class D, and it is controlled airspace, it is Class E airspace. Class E airspace extends upward from either the surface or a designated altitude to the overlying or adjacent controlled airspace. When designated as a surface area, the airspace will be configured to contain all instrument procedures. Also in this class are Federal airways, airspace beginning at either 700 or 1,200 feet AGL used to transition to/from the terminal or enroute environment, enroute domestic, and offshore airspace areas designated below 18,000 feet MSL. Unless designated at a lower altitude, Class E airspace begins at 14,500 MSL over the United States, including that airspace overlying the waters within 12 nautical miles of the coast of the 48 contiguous States and Alaska, Class E airspace does not include the airspace 18,000 MSL or above.

CONTROLLED DEPARTURE TIME [CDT] PROGRAMS—

These programs are the flow control process whereby aircraft are held on the ground at the departure airport when delays are projected to occur in either the en route system or the terminal of intended landing. The purpose of these programs is to reduce congestion in the air traffic system or to limit the duration of airborne holding in the arrival center or terminal area. A CDT is a specific departure slot shown on the flight plan as an expected departure clearance time [EDCT].

CONVECTIVE SIGMET—

A weather advisory concerning convective weather significant to the safety of all aircraft. Convective SIGMET's are issued for tornadoes, lines of thunderstorms, embedded thunderstorms of any intensity level, areas of thunderstorms greater than or equal to VIP level 4 with an area coverage of 4/10 (40%) or more, and hail 3/4 inch or greater. (See AWW) (See SIGMET) (See CWA) (See AIRMET) (Refer to AIM)

COUPLED APPROACH—

A coupled approach is an instrument approach performed by the aircraft autopilot which is receiving position information and/or steering commands from onboard navigation equipment. In general, coupled nonprecision approaches must be discontinued and flown manually at altitudes lower than 50 feet below the minimum descent altitude, and coupled precision approaches must be flown manually below 50 feet ALG (See Autoland Approach).

Note: Coupled and autoland approaches are flown in VFR and IFR. It is common for carriers to require their crews to fly coupled approaches and autoland approaches (if certified) when the weather conditions are less than approximately 4,000 RVR.

CROSS (FIX) AT (ALTITUDE)—

Used by ATC when a specific altitude restriction at a specified fix is required.

CROSS (FIX) AT OR ABOVE (ALTITUDE)—

Used by ATC when an altitude restriction at a specified fix is required. It does not prohibit the aircraft from crossing the fix at a higher altitude than specified; however, the higher altitude may not be one that will violate a succeeding altitude restriction or altitude assignment. (See Altitude Restriction) (Refer to AIM)

CROSS (FIX) AT OR BELOW (ALTITUDE)—

Used by ATC when a maximum crossing altitude at a specific fix is required. It does not prohibit the aircraft from crossing the fix at a lower altitude; however, it must be at or above the minimum IFR altitude. (See Minimum IFR Altitude) (See Altitude Restriction) (Refer to FAR 91)

CROSSWIND COMPONENT—

The wind component measured in knots at 90 degrees to the longitudinal axis of the runway.

CRUISE—

Used in an ATC clearance to authorize a pilot to conduct flight at any altitude from the minimum IFR altitude up to and including the altitude specified in the clearance. The pilot may level off at any intermediate altitude within this block of airspace. Climb/descent within the block is to be made at the discretion of the pilot. However, once the pilot starts descent and verbally reports leaving an altitude in the block, he may not return to that altitude without additional ATC clearance. Further, it is approval for the pilot to proceed to and make an approach at destination airport and can be used in conjunction with:

1. An airport clearance limit at locations with a standard/special instrument approach procedure. The FAR's require that if an instrument letdown to an airport is necessary, the pilot shall make the letdown in accordance with a standard/special instrument approach procedure for that airport, or

2. An airport clearance limit at locations that are within/below/outside controlled airspace and without a standard/special instrument approach procedure. Such a clearance is NOT AUTHORIZATION for the pilot to descend under IFR conditions below the applicable minimum IFR altitude nor does it imply that ATC is exercising control over aircraft in uncontrolled airspace; however, it provides a means for the aircraft to proceed to destination airport, descend, and land in accordance with applicable FAR's governing VFR flight operations. Also, this provides search and rescue protection until such time as the IFR flight plan is closed. (See Instrument Approach Procedure)

DECISION HEIGHT [DH]—

With respect to the operation of aircraft, means the height at which a decision must be made during an ILS, MLS, or PAR instrument approach to either continue the approach or to execute a missed approach.

DF APPROACH PROCEDURE—

Used under emergency conditions where another instrument approach procedure cannot be executed. DF guidance for an instrument approach is given by ATC facilities with DF capability. (See DF Guidance) (See Direction Finder) (Refer to AIM)

DIRECTION FINDER [DF] [UDF] [VDF] [UVDF]—

A radio receiver equipped with a directional sensing antenna used to take bearings on a radio transmitter. Specialized radio direction finders are used in aircraft as air navigation aids. Others are ground-based, primarily to obtain a "fix" on a pilot requesting orientation assistance or to locate downed aircraft. A location "fix" is established by the intersection of two or more bearing lines plotted on a navigational chart using either two separately located Direction Finders to obtain a fix on an aircraft or by a pilot plotting the bearing indications of his DF on two separately located ground-based transmitters, both of which can be identified on his chart. UDF's receive signals in the ultra high frequency radio broadcast band; VDF's in the very high frequency band; and UVDF's in both bands. ATC provides DF service at those air traffic control towers and flight service stations listed in the Airport/Facility Directory and the DOD FLIP IFR En Route Supplement. (See DF Guidance) (See DF Fix)

DISCRETE CODE—

As used in the Air Traffic Control Radar Beacon System [ATCRBS], any one of the 4096 selectable Mode 3/A aircraft transponder codes except those ending in zero zero; e.g., discrete codes: 0010, 1201, 2317, 7777; non-discrete codes: 0100, 1200, 7700. Non-discrete codes are normally reserved for radar facilities that are not equipped with discrete decoding capability and for other purposes such as emergencies (7700), VFR aircraft (1200), etc. (See Radar) (Refer to AIM)

DISCRETE FREQUENCY—

A separate radio frequency for use in direct pilot-controller communications in air traffic control which reduces frequency congestion by controlling the number of aircraft operating on a particular frequency at one time. Discrete frequencies are normally designated for each control sector in en route/terminal ATC facilities. Discrete frequencies are listed in the Airport/Facility Directory and the DOD FLIP IFR En Route Supplement. (See Control Sector)

EMERGENCY LOCATOR TRANSMITTER [ELT]—

A radio transmitter attached to the aircraft structure which operates from its own power source on 121.5 MHz and 243.0 MHz. It aids in locating downed aircraft by radiating a downward sweeping audio tone, 2-4 times per second. It is designed to function without human action after an accident. (Refer to FAR 91.3) (Refer to AIM)

EXECUTE MISSED APPROACH—

Instructions issued to a pilot making an instrument approach which means continue inbound to the missed approach point and execute the missed approach procedure as described on the Instrument Approach Procedure Chart or as previously assigned by ATC. The pilot may climb immediately to the altitude specified in the missed approach procedure upon making a missed approach. No turns should be initiated prior to reaching the missed approach point. When conducting an ASR or PAR approach, execute the assigned missed approach procedure immediately upon receiving instructions to "execute missed approach." (Refer to AIM)

FAST FILE—

A system whereby a pilot files a flight plan via telephone that is tape recorded and then transcribed for transmission to the appropriate air traffic facility. Locations having a fast file capability are contained in the Airport/Facility Directory. (Refer to AIM)

FEEDER ROUTE—

A route depicted on instrument approach procedure charts to designate routes for aircraft to proceed from the en route structure to the initial approach fix [IAF]. (See Instrument Approach Procedure)

FINAL APPROACH COURSE—

A published MLS course, a straight line extension of a localizer, a final approach radial/bearing, or a runway centerline all without regard to distance. (See Final Approach-IFR (See Traffic Pattern)

FINAL APPROACH FIX [FAF]—

The fix from which the final approach (IFR) to an airport is executed and which identifies the beginning of the final approach segment. It is designated on Government charts by the Maltese Cross symbol for nonprecision approaches and the lightning bolt symbol for precision approaches; or when ATC directs a lower-than-published Glideslope/path Intercept Altitude, it is the resultant actual point of the glideslope/path intercept. (See Final Approach Point (See Glideslope/path Intercept Altitude (See Segments of an Instrument Approach Procedure)

FINAL APPROACH-IFR—

The flight path of an aircraft which is inbound to an airport on a final instrument approach course, beginning at the final approach fix or point and extending to the airport or the point where a circle-to-land maneuver or a missed approach is executed. (See Segments of an Instrument Approach Procedure (See Final Approach Fix (See Final Approach Course (See Final Approach Point)

GATE HOLD PROCEDURES—
Procedures at selected airports to hold aircraft at the gate or other ground location whenever departure delays exceed or are anticipated to exceed 15 minutes. The sequence for departure will be maintained in accordance with initial call-up unless modified by flow control restrictions. Pilots should monitor the ground control/clearance delivery frequency for engine start/taxi advisories or new proposed start/taxi time if the delay changes. (See Flow Control)

GLIDESLOPE—
Provides vertical guidance for aircraft during approach and landing. The glideslope/glidepath is based on the following:

1. Electronic components emitting signals which provide vertical guidance by reference to airborne instruments during instrument approaches such as ILS/MLS, or

2. Visual ground aids, such as VASI, which provide vertical guidance for a VFR approach or for the visual portion of an instrument approach and landing.

3. PAR. Used by ATC to inform an aircraft making a PAR approach of its vertical position (elevation) relative to the descent profile.

GLIDESLOPE INTERCEPT ALTITUDE—
The minimum altitude to intercept the glideslope/path on a precision approach. The intersection of the published intercept altitude with the glideslope/path, designated on Government charts by the lightning bolt symbol, is the precision FAF; however, when ATC directs a lower altitude, the resultant lower intercept position is then the FAF. (See Final Approach Fix) (See Segments of an Instrument Approach Procedure)

GROUND CONTROLLED APPROACH [GCA]—
A radar approach system operated from the ground by air traffic control personnel transmitting instructions to the pilot by radio. The approach may be conducted with surveillance radar [ASR] only or with both surveillance and precision approach radar [PAR]. Usage of the term "GCA" by pilots is discouraged except when referring to a GCA facility. Pilots should specifically request a "PAR" approach when a precision radar approach is desired or request an "ASR" or "surveillance" approach when a nonprecision radar approach is desired. (See Radar Approach)

HAZARDOUS INFLIGHT WEATHER ADVISORY SERVICE [HIWAS]—
Continuous recorded hazardous inflight weather forecasts broadcast to airborne pilots over selected VOR outlets defined as an HIWAS BROADCAST AREA.

HAZARDOUS WEATHER INFORMATION—
Summary of significant meteorological information (SIGMET/WS), convective significant meteorological information (convective SIGMET/WST), urgent pilot weather reports (urgent PIREP/UUA), center weather advisories (CWA), airmen's meteorological information (AIRMET/WA) and any other weather such as isolated thunderstorms that are rapidly developing and increasing in intensity, or low ceilings and visibilities that are becoming widespread which is considered significant and are not included in a current hazardous weather advisory.

HEIGHT ABOVE AIRPORT [HAA]—
The height of the Minimum Descent Altitude above the published airport elevation. This is published in conjunction with circling minimums. (See Minimum Descent Altitude)

HEIGHT ABOVE TOUCHDOWN [HAT]—
The height of the Decision Height or Minimum Descent Altitude above the highest runway elevation in the touchdown zone (first 3,000 feet of the runway). HAT is published on instrument approach charts in conjunction with all straight-in minimums. (See Decision Height) (See Minimum Descent Altitude)

HOLD PROCEDURE— A predetermined maneuver which keeps aircraft within a specified airspace while awaiting further clearance from air traffic control. Also used during ground operations to keep aircraft within a specified area or at a specified point while awaiting further clearance from air traffic control. (See Holding Fix) (Refer to AIM)

HOLDING FIX— A specified fix identifiable to a pilot by NAVAID's or visual reference to the ground used as a reference point in establishing and maintaining the position of an aircraft while holding. (See Fix) (See Visual Holding) (Refer to AIM)

IFR TAKEOFF MINIMUMS AND DEPARTURE PROCEDURES— FAR, Part 91, prescribes standard takeoff rules for certain civil users. At some airports, obstructions or other factors require the establishment of nonstandard takeoff minimums, departure procedures, or both to assist pilots in avoiding obstacles during climb to the minimum en route altitude. Those airports are listed in NOS/DOD Instrument Approach Charts (IAP's) under a section entitled "IFR Takeoff Minimums and Departure Procedures." The NOS/DOD IAP chart legend illustrates the symbol used to alert the pilot to nonstandard takeoff minimums and departure procedures. When departing IFR from such airports or from any airports where there are no departure procedures, SID's, or ATC facilities available, pilots should advise ATC of any departure limitations. Controllers may query a pilot to determine acceptable departure directions, turns, or headings after takeoff. Pilots should be familiar with the departure procedures and must assure that their aircraft can meet or exceed any specified climb gradients.

INITIAL APPROACH FIX [IAF]— The fixes depicted on instrument approach procedure charts that identify the beginning of the initial approach segment(s). (See Fix (See Segments of an Instrument Approach Procedure)

ILS CATEGORIES— 1. ILS Category I—An ILS approach procedure which provides for approach to a height above touchdown of not less than 200 feet and with runway visual range of not less than 1,800 feet.
2. ILS Category II—An ILS approach procedure which provides for approach to a height above touchdown of not less than 100 feet and with runway visual range of not less than 1,200 feet.
3. ILS Category III:
a. IIIA—An ILS approach procedure which provides for approach without a decision height minimum and with runway visual range of not less than 700 feet.
b. IIIB—An ILS approach procedure which provides for approach without a decision height minimum and with runway visual range of not less than 150 feet.
c. IIIC—An ILS approach procedure which provides for approach without a decision height minimum and without runway visual range minimum.

INNER MARKER [IM]— A marker beacon used with an ILS (CAT II) precision approach located between the middle marker and the end of the ILS runway, transmitting a radiation pattern keyed at six dots per second and indicating to the pilot, both aurally and visually, that he is at the designated decision height (DH), normally 100 feet above the touchdown zone elevation, on the ILS CAT II approach. It also marks progress during a CAT III approach. (See Instrument Landing System) (Refer to AIM)

INSTRUMENT APPROACH PROCEDURE [IAP]— A series of predetermined maneuvers for the orderly transfer of an aircraft under instrument flight conditions from the beginning of the initial approach to a landing or to a point from which a landing may be made visually. It is prescribed and approved for a specific airport by competent authority. (See Segments of an Instrument Approach Procedure) (Refer to FAR 91 (See AIM)

1. U. S. civil standard instrument approach procedures are approved by the FAA as prescribed under FAR 97 and are available for public use.

2. U.S. military standard instrument approach procedures are approved and published by the Department of Defense.

3. Special instrument approach procedures are approved by the FAA for individual operators but are not published in FAR 97 for public use.

INSTRUMENT LANDING SYSTEM [ILS]—

A precision instrument approach system which normally consists of the following electronic components and visual aids:

1. Localizer. (See Localizer)

2. Glideslope. (See Glideslope)

3. Outer Marker. (See Outer Marker)

4. Middle Marker. (See Middle Marker)

5. Approach Lights. (See Airport Lighting)

(Refer to FAR 91 (See AIM)

INSTRUMENT RUNWAY—

A runway equipped with electronic and visual navigation aids for which a precision or nonprecision approach procedure having straight-in landing minimums has been approved.

INTERMEDIATE FIX [IF]—

The fix that identifies the beginning of the intermediate approach segment of an instrument approach procedure. The fix is not normally identified on the instrument approach chart as an intermediate fix (IF). (See Segments of an Instrument Approach Procedure)

LANDING MINIMUMS—

The minimum visibility prescribed for landing a civil aircraft while using an instrument approach procedure. The minimum applies with other limitations set forth in FAR 91 with respect to the Minimum Descent Altitude [MDA] or Decision Height [DH] prescribed in the instrument approach procedures as follows:

1. Straight-in landing minimums-A statement of MDA and visibility, or DH and visibility, required for a straight-in landing on a specified runway, or

2. Circling minimums-A statement of MDA and visibility required for the circle-to-land maneuver.

Descent below the established MDA or DH is not authorized during an approach unless the aircraft is in a position from which a normal approach to the runway of intended landing can be made and adequate visual reference to required visual cues is maintained. (See Straight-in Landing) (See Circle-to-Land Maneuver) (See Decision Height) (See Minimum Descent Altitude) (See Visibility) (See Instrument Approach Procedure) (Refer to FAR 91)

LOCAL AIRPORT ADVISORY [LAA]—

A service provided by flight service stations or the military at airports not serviced by an operating control tower. This service consists of providing information to arriving and departing aircraft concerning wind direction and speed, favored runway, altimeter setting, pertinent known traffic, pertinent known field conditions, airport taxi routes and traffic patterns, and authorized instrument approach procedures. This information is advisory in nature and does not constitute an ATC clearance. (See Airport Advisory Area)

LOCALIZER TYPE DIRECTIONAL AID [LDA]—

A NAVAID used for nonprecision instrument approaches with utility and accuracy comparable to a localizer but which is not a part of a complete ILS and is not aligned with the runway. (Refer to AIM)

LORAN—
An electronic navigational system by which hyperbolic lines of position are determined by measuring the difference in the time of reception of synchronized pulse signals from two fixed transmitters. Loran A operates in the 1750-1950 kHz frequency band. Loran C and D operate in the 100-110 kHz frequency band. (Refer to AIM)

LOW APPROACH—
An approach over an airport or runway following an instrument approach or a VFR approach including the go-around maneuver where the pilot intentionally does not make contact with the runway. (Refer to AIM)

MARKER BEACON—
An electronic navigation facility transmitting a 75 MHz vertical fan or boneshaped radiation pattern. Marker beacons are identified by their modulation frequency and keying code, and when received by compatible airborne equipment, indicate to the pilot, both aurally and visually, that he is passing over the facility. (See Outer Marker) (See Middle Marker) (See Inner Marker) (Refer to AIM)

MAXIMUM AUTHORIZED ALTITUDE [MAA]—
A published altitude representing the maximum usable altitude or flight level for an airspace structure or route segment. It is the highest altitude on a Federal airway, jet route, area navigation low or high route, or other direct route for which an MEA is designated in FAR 95 at which adequate reception of navigation aid signals is assured.

MICROWAVE LANDING SYSTEM [MLS]—
A precision instrument approach system operating in the microwave spectrum which normally consists of the following components:
1. Azimuth Station.
2. Elevation Station.
3. Precision Distance Measuring Equipment. (See MLS Categories)

MIDDLE MARKER [MM]—
A marker beacon that defines a point along the glideslope of an ILS normally located at or near the point of decision height (ILS Category I). It is keyed to transmit alternate dots and dashes, with the alternate dots and dashes keyed at the rate of 95 dot/dash combinations per minute on a 1300 Hz tone, which is received aurally and visually by compatible airborne equipment. (See Marker Beacon) (See Instrument Landing System) (Refer to AIM)

MINIMUM CROSSING ALTITUDE [MCA]—
The lowest altitude at certain fixes at which an aircraft must cross when proceeding in the direction of a higher minimum en route IFR altitude [MEA]. (See Minimum En Route IFR Altitude)

MINIMUM DESCENT ALTITUDE [MDA]—
The lowest altitude, expressed in feet above mean sea level, to which descent is authorized on final approach or during circle-to-land maneuvering in execution of a standard instrument approach procedure where no electronic glideslope is provided. (See Nonprecision Approach Procedure)

MINIMUM EN ROUTE IFR ALTITUDE [MEA]—
The lowest published altitude between radio fixes which assures acceptable navigational signal coverage and meets obstacle clearance requirements between those fixes. The MEA prescribed for a Federal airway or segment thereof, area navigation low or high route, or other direct route applies to the entire width of the airway, segment, or route between the radio fixes defining the airway, segment, or route. (Refer to FAR 91) (Refer to FAR 95) (Refer to AIM)

MINIMUM FUEL—
Indicates that an aircraft's fuel supply has reached a state where, upon reaching the destination, it can accept little or no delay. This is not an emergency situation but merely indicates an emergency situation is possible should any undue delay occur. (Refer to AIM)

MINIMUM HOLDING ALTITUDE [MHA]—

The lowest altitude prescribed for a holding pattern which assures navigational signal coverage, communications, and meets obstacle clearance requirements.

MINIMUM IFR ALTITUDES [MIA]—

Minimum altitudes for IFR operations as prescribed in FAR 91. These altitudes are published on aeronautical charts and prescribed in FAR 95 for airways and routes, and in FAR 97 for standard instrument approach procedures. If no applicable minimum altitude is prescribed in FAR 95 or FAR 97, the following minimum IFR altitude applies:

1. In designated mountainous areas, 2,000 feet above the highest obstacle within a horizontal distance of 5 statute miles from the course to be flown; or

2. Other than mountainous areas, 1,000 feet above the highest obstacle within a horizontal distance of 5 statute miles from the course to be flown; or

3. As otherwise authorized by the Administrator or assigned by ATC. (See Minimum En Route IFR Altitude) (See Minimum Obstruction Clearance Altitude) (See Minimum Crossing Altitude) (See Minimum Safe Altitude) (See Minimum Vectoring Altitude) (Refer to FAR 91)

MINIMUM OBSTRUCTION CLEARANCE ALTITUDE [MOCA]—

The lowest published altitude in effect between radio fixes on VOR airways, off-airway routes, or route segments which meets obstacle clearance requirements for the entire route segment and which assures acceptable navigational signal coverage only within 25 statute (22 nautical) miles of a VOR. (Refer to FAR 91) (Refer to FAR 95)

MINIMUM RECEPTION ALTITUDE [MRA]—

The lowest altitude at which an intersection can be determined. (Refer to FAR 95)

MINIMUM SAFE ALTITUDE [MSA]—

1. The minimum altitude specified in FAR 91 for various aircraft operations.

2. Altitudes depicted on approach charts which provide at least 1,000 feet of obstacle clearance for emergency use within a specified distance from the navigation facility upon which a procedure is predicated. These altitudes will be identified as Minimum Sector Altitudes or Emergency Safe Altitudes and are established as follows:

a. Minimum Sector Altitudes-Altitudes depicted on approach charts which provide at least 1,000 feet of obstacle clearance within a 25-mile radius of the navigation facility upon which the procedure is predicated. Sectors depicted on approach charts must be at least 90 degrees in scope. These altitudes are for emergency use only and do not necessarily assure acceptable navigational signal coverage.

[ICAO] Minimum Sector Altitude—The lowest altitude which may be used under emergency conditions which will provide a minimum clearance of 300 m (1,000 feet) above all obstacles located in an area contained within a sector of a circle of 46 km (25 NM) radius centered on a radio aid to navigation.

b. Emergency Safe Altitudes-Altitudes depicted on approach charts which provide at least 1,000 feet of obstacle clearance in nonmountainous areas and 2,000 feet of obstacle clearance in designated mountainous areas within a 100-mile radius of the navigation facility upon which the procedure is predicated and normally used only in military procedures. These altitudes are identified on published procedures as ''Emergency Safe Altitudes.''

MINIMUM SAFE ALTITUDE WARNING [MSAW]—

A function of the ARTS III computer that aids the controller by alerting him when a tracked Mode C—

equipped aircraft is below or is predicted by the computer to go below a predetermined minimum safe altitude. (Refer to AIM)

MINIMUM VECTORING ALTITUDE [MVA]—

The lowest MSL altitude at which an IFR aircraft will be vectored by a radar controller, except as otherwise authorized for radar approaches, departures, and missed approaches. The altitude meets IFR obstacle clearance criteria. It may be lower than the published MEA along an airway or J-route segment. It may be utilized for radar vectoring only upon the controller's determination that an adequate radar return is being received from the aircraft being controlled. Charts depicting minimum vectoring altitudes are normally available only to the controllers and not to pilots. (Refer to AIM)

MISSED APPROACH POINT [MAP]— A point prescribed in each instrument approach procedure at which a missed approach procedure shall be executed if the required visual reference does not exist. (See Missed Approach) (See Segments of an Instrument Approach Procedure)

MODE— The letter or number assigned to a specific pulse spacing of radio signals transmitted or received by ground interrogator or airborne transponder components of the Air Traffic Control Radar Beacon System [ATCRBS]. Mode A (military Mode 3) and Mode C (altitude reporting) are used in air traffic control. (See Transponder) (See Interrogator) (See Radar) (Refer to AIM)

MULTICOM— A mobile service not open to public correspondence used to provide communications essential to conduct the activities being performed by or directed from private aircraft.

NAVAID CLASSES— VOR, VORTAC, and TACAN aids are classed according to their operational use. The three classes of NAVAID's are:
  T—Terminal.
  L—Low altitude.
  H—High altitude.
The normal service range for T, L, and H class aids is found in the AIM. Certain operational requirements make it necessary to use some of these aids at greater service ranges than specified. Extended range is made possible through flight inspection determinations. Some aids also have lesser service range due to location, terrain, frequency protection, etc. Restrictions to service range are listed in Airport/Facility Directory.

NO GYRO APPROACH— A radar approach/vector provided in case of a malfunctioning gyro-compass or directional gyro. Instead of providing the pilot with headings to be flown, the controller observes the radar track and issues control instructions "turn right/left" or "stop turn" as appropriate. (Refer to AIM)

NONAPPROACH CONTROL TOWER— Authorizes aircraft to land or takeoff at the airport controlled by the tower or to transit the associated Class D airspace. The primary function of a nonapproach control tower is the sequencing of aircraft in the traffic pattern and on the landing area. Nonapproach control towers also separate aircraft operating under instrument flight rules clearances from approach controls and centers. They provide ground control services to aircraft, vehicles, personnel, and equipment on the airport movement area.

NONDIRECTIONAL BEACON [NDB]— An L/MF or UHF radio beacon transmitting nondirectional signals whereby the pilot of an aircraft equipped with direction finding equipment can determine his bearing to or from the radio beacon and "home" on or track to or from the station. When the radio beacon is installed in conjunction with the Instrument Landing System marker, it is normally called a Compass Locator. (See Compass Locator (See Automatic Direction Finder)

NONPRECISION APPROACH PROCEDURE— A standard instrument approach procedure in which no electronic glideslope is provided; e.g., VOR, TACAN, NDB, LOC, ASR, LDA, or SDF approaches.

OPTION APPROACH—

An approach requested and conducted by a pilot which will result in either a touch-and-go, missed approach, low approach, stop-and-go, or full stop landing. (See Cleared for the Option) (Refer to AIM)

OUTER AREA (associated with Class C airspace)—

Nonregulatory airspace surrounding designated Class C airspace airports wherein ATC provides radar vectoring and sequencing on a full-time basis for all IFR and participating VFR aircraft. The service provided in the outer area is called Class C service which includes: IFR/IFR- and VFR/VFR-traffic advisories and, as appropriate, safety alerts. The normal radius will be 20 nautical miles with some variations based on site-specific requirements. The outer area extends outward from the primary Class C airspace airport and extends from the lower limits of radar/radio coverage up to the ceiling of the approach control's delegated airspace excluding the Class C charted area and other airspace as appropriate. (See Controlled Airspace). (See Conflict Resolution)

OUTER FIX—

A general term used within ATC to describe fixes in the terminal area, other than the final approach fix. Aircraft are normally cleared to these fixes by an Air Route Traffic Control Center or an Approach Control Facility. Aircraft are normally cleared from these fixes to the final approach fix or final approach course.

OUTER MARKER [OM]—

A marker beacon at or near the glideslope intercept altitude of an ILS approach. It is keyed to transmit two dashes per second on a 400 Hz tone, which is received aurally and visually by compatible airborne equipment. The OM is normally located four to seven miles from the runway threshold on the extended centerline of the runway. (See Marker Beacon) (See Instrument Landing System) (Refer to AIM)

PRECISION APPROACH RADAR [PAR]—

Radar equipment in some ATC facilities operated by the FAA and/or the military services at joint-use civil/military locations and separate military installations to detect and display azimuth, elevation, and range of aircraft on the final approach course to a runway. This equipment may be used to monitor certain nonradar approaches, but is primarily used to conduct a precision instrument approach [PAR] wherein the controller issues guidance instructions to the pilot based on the aircraft's position in relation to the final approach course (azimuth), the glidepath (elevation), and the distance (range) from the touchdown point on the runway as displayed on the radar scope. (See Glidepath) (See PAR) (Refer to AIM)

The abbreviation "PAR" is also used to denote preferential arrival routes in ARTCC computers. (See Preferential Routes)

PREFERENTIAL ROUTES—

Preferential routes (PDR's, PAR's, and PDAR's) are adapted in ARTCC computers to accomplish inter/intrafacility controller coordination and to assure that flight data is posted at the proper control positions. Locations having a need for these specific inbound and outbound routes normally publish such routes in local facility bulletins, and their use by pilots minimizes flight plan route amendments. When the workload or traffic situation permits, controllers normally provide radar vectors or assign requested routes to minimize circuitous routing. Preferential routes are usually confined to one ARTCC's area and are referred to by the following names or acronyms:

1. Preferential Departure Route [PDR]—A specific departure route from an airport or terminal area to an en route point where there is no further need for flow control. It may be included in a Standard Instrument Departure [SID] or a Preferred IFR Route.

2. Preferential Arrival Route [PAR]—A specific arrival route from an appropriate en route point to an airport or terminal area. It may be included in a Standard Terminal Arrival [STAR] or a Preferred IFR Route. The abbreviation "PAR" is used primarily within the ARTCC and should not be confused with the abbreviation for Precision Approach Radar.

3. Preferential Departure and Arrival Route [PDAR]—A route between two terminals which are within or immediately adjacent to one ARTCC's area. PDAR's are not synonymous with Preferred IFR Routes but may be listed as such as they do accomplish essentially the same purpose. (See Preferred IFR Routes) (See NAS Stage A)

PREFERRED IFR ROUTES— Routes established between busier airports to increase system efficiency and capacity. They normally extend through one or more ARTCC areas and are designed to achieve balanced traffic flows among high density terminals. IFR clearances are issued on the basis of these routes except when severe weather avoidance procedures or other factors dictate otherwise. Preferred IFR Routes are listed in the Airport/Facility Directory. If a flight is planned to or from an area having such routes but the departure or arrival point is not listed in the Airport/Facility Directory, pilots may use that part of a Preferred IFR Route which is appropriate for the departure or arrival point that is listed. Preferred IFR Routes are correlated with SID's and STAR's and may be defined by airways, jet routes, direct routes between NAVAID's, Waypoints, NAVAID radials/DME, or any combinations thereof. (See Standard Instrument Departure) (See Standard Terminal Arrival) (See Preferential Routes) (See Center's Area) (Refer to Airport/Facility Directory) (Refer to Notices to Airmen Publication)

PROCEDURE TURN [PT]— The maneuver prescribed when it is necessary to reverse direction to establish an aircraft on the intermediate approach segment or final approach course. The outbound course, direction of turn, distance within which the turn must be completed, and minimum altitude are specified in the procedure. However, unless otherwise restricted, the point at which the turn may be commenced and the type and rate of turn are left to the discretion of the pilot.

PROCEDURE TURN INBOUND— That point of a procedure turn maneuver where course reversal has been completed and an aircraft is established inbound on the intermediate approach segment or final approach course. A report of "procedure turn inbound" is normally used by ATC as a position report for separation purposes. (See Final Approach Course) (See Procedure Turn) (See Segments of an Instrument Approach Procedure)

PROFILE DESCENT— An uninterrupted descent (except where level flight is required for speed adjustment; e.g., 250 knots at 10,000 feet MSL) from cruising altitude/level to interception of a glideslope or to a minimum altitude specified for the initial or intermediate approach segment of a nonprecision instrument approach. The profile descent normally terminates at the approach gate or where the glideslope or other appropriate minimum altitude is intercepted.

RADAR— A device which, by measuring the time interval between transmission and reception of radio pulses and correlating the angular orientation of the radiated antenna beam or beams in azimuth and/or elevation, provides information on range, azimuth, and/or elevation of objects in the path of the transmitted pulses.

1. Primary Radar—A radar system in which a minute portion of a radio pulse transmitted from a site is reflected by an object and then received back at that site for processing and display at an air traffic control facility.

2. Secondary Radar/Radar Beacon [ATCRBS]—A radar system in which the object to be detected is fitted with cooperative equipment in the form of a radio receiver/transmitter (transponder). Radar pulses transmitted from the searching transmitter/receiver (interrogator) site are received in the cooperative equipment and used to trigger a distinctive transmission from the transponder. This reply transmission, rather than a reflected signal, is then received back at the transmitter/receiver site for processing and display at an air traffic control facility. (See Transponder) (See Interrogator) (Refer to AIM)

RADAR APPROACH CONTROL FACILITY— A terminal ATC facility that uses radar and nonradar capabilities

267

to provide approach control services to aircraft arriving, departing, or transiting airspace controlled by the facility (See Approach Control Service). Provides radar ATC services to aircraft operating in the vicinity of one or more civil and/or military airports in a terminal area. The facility may provide services of a ground controlled approach [GCA]; i.e., ASR and PAR approaches. A radar approach control facility may be operated by FAA, USAF, US Army, USN, USMC, or jointly by FAA and a military service. Specific facility nomenclatures are used for administrative purposes only and are related to the physical location of the facility and the operating service generally as follows:

Army Radar Approach Control [ARAC] (Army).

Radar Air Traffic Control Facility [RATCF] (Navy/FAA).

Radar Approach Control [RAPCON] (Air Force/FAA).

Terminal Radar Approach Control [TRACON] (FAA).

Tower/Airport Traffic Control Tower [ATCT] (FAA). (Only those towers delegated approach control authority.)

RADIO MAGNETIC INDICATOR [RMI]—

An aircraft navigational instrument coupled with a gyro compass or similar compass that indicates the direction of a selected NAVAID and indicates bearing with respect to the heading of the aircraft.

REMOTE COMMUNICATIONS AIR/ GROUND FACILITY [RCAG]—

An unmanned VHF/UHF transmitter/receiver facility which is used to expand ARTCC air/ground communications coverage and to facilitate direct contact between pilots and controllers. RCAG facilities are sometimes not equipped with emergency frequencies 121.5 MHz and 243.0 MHz. (Refer to AIM)

REQUEST FULL ROUTE CLEARANCE [FRC]—

Used by pilots to request that the entire route of flight be read verbatim in an ATC clearance. Such request should be made to

ROUTE SEGMENT—

As used in Air Traffic Control, a part of a route that can be defined by two navigational fixes, two NAVAID's, or a fix and a NAVAID. (See Fix) (See Route)

RUNWAY PROFILE DESCENT—

An instrument flight rules [IFR] air traffic control arrival procedure to a runway published for pilot use in graphic and/or textual form and may be associated with a STAR. Runway Profile Descents provide routing and may depict crossing altitudes, speed restrictions, and headings to be flown from the en route structure to the point where the pilot will receive clearance for and execute an instrument approach procedure. A Runway Profile Descent may apply to more than one runway if so stated on the chart. (Refer to AIM)

SEE AND AVOID—

A visual procedure wherein pilots of aircraft flying in visual meteorological conditions [VMC], regardless of type of flight plan, are charged with the responsibility to observe the presence of other aircraft and to maneuver their aircraft as required to avoid the other aircraft. Right-of-way rules are contained in FAR 91. (See Instrument Flight Rules) (See Visual Flight Rules) (See Visual Meteorological Conditions) (See Instrument Meteorological Conditions)

SEGMENTS OF AN INSTRUMENT APPROACH PROCEDURE—

An instrument approach procedure may have as many as four separate segments depending on how the approach procedure is structured.

1. Initial Approach—The segment between the initial approach fix and the intermediate fix or the point where the aircraft is established on the intermediate course or final approach course.

*[ICAO] Initial Approach Segment—*That segment of an instrument approach procedure between the initial approach fix and the intermediate approach fix or, where applicable, the final approach fix or point.

2. Intermediate Approach—The segment between the intermediate fix or point and the final approach fix.

[ICAO] Intermediate Approach Segment—That segment of an instrument approach procedure between either the intermediate approach fix and the final approach fix or point, or between the end of a reversal, race track or dead reckoning track procedure and the final approach fix or point, as appropriate.

3. Final Approach—The segment between the final approach fix or point and the runway, airport, or missed approach point.

[ICAO] Final Approach Segment—That segment of an instrument approach procedure in which alignment and descent for landing are accomplished.

4. Missed Approach—The segment between the missed approach point or the point of arrival at decision height and the missed approach fix at the prescribed altitude. (Refer to FAR 97)

[ICAO] Missed Approach Procedure—The procedure to be followed if the approach cannot be continued.

SHORT RANGE CLEARANCE— A clearance issued to a departing IFR flight which authorizes IFR flight to a specific fix short of the destination while air traffic control facilities are coordinating and obtaining the complete clearance.

SIDESTEP MANEUVER— A visual maneuver accomplished by a pilot at the completion of an instrument approach to permit a straight-in landing on a parallel runway not more than 1,200 feet to either side of the runway to which the instrument approach was conducted. (Refer to AIM)

SIGMET [WS]— A weather advisory issued concerning weather significant to the safety of all aircraft. SIGMET advisories cover severe and extreme turbulence, severe icing, and widespread dust or sandstorms that reduce visibility to less than 3 miles. (See AWW) (See Convective SIGMET) (See CWA) (See AIRMET) (Refer to AIM)

SIMPLIFIED DIRECTIONAL FACILITY [SDF]— A NAVAID used for nonprecision instrument approaches. The final approach course is similar to that of an ILS localizer except that the SDF course may be offset from the runway, generally not more than 3 degrees, and the course may be wider than the localizer, resulting in a lower degree of accuracy. (Refer to AIM)

SPECIAL USE AIRSPACE— Airspace of defined dimensions identified by an area on the surface of the earth wherein activities must be confined because of their nature and/or wherein limitations may be imposed upon aircraft operations that are not a part of those activities. Types of special use airspace are:

1. Alert Area—Airspace which may contain a high volume of pilot training activities or an unusual type of aerial activity, neither of which is hazardous to aircraft. Alert Areas are depicted on aeronautical charts for the information of nonparticipating pilots. All activities within an Alert Area are conducted in accordance with Federal Aviation Regulations, and pilots of participating aircraft as well as pilots transiting the area are equally responsible for collision avoidance.

2. Controlled Firing Area—Airspace wherein activities are conducted under conditions so controlled as to eliminate hazards to nonparticipating aircraft and to ensure the safety of persons and property on the ground.

3. Military Operations Area [MOA]—An MOA is an airspace assignment of defined vertical and lateral dimensions established outside Class A airspace to separate/segregate certain military activities from IFR traffic and to identify for VFR traffic where these activities are conducted. (Refer to AIM)

4. Prohibited Area—Designated airspace within which the flight of aircraft is prohibited. (Refer to En Route Charts, AIM).

5. Restricted Area—Airspace designated under FAR, Part 73, within which the flight of aircraft, while not wholly prohibited, is subject to restriction. Most restricted areas are designated joint use and IFR/VFR operations in the area may be authorized by the controlling

SPEED ADJUSTMENT—

An ATC procedure used to request pilots to adjust aircraft speed to a specific value for the purpose of providing desired spacing. Pilots are expected to maintain a speed of plus or minus 10 knots or 0.02 mach number of the specified speed.

Examples of speed adjustments are:

1. "Increase/reduce speed to mach point (number)."
2. "Increase/reduce speed to (speed in knots)" or "Increase/reduce speed (number of knots) knots."

STANDARD INSTRUMENT DEPARTURE [SID]—

A preplanned instrument flight rule [IFR] air traffic control departure procedure printed for pilot use in graphic and/or textual form. SID's provide transition from the terminal to the appropriate en route structure. (See IFR Takeoff Minima and Departure Procedures) (Refer to AIM)

STANDARD RATE TURN—

A turn of three degrees per second.

STANDARD TERMINAL ARRIVAL [STAR]—

A preplanned instrument flight rule [IFR] air traffic control arrival procedure published for pilot use in graphic and/or textual form. STAR's provide transition from the en route structure to an outer fix or an instrument approach fix/arrival waypoint in the terminal area.

STRAIGHT-IN APPROACH-IFR—

An instrument approach wherein final approach is begun without first having executed a procedure turn, not necessarily completed with a straight-in landing or made to straight-in landing minimums. (See Straight-in Landing) (See Landing Minimums) (See Straight-in Approach-VFR)

STRAIGHT-IN APPROACH-VFR—

Entry into the traffic pattern by interception of the extended runway centerline (final approach course) without executing any other portion of the traffic pattern. (See Traffic Pattern)

STRAIGHT-IN LANDING—

A landing made on a runway aligned within 30° of the final approach course following completion of an instrument approach. (See Straight-in Approach-IFR)

SUBSTITUTE ROUTE—

A route assigned to pilots when any part of an airway or route is unusable because of NAVAID status. These routes consist of:

1. Substitute routes which are shown on U.S. Government charts.
2. Routes defined by ATC as specific NAVAID radials or courses.
3. Routes defined by ATC as direct to or between NAVAID's.

SUPER HIGH FREQUENCY [SHF]—

The frequency band between 3 and 30 gigahertz (gHz). The elevation and azimuth stations of the microwave landing system operate from 5031MHz to 5091MHz in this spectrum.

SURVEILLANCE APPROACH—

An instrument approach wherein the air traffic controller issues instructions, for pilot compliance, based on aircraft position in relation to the final approach course (azimuth), and the distance (range) from the

TACTICAL AIR NAVIGATION [TACAN]—

An ultra-high frequency electronic rho-theta air navigation aid which provides suitably equipped aircraft a continuous indication of bearing and distance to the TACAN station. (See VORTAC) (Refer to AIM)

TERMINAL RADAR SERVICE AREA [TRSA]—

Airspace surrounding designated airports wherein ATC provides radar vectoring, sequencing, and separation on a full-time basis for all IFR and participating VFR aircraft. Service provided in a TRSA is called Stage III Service. The AIM contains an explanation of TRSA. TRSA's are depicted on VFR aeronautical charts. Pilot participation is urged but is not mandatory. (See Terminal Radar Program) (Refer to AIM) (Refer to Airport/Facility Directory)

TERMINAL-VERY HIGH FREQUENCY OMNIDIRECTIONAL RANGE STATION [TVOR]—

A very high frequency terminal omnirange station located on or near an airport and used as an approach aid. (See Navigational Aid) (See VOR)

TOUCHDOWN ZONE—

The first 3,000 feet of the runway beginning at the threshold. The area is used for determination of Touchdown Zone Elevation in the development of straight-in landing minimums for instrument approaches.

TRAFFIC MANAGEMENT PROGRAM ALERT—

A term used in a Notice to Airmen NOTAM) issued in conjunction with a special traffic management program to alert pilots to the existence of the program and to refer them to either the Notices to Airmen publication or a special traffic management program advisory message for program details.

TRANSPONDER—

The airborne radar beacon receiver/transmitter portion of the Air Traffic Control Radar Beacon System [ATCRBS] which automatically receives radio signals from interrogators on the ground, and selectively replies with a specific reply pulse or pulse group only to those interrogations being received on the mode to which it is set to respond. (See Interrogator) (Refer to AIM)

UNPUBLISHED ROUTE—

A route for which no minimum altitude is published or charted for pilot use. It may include a direct route between NAVAIDS, a radial, a radar vector, or a final approach course beyond the segments of an instrument approach procedure. (See Published Route) (See Route)

VERY HIGH FREQUENCY [VHF]—

The frequency band between 30 and 300 MHz. Portions of this band, 108 to 118 MHz, are used for certain NAVAIDS; 118 to 136 MHz are used for civil air/ground voice communications. Other frequencies in this band are used for purposes not related to air traffic control.

VISIBILITY—

The ability, as determined by atmospheric conditions and expressed in units of distance, to see and identify prominent unlighted objects by day and prominent lighted objects by night. Visibility is reported as statute miles, hundreds of feet or meters. (Refer to FAR 91) (See AIM)

1. Flight Visibility—The average forward horizontal distance, from the cockpit of an aircraft in flight, at which prominent unlighted objects may be seen and identified by day and prominent lighted objects may be seen and identified by night.

2. Ground Visibility—Prevailing horizontal visibility near the earth's surface as reported by the United States National Weather Service or an accredited observer.

3. Prevailing Visibility—The greatest horizontal visibility equaled or exceeded throughout at least half the horizon circle which need not necessarily be continuous.

4. Runway Visibility Value [RVV]—The visibility determined for a particular runway by a transmissometer. A meter provides a continuous indication of the visibility (reported in miles or fractions of miles) for the runway. RVV is used in lieu of prevailing visibility in determining minimums for a particular runway.

5. Runway Visual Range [RVR]—An instrumentally derived value, based on standard calibrations, that represents the horizontal distance a pilot will see down the runway from the approach end. It is based on the sighting of either high intensity runway lights or on the visual contrast of other targets whichever yields the greater visual range. RVR, in contrast to prevailing or runway visibility, is based on what a pilot in a moving aircraft should see looking

down the runway. RVR is horizontal visual range, not slant visual range. It is based on the measurement of a transmissometer made near the touchdown point of the instrument runway and is reported in hundreds of feet. RVR is used in lieu of RVV and/or prevailing visibility in determining minimums for a particular runway.

a. Touchdown RVR—The RVR visibility readout values obtained from RVR equipment serving the runway touchdown zone.

b. Mid-RVR—The RVR readout values obtained from RVR equipment located midfield of the runway.

c. Rollout RVR—The RVR readout values obtained from RVR equipment located nearest the rollout end of the runway.

VISUAL APPROACH— An approach wherein an aircraft on an IFR flight plan, operating in VFR conditions under the control of an air traffic control facility and having an air traffic control authorization, may proceed to the airport of destination in VFR conditions.

VISUAL DESCENT POINT [VDP]— A defined point on the final approach course of a nonprecision straight-in approach procedure from which normal descent from the MDA to the runway touchdown point may be commenced, provided the approach threshold of that runway, or approach lights, or other markings identifiable with the approach end of that runway are clearly visible to the pilot.

VOR— A ground-based electronic navigation aid transmitting very high frequency navigation signals, 360 degrees in azimuth, oriented from magnetic north. Used as the basis for navigation in the National Airspace System. The VOR periodically identifies itself by Morse Code and may have an additional voice identification feature. Voice features may be used by ATC or FSS for transmitting instructions/information to pilots. (See Navigational Aid) (Refer to AIM)

VORTAC— A navigation aid providing VOR azimuth, TACAN azimuth, and TACAN distance measuring equipment [DME] at one site. (See Distance Measuring Equipment) (See Navigational Aid) (See TACAN) (See VOR) (Refer to AIM)

BIBLIOGRAPHY

Air Navigation: Flying Training, AF Manual 51-40, NAVAIR 00-80V-49, U.S. Department of the Air Force, U.S. Department of the Navy, Washington, DC. 1983

Air Traffic Control Handbook, 7110.65F. U.S. Department of Transportation, Federal Aviation Administration. 1989

Airman's Information Manual, Basic Flight Information and ATC Procedures. U. S. Department of Transportation, Federal Aviation Administration. 1993

Airport/Facility Directory, U. S. Department of Commerce, National Oceanic and Atmospheric Administration. 1993

Aviation Weather, AC 00-6A. U. S. Department of Transportation, Federal Aviation Administration. 1975.

Aviation Weather Services (A Supplement to Aviation Weather), AC-0045C. U. S. Department of Transportation, Federal Aviation Administration. 1985

Flight Services Handbook, 7110.10I. U. S. Department of Transportation, Federal Aviation Administration. 1989

Holding Pattern Criteria, 7130.3. U. S. Department of Transportation, Federal Aviation Administration. 1967

Instrument Flying Handbook, AC 61-27C. U. S. Department of Transportation, Federal Aviation Administration. 1980

Instrument Rating, Practical Test Standards, U. S. Department of Transportation, Federal Aviation Administration, 1989

Jeppesen Airway Manual, Jeppesen-Sanderson, Inc., 55 Inverness Drive East, Englewood, CO. 1989

Loran-C User Handbook, COMDTINST MI6562.3, U.S. Coast Guard, U.S. Department of Transportation. 1980

United States Standard for Terminal Instrument Procedures (TERPS), 8260.3B. 1976 (changes through 1984)

Buck, Robert N., **Weather Flying**. Macmillan Publishing Co., Inc., New York, N.Y. 1988

Carden, Skip, **ADF Directory and Manual**. Skip Carden, Durham, NC. 1988

Clausing, Donald J., **The Aviator's Guide to Modern Navigation**, TAB Books Inc., Blue Ridge Summit, PA. 1987

Collins, Richard L., **Flying IFR**. Macmillan Publishing Company/Eleanor Friede, New York, NY. 1983

Connes, Keith, **The Loran, RNAV, and NAV/COMM Guide**, Butterfield Press, San Anselmo, CA. 1987

Ferrara, John M., **Every Pilot's Guide to Aviation Electronics, Comm. Nav. & Pulse Systems and Equipment**. Air & Space Company, Yardley, PA. 1985

Hurt, H. H. Jr., **Aerodynamics For Naval Aviators**. Issued by The Office of the Chief of Naval Operations, Aviation Training Division. January 1965

Kendal, Brian, **Manual of Avionics**, BSP Professional Books, London, England. 1987

Kershner, William K., **The Instrument Flight Manual**. Iowa State University Press, Ames, IA. 1991

Kershner, William K., **The Advanced Pilot's Flight Manual**. Iowa State University Press, Ames, IA. 1985

Lagewiesche, Wolfgang, **Stick and Rudder**. McGraw-Hill Book Company, New York. 1972

Melton, Luke, **The Complete Loran-C Handbook**, International Marine Publishing Co., Camden, ME. 1986

Newton, Dennis, **Severe Weather Flying**. McGraw-Hill Book Company. New York. 1983

Taylor, Richard L., **Instrument Flying**. Macmillan Publish **Instrument Flying**. Macmillan Publishing Co., Inc., New York, N.Y. 1986

Taylor, Richard L. and Guinther, William M., **Positive Flying**. Macmillan Publishing Co./Eleanor Friede, New York. 1983

Index

A

Abeam 125,126,135
ADF 108
Acronyms 234
Airborne checkpoint (designated) 87
Airborne checkpoint (homemade) 87
AIRMETs 59
Airport surveillance radar (ASR) 153
Airport traffic areas 66
Airspace Structure 65
Airspeed 148
  Calibrated 22
  Indicated 22
  True 22
Airspeed indicator 22
Alternate minimums 71
Altimeter 18
Altitude 76,147
  Absolute 19
  Density 20
  Indicated 19
  Pressure 20
  True 19
Ammeter 26
Angular deviation 189
Approach Architecture 149
Approach Descent 41
Approach Level 39
Approach from a Hold 156
Approach lighting system (ALS) 168
Approach plate clip 77
Approach plates and charts 77
Area forecast 59
Area Navigation 187
Artificial Horizon 12
ATC Communications 76
ATC System 8
Attitude Indicator 12
Automatic Direction Finder (ADF) 108

B

Back Course (BC) 152
Bank Angle 147
Bearing 110

C

Checklist 233
Circle-to-Land 146
Clearance limit 74
"Cleared for the Approach" 143

Climbing and Descending Turns 44
Climbs 34
Cockpit Organization 77
Communications Failure 198
Compass Turns 48
Compass locator 168
Compensating For The Wind 129
Cone of confusion 90
Contact approaches 153
Course deviation indicator 89
Course line computer (CLC) 188
Cruise Descent 38

D

DME 85
DME Arc 156,158
Decision Height (DH) 171
Departure instructions 75
Dip errors 23
Directional Gyro 13
Dual VOR check 87
DUAT 62

E

Electrical Failure 205
Engine Failure 199
Engine Instruments 25,26
Expect further clearance (EFC) 132

F

FAR's 236
Feeder routes 143
Final approach courses 155
Final approach fix (FAF) 144
Final approach segment 144
Five T's 101
Flight Plan 67
Flight strip 72
Flight Test Preparation 213
Freezing level charts 61
Full approach 154

G

Glide Slope 168
Glossary of Terms 253
Ground checkpoint 87
Ground instruction 4
Gyro Instruments 10

H

Heading 87,147
Headset 78
Height above touchdown (HAT) 146
Height above airport (HAA) 146
Hold entries 127
  Direct 128
  Teardrop 129,135
  Parallel 129,135
Holding 123,125
Holding at other types of fix 134
Holding Clearance 132
Holding Pattern Terminology 125
Holding at a VOR 125
Holding course 125
Holding fix 125
Holding side 125
Horizontal situation indicator (HSI) 97
HSI 97

I

Ice 208
IFR Clearance 72
Inbound leg 125,126,135
Inbound turn 125,127,135
Initial approach fix 143
Initial segment 143
Instructors 6
Instrument Classification 32
Instrument Currency 215
Instrument Scan 29
Instrument skills 7
Instrument landing system (ILS) 167
Intercept angle 111
Intermediate fix 143
Intermediate segment 143

L

Lap board 77
Lead radials 158
Legal Requirements 64
Level cruise 37
Localizer 152,168
Localizer type directional aid (LOA) 153
Locator middle marker (LMM) 168
Locator outer marker (LOM) 168
LORAN-C 188,193

M

Magnetic Compass 23
Magnetic bearing 110
Marker beacon 171

Maximum Authorized Altitude (MAA) 67
Maximum legal holding speed 125
Microwave landing system (MLS) 166
Middle marker 168
Minimum Crossing Altitude (MCA) 67
Minimum Enroute Altitude (MEA) 67
Minimum Fuel Advisory 208
Minimum Obstruction Clearance Altitude 67
Minimum Reception Altitude (MRA) 67
Minimum Safe Altitudes (MSA) 143
Minimum Descent Altitude 144
Missed Approach 148,178
Missed approach point (MAP) 144
Missed approach segment 146

N

NoPt Transition 156
Non-holding side 125
Nonprecision Approaches 149
Nonprecision Descent 42
NOTAM 62

O

Omni-bearing selector 89
Outbound leg 125,127,135
Outbound turn 125,126,135
Outer marker 168

P

Partial Panel 48
Partial Panel Turns 47
Phugoid oscillation 49
PIREPS 61
Pitch, Power and Trim 30
Pitot-Static System 17
Poor Man's RMI 109
Power Instruments 17
Precession 11
Precision approach radar (PAR) 166
Pressure Instruments 17
Procedure turn 102,119
Proceed Direct 100

R

Radar Vectors 155
Radar summary chart 62
Radial 89
Radio magnetic indicator (RMI) 111
Radio shop check 87
Rate Climbs and Descents 48
Reference descent rate 177

Reference heading 115,176
Relative bearing 110
Reported visibility 174
Requirements for the Instrument Rating 2
RMI 111
RNAV 187
RNAV approaches 192
Route legs 77

S
Scan 8, 29
Sequence reports 59
SIGMETs 59
Simplified directional facility (SDF) 153
Simulator 5,7
Six Configurations 33
Slant range 86
Stalls 50
Station passage 126,135
Steep Turns 45
Stepdown fixes 149
Stormscope 62
Straight-in Approaches 154
Straight-in landing 146
Synopsis (weather) 59

T
TACAN 85
Tangent heading 160
Tangents 159
Terminal forecasts 61
Terminal routes 143
TERPS Manual 230
Threshold crossing height (TCH) 168
Thunderstorms 208
Timed Turns 47

Timer 77
TO-FROM flag 89
Touchdown zone elevation (TDZE) 146
Tracking 115,118,120
Tracking errors 66
Transitions 143
Transponder code 76
Turn Instrument 14
Turn coordinator 15
Turn indicator 15
Turns 42

U
Unusual Attitudes 49

V
Vacuum Failure 207
Vertical Speed Indicator 21
Visual Approaches 153
Visualization 8
VOR
  (H) class 83
  (L) class 84
VOR DME 151,188
VOR Orientation 87
VOR System 83
VOR Testing 86
VOR test facility (VOT) 86

W
Weather radar 61
Winds aloft forecast 61

Z
Zone of ambiguity 89